CYBER CRIMINALS ON TRIAL

As computer-related crime becomes more important globally, both scholarly and journalistic accounts tend to focus on the ways in which the crime has been committed and how it could have been prevented. Very little has been written about what follows: the capture, possible extradition, prosecution, sentencing and incarceration of the cyber criminal.

This book provides the first international study of the manner in which cyber criminals have been dealt with by the judicial process, and anticipates how prosecutors will try to bring criminals to the courts in future. It is a sequel to the groundbreaking *Electronic Theft: Unlawful Acquisition in Cyberspace* by Grabosky, Smith and Dempsey (Cambridge University Press, 2001). Some of the most prominent cases from around the world have been presented in an attempt to discern trends in the handling of cases, and common factors and problems that emerged during the processes of prosecution, trial and sentencing.

This is a valuable resource for all those who seek to understand how the difficult task of convicting cyber criminals can be achieved in a borderless world.

Russell G. Smith, BA (Hons), LLM, DipCrim (Melb.), PhD (London), Solicitor of the Supreme Court of England and Wales, Barrister and Solicitor of the Supreme Court of Victoria and the Federal Courts of Australia, is Deputy Director of Research at the Australian Institute of Criminology. He is co-author of the books *Electronic Theft: Unlawful Acquisition in Cyberspace* and *Crime in the Digital Age.*

Peter Grabosky, BA (Colby), MA, PhD (Northwestern), FASSA, is a Professor in the Regulatory Institutions Network at the Australian National University, a former Deputy Director at the Australian Institute of Criminology, and current Deputy Secretary General of the International Society of Criminology. He is a co-author of *Electronic Theft: Unlawful Acquisition in Cyberspace* and *Crime in the Digital Age,* and co-editor of *The Cambridge Handbook of Australian Criminology.*

Gregor Urbas, BA (Hons), LLB (Hons), PhD (ANU), Barrister and Solicitor of the Supreme Court of the Australian Capital Territory and the Federal Courts of Australia, is a Lecturer in Law at the Australian National University and a former Research Analyst at the Australian Institute of Criminology. With Russell Smith, he is a co-author of *Controlling Fraud on the Internet.*

CYBER CRIMINALS ON TRIAL

RUSSELL G. SMITH

Australian Institute of Criminology

PETER GRABOSKY

Australian National University

GREGOR URBAS

Australian National University

CAMBRIDGE
UNIVERSITY PRESS

PUBLISHED BY THE PRESS SYNDICATE OF THE UNIVERSITY OF CAMBRIDGE
The Pitt Building, Trumpington Street, Cambridge, United Kingdom

CAMBRIDGE UNIVERSITY PRESS
The Edinburgh Building, Cambridge, CB2 2RU, UK
40 West 20th Street, New York, NY 10011–4211, USA
477 Williamstown Road, Port Melbourne, VIC 3207, Australia
Ruiz de Alarcón 13, 28014 Madrid, Spain
Dock House, The Waterfront, Cape Town 8001, South Africa

http://www.cambridge.org

First published by Cambridge University Press 2004

Printed in Australia by Ligare Pty Ltd

Typeface New Baskerville (Adobe) 10.5/12 pt.   *System* LaTeX 2_ε [TB]

A catalogue record for this book is available from the British Library

National Library of Australia Cataloguing in Publication data
Smith, Russell G.
Cyber criminals on trial.
Bibliography.
Includes index.
ISBN 0 521 84047 3.
1. Internet fraud.   2. Computer crimes.   3. Trials.
I. Grabosky, Peter N., 1945–.   II. Urbas, Gregor.   III. Title.
345.0268

ISBN 0 521 84047 3 hardback

Foreword

Crime has been with us since society began and will be with us forever. As long as we have rules to regulate the conduct of humans, we will have rule-breakers. The best we can ever hope to achieve in countering this tendency is a socially acceptable level of control of such behaviour. We exercise such control by prevention and, where that fails, punishment.

The motivations for rule-breaking have not changed greatly because they arise from human nature. Criminals are motivated by passion, greed, revenge, curiosity, need, abnormal perceptions of themselves or society, or just plain evil. Some simply enjoy the challenge of offending and not being caught. Sometimes, rules are broken because they are not appropriate to the people, the place or the time to which they purport to apply.

But the ways in which crime may be committed change significantly over time. In most developed countries, highway robbery is a thing of the past. Now, among other developments, we have moved into the realm of cyber crime.

The present authors are well qualified to write about it and they do so in a comprehensive and easily understandable fashion. They present an up-to-date and truly international perspective on responses to the novel legal problems thrown up by the criminal use of computer technology.

The authors define cyber crime as encompassing 'any proscribed conduct perpetrated through the use of, or against, digital technologies'. Simple! They focus on what is known as 'tertiary crime prevention' – criminal justice system action that might deter, incapacitate or rehabilitate offenders. Therefore the book will be of primary interest to investigators, prosecutors, judicial officers and others engaged in the process of bringing offenders to justice. It also provides valuable insights and suggestions for academics, students and lawmakers.

The criminal law is inherently conservative in its development (as it should be), but significant changes have occurred in response to social pressures. At one time in parts of the United States, as the authors point out, it was an offence to harbour a runaway slave, while in other parts slavery was prohibited. At the time of the industrial revolution in the United Kingdom the legislature was obliged to act to create statutory offences, on top of and superseding the common law, to provide a better measure of protection for factory and mine workers. In the information technology age it has become necessary to develop new approaches to crimes that are motivated by the old forces but committed by new means in the 'wired world' of cyberspace.

There are many challenges to be confronted. At first prosecutors tried to squeeze new criminal acts into old laws; now laws are being made to address the conduct directly. The question of the appropriate jurisdiction in which to proceed is vexed, given that electronic impulses may traverse many nations before hitting their targets. What priority should be given to the pursuit of cyber criminals where in some cases there may be substantial loss and in others not much more than nuisance value? If there are no flesh and blood victims, does it make a difference? Juveniles are empowered as never before by information technology – how should juvenile cyber criminals be treated? What strategies have been adopted by investigators and prosecutors to meet the modern challenges? What are some of the defences that have been tried so far? And what punishments are appropriate for these types of offences? These issues and more are addressed in the chapters that follow, and compelling arguments are presented for the need for the law to develop and move in step with the enormous technological changes that have occurred in recent decades.

This is not just a book about the place of computers in the commission of crime. The reader is treated to an examination of specific cases in many jurisdictions, chosen to illustrate the ways in which novel problems are being addressed. Apparently simple measures, such as a greater degree of harmonisation of substantive and procedural laws between jurisdictions, would go a long way towards lowering the cost to societies of prevention and punishment. The authors describe ways in which such developments could occur and the extent to which they have begun. They raise specific issues that require further consideration by us all.

In the meantime, trial and punishment proceed under existing regimes and the ways in which they occur are the focus of the book.

This is a timely and trailblazing work. It is indeed, as the authors say: '. . . the first international study of the ways in which cyber criminals have been dealt with by the judicial process'. It provides extremely valuable assistance to those of us in the law, wherever we are, who are interested in learning how to deal with the novel considerations raised by the development of cyber crime.

Nicholas Cowdery AM QC
Director of Public Prosecutions, New South Wales, Australia
President, International Association of Prosecutors

Contents

Figures and Tables

Acknowledgments

In researching this book we have been fortunate in having had discussions with many people involved in the investigation, prosecution, trial and regulation of cyber crime around the world. Others have read drafts of chapters and provided important sources of information and advice. In particular we wish to thank the following.

In Australia: Paul Coghlan QC (Director, Victorian Office of Public Prosecutions), Richard Refshauge SC (Director, Director of Public Prosecutions, Australian Capital Territory), Geoff Gray (Office of the Commonwealth Director of Public Prosecutions), Geoff Denman (Office of the Director of Public Prosecutions, New South Wales), David Morters (Office of the Director of Public Prosecutions, Australian Capital Territory), and Alastair MacGibbon (Australian High Tech Crime Centre).

In the European Union: Henrik Kaspersen (Vrije Universiteit, Amsterdam).

In the United Kingdom: Evan Bell (Department of the Director of Public Prosecutions for Northern Ireland), Andrew Laing (Fraud and Special Services Unit, Crown Office, Scotland), Adrian Culley (Metropolitan Police, New Scotland Yard, Computer Crime Unit), Dick Woodman (Metropolitan Police, S06 Specialist Crime Unit), Len Hynds (Head, National High Tech Crime Unit, National Crime Squad), Sheridan Morris (Home Office, Policing and Reducing Crime Unit), Terry Palfrey (Casework Directorate, Crown Prosecution Service), Ian N. Walden (Centre for Commercial Law Studies, Senior Research Fellow, Queen Mary & Westfield College), Bill Wheeldon (Casework Directorate, Crown Prosecution Service), Peter Parker (Head Internet Unit, Financial Services Authority), John Doran (Internet Unit, Financial Services Authority), Tricia Howse (Assistant Director, Serious Fraud Office), Steve Edwards (Computer Crime Division, Serious Fraud Office) and Tim Wright (Head Hi Tech Crime Team, Home Office).

In the United States: Orin Kerr (George Washington University Law School) and his immensely informative website at <http://hermes.circ.gwu.edu/archives/cybercrime.html>, Chris Painter, Todd Hinnen, Joel Schwartz and Michael Sussmann (Computer Crime and Intellectual Property Section, Criminal Division, United States Department of Justice), Gregory Schaffer (PricewaterhouseCoopers) and Susan Brenner (University of Dayton School of Law).

We wish also to thank the Australian Institute of Criminology and the Australian National University for their institutional support and for generously providing funding for the engagement of the following research assistants: Julie Ayling, Michael Cook, Simon MacKenzie, Yuka Sakurai, Alex Strang, Neale Williams and Heidi Yates. Sascha Walkley, a doctoral student at the Australian National University, also read and commented on the manuscript.

Finally, we are particularly grateful to our publishers, Cambridge University Press, for their guidance and encouragement, for Peter Debus's enthusiasm and support throughout and for Elaine Miller's meticulous editing of the manuscript which improved its accuracy and style immensely. We remain, of course, entirely responsible for this final published version.

Russell G. Smith
Melbourne
Peter N. Grabosky and Gregor F. Urbas
Canberra
March 2004

Preface

The material presented in this book comes from a wide range of sources. Apart from recourse to secondary sources and commentaries on the judicial process in this area, we have drawn on a number of government reports dealing with cyber crime. The Internet itself provides a good deal of information, and of course many unreported judicial decisions are now available online.

In addition, we sought input and advice from senior practitioners in the field. This was achieved through informal discussions with personal contacts and, more formally, by holding a number of Roundtable Discussions in which we called together the most senior people in a variety of jurisdictions who are involved in the investigation and prosecution of cyber crime. The purpose of these was to seek their understanding of the key issues that affect their daily work.

Two such Roundtable Discussions were held, one in Canberra on 4 April 2002 at the Australian Institute of Criminology and one in London on Tuesday 16 July 2002 at the Home Office. In the United States, discussions were held with key informants in Washington DC on 7 and 8 November 2002. Attending each were senior police, prosecutors and/or representatives from regulatory agencies in each country, with each discussion facilitated by one of the authors. Each discussion followed the plan of the chapters of this book.

Our primary focus was, however, on cases that have reached the courts, and we attempted to identify the most significant cases that have been dealt with by the courts in North America, the United Kingdom and Australasia. Of course, some cases have been omitted, but we are confident that we have examined the key decisions over the last thirty years. Each case was analysed with respect to the judicial processes involved in prosecution, trial and sentencing.

The present work does not purport to be a scientific, empirical analysis of cases decided in the courts, although we have presented some descriptive statistics of sentencing outcomes, aggravating and mitigating factors. We also present the results of a small study of sentencing in serious fraud cases involving computer-assisted crimes decided by Australian and New Zealand courts in the calendar years 1998 and 1999.

We have included a selection of cases involving cyber crimes that have been determined in the courts, identifying as many as we were able to locate from jurisdictions involving adversarial court processes (principally, Australia, the United

Table 1 – *Number of cyber crime cases examined, 1972–2003*

Year	USA	Australia and New Zealand	Asia	UK	Canada	EU	Subtotal	Total
Number	(2)						(2)	2
Date								
1972	1						1	1
1973		(1)					(1)	1
1974	(1)						(1)	1
1984				1			1	1
1986		1	1				2	2
1987		2			1		3	3
1988				(1)			(1)	1
1989			(1)				(1)	1
1990	(1)						(1)	1
1991	1 (1)			1			2 (1)	3
1992	1	1	(1)	2	(1)		4 (2)	6
1993	1	1		1 (1)	(2)		3 (3)	6
1994	1 (1)		(1)	1			2 (2)	4
1995		3		1	2 (1)		6 (1)	7
1996	2			2 (1)	1		5 (1)	6
1997	1 (2)		1	3(1)			5 (3)	8
1998	4 (1)	3	1	(2)			8 (3)	11
1999	7 (2)	3	6 (1)	3 (1)		(1)	19 (5)	24
2000	11 (7)	(1)	6 (1)	2			19 (9)	28
2001	16 (3)	4 (2)	3	3		1	27 (5)	32
2002	15 (10)	2 (2)	4 (4)	4	1		26 (16)	42
2003	15 (16)	12 (1)	1	2		1 (1)	31 (18)	49
sub-totals	76 (47)	32 (7)	23 (9)	26 (7)	5 (4)	2 (2)	164 (76)	240
Total	123	39	32	33	9	4	240	

Note: Numbers represent the number of cases from each jurisdiction set out in Appendix A and (in parentheses, the number of additional cases not included in Appendix A).
Information is current, and URLs were operational, at 31 March 2004 unless otherwise indicated.

Kingdom, United States, Canada, New Zealand and Hong Kong), with some reference to other countries to illustrate alternative ways in which cases have been dealt with. The work is not, however, a comparative analysis of prosecution and sentencing in the countries examined. Rather, it attempts to identify issues that are common to prosecutors and judges in these jurisdictions.

We conducted extensive online searches of databases of cases and legislation publicly available for legal research. Cases were identified for analysis if they resulted in a judicial determination and imposition of a sanction, although reference is also made to some striking examples of cases which could not be prosecuted due to legislative or procedural difficulties, or which resulted in an acquittal of the accused or in which the accused's appeal was successful. We were also only able to refer to cases that had been publicly reported, which of course excludes some cases heard in lower courts. We are confident that we have isolated for examination those cases which best illustrate the points under discussion from the various jurisdictions under consideration. This methodology reflects the way in which judges rely upon precedents in decision-making, reasoning analogically from similar cases – although, strictly speaking, many of the decisions we cite would be of limited binding or persuasive authority, coming as they do in many cases from courts in other jurisdictions or from lower courts.

In all, we examined some 240 cases. Of these, 164 cases involved a conviction or a guilty plea by the accused (see Table 1). We have been able to locate sentencing outcomes in respect of 139 of these cases. To assist readers in understanding the salient facts and outcomes of the cases selected for examination, we include Appendix A, which contains the essential details of each case, identified by [**Case No.**] where referred to in the text. Again, this information is provided for illustrative purposes rather than as the basis of an empirical database. In time, when more cases have reached the courts, it may be possible to undertake a more rigorous analysis of the circumstances and outcomes of these cases. In the remaining 76 cases, the accused was acquitted at trial or the accused's appeal was allowed or conviction quashed. These latter cases have not been included in Appendix A, although some are referred to in the discussion. It is apparent that most cases have emanated from the United States and that there has been an increasing number of cases coming before the courts in recent times.

Abbreviations

Where cases are cited in the text, the following abbreviations are used. Some abbreviations refer to law report series; others simply provide case identification (if, for example, the case is unreported).

Australia

ACL Rep	Australian Current Law Reporter
A Crim R	Australian Criminal Reports
ACT CA	Australian Capital Territory Court of Appeal
ACT SC	Australian Capital Territory Supreme Court
CLR	Commonwealth Law Reports
FCA	Federal Court of Australia
NSWCCA	New South Wales Court of Criminal Appeal
Qd R	Queensland Reports
VICSC	Victorian Supreme Court
VSCA	Victorian Supreme Court, Court of Appeal
VR	Victorian Reports

Canada

BCJ	British Columbia Judgment (followed by court number)
BC Prov Court	British Columbia Provincial Court
LAC	Labour Arbitration Cases
OJ	Ontario Judgment (followed by court number)
ONCA	Ontario Court of Appeal
OR	Ontario Reports

Hong Kong

CACC	Court of Appeal Criminal Case (followed by court number/year)
DCCC	District Court Criminal Case (followed by court number/year)
HKC	Hong Kong Cases
HKCA	Hong Kong Court of Appeal

HCMA   Hong Kong Magistracy Appeal (followed by court
                        number/year)

New Zealand

NZCA   Court of Appeal of New Zealand

United Kingdom

AC   Appeal Cases
All ER   All England Law Reports
CA (Crim Div)   Court of Appeal (Criminal Division)
Crim App R   Criminal Appeal Reports
Crim App R (S)   Criminal Appeal Reports (Sentencing)
Crim LR   Criminal Law Review
EWCA Crim   England and Wales Court of Appeal (Criminal) Reports
IPR   Intellectual Property Reports
QB   Law Reports, Queen's Bench Division
WLR   Weekly Law Reports

United States of America

F   Federal Reporter
F 2d   Federal Reporter, Second Series
F 3d   Federal Reporter, Third Series
F Supp   Federal Supplement (District Court Reports)
NY App Div   New York Appellate Division
NYS   New York Supreme Court
WI App   Wisconsin Court of Appeals

US Federal Courts

US federal judicial circuits comprise a number of districts from different states.
CD   Central District
Cir   Circuit
ND   Northern District
SD   Southern District

Currency exchange rates

Monetary amounts are generally provided in US dollars (US$). The conversions from other currencies were done using the following exchange rates.

Australia	A$1 = US$0.75
Canada	Can$1 = US$0.75
China	1 RMB = US$0.12
European Union	€1 = US$1.22
Hong Kong	HK$1 = US$0.13
New Zealand	NZ$1 = US$0.65
Philippines	P1 = US$0.017
Singapore	S$1 = US$0.58
United Kingdom	£1 = US$1.80

CHAPTER ONE

Introduction

... you have pleaded guilty to fourteen counts of what might conveniently be described as 'hacking' offences under Part 6A, being offences relating to computers. ... You were 20 at the time of the commission of these offences. You are a final year accountancy student at the Royal Melbourne Institute of Technology ... you have no previous convictions and have an unblemished record ... it is accepted that your motive was no more than to test your computer skills ... it was said by your counsel that you became addicted to your computer in much the same way as an alcoholic becomes addicted to the bottle ...

I formed the view that a custodial sentence is appropriate in respect of each of these offences because of the seriousness of them, and having regard to the need to demonstrate that the community will not tolerate this type of offence. Our society is being increasingly served by and dependent upon the use of computer technology. Conduct of the kind in which you engaged poses a threat to the usefulness of that technology, and I think it is incumbent upon the courts in appropriate cases to see to it that the sentences they impose reflect the gravity of this kind of criminality ...

You are convicted and sentenced to a term of imprisonment of six months ... but you may be released forthwith upon your giving security by recognisance in each instance in the sum of $500 to be of good behaviour for a term of six months.

County Court of Victoria, at Melbourne, 3 June 1993, *per* Judge Smith

The above sentencing remarks were made after the successful prosecution of a young hacker in Victoria, Australia, at a time when courts were just beginning to deal with the emerging phenomenon of cyber crime and its societal consequences (see **[Case No. 15]**). The case itself is not remarkable – on the contrary, it resembles many other prosecutions of computer-literate offenders motivated more by curiosity than obvious criminality, and the sentence imposed was also fairly typical. However, the judge's remarks illustrate the difficulties faced by prosecutors and courts in responding appropriately to emerging threats created by new technologies.

Since this case was heard over ten years ago, cyber crime has come a long way. Along with its inexorable growth has come a corresponding increase in the number of cases appearing in the courts. The trajectory of the growth of cyber crime and the emerging capacity of governments to respond will almost certainly lead to more and more cases entering the judicial process. These cases will pose some familiar challenges for prosecutors and judges, and also many new ones.

Until recently, both scholarly and journalistic accounts of cyber crime have tended to focus on the ways in which the crime has been committed and how it could have been prevented. This can be explained in part by the fact that most cyber crimes, like crimes in general, never result in prosecution – much less in conviction and punishment of the perpetrators.

This book provides the first international study of the manner in which cyber criminals are dealt with by the judicial process. Some of the most prominent cases from around the globe have been selected for presentation and discussion in an attempt to discern trends in the disposition of cases, and common factors and problems that emerged during the processes of prosecution, trial and sentencing.

Although the book does not purport to be a global handbook for prosecutors, lawyers, or judges with a professional interest in cases involving cyber crime, we hope that it will be a valuable resource for all those who seek to recall the facts of some of the world's most famous prosecutions and to know the reasons why particular sentences were imposed. As with other types of crime, to gain some understanding of sentencing it is necessary to have a detailed knowledge of the circumstances in which cyber crimes are committed and the personal character-istics of those found guilty of criminal conduct.

Although our inquiry encompasses cases adjudicated in courts from around the globe, responses to cyber crime in different jurisdictions have many common features, as offences of this nature are often committed for similar motivations of greed, curiosity or revenge. Offenders from different countries also tend to have similar characteristics, often being well-educated, middle-class, young and male. As digital technologies become more prevalent, however, it is to be expected that this profile will alter and that individuals from different social and educational backgrounds will become involved, as will female users of digital technologies.

Previous studies have carefully described the kinds of crimes that can take place in the digital age as well as a wide range of preventive measures that may be appropriate to address these crimes (Grabosky and Smith 1998; Grabosky, Smith and Dempsey 2001). In the present volume, however, we focus on the operation of what is known as 'tertiary crime prevention' – that is, criminal justice system action designed to prevent crime after offences have occurred. This can operate directly through deterrence, incapacitation, and rehabilitation of offenders, or indirectly through the promotion of social norms that seek to characterise criminal conduct as unacceptable in the eyes of the community generally (Layton-Mackenzie 2002).

Of course, the success of tertiary crime prevention requires that cases be pros-ecuted and come before the courts, with all the attendant publicity that this may involve. This is now starting to occur in the world of cyber crime, and it is hoped that the effects will be fruitful. Our objective is, therefore, to find out what has happened to cyber criminals who have been prosecuted and what impediments have arisen with respect to successful prosecution and punishment. The common theme lies not so much in the nature of the illegality, but in the fact that it resulted in prosecution and trial of those alleged to have committed such crimes. The focus is, therefore, on uncovering the ways in which prosecutors, lawyers, and judges have dealt with these often complex cases.

Structure and Plan

Three principal hypotheses are addressed in the chapters that follow. These are:

(a) that the prosecution and judicial disposition of cases involving cyber crime are no different from conventional crime;

(b) that the prosecutorial and judicial responses to cyber crime have been similar in North America, Britain and Australasia; and

(c) that the presence of computers in the commission of crime does not affect the severity with which courts deal with those convicted of crimes.

Each substantive chapter will be structured in such a way as to identify the key issues under discussion, to illustrate these by reference to decided cases and legislation, and to examine relevant evidence supporting and rebutting each of the hypotheses, where appropriate.

The remainder of this book is divided into eight chapters.

Chapter Two considers the definition and scope of cyber crime and its theoretical interaction with white collar crime, economic crime, intellectual property infringement, telecommunications crime and civil redress. A formal classification is proposed that is used to delimit the scope of the present discussion. We also review current knowledge concerning the incidence and threat of cyber crime as disclosed in official administrative data and victimisation surveys, particularly in the business and corporate environment.

Chapter Three focuses on the prosecution of cases in both adversarial and inquisitorial systems. It will examine the difficult policy and practical questions associated with deciding which cases to prosecute, and the application of the various prosecution policies that are used in the regions concerned. This chapter will also discuss the role of the prosecutor in criminal investigation, comparing the more direct 'upstream' involvement in the United States and in inquisitorial systems with the Anglo-Australian model of detached independence. It will also address the vexed question of whether to prosecute juveniles.

Chapter Four considers the problem of prosecuting cyber crime that involves a cross-border element (within federal systems as well as cross-nationally). The chapter includes discussion of legal questions of jurisdiction and conflicts of law as well as forensic and practical issues associated with obtaining evidence, extradition of offenders, and reliance on arrangements for mutual assistance internationally. It reviews, among others, the cases of a fifteen-year-old Canadian youth who was charged with the distributed denial-of-service attacks against major e-commerce sites in February 2000, and the Philippine former computer science student alleged to have been the architect of the 'Love Bug' virus, who avoided prosecution because of the lack of dual criminality under Philippine law. The chapter concludes with an examination of some of the practical impediments to the successful prosecution of cross-border cyber crimes.

Chapter Five concerns the trial of cyber criminals and, in particular, compares the contending strategies of prosecution and defence. It notes how in common law systems, the defence often seeks to exclude evidence likely to be inculpatory, by challenging the legality of the investigative processes by which the evidence was derived, and how the prosecution responds to these challenges. In addition, it compares defence tactics in jury trials to make the evidence appear unduly complex (and thereby introduce doubt) with the prosecution's efforts to make the evidence simple and intelligible to the jury. This is particularly challenging in circumstances where the evidence may have been rendered inaccessible or difficult to detect through technical means such as encryption. The chapter also discusses various defences that may be raised to suggest a lack of criminal intent on the part of the accused.

Chapter Six looks at the initiatives that have been taken to reform laws to accommodate cyber crime. It considers the applicability of existing criminal offences to a range of computer misconduct, noting areas in which new laws have had to be enacted, and reviews model legislative reforms and the processes of harmonisation that have been implemented globally to deal with these new offences. Foremost among these is the Council of Europe's *Convention on Cybercrime.*

Chapter Seven considers the nature and purposes of punishment for cyber crimes. It discusses the objectives of punishment, under the two broad categories of retributive and consequentialist approaches, and some of the specific features that punishment should have in order to achieve its purpose under one or the other of these approaches. The chapter then considers, with reference to recent cases, how each of these features applies in the case of cyber crime.

Chapter Eight examines the process of sentencing cyber criminals. It reviews questions of fact-finding and then examines the various factors that courts are required to take into consideration when determining sentence, including aggravating factors, or what are known in the United States as 'enhancements', as well as mitigating factors raised on behalf of the defendant. The vexed issue of consistency of approach is also addressed. Some empirical evidence is presented concerning the extent to which specific punishments are actually used in cases involving cyber crime. The chapter discusses novel sentencing options for dealing with often rationally motivated economic offenders and how conditional non-custodial sanctions can be used to achieve lasting deterrent effects. Finally, the role of publicity as a sanction is considered. Cases to be discussed include offenders whose substantial sentences and stringent release conditions have engendered public controversy.

Chapter Nine, the final chapter, draws the evidence together and provides an assessment of the extent to which each of the hypotheses referred to above has been accepted or rejected. It also identifies whether, and if so, why, cyber criminals are dealt with differently from other offenders in the judicial process, and how different countries' legal systems have responded to the continuing problem of cyber crime. We offer some suggestions for reforming laws and procedures in order to deal with such cases more efficiently, and to reduce the sometimes considerable resources that governments expend in the effort to achieve justice in cyberspace. Finally, we seek to identify the most productive ways in which legislatures, prosecutors and the courts can proceed in the future, as well as to isolate the most urgent areas for further data collection, reporting and research.

Conclusion

Our aim in this book is to shed light on how the prosecutorial and judicial process could be improved in order to handle more effectively the complex legal and technical difficulties that arise in cyber crime cases. We also seek to illuminate directions for policy and law reform in the future, in order to deal with the many problems that tend to be common across countries in cases of this nature. Finally, we respond to the basic question: how are cyber crime cases different from ordinary criminal cases?

CHAPTER TWO

Defining and Measuring Cyber Crime

Before proceeding with our substantive discussion it is important to examine the definition, nature and scope of cyber crime, in order to delimit our inquiry as well as to place the discussion of the cases we have chosen for analysis in some theoretical context. In the following discussion we shall examine some of the key terms and their relationship to other descriptive categories of crime that overlap to some extent with our topic of inquiry.

Clearly, digital technologies lie at the heart of cyber crime and these include computers, communication technologies and networked services. Grabosky and Smith (1998) describe the wide range of services included within the concept of digital technologies and for the purposes of the present discussion we shall assume that computers, communications technologies and other networked services form the infrastructure in which cyber crime may be committed. References to computers and digital technologies will be used interchangeably.

Cyber Crime Not Cybercrime

There is, at present, a wide range of adjectives used to describe computer crime – virtual, online, cyber-, digital, high-tech, computer-related, Internet-related, telecommunications-related, computer-assisted, electronic, and 'e-' (as in 'e-crime'). In the same way that the term 'white collar crime' sparked fifty years of discussion and controversy, these terms coined to delimit the scope of computer-related misconduct are likely to be similarly problematic.

For present purposes we have chosen to adopt the term 'cyber crime' to describe our subject matter, although any of the other terms could justifiably have been chosen. 'Cyber crime' is used generically to describe a range of criminal offences, only some of which specifically relate to computers and the telecommunications infrastructure that supports their use. In this sense, it is similar to terms such as 'fraud', which are generally not used in legislation (statute drafters preferring legalisms such as 'obtaining financial advantage by deception'), but rather, are used by criminal justice personnel to describe a range of offences, all of which contain an element of dishonesty. Similarly, 'cyber crime', spelt as a single word in the titles of some recent pieces of legislation such as the Australian *Cybercrime Act 2001* (Cth) and the Council of Europe's *Convention on Cybercrime*, is a way of

describing conduct that could entail a range of offences, many of which have
nothing to do with computers in their legislative descriptions.

Defining the term 'cyber crime' raises conceptual complexities. The term
'cyberspace' was first coined by William Gibson in his novel *Neuromancer* (1984) to
describe a high-tech society in which people inhabit a virtual world divorced from
terrestrial life. It has been used since then in a wide range of contexts to describe
almost anything to do with computers, communications systems, the Internet, or,
indeed, life in the twenty-first century. Chatterjee (2001, p. 81) reviews the many
ways in which the term 'cyberspace' has been used, as well as the disparate other
terms used to describe computer-related activities including those that infringe
criminal laws. She also refers to the observation by Crang, Crang and May (2001,
pp. 1–18) that 'the value in cyberspace lies in its ability to resist singular interpretation, and . . . it would be a mistake to try to impose one'. Unfortunately, our
discussion requires that cases which do involve cyberspace be distinguished from
those which do not.

Arguably a distinction could be made between cybercrime (a singular concept
of crime that could encompass new criminal offences perpetrated in new ways)
and cyber crime (a descriptive term for a type of crime involving conventional
crimes perpetrated using new technologies). Criminal offences that fall into the
former category might include cyberstalking and cyberterrorism.

Some have argued that virtual crime should be characterised as separate from
and less serious than terrestrial crime, although Williams (2001, pp. 152–3)
believes that 'the "real" and the "virtual" are not separate experiences and as
such the nature of online communication enables a perpetrator to inflict recog-
nisable levels of harm upon a victim via textual slurs and abuse'. We prefer to
use the term 'cyber crime' to encompass any proscribed conduct perpetrated
through the use of, or against, digital technologies. Hence, we would argue that
cyber stalking should simply be defined as the pursuit or harassment of a victim by
means of computers, and that this does not normally entail any new type of crime;
the only new element is the means by which it is committed. Similarly, the theft of
funds electronically is no different in terms of financial loss from the theft of currency from a bank, and the display of obscene images online (whether involving
real human actors or images of people created electronically) involves the same
affront to those who view the images as when they see them in a magazine. There
may be differences in the extent and scale of the impact, but the effects of the
acts themselves remain the same.

Our view that cyber crime raises essentially conventional legal concepts is rein-
forced by the scope of our present study, which is restricted to cases that have been
prosecuted before the courts under existing criminal laws. Some have involved
the use of recently enacted laws targeting offences specifically related to computers, such as unauthorised access or modification of data, but the majority
involve conventional crimes such as theft and other regulatory offences. The
future will undoubtedly see new criminal laws enacted that have particular relevance to computers and new technologies, but we suspect that few will raise
truly novel legal considerations. Rather, they will simply apply existing rules
to digital technologies and computer-based activities. For the moment, however, we focus on those instances of cyber crime that have actually gone to
court.

A Classification of Cyber Crime

The concept of cyber crime we have chosen to adopt derives from the now widely accepted conception of cyber crime as entailing conduct proscribed by legislation and/or common law as developed in the courts, that:

- involves the use of digital technologies in the *commission of the offence*; or
- is *directed at* computing and communications technologies themselves; or
- is *incidental* to the commission of other crimes.

Such activities may be prosecuted through the use of traditional offence categories such as theft or obtaining financial advantage by deception, or recently enacted offences such as gaining unauthorised access to computers or modifying data. Indeed, as the categories are not mutually exclusive (for example, where offenders hack into a bank's customer database in order to obtain credit details, which are then used to effect fraudulent transactions), a combination of such offences may be involved.

Within the first category are cases involving dissemination of offensive material electronically, online fraud and financial crime, electronic manipulation of sharemarkets, and the dissemination of misleading advertising information, to name but a few. Also included are traditional crimes such as fraud or deception in which the involvement of computers constitutes a statutory aggravating element. Examples within the second category include unauthorised access to computers and computer networks (so-called 'hacking' or 'cracking'), crimes involving vandalism and invasion of personal space, such as cyber stalking and denial of service attacks, and theft of telecommunications and Internet services. The third category involves conduct that has been described as 'computer-supported crime' (Kowalski 2002, p. 6). This includes the use of encryption (the translation of data into secret code) or steganography (in which information is embedded within other, seemingly harmless data such as pictures) to conceal communications or information from law enforcement. It also includes the use of electronic databases to store and to organise information concerning proposed or completed criminal activities. The issues raised for investigators therefore generally involve access to evidence rather than specifically proscribed conduct.

These are just some examples, and the full range of potential conduct is limited only by the extent of one's criminal imagination.

Causal Connection

The involvement of computers in the commission of crime can extend from being clear and direct to being peripheral and of minor importance. The definition of computer crime adopted by the National Criminal Intelligence Service's *Project Trawler* (1999) in Britain, for example, is 'an offence in which a computer network is directly and significantly instrumental in the commission of the crime. Computer interconnectivity is the essential characteristic.' Such a definition would exclude many instances involving non-networked computers and is, we believe, overly restrictive.

Clearly, there are certain crimes in which computing and communications technologies *facilitate* the commission of the offence but are not *essential* to its commission. Examples include the theft of funds by creating fictitious invoices on a company's computer, an offence which could just as easily be committed on paper. The opportunity to manipulate paper accounts might not, however, be immediately apparent to a potential offender, whereas the theft of funds electronically might seem more likely to be successful and not as easily detected. Hence there is a need to consider cases in which the use of a computer is of peripheral relevance.

A good example of the subtle differentiation between crimes in which computers are instrumental and crimes in which computers are incidental can be seen in instances of sexual abuse of children whom an offender has located online. In **[Case No. 159]**, for example, the offender met a number of young girls under the age of sixteen through an Internet chat room and, after winning their confidence, arranged to meet them in person. He then persuaded them to engage in various acts of indecency in return for money, cigarettes or alcohol which he provided. He also took obscene photographs of the girls, again in return for money and goods. He was convicted and sentenced to eight years' imprisonment with a non-parole period of six years.

Although such conduct could have been carried out without the use of the Internet – for example, following a chance meeting with a young person in any public place – it seems probable that chat rooms provided an easy and efficient way in which to meet potential victims and to cultivate their interest. The court in sentencing this offender imposed a heavy penalty because of the physical acts perpetrated rather than because the contact had been initiated electronically. Recently, however, legislators have begun to consider specifically proscribing so-called 'grooming' of children by online predators, which would make such discussions in chat rooms illegal even if a physical meeting did not eventuate. In the Australian state of Queensland, a recently enacted provision of the Criminal Code (s. 218A) prohibiting the use of the Internet or e-mail to procure a child under 16 has been used to charge a man after he allegedly sought sexual contact with a chat room visitor he believed was a 13-year-old girl – it was actually a Crime and Misconduct Commission officer using the name 'BettyBoo13' (Wenham 2004).

Such cases are likely to become more prevalent as investigative authorities devote greater resources to 'sting operations', which can include the creation by police of fake websites specifically designed to be attractive to those who search for images of child pornography (AHTCC 2003). Of course, any criminal prosecution based only on evidence that such a site was visited would raise defence arguments of entrapment, but it should be noted that in many jurisdictions, including Australia, the exclusion of illegally or improperly obtained evidence is a matter for judicial discretion rather than a general statutory prohibition (see *Evidence Act 1995* (Cth), s. 138).

In another recent case, a 17-year-old who had been befriended for the purpose of sexual contact by a man he had met in an Internet chat room was alleged to have attempted to murder the man during a sexual encounter they had arranged. As part of the youth's bail conditions, he was prohibited from using the Internet except for the purposes of schoolwork (Melbourne Magistrates Court, 28 October 2003; see Milovanovic 2003).

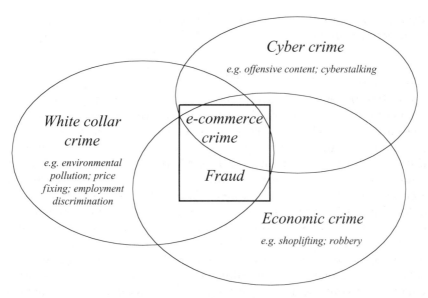

Figure 1 – The interrelationship between white collar crime, economic crime and cyber crime

There are other cases in which computers are involved in the *actus reus* (physical elements) of the crime as the object of the illegality, such as cases involving theft of computer hardware or components, but which have no other connection with digital technologies in terms of how the offence was perpetrated or the ultimate effect of the illegality. These cases, which could include theft of mobile telephones or hand-held personal organisers, or interference with automatic teller machines, vending machines or even modern motor vehicles which have computers on board, will not be considered in our present discussion.

Cyber Crime and Economic Crime

The interrelationship between cyber crime and economic crime raises difficult definitional questions. This is in part because most property crimes involving fraud or dishonesty that have been committed in recent years have involved the use of computers, simply because modern businesses rely so heavily on digital technologies for accounting purposes and for transfer of funds. Moreover, some (though not all) economic crime overlaps with 'white collar' crime, distinguished by its relative sophistication and the background of its usual perpetrators. Figure 1 provides an illustration of the interrelationship between the concepts of white collar crime, economic crime and cyber crime.

We can see that cyber crime has connections with both white collar crime and economic crime. Only a subset of cyber crimes has no economic component, that is, no financial benefit sought to be derived from the activity. Included are cases of cyber stalking or cyber vandalism in which computers are used to threaten or to harass. Many cases of hacking are also carried out for non-economic reasons. The dissemination of offensive content could be either financially motivated (for example, online businesses' distribution of child pornography for a fee) or not (for example, the publication of other offensive content such as racist material generally, with no fee demanded for access).

Cyber Crime and White Collar Crime

The definition of white collar crime has been an enduring topic of debate over the past century (see Smith 2002 and the extensive review of definitions of white collar crime conducted by Geis 1991). It has been observed that white collar crime is 'a social rather than a legal concept, one invented not by lawyers but by social scientists' (Weisburd, Wheeler and Waring 1991, p. 3). There is no specific offence or group of offences that can be identified as white collar crime. As such, white collar crime is a concept similar to cyber crime in definitional difficulties.

The traditional definition of white collar crime focused on crimes committed by persons of high status and social repute in the course of their occupation (Sutherland 1940). Included in this definition were crimes committed by company officers, public servants, and professional people such as doctors and lawyers. The original emphasis was on economic crime, although over time, white collar crime has come to include any acts of occupational deviance involving a breach of the law or ethical principles. As such, it has been suggested that white collar crime now includes almost any form of illegality other than conventional street crimes (Freiberg 1992).

Technological developments over the past decade have created further complexities surrounding the types of persons able to commit white collar crime. The perpetrator of an online fraud, for example, might just as easily be a self-taught teenager using a personal computer at home as an educated professional in the workplace.

A simple categorisation distinguishes crimes committed by specified types of offenders (mainly professionals and individuals employed by corporations) from crimes perpetrated in specified ways (mainly economic crimes that involve sophistication, planning, or the use of technology in their commission). The essence of white collar crime, however, remains rooted in abuse of power and breach of trust, usually involving the pursuit of financial gain as a motive.

Clearly, not all white collar crimes involve the use of digital technologies, although in recent times the vast majority have. Examples of those which do not include acts of violence committed in the workplace, such as sexual assault of patients by doctors, and some environmental crimes such as pollution, although even the latter can be committed electronically (see for example [**Case No. 101**], in which the offender manipulated a local council's computer system, deliberately releasing hundreds of thousands of litres of raw sewage into public waterways).

The category of fraud, or financial crimes of dishonesty, intersects with white collar crime, economic crime, and cyber crime. Overlying the other concepts are the categories of property crime and corporate crime. Property crime is sometimes used synonymously with economic crime, although trespass, for example, or acts of vandalism would not be economic but nonetheless clearly property-related. Problems also arise in relation to the types of property protected by the criminal law. Notably, at least until recently, information usually has been regarded as being outside the scope of criminal prosecutions, dealt with instead by a range of intellectual property regimes such as copyright, patents, designs, and protection of confidential information.

Cyber Crime and Corporate Crime

Corporate crime can be defined in numerous ways (Smith 2002). Tomasic (1993), for example, provides a fourfold classification: corporate crime committed by a corporation itself for the benefit of that corporation; corporate crime committed by the agents or controllers of a corporation for the benefit of that corporation; corporate crime committed by a corporation itself against the interests of another corporation; and corporate crime committed by the agents or controllers of a corporation against the interests of the corporation.

Examples of corporate crimes and other forms of corporate illegality include infringements of corporations laws, taxation and revenue offences, non-compliance with occupational health and safety laws and anti-discrimination legislation, breach of environmental protection laws, consumer protection offences relating to deceptive practices and the sale of dangerous or unhealthy products, infringement of trade practices and competition legislation, intellectual property piracy, bribery and corrupt practices in dealing with government agencies, and various economic offences concerning employees such as breaches of industrial awards and non-payment of wages and superannuation (Grabosky 1984).

Clearly some of these activities would fall within the definition of cyber crime as conduct that involves the use of computers, although to date corporations have rarely been prosecuted for such activities, although their officers have. To limit the scope of the present discussion, we shall focus on cyber crimes perpetrated by individuals rather than by corporate entities. In time, we shall see a much greater interest being taken in corporate cyber crime (see, for example, Clough and Mulhern 2002).

Cyber Crime and Electronic Commerce

Electronic commerce encompasses a wide range of activities but essentially involves the use of computing and communications technologies to advertise, trade in and pay for goods and services. Various technologies can be used for electronic commerce including electronic mail, facsimile transfers, and a variety of web-based systems for the sharing and exchange of information. Acts of dishonesty, deception and misrepresentation relating to any of these technologies are included within the scope of our discussion.

Cyber Crime and Intellectual Property Infringement

Infringement of intellectual property laws can entail both civil and criminal consequences, and in the majority of cases computers are the primary means by which infringements take place. Using the classification of cyber crime described above on p. 7, infringements include:

- crimes *committed through the use of* computing and telecommunications technologies (such as unauthorised copying of digital information using computers and unlawful dissemination of data such as trade secrets, trade marks and logos using e-mail attachments, or the use of computers to fabricate documents);

- crimes *directed at* computing and communications technologies (such as direct theft of software or infringement of patents, designs, trade marks or circuit layouts relating to computer hardware); and
- crimes in which computing and communications technologies are *incidental*, but nonetheless involved in the commission of crime (such as the use of encryption to prevent the disclosure of communications between offenders, the use of steganography to conceal the transmission of infringing material, or the use of databases to record the movement of stolen data).

Arguably the first cases of cyber crime to reach the courts were those against the 'phone phreakers' in the mid 1970s. These were cases involving theft of telecommunications services, such as the famous 1969 case in which a Californian offender was sentenced to two months' imprisonment for repeatedly using a toy whistle to evade charges for long distance phone calls (see [**Case No. 1**]). Details of these and other cases involving manipulation of the billing systems of telecommunications systems are provided by Glough and Mungo (1992) and Grabosky and Smith (1998). As telecommunications systems are invariably controlled by computers, theft of services provides a clear example of crime directed at computers as the targets of illegality.

Cross-Border Cyber Crime

In addition to involving computers, the other feature of cyber crime (to be discussed more fully in Chapter Four) is that it often takes place across jurisdictional boundaries. Cyberspace has been characterised as divorced from terrestrial life, existing in digital data streams that are transmitted via telephone lines and satellites. Often criminal conduct is committed remotely with offenders, victims, and others implicated in the offences located in different countries. Examples include various frauds committed by Russian criminals against banks and other businesses in the West, or the online stalking of a victim on the other side of the globe, as discussed in Chapter Four. In another recent example, offenders in Romania allegedly used e-mail messages to attempt to extort funds by threatening to sell hacked details of the computerised control systems of an Antarctic research facility (FBI 2003).

The use of the Internet and other networked services clearly makes such activities possible and creates jurisdictional questions about the most appropriate place in which legal proceedings should be brought. This question will be explored in much greater depth in Chapter Four on cross-border matters.

Cyber Crime and Civil Wrongs

In delimiting the scope of cyber crime, it is also important to distinguish between incidents that might result in criminal proceedings and those for which civil action for compensation may be taken. Where both criminal and civil remedies are available, there may be uncertainty as to the most appropriate legal response, and in some cases, argument over whether the public authorities or the affected private interest should bear the cost of legal proceedings. A particularly complex area is the infringement of intellectual property rights, such as copyright and trade marks, where the same conduct can have both civil and criminal consequences. Choosing the appropriate response raises difficult questions for victims, police, and prosecutors alike.

Criminal proceedings have been brought in a number of cases involving copyright infringement, particularly where software has been made available via the Internet. A recent example concerns the prosecution of a 21-year-old man in the United States for making 142 software programs available from his website. On 30 January 2001, he was sentenced to three years' probation, including 180 days of home confinement and a tether, as well as 40 hours of community service. He was ordered to make restitution to the software manufacturers, and prohibited from engaging in Internet activity without approval of the Probation Department. See **[Case No. 82]** (United States Department of Justice 2001a).

To date, only civil defamation proceedings have been brought in connection with the electronic publication of material, and while criminal proceedings for defamation remain a possibility in some countries, their use is rare. In the famous civil case of *Dow Jones & Company Inc. v Gutnick* [2002] HCA 56, the High Court of Australia affirmed an Australian businessman's standing to sue an American publisher for publishing an online version of its magazine, in which allegedly defamatory remarks were made. The fact that the server was located in the United States did not deprive an Australian court from exercising jurisdiction as the plaintiff resided and conducted business in Australia, where his reputation was affected. Moreover, the substantive case was to be decided under applicable Australian defamation law, which does not include the same level of protection for public comment that might be available to American publishers under the First Amendment to the Constitution of the United States. It is conceivable that where such offences exist, criminal proceedings for defamation in the online environment may follow in time.

The circumstances of various types of cyber crime can also give rise to civil consequences and remedies, such as in tort, contract or equity. In relation to e-commerce, for example, it is the civil law that will most likely be used where dishonest practices occur rather than clearly criminal acts. The same is true to a large extent in cases of digital copyright infringement, as illustrated in recent litigation over Internet file-sharing services, though criminal charges for commercial dealings in pirated material are of course also available. Case law is also developing with respect to the tort of privacy invasion committed electronically (see *Theofel v Farey-Jones*, F 3d 978 (9th Cir, 2003) (Kozinski J)).

Where computers are involved in the commission of acts infringing intellectual property laws or other civil matters and criminal proceedings have been brought, we will include these within the scope of our discussion of cyber crime.

Surveying Cyber Crime

On the basis of currently available information, we are not able to determine exactly how many individuals have been successfully prosecuted and punished around the world in respect of cyber crimes – principally because inadequate recording and classification of these offences in official statistics make it impossible to know the extent to which computers were involved in the commission of a crime or the extent to which they were the target of an offender. Similarly, little is known about those who have escaped prosecution and punishment, as many cyber crimes are not reported officially and, of course, it cannot be reliably concluded that an offence has been committed and an individual is guilty until a trial has taken place and a conviction recorded.

What is known, however, is that there are high levels of concern in the community about the level of cyber crime and that businesses and government believe that victimisation is widespread. One recent estimate puts the cost of cyber crime to companies worldwide at US$2.25 trillion annually (Taylor 2001). Before examining the incidence of cases that go to court, it is useful to review some of the information obtained from victimisation surveys as to the perceived and actual incidence of crimes of this nature. None of these can be regarded as a perfect measuring instrument. But taken together, they provide an aggregate picture that may give some sense of the risks and vulnerabilities that characterise the digital age.

Organisational Victimisation Surveys

In Ernst & Young's (2003) *Fraud: The Unmanaged Risk: 8th Global Survey*, 51 per cent of respondents considered that computer crime was of most concern to their organisation, ahead of corruption, organised crime, and financial statement fraud. Only asset misappropriation was viewed as being more problematic (63 per cent of respondents).

In early 2002, the Computer Security Institute and the FBI's Computer Intrusion Squad based in San Francisco released the seventh *Computer Crime and Security Survey* (Computer Security Institute 2002). This was a survey of over 500 computer security practitioners in corporations, government agencies, financial institutions, medical institutions and universities in the United States. Ninety per cent of respondents (primarily large corporations and government agencies) detected computer security breaches within the preceding 12 months, up from 85 per cent the previous year. Eighty per cent acknowledged financial losses due to computer breaches (64 per cent the year before). Forty-four per cent (223 respondents) provided quantification of their financial losses, which amounted to US$455,848,000. The year before, 35 per cent (186 respondents) reported total losses of US$377,828,700, and the losses from 249 respondents in the 2000 survey totalled only US$265,589,940. The average annual loss reported over the three years prior to 2000 was US$120,240,180.

As in previous years, the most serious losses occurred through theft of proprietary information and financial fraud. For the fifth year in a row, more respondents (74 per cent) cited their Internet connection as a frequent point of attack than cited their internal systems (33 per cent). Thirty-four per cent of respondents reported the intrusions to law enforcement. In 2001 the figure was 36 per cent; 25 per cent in 2000; and just 16 per cent in 1996.

In terms of reported incidents relating to electronic commerce, the survey found that of the 98 per cent of respondents who maintained websites, 38 per cent suffered unauthorised access or misuse within the preceding 12 months, while 21 per cent said that they did not know whether there had been unauthorised access or misuse of their sites. Twenty-five per cent of those acknowledging attacks reported between two and five incidents while 39 per cent reported 10 or more incidents. Twelve per cent reported theft of transaction information, and six per cent claimed financial fraud (8 per cent in 2001, 3 per cent in the 2000 survey).

Although solely based on corporations in the United States, these figures give some indication of the likely risk levels that are present in those countries with similar levels of computer usage.

In relation to financial crime, computers are seen as being a key risk area. In 2003, for example, PricewaterhouseCoopers in conjunction with Wilmer, Cutler and Pickering (2003) conducted 3623 interviews with senior managers in the top 1000 companies in 50 countries. Cyber crime (defined as illegal access to a computer or computer network to cause damage or theft) was considered by 31 per cent of respondents to be the type of crime of greatest concern for the future, second only to asset misappropriation. However, only 15 per cent of respondents had actually suffered cyber crime in the preceding two years. Although over two-thirds of the victims of cyber crime could not quantify their losses, the average financial cost of cyber crime over the preceding two years was US$812,318.

In relation to the influence of security risks on electronic commerce, KPMG in 2000 conducted a *Global eFraud Survey* of more than 14,000 senior executives in large public and private companies in 12 countries. Responses were obtained from 92 companies in Australia. In total, 1253 responses were received (KPMG 2001).

Thirty-nine per cent of the 1253 respondents said that security and privacy issues prevented their company from implementing an electronic commerce system, with 50 per cent of respondents saying that cost was the main impediment to establishing such a system. Seventy-nine per cent of respondents indicated that a security breach to their electronic commerce system would most likely be caused via the Internet or other external access. When asked to name the primary type of risk associated with their electronic commerce system, 72 per cent of respondents identified risk of damage to the company's reputation.

Only nine per cent of respondents indicated that a security breach had actually occurred within the preceding 12-month period, although 23 per cent of respondents from India reported a security breach of their electronic commerce systems, the highest percentage of any country surveyed. The types of security breaches reported included viruses, system crashes, website defacement or alteration, and system resources being redirected or misappropriated. In approximately half of reported cases, the victim was unable to identify the perpetrator.

The results of these surveys show high levels of business victimisation involving computers, with many attacks conducted remotely by offenders external to organisations and physically located in other countries.

The Australian Computer Crime and Security Survey (2003) found that 42 per cent of the 214 public and private sector organisations surveyed reported some level of computer crime or abuse in the preceding twelve months, considerably fewer than the 67 per cent of respondents who reported attacks in the comparable 2002 survey. Possible reasons for this decline may include the fact that a larger sample was present in 2003 and that the definition of 'computer security incident' was more stringent than in 2002. As in the 2002 survey, the most prevalent source of attack was the Internet (60 per cent in 2003) with viruses representing the most common type of attack (80 per cent in 2003). As in 2002, the two highest economic losses arose out of theft of laptops and virus attacks, each accounting for over US$1.5 million aggregate cost over the preceding 12-month period. Only financial fraud involved higher total losses in 2003, amounting to US$2.625 million lost by those 126 respondents reporting quantified losses (Australian Computer Crime and Security Survey 2003).

Viruses and hacking were also the two most frequent incidents reported by 105 respondents to the British Fraud Advisory Panel's *Cybercrime Survey* (2001), with 66 per cent of respondents reporting a serious incident of any kind in the preceding twelve months.

Although some of these figures are indeed disturbing, they need to be placed in context. Any increase in cyber crime has to be considered in light of the substantial increase in use of digital technologies. Business is now heavily dependent on computers and it is predictable that incidents of cyber crime will increase in direct proportion to usage. It has been found, however, that victimisation has not increased at exactly the same rate as the increase in usage. Internet usage surveys carried out by the Australian Bureau of Statistics (1998, 2001), for example, have found an increase of sixty-one per cent in the number of adults in Australia who had gained access to the Internet between November 1998 and November 2000 – from 4.2 million adults (31 per cent of the adult population) to 6.9 million adults (50 per cent of the adult population).

The surveys also found a 367 per cent increase in the number of adults who had used the Internet to purchase or order goods or services for their own private use between November 1998 and November 2000 – from 286,000 (2.6 per cent of Australian adults) in the twelve months prior to November 1998 to 1,335,000 (10 per cent of Australian adults) in the 12 months prior to November 2000.

In terms of electronic funds transfers, Australian statistics compiled by the Australian Securities and Investments Commission (2000) on the operation of the Electronic Funds Transfer Code of Conduct show that 106,719 complaints were made arising out of the 1.6 billion electronic transactions carried out in the year 1999–2000 (only 0.006 per cent). Only 28 per cent of complaints concerned unauthorised transactions, not all, of course, involving crime.

In addition, many of the problems associated with cyber crime relate only to a relatively small proportion of the world's population. Even in Australia, only ten per cent of the adult population used the Internet to purchase goods or services online in the year to November 2000. Even if usage rates in developed countries increase, third-world populations are unlikely to use computers extensively in the foreseeable future.

Finally, a number of the surveys that have been conducted cannot be said to have examined the incidence of cyber crime objectively. Some have used clearly leading questions when asking respondents about their experiences. Others have been overly general in seeking information – often not even defining or explaining what cyber crime actually means. For example, the National Consumers League in the United States found that American consumers lost US$3.2 million to online scams in 1999 alone. However, 97 per cent of cases involved consumers paying for goods using cheques and money orders, making the online component of the fraud simply the fact that the goods were advertised electronically (National Office for the Information Economy and the Australian Computer Society 2000). In essence, these were no more than traditional cases of cheque or money order fraud, although, of course, locating victims online is now considerably easier than in the past.

Table 2 – *Methods of acquiring intellectual property identified in the PricewaterhouseCoopers survey*

Method	Number of Respondents	Percentage
Copyright breach	33	28.7
Trade mark infringement	30	25.9
Theft	22	19.4
Unauthorised use	20	17.6
Other	9	8.4
Total	114	100.0

Source: PricewaterhouseCoopers (2002), p. 10

Intellectual Property Loss Surveys

Surveys have also been carried out to determine the extent of intellectual property losses sustained by business. Although not all incidents would involve the use of computers, it is reasonable to assume that the vast majority would, particularly those involving software and other digital products.

In June 2001, for example, PricewaterhouseCoopers (2002) conducted a survey of 1200 of Australia's largest private and public sector organisations to determine the nature and extent of intellectual property losses in Australia. 114 responses were received (approximately 10 per cent). Almost one-third of respondents had experienced at least one intellectual property loss incident (108 incidents of loss were reported by the 114 respondents). As shown in Table 2, copyright breach was the most common method of acquiring intellectual property (29 per cent) followed by trade mark infringement (26 per cent) and theft (19 per cent). The most frequently reported category of property stolen was customer lists and data, followed by research and development. Unfortunately, the survey did not distinguish between incidents that were computer-assisted and those that were not. Some 82 per cent of respondents reporting an incident were unable to report a known loss (18 per cent reported incidents involving financial losses). Actual losses ranged from US$375 to US$225,000 with an average loss of US$34,500. The potential financial impact was estimated by 26 per cent of respondents to be between US$750 and $3.75 million with an average potential impact of US$.75 million.

In 1999, the International Intellectual Property Alliance (2000) estimated that infringement of copyright laws in Australia caused losses to the motion picture industry equivalent to 4 per cent of total sales, and losses to software companies equivalent to 32 per cent of business software sales, constituting a total loss to industry of US$143 million.

More recently, the Australasian Film and Visual Security Office reported that the Australian cinema and video industry lost approximately US$75 million to piracy in 2002, with an additional $45 million lost to pirated video games. The illegal market in Australia is now estimated to amount to 8 per cent of motion picture sales (Urban 2003).

The Business Software Alliance's (2003) annual survey of software piracy indicates that software piracy rates have declined slightly since 1994, with financial losses increasing only slightly. Piracy rates are calculated by comparing the

Table 3 – *Global software piracy rates and US dollar losses*

Year	Software Piracy Rate (%)	Losses (US$ 000s)
1994	49	12,346,452
1995	46	13,332,654
1996	43	11,306,160
1997	40	11,440,079
1998	38	10,976,395
1999	36	12,163,161
2000	37	11,750,359
2001	40	10,975,780
2002	39	13,075,301

Source: <http://www.bsa.org/asia-eng> and <http://global.bsa.org/
globalstudy/2003_GSPS.pdf> (Business Software Alliance 2003)

difference between software applications installed (demand) and software applications legally shipped (supply). The piracy rate was thus defined as the volume
of software pirated as a percentage of total software installed: Table 3. Countries
such as China and Vietnam have consistently had software piracy rates in excess
of 90 per cent each year since 1994 (Business Software Alliance 2003).

Consumer Victimisation Surveys

In the United States during 2002, the Internet Fraud Complaint Center, organised by the United States Department of Justice and the Federal Bureau of Investigation, received 75,063 complaints relating to matters such as auction fraud,
credit/debit card fraud, computer intrusions, spam and child pornography. Of
these, 48,252 were fraud complaints, a threefold increase from the previous year.
US$54 million was lost in relation to these fraud cases, a US$37 million increase
from 2001. The average (median) monetary loss per referred complaint was
US$299, with 46 per cent of complaints relating to auction fraud (Internet Fraud
Complaint Center 2003).

The Federal Trade Commission's fraud database, 'Consumer Sentinel', which
compiles identity theft and consumer fraud data from United States and Canadian
agencies, recorded over 380,103 fraud and identity theft complaints in the calendar year 2002 (Federal Trade Commission 2003). This compares with 220,089
complaints received in 2001, and 139,007 in 2000. The proportion of these
complaints that relate to identity theft has increased over the past three years,
from 22 per cent in 2000 to 43 per cent in 2002. Fraud complaints accounted
for the other 57 per cent of complaints in 2002. Of these fraud complaints,
47 per cent were Internet-related in 2002, compared with only 31 per cent in
2000.

Finally, in a telephone survey of 1006 online consumers conducted for the
National Consumers League in the United States between April and May 1999,
24 per cent said they had purchased goods and services online.

However, seven per cent, which represents 6 million people, said that they had
experienced fraud or unauthorised use of credit card or personal information
online (Louis Harris and Associates Inc. 1999).

In 2002, the top three countries from which complaints had been registered by the Internet Fraud Complaint Center were the United States (92.9 per cent), Canada (2.5 per cent) and Australia (0.6 per cent). Others in the top ten countries reporting Internet fraud were Great Britain (0.4 per cent), Germany (0.3 per cent), Japan (0.2 per cent), the Netherlands, Italy, India and France (0.1 per cent each). The top countries from which perpetrators operated – of those cases in which their location could be ascertained – were the United States (76.5 per cent), Nigeria (5.1 per cent), Canada (3.5 per cent), South Africa (2.0 per cent), Romania (1.7 per cent), Spain (1.3 per cent), Indonesia (0.9 per cent), Russia (0.7 per cent), the Netherlands (0.6 per cent) and Togo (0.5 per cent) (Internet Fraud Complaint Center 2003). These statistics are obviously heavily weighted towards the North American and English-speaking segments of the online community, but the contents of and contrasts between these lists of countries point to the global nature of the problem.

The top ten types of Internet fraud recorded by the United States Internet Fraud Watch between 1999 and 2002 revealed that websites were by far the most common means by which consumers were solicited for fraudulent Internet offers (90 per cent in 1999 and 94 per cent in 2002). In some of the most frequently reported Internet frauds, many of the offers came by e-mail: 97 per cent of Nigerian money offers; 24 per cent of work-at-home schemes; 28 per cent of bogus credit card offers; and 36 per cent of fraudulent business opportunities and franchises (Internet Fraud Watch 2002).

The average dollar losses sustained in Internet fraud recorded by Internet Fraud Watch between 1999 and 2001 showed that the amount of money consumers lost to Internet fraud increased, with the average loss per person rising from US$310 in 1999 to US$518 in 2001. Losses overall were US$6,152,070 in 2001, almost double the total amount lost in 2000.

There were also differences in the methods of payment used by the victims of Internet fraud. In 2002, for the first time, credit cards overtook money orders as the most common way in which the victims of Internet fraud in the United States paid for their products or services, with 34 per cent using credit cards and 30 per cent using money orders (Internet Fraud Watch 2002). The overall increase in credit card use, however, is inconsistent with the fact that while some fraud categories show a large increase in credit cards for payments, others such as Nigerian money offers continue to show bank account debits and wire services as the most common payment method (Internet Fraud Watch 2002).

In Canada, the 2000 General Social Survey (GSS) collected detailed information on individual use of technology. Although not designed specifically to capture information on cyber crime, the 2000 GSS collected information on offensive content and security issues relating to the Internet. In 2000, 53 per cent of Canadians 15 years of age and over said they used the Internet at home, at work or somewhere else in the last 12 months, a dramatic increase since 1994 when only 18 per cent of people surveyed were Internet users (Kowalski 2002).

Offensive content, including the collection and distribution of obscene material, hate material and pornography, continued to pose a concern for criminal justice officials as well as for parents of young children in Canada. Results of the 2000 GSS indicated that some 6 per cent of parents reported that their child had come across offensive content on the Internet; half (49 per cent) of Canadians had come across websites that contained pornography. Of those who had come across pornographic websites, 83 per cent came across them unexpectedly and 46 per cent found them offensive. Some 13 per cent of Internet users had come across content that promoted hate or violence toward a particular group and 8 per cent of Canadians who used the Internet had received threatening or harassing e-mail (Kowalski 2002).

According to results from the GSS, 5 per cent of Canadians who had used the Internet in the past year experienced problems associated with security. Forty-five per cent of respondents indicated problems with a virus, 32 per cent reported someone hacking into their e-mail accounts or computer files, 11 per cent said their personal information was made public and 9 per cent indicated receiving threatening e-mail (Kowalski 2002).

Administrative Data on Criminal Justice Procedures

In addition to information gathered from victims of cyber crime, data on the extent of prosecution and punishment are also gathered by the various criminal justice agencies involved: police, court and correctional agencies. Unfortunately, these agencies rarely have information that distinguishes cyber crime from other forms of property crime.

United States

In the United States, the National Incident Based Reporting System (NIBRS) collects incident and arrest-level crime data maintained in law enforcement records, including a category that captures data on computer crime incidents. NIBRS provides the capability to indicate whether a computer was the object of the crime and to indicate whether the offender(s) used computer equipment to perpetrate a crime.

In 2000, of the 45,950 computer crimes reported by the NIBRS, 5744 were crimes where the computer was the tool and 40,211 were crimes where the computer was the object. The most common type of computer crime for both definitions was larceny/theft. Table 4 provides a breakdown of offences reported through the NIBRS in which the offender was suspected of using a computer to commit the offence and in which the computer was the object of the crime. Of course, in some of these cases, computers would have been involved only indirectly, such as where a sexual offender maintained details of potential victims in a computerised database (Kowalski 2002). Where a computer was said to be the object of a sexual offence, the connection would presumably arise out of an individual's property, such as a computerised personal organiser or mobile telephone being damaged or stolen during the commission of a sexual offence. Again, this provides a peripheral link only. In 2001, the United States Bureau of Justice Statistics conducted a survey of 114 State Court prosecutors' offices in large districts with a population of 500,000 or more (in the United States there are 2341 prosecutors' offices nationwide). The 114 offices surveyed serviced 45 per cent of the US population in 1999 (De Frances 2001). Overall, some 83 per cent of offices handled some form of computer crime, with 75 per cent of offices prosecuting matters relating to child pornography (Table 5). An indication of the attrition that occurs between reporting and trial in the United States is that in 1998, although some 419 cases involving computer viruses were sent to federal prosecutors, only

Table 4 – *Computer crime offences by type in the United States in 2000*

	Computer was:	
	Tool	Object
Assault offences	878	282
Sex offences, forcible	73	15
Kidnapping/Abduction	12	32
Sex offences, non-forcible	5	0
Murder and non-negligent manslaughter	0	1
Crimes against the person	**968**	**330**
Drug/Narcotic offences	605	606
Weapon law violations	36	52
Pornography/Obscene material	108	1
Gambling offences	6	4
Prostitution offences	9	0
Crimes against society	**764**	**663**
Larceny/Theft offences	1,589	19,950
Destruction/Damage/Vandalism of property	485	2,990
Burglary/Breaking and entering	373	14,174
Fraud offences	756	595
Counterfeiting/Forgery	525	293
Motor vehicle theft	110	386
Embezzlement	84	277
Robbery	37	220
Stolen property offences	31	283
Arson	10	39
Extortion/Blackmail	7	10
Bribery	5	1
Crimes against property	**4,012**	**39,213**
Total	**5,744**	**40,211**

69 agencies submitted data where an offender was suspected of using computer equipment to commit a crime. 102 agencies submitted data where computer hardware/software was the object of the crime in 2000. The NIBRS represents 13 per cent of police agencies in the United States accounting for 16 per cent of the US population.
Source: National Incident Based Reported System. Federal Bureau of Investigation, US Department of Justice

83 cases proceeded and of these only 21 convictions resulted (Zmontana 2000). Further data on the attrition of cases presented for prosecution in the United States are presented in Chapter Three below.

Canada

In Canada, the Adult Criminal Courts Survey (ACCS) collects data on federal statute charges disposed of in provincial and territorial adult criminal and superior courts. The data represent seven provinces and one territory and account for 80 per cent of the national adult court caseload. To date, the technology-specific offences that are in the Criminal Code at present include unauthorised use of computer (s. 342.1), possession of device to obtain computer service (s. 342.2), possession of device to obtain telecommunication facility or service (s. 327),

Table 5 – *Types of computer crimes prosecuted in prosecutors' offices in large districts of the United States in 2001*

Type of computer crime prosecuted	Percentage of prosecutors' offices in large districts		
	All offices in large districts	Offices serving a population of –	
		1,000,000 or more	500,000 to 999,999
Any computer related crime	83.3%	97.0%	77.3%
Credit card fraud	73.3	93.5	64.9
Bank card fraud[a]	65.7	83.3	58.0
Computer forgery[b]	53.4	63.0	49.2
Computer sabotage[c]	29.1	53.6	17.2
Unauthorised access to computer system[d]	42.7	60.7	34.4
Unauthorised copying or distribution of computer programs[e]	25.0	53.8	11.1
Cyberstalking[f]	66.0	76.7	60.9
Theft of intellectual property	23.5	40.7	14.8
Transmitting child pornography	75.0	87.1	69.6
Identity theft	67.7	80.0	62.3

Note: Data on prosecution of any computer-related crimes under their state's computer statutes were available for 108 offices. Data were available on credit card fraud for 105 prosecutors' offices in large districts, bank card fraud 99 offices, forgery 88 offices, sabotage 86 offices, unauthorised access to computer system 89 offices, unauthorised copying or distribution of computer programs 80 offices, cyberstalking 94 offices, theft of intellectual property 81 offices, transmitting child pornography 100 offices, identity theft 99 offices.
[a] ATM or debit.
[b] Alteration of computerised documents.
[c] To hinder the normal function of a computer system through the introduction of worms, viruses, or logic bombs.
[d] Hacking.
[e] Software copyright infringement.
[f] The activity of users sending harassing or threatening e-mail to other users.
Source: De Frances (2001)

mischief in relation to data (s. 430(1.1)), and theft of telecommunication service (s. 326). Table 6 reveals that there were no consistent trends in relation to any of these five offences between 1995 and 2001. Possession of a device to obtain a telecommunication facility or service, and theft of telecommunication service, were more predominant than the other technology-specific offences (Kowalski 2002).

Data from police in various Canadian provinces have also been examined to determine the extent to which cyber crimes have been reported to these agencies (Kowalski 2002). Some of the findings were as follows.

The number of cyber crimes dealt with by the RCMP has increased from 54 incidents in 1997 to 768 incidents in 2001. In 2001, the most common cyber crimes reported were mischief to data (376), child pornography (110) and unauthorised use of a computer (58).

In Halifax, in 2001, 41 cyber crimes were reported, most commonly child pornography (8) and fraud (5).

Table 6 – *Technology-specific offences: Number of charges in Canadian courts 1995–96 to 2000–01*

Criminal Code offence	1995/96	1996/97	1997/98	1998/99	1999/00	2000/01
Mischief in relation to data – CC 430.(1.1)	64	19	61	20	15	16
Theft of telecommunication service – CC 326	433	443	520	396	301	270
Possession of device to obtain telecommunication facility or service – CC 327	357	220	262	238	599	133
Unauthorised use of computer – CC 342.1	25	26	57	113	43	58

There were no charges reported for possession of a device to obtain computer services (CC 342.2) for 1995/96 through to 2000/01.
Note: Adult Criminal Court Survey data are from 7 provinces and one territory, representing 80 per cent of the national adult court caseload.
Source: Adult Criminal Court Survey, Canadian Centre for Justice Statistics Canada

The number of cyber crimes on which the Montreal Urban Community Police has provided assistance declined 23 per cent between 2000 and 2001, from 275 to 213 incidents.

Between January and September 2002, the Division of Cyber Surveillance and Monitoring in Quebec provided assistance in 309 incidents, which it classified into the categories of morality incidents, such as child pornography (185), economic crime incidents (99) and incidents against the person (99).

Ottawa Police Service's High-Tech Crime Unit dealt with 143 cases of Internet-related crime in 2000 and 155 cases in 2001.

In 2001, the e-Crime Section of the Ontario Provincial Police received a total of 191 requests for service, of which 70 per cent were Internet-related. The most common Internet-related offences were fraud (19), uttering threats (16), mischief to data (10), child pornography (9), sexual assault (9) and criminal harassment (6). The OPP also has the Child Pornography Unit, which investigates child pornography including that which involves computers and the Internet. The Child Pornography Unit has a system in place within their records management system that captures Internet investigation statistics. In the year 2001, the Child Pornography Unit responded to 410 investigations, executed 91 search warrants, and laid 75 charges against 37 persons.

The other provinces do not have systems to distinguish cyber crime from other types of offence.

United Kingdom

A similar trend is evident in the United Kingdom, where very few convictions have been obtained in respect of offences under the *Computer Misuse Act 1990* (UK) in recent years. Although there has been a gradual increase in convictions, the data in Table 7 relate only to cases in which computers were instrumental, excluding the many possible other cases of incidental computer involvement.

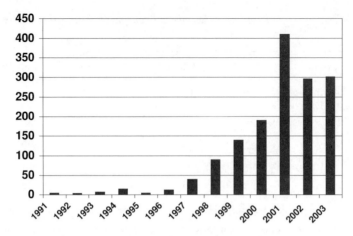

Figure 2 – Number of electronic crime referrals to the Australian Federal Police, 1991–2003
Source: Australian Federal Police, *Annual Reports* 1991–2003

Table 7 – *Convictions in England and Wales under the* Computer Misuse Act 1990

Section	1997	1998	1999
Unauthorised access to computer material	Not available	3	3
Unauthorised access with intent to commit or facilitate the commission of a further offence	0	2	1
Unauthorised modification of computer material	3	4	7

Source: Bell (2002), p. 321

   One can imagine that since the establishment of the National High Tech Crime Unit in the United Kingdom in 2001, the attention paid to crimes of this nature will have increased and, in time, the number of prosecutions and convictions will also increase.

Australia

In Australia, the last twenty years or so have seen an increased number of computer offences reported to law enforcement agencies for investigation. In the year 2002–03, the Australian Federal Police, for example, received 301 electronic crime referrals, 61 per cent of which related to child pornography and paedophile activity on the Internet. Eleven per cent of referrals involved threats and harassment over the Internet; nine per cent unauthorised access to systems; eight per cent denial of service attacks, spamming and computer viruses; and eleven per cent involved other offences such as fraud, intellectual property infringements and the sale of illegal items via the Internet (Australian Federal Police 2003, p. 74). Over the past twelve years, the computer crime caseload has increased substantially, as can be seen from Figure 2. These, however, represent only the tip of the iceberg, as the rate cyber crime is reported remains extremely low (see Geurts 2000).

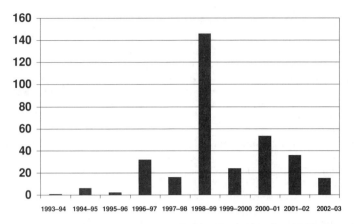

Figure 3 – Computer-related offences recorded by Victoria Police 1993–94 to 2002–03
Source: Victoria Police, *Statistical Review of Crime 1993–2003*

As in the case of the United Kingdom, the establishment of the Australian High-Tech Crime Centre in September 2003 will undoubtedly result in many more cases being reported and investigated in the future.

In Australia, state and territory authorities have jurisdiction over most criminal law matters, including computer crime, as does the Commonwealth. In Victoria, since 1993–94, there has been an increase in computer-related crime recorded by police as shown in Figure 3, although these data refer to computer-related offences officially recorded under Victorian legislation rather than all matters referred for investigation as shown in Figure 2. In addition, these matters are only those that involve alleged infringements of specific computer crime offences, and not cases in which computer usage may have been incidental to the commission of the crime.

In New South Wales, the Judicial Commission of New South Wales publishes data on the number of cases in which court sentences were handed down each year. The statistics reported in Table 8 present the data available concerning computer crime cases in 2001–02.

Clearly, then, it is apparent that very few cases involving cyber crime have come before the courts in recent years. Although the problem is perceived as a serious one, and although many cases are reported to the police, few seem to make their way through the remaining stages of investigation, prosecution, trial, and sentencing. We now consider some of the possible reasons why such attrition in numbers occurs.

Impediments to Prosecution and Punishment

With all crimes, there is a considerable attrition in numbers of crimes that we in the community believe are being perpetrated against us, the number that we report to the police and other official agencies for investigation, and the number that result in judicial proceedings and (on occasions) punishment of offenders. This is no different for cyber crimes. In Australia, for example, over ninety per cent of organisations report cyber crime victimisation, while only 301 matters were referred to the Australian Federal Police in 2002–03.

Table 8 – *New South Wales computer crime cases in which sentences were imposed,*
2001–02

Offence *Crimes Act 1900* (NSW)	Lower courts (Local courts NSW)	Higher courts (District and Supreme Courts NSW)
Unauthorised computer function with intent to commit a serious indictable offence (s. 308 C(1))	1	
Producing, supplying or obtaining data with intent to commit serious computer offence (s. 308 G(1))	1	
Unauthorised access to or modification of restricted data held in a computer (s. 308 H(1))	5	
Unauthorised impairment of data held in a computer disk, credit card or other device (s. 308 I(1))	1	
Unlawful access to data in computer (s. 309(1) repealed)	15	
Obtaining access to data in computer with intent to obtain financial advantage (s. 309(2) repealed)	2	1
Obtaining access to computer data with confidential information (s. 309(3) repealed)	2	1
Unlawfully altering, erasing or inserting data in a computer (s. 310(a) repealed)	3	3
Total	30	5

Source: Judicial Commission of New South Wales

There are many reasons why so few cases are dealt with by the criminal justice system. First is the problem of victims failing to report cyber crimes to the police. This might be because some victims are unaware that they have been victimised or that their computer security has been breached, for example in cases where fraudulent charitable solicitation is carried out online. Victims, particularly businesses, are also often unwilling to report cases through fear of bad publicity and reluctance to send good money after bad in terms of the cost of prosecution.

Many consumer frauds involve small losses which victims may be unwilling to spend time and money in pursuing. When duplicated hundreds or thousands of times, however, considerable sums can be involved. Sometimes businesses may be unable to calculate exactly how much they have lost, in terms of both direct losses and loss of reputation and goodwill. The costs of re-establishing one's good name can also be difficult to quantify.

Finally, the costs of reporting and prosecuting a case may well exceed the amount lost, making it commercially not viable to follow up the matter with the police.

The second major impediment to prosecution of cyber crime concerns the difficulties that may exist in identifying and locating the accused person. There are many ways of disguising one's identity online. Technologies such as encryption, steganography, the use of prepaid anonymous services, and even simply entering into contracts using a false name make it difficult to locate offenders. Sometimes anonymous re-mailing services can be used to make the task of identifying individuals in cyberspace difficult for the authorities.

Occasionally, police will, despite their best endeavours, arrest the wrong person. In March 2003, a 72-year-old man was being investigated by the FBI in connection with alleged telemarketing fraud involving millions of dollars in the United States. Since 1989, he had been making use of the identity of a 72-year-old retired businessman from Bristol in the United Kingdom, who had never met the alleged offender and had no connection with his alleged crimes at all. The FBI issued a warrant for the arrest of the alleged offender and this was executed by South African Police in Durban on 6 February 2003 in the name of the English retired businessman. Unfortunately, the retired businessman, who was on holiday with his wife, was arrested instead of the real suspect.

The police relied on the facts that the name on the warrant corresponded, he was the correct age, looked similar, and had the same passport number. The retired English businessman was held in custody at police headquarters in Durban until 26 February 2003, when he was released following the arrest of the real suspect the day before in Las Vegas (BBC News 2003).

As we shall see in Chapter Three, difficult decisions can also arise in deciding which country has jurisdiction to mount a prosecution. On occasion, more than one country may be able to take action and some may be more reluctant than others to act. Once an offender has been located, the assistance of other countries may be needed to enable his or her extradition to stand trial. Some countries may refuse to allow their nationals to be deported to other countries where particularly severe punishments are used or where judicial procedures are seen to be unfair.

Finally, even if extradition arrangements exist between the countries concerned, problems of delay and cost can be significant.

The third area of difficulty lies in obtaining evidence. It is often very expensive to obtain electronic evidence, as forensic accountancy services may need to be used and large amounts of data examined. In cross-border cases, the procedures for obtaining mutual legal assistance are also slow and some countries are not parties to international conventions. This is a problem where offenders can move around quickly and destroy critical evidence.

Traditional search warrants are often inadequate to deal with electronic evidence, and there is also the problem of seizing entire hard drives or servers in order to obtain only small amounts of data that may be relevant to the case. If data have been encrypted, then either the owner of the key must agree to disclose it, a court order must be obtained to have the data produced in readable form, or else the data must be decrypted electronically – which is often too difficult or expensive to be practicable. As discussed in Chapter Six, legislative amendments have been introduced in several jurisdictions to enable investigating authorities to force computer operators to disclose passwords or provide decryption assistance, with criminal penalties for refusal. Not surprisingly, issues of privacy, the right against self-incrimination, and claims to legal professional privilege often arise in these contexts.

Finally, once data have been seized and decrypted, the sheer volume of material can make location of relevant evidence impossible. It is now not unusual for police to have to examine gigabytes of data amounting to millions of pages of text.

As we shall see in Chapter Three, prosecution policies can represent a real impediment to cases proceeding to the courts. It may be difficult to satisfy the requirement that cyber crimes are matters of sufficient seriousness, in cases where no physical violence is involved. Even where cases are successfully prosecuted, victim impact statements are rarely used at sentencing, or it may be impossible to determine the full extent of the impact.

A conviction is less likely to be obtained where laws are out of date or inadequate to deal with the nature of the crimes involved. If offenders or witnesses cannot be located, the likelihood of success may be remote. Similarly, satisfying the test of the public interest is also problematic where a prosecution may be complex, slow and costly due to the cross-border nature of the activity and the difficulty of bringing witnesses from other places.

Even if prosecutors are satisfied with the evidence in a case, finding suitable criminal offences with which to charge an accused may prove impossible. Many jurisdictions have not reformed their computer crime laws, making it impossible to prosecute some matters. McConnell International (2000), for example, recently carried out a survey of laws in 52 countries and found that 33 of the countries surveyed had not yet updated their laws to address any type of computer crime. Of the remaining countries, nine had enacted legislation to address five or fewer types of computer crime, and ten had updated their laws to prosecute six or more of the ten types of computer crime identified.

Further, many new computer crime laws have not yet been tested in the courts. Until recently, for example, the absence of laws that proscribed deception of computers as opposed to human actors made it difficult to prosecute ATM-related fraud. New laws governing electronic transactions and cyber stalking may well have problems that are yet to be discovered in the courts.

Finally, computer crimes have traditionally attracted relatively low maximum penalties, although this is now beginning to change in many countries, as we shall see in Chapter Eight. In cases involving fraud as opposed to violence, however, very high penalties are not often used.

Once a case proceeds to court, some accused persons with competent legal advice may employ tactics that make securing a conviction extremely difficult. For example, prosecution witnesses may be subject to excessive cross-examination on technical points; overly detailed evidence may be adduced by the defence concerning the operation of electronic systems, tending to confuse a jury; or excessive procedural applications may be made with a view to delaying trial. The absence of competent legal advice can also threaten the viability of a prosecution. Few individuals are able to afford the costs associated with a long and complex criminal trial, and publicly funded legal services may not be available where an accused wishes to contest the charges. In such circumstances, a trial judge may be obliged to stay proceedings until adequate legal representation can be arranged, in order to prevent an unfair trial or abuse of process. Defendants charged with serious computer crimes may be able to arrange their financial circumstances in such a way as to make themselves appear indigent and thus able to take advantage of such judicial obligations. The effect may well be that a long and complex litigation will be stayed indefinitely.

Cases involving serious and complex computer crime, especially if cross-border conduct is involved, also take a considerable time to process – sometimes more than five years. This detracts from the principle that justice should be afforded in a timely manner, and also lessens any deterrent effects of punishment. Defendants are also often able to slow proceedings by acting in an uncooperative way. The use of frequent interlocutory applications, appeals and other devices can delay proceedings, increase prosecution costs, and often lead to evidence being lost or witnesses eventually unavailable.

Even if a conviction has been obtained, offenders may be able to secure relatively lenient sentences in cases involving cyber crime, as the conduct may have only indirect impact on individuals, personal violence is unlikely to be involved, and offenders are invariably well-placed to exploit exculpatory submissions. Cyber criminals often have available to them the most attractive range of mitigating factors to take into account. These include youth, lack of violent crime, cooperation with police, lack of prior offences, remorse, lack of intention to cause serious harm, and good chances of rehabilitation.

Arguably, greater efforts need to be made in obtaining evidence of the impact of computer crime for sentencing purposes. Sometimes this may require more extensive use of forensic accountants. Lawyers also need to be trained to make knowledgeable decisions about what sort of material to present in court. In times of limited resources for public prosecution agencies, these cases are sometimes not fully investigated in terms of submissions that are made prior to sentencing. Again, the state needs to be able to spend money to obtain and present expert evidence.

Finally, judicial proceedings involving cyber crime often raise novel legal problems concerning new pieces of legislation, making it easier to succeed in an appeal against conviction or sentence. Similarly, new technologies of crime may appear less serious to appeal courts, resulting in reduced sentences. Appeal courts may also find it difficult to review the evidence that was given during a trial involving complex electronic communications, particularly if the appeal court does not have counsel capable of explaining the matter in the same way as it was explained during the trial.

The result is that the relatively small proportion of cases that are reported to police can founder during the preparation of prosecution briefs, during hearings, and on appeal. It is little wonder, therefore, that cyber criminals rarely go to prison.

Conclusion

This chapter has discussed the difficult conceptual and definitional problems that arise when examining cyber crime. Arguably, adopting the term 'cyber crime' adds little to our understanding of this new area of criminality and, as occurred in the case of 'white collar crime', the introduction of a new term into an already crowded lexicon could be said to have made the debate more difficult and protracted. 'Cyber crime' has, however, taken on a life of its own to some extent, and entered popular discourse, and so we propose to retain it in the present work – with all the limitations that this might entail.

In terms of our three central arguments, the discussion of definitions and the review of data and surveys enable some initial observations. First, we have seen that although cyber crime overlaps with a number of other areas of economic crime and white collar crime, there are some aspects that are unique. Some forms of illegality simply could not have been committed prior to the introduction of computers and so, in this sense, cyber crimes (or at least elements of them) are dissimilar from conventional crimes. In addition, with cyber crime the level of apprehension of victimisation felt by many businesses, as disclosed in surveys, is far greater than what appears to be the actual incidence of offences – although, of course, our current knowledge base is imperfect.

Secondly, it is clear that cyber crime is a global problem that affects computer users and others in all developed countries that rely heavily on computing and communications technologies. The need to respond effectively has, therefore, been a common theme throughout the networked world, although the level of concern and the impetus for reform have been closely correlated with the degree of usage and hence the risk of victimisation. Those countries with the highest usage levels tend to have taken greater steps with respect to regulation and law reform.

Finally, we have seen from some victimisation surveys that the presence of computers in the commission of crime has enhanced the seriousness with which these crimes are viewed, at least in the minds of those at risk of victimisation and those who have actually suffered from these crimes. It remains to be seen whether the courts deal with persons convicted of cyber crimes in ways similar to, or dissimilar from, the ways in which they treat those convicted of conventional crimes.

CHAPTER THREE

The Prosecutor as Gatekeeper

Prosecuting Cyber Crime

The extent of the prosecutor's involvement with cyber crime will vary from one country to another depending upon the prosecutor's role in the criminal justice system and on constitutional issues more generally. In civil law countries, the decision to begin an investigation may rest with the prosecutor, depending on whether coercive measures are necessary or special proceedings are required. Japanese prosecutors routinely direct investigations (Johnson 2002). Prosecutors also play a central investigative role in Korea and China (UNAFEI 1995). In the United States, especially at the federal level, prosecutors are involved well before a criminal charge is brought, and are often engaged in the planning, organisation and execution of criminal investigations. This early involvement tends to arise from constitutional restraints on criminal investigation that invite detailed and exacting prosecutorial oversight. The National District Attorneys Association, the peak body of all US prosecutors, has specified that the office of the prosecutor should review and approve all applications for search warrants, arrest warrants, and all applications for the use of electronic surveillance (National District Attorneys Association 1991, Standards 40.1–40.3).

In Scotland, the office of the Procurator Fiscal has direct involvement with the investigation of offences from the outset. In Northern Ireland, prosecutors have traditionally been relatively 'passive' recipients of evidence collected and presented to them by police. This reflects the British tradition of prosecutorial independence, which favours a degree of insulation from the police and from executive government. This relatively passive role also characterises nations that have been influenced by British legal traditions, such as India, Malaysia, and Singapore (UNAFEI 1995). In Australia and the United Kingdom, the tradition of prosecutorial passivity is slightly tempered by the occasional practice of offering advice early in the course of an investigation, but only in serious or complex cases or where unusual legal issues were involved. (Minor crimes in British and in many Australian jurisdictions are still prosecuted by the police.)

The role of the prosecutor in the criminal justice system in turn reflects the role of the prosecutor in the governmental system. In the United States, federal prosecutors are appointed by the president, while their state counterparts are elected at the county level. In Japan, prosecutors are career bureaucrats within the Ministry of Justice (Johnson 2002). In Australia, they may be public servants, or from time to time, private barristers engaged on a temporary basis by the relevant Commonwealth state or territory director of public prosecutions (DPP).

Deciding whether to prosecute

As noted in the introduction, a great deal of cyber crime never comes to prosecutorial attention. Consensual criminal activities, such as the exchange of illicit images among members of a closed network, often come to light only when a member of the network attracts law enforcement attention for other reasons. A great deal of online illegality, consensual or otherwise, goes undiscovered. In the case of fraud, the most skilfully executed offences are never detected by the victim. Of those that are detected, many are dealt with privately. Some, especially the more trivial matters, are brushed aside or ignored. Many readers will have received cyber variations on the Nigerian advanced fee fraud letter (Smith, Holmes and Kaufman 1999). Few will have called the police about it. In other matters involving crimes against a company's computer systems, police may not be called because the resulting adverse publicity will be bad for business. No financial institution wants the world to know that its depositors' accounts have been accessed by criminals. It can also be bad for the corporate security professional, who may be disinclined to publicise his or her shortcomings. As one commentator noted, '[I]f you were the person in charge of security at a major corporation, do you want to admit that, while you were on watch, your company lost $4 million? No.' (quoted in United States Sentencing Commission 2000, p. 218).

In this respect, cyber crime differs little from crime in terrestrial space, where, similarly, most incidents never reach police attention.

When matters *are* reported to police, the attrition continues. Police, who themselves tend to have more business than they can handle, may lack the legal or technical capacity to investigate computer crime. Although law enforcement agencies in most Western industrial nations are improving their computer forensics capabilities, there is still such a thing as a 'too hard' basket.

While a 2001 survey of prosecutors at the local level in the United States found that 42 per cent of the 2341 agencies surveyed had prosecuted computer-related crimes, experience in other nations has been different. When we organised a workshop with a group of Australian prosecutors in April 2002, we asked about their exercise of discretion in the prosecution of computer crime cases. Coming from the Anglo-Australian tradition, these prosecutors tended not to be involved in investigative activities. 'What's different about cyber crime?' we asked. 'Where are the cases?' came the reply. And so, prosecutors deal with only the tip of the iceberg of computer cases.

Despite the decrease in the number of cases that occurs before prosecutors even enter the picture, prosecutors must still be selective. Like busy people everywhere, prosecutors tend to have an unremitting workload (Japan makes for interesting comparison: see Johnson 2002). Faced with these pressures, prosecutors must decide which cases they take on.

One of the fundamental decisions a prosecutor must make, in matters relating to both cyber crime and terrestrial illegality, is whether or not to prosecute. In most Western jurisdictions, the principles by which such decisions are reached are set out formally in a prosecution policy. They are remarkable in their similarity.

- Australia has the Prosecution Policy of the Commonwealth: <http://www.cdpp. gov.au/Prosecutions/Policy>;
- The United States has Principles of Federal Prosecution: <http://www.usdoj. gov/usao/eousa/foia_reading_room/usam/title9/27mcrm.htm>;
- The United Kingdom has its Code for Crown Prosecutors: <http://www.cps. gov.uk/Home/CodeForCrownProsecutors/>
- The Hong Kong Special Administrative Region has its Statement of Prosecution Policy and Practice: <http://www.info.gov.hk/justice/new/sitemap/index-depart.htm>.

Essentially, the prosecutor's decision is determined by two factors: the seriousness of the offence and the sufficiency of the evidence. The first of these is fairly objective; the available sentence will give some relative indication of the gravity with which an offence is regarded. Sufficiency of evidence may entail more of a judgment call, although experienced prosecutors will be able to assess the probability of conviction with a fair degree of accuracy.

Japan is different, as the likelihood of a confession figures prominently in the decision to prosecute (Johnson 2002).

Looming over the decision to prosecute is the question of resources. The fiscal crisis of the state, a term coined more than thee decades ago (O'Connor 1973), is a reality in most Western jurisdictions. Prosecutors have in a real sense become managers, responsible for getting the most out of limited resources. The threshold of what constitutes an acceptable case will vary, depending on how much is left in the year's budget. This is especially relevant in cases where the offender, or the evidence, is located in another jurisdiction, whether in another state or another country. The cost of bringing a representative of an ISP from France to testify in an Australian court is not trivial. A prosecutor can quickly blow her budget in pursuit of transnational cyber crime (Brenner and Schwerha 2002).

Some prosecutors will also invoke 'the public interest' as a determinant of the decision to prosecute. The term 'public interest' is an elastic one, often meaning many things to many people. In general, it refers to the impact that the offence has had on society, the deterrent or educative potential of a successful conviction, and whether there are any special factors in favour of or against prosecution. For example, all else being equal, the public interest might militate against prosecution of a terminally ill grandmother, but weigh in favour of pursuing a notorious recidivist.

As we shall see in the following chapter, the borderless nature of cyberspace entails a great deal of cross-national offending. Offences committed within the borders of 'Country A' may have little impact there, but may have significant effects in 'Country B'. Len Hynds of the United Kingdom National High Tech Crime Unit has observed that the impact of a case in a foreign jurisdiction may bear upon one's own domestic public interest. This need not be based on altruistic considerations: authorities in 'Country A' may not wish their country to be regarded as the home of transnational cyber criminals. Moreover, in the event that the tables turn and 'Country A' becomes the target of offenders situated in other countries, authorities in 'Country A' may well appreciate the attentiveness of foreign authorities.

In the terrestrial world, as in cyberspace, prosecutors are more likely to pursue cases that pose 'trouble for society', resources permitting (Stanko 1981, p. 225). This will vary over time and place, and in the degree to which priorities are articulated. What is deemed to be serious in Saudi Arabia (e.g. consumption of alcohol in a public place) may be regarded as entirely acceptable in France. What is regarded as 'trouble for society' may also vary within a jurisdiction over time. In many common law jurisdictions, domestic violence and sexual assault were accorded relatively low priority by police and prosecutorial authorities until the 1970s, when the women's movement drove them higher on the public agenda.

Activities in cyberspace will also pose trouble for society, and again, the magnitude of this trouble will vary over time and place. Attacks on national infrastructure (i.e. energy, power, transport, communications, and financial systems, *inter alia*) are regarded as serious in all nations. To the extent that elements of a nation's infrastructure are connected to the Internet, the risk of cyber attack will be that much greater, and those nations that do experience attacks will regard them as more serious.

National interests tend to be defined by the state, informed to varying degrees by public opinion or at least by the views of powerful interests. In the United States, the economic and political clout of the entertainment and software industries has helped to elevate theft of intellectual property to the level of a very serious matter. Indeed, the section of the Department of Justice with primary responsibility for computer crime is called the Computer Crime and Intellectual Property Section (CCIPS). By contrast, authorities in Australia have tended to accord lower priority to the investigation and prosecution of intellectual property offences.

Internet child pornography tends to be regarded as very serious in the United States, Canada, the United Kingdom and Australia, but less so in Japan. Neo-Nazi content on the World Wide Web is regarded as abhorrent in Germany, but as protected speech in the United States. In the People's Republic of China, online criticism of the state, pornography of any kind, and material advocating the independence of Taiwan and Tibet can land one in serious trouble. By contrast, such content would fail to raise an eyebrow in the Netherlands.

There are, of course, situational factors that may also bear upon a prosecutor's choices. There may be a preference for investing prosecutorial resources in such high-profile terrestrial cases as homicides and armed robberies. Interest in and familiarity with digital technology may contribute to a decision to prosecute a cybercrime case. At present, where some prosecutors may not be entirely comfortable with it, there may be some aversion to taking on such a case. In jurisdictions where 'tech-savvy' younger prosecutors are able to command a higher salary in the private sector, there may be something of a 'brain drain' and a lack of accumulated wisdom with regard to the handling of cyber crime cases.

Presumably with the passage of time, all prosecutors will command a degree of technological literacy. But steps are being taken in the short term to ensure a degree of prosecutorial familiarity with digital technology. In Korea, the Supreme Public Prosecutor's Office established the Computer Crime Investigation Division under the direction of its Central Investigation Department in February 2000 (Park 2001). In the United States, US Attorneys' offices in every federal judicial district have at least one assistant designated as the Computer and Telecommunications Coordinator (CTC). Each has received specialised training in computer crime and is primarily responsible for providing technical expertise within that district (United States Department of Justice 2001c, p. 5). Even so, the budget of local offices may be strained by the cost of training, and there may be a limit to the extent to which local prosecutors can rely on federal authorities for assistance (Brenner and Schwerha 2002, pp. 374–6).

Although high-tech crime may not explicitly figure in prosecution policies, certain aspects of cyber crime will accord it relatively high priority. The current global movement against child pornography, and the degree to which its creation and dissemination have been facilitated by digital technology (Grant, David and Grabosky 1997), have attracted increased law enforcement and prosecutorial attention.

Beyond the specialised matter of child pornography, it is becoming increasingly apparent that we live in a wired world. Much of the infrastructure on which modern societies depend – communications, electric power, water, transportation, financial systems – is based on digital technology. More and more commercial activity occurs online. These systems are vulnerable to attack, and offences against them are regarded as particularly serious. Attacks on infrastructure have led to the prosecution of juveniles. In extreme cases, as we shall see, they have resulted in custodial sanctions.

One of the factors that may weigh informally on the decision to prosecute is what is termed 'jury appeal'. If the case is likely to come before a jury, the prosecutor must assess whether the jury will sympathise with the prosecution or with the accused. There are three basic elements to which the jury can relate: the defendant, the victim witness (where appropriate), and the offence itself.

One issue that tends to differentiate the cyber world from the terrestrial world relates to victims. Victims of conventional crimes such as assault, rape or robbery will vary in their attractiveness and credibility to a jury. Stanko (1981) and Frohmann (1997) both show how social class, sex, race and lifestyle are used as indicators of credibility by prosecutors. To the extent that a victim comes from outside the mainstream, prosecutors may regard him or her as less attractive to the jury, and less sympathetic.

The harm suffered by victims in many cyber crime cases may be less immediate and obvious than in 'flesh and blood' cases. This may result in juries being somewhat unsympathetic to the interests of the victim, which may be a large, rich and powerful institution. By contrast, a young and adventurous offender can be seen as less culpable if the victim has created the very system by which it has been victimised.

Jurors too may regard some crimes as more heinous than others. Persons accused of possessing or transmitting child pornography, or of using the Internet to arrange assignations with minors, will find few sympathisers. By contrast, offences of information piracy, particularly cases in which the perpetrator derives no financial gain, are less likely to cause affront to jurors. One former prosecutor in the United States referred to resource constraints and their bearing upon the decision to prosecute a defendant who did not profit from piracy:

> I had more good cases than I could prosecute all the time, and I don't think you're going to find US Attorneys sympathetic to bringing criminal cases against somebody who is not deriving a profit from the activity, you know, the Robin Hood defense. How excited is a jury going to get about somebody who is giving away free [sic] on the Internet? (Quoted in United States Sentencing Commission 2000, Intellectual Property/Copyright Infringement: Group Breakout Session Two, Day Two, p. 249.)

One convenient measure for judging the severity of a matter for purposes of deciding whether to prosecute or not is the likely sentence in the event of conviction. Given the resource constraints under which most prosecutors labour, a case that is unlikely to result in any significant punishment may not be taken up.

> I see no problem with a prosecutor who has limited resources not prosecuting these situations, not because they aren't crimes, but simply because you have limited resources and there's not much punishment. (Quoted in United States Sentencing Commission 2000, Intellectual Property/Copyright Infringement: Group Breakout Session Two, Day Two, p. 255.)

The suggestion that some victims of crime make less sympathetic witnesses because they placed themselves in a position of vulnerability and thereby facilitated the offence is anathema to many victim advocates, especially feminists. Nevertheless, prosecutors often take the antecedent conduct of the victim into consideration in assessing a case's jury appeal.

The same principles apply in some cyber crime cases, especially those in which the victim may have been lax in maintaining the security of its IT systems. In discussing cases involving economic espionage generally, one prosecutor commented:

> For us prosecutors, we're asking those questions. We're saying we have to prove to a jury that this is reasonable. 'What measures did you take to protect it?' And if they say, 'Well, none, but we hoped that they know that this was wrong,' we're going to evaluate that in deciding whether to bring the case. (D. Green, quoted in United States Sentencing Commission 2000, Intellectual Property/Copyright Infringement: Group Breakout Session Three, Day Two, p. 282.)

One aspect of offence severity that may weigh on the decision to prosecute is the amount of loss occasioned by the alleged criminal act. As discussed below in the chapter on sentencing (Chapter Eight), this has often challenged policy-makers.

Some prosecutors' offices (and, further upstream, law enforcement agencies) establish a monetary threshold that will determine whether or not they will pursue a case. All else being equal, this threshold will vary, depending on the size and resources of the prosecutor's office and the volume of cases they are handling. In some jurisdictions the threshold may run to six figures (United States Department of Justice 1997, p. 33). For obvious reasons, these guidelines are not publicised, although one could argue that the principle of fairness would require transparency.

The question of whether this is measured in terms of the offender's gain or the victim's loss has been a challenging one. As we have noted, some offenders, driven by motives other than profit, achieve no financial gain. They may feel avenged, or enjoy notoriety, but they don't profit financially. The successful campaign in the United States to place greater weight on loss to the victim in electronic piracy cases was part of the movement to increase the priority of intellectual property prosecutions.

Civil Remedies or Criminal Prosecution

Another factor that may bear on the prosecutor's decision is the availability of civil remedies, either to the government or to a private party. In many cases of securities fraud, for example, regulatory authorities may be content to recover the offender's ill-gotten gains (and, in some cases, a civil fine), and to obtain an undertaking to refrain from further inappropriate conduct. Referrals for criminal prosecution are reserved for only the most serious cases. Under several European systems the victim is entitled to claim damages as part of the criminal proceedings, and the decision to prosecute may be based in part on deference to the victim's financial interest.

In cases of copyright infringement, individual victims often command substantial resources of their own, and may avail themselves of extensive civil remedies. Prosecutors may consider the deterrent effects of these remedies, and assess whether criminal prosecution will add any value. In cases where offenders have arranged their affairs so that they are judgment-proof, or have concealed their assets offshore in a relatively inaccessible location, the civil path may be less fruitful, and circumstances may militate in favour of prosecution.

In cases where the victim has ample resources, the victim may encourage prosecution as well as pursuing private civil remedies. The following remarks by a senior executive of the Walt Disney Company illustrate that even very large and powerful organisations don't always get what they want:

> Whether we go criminally or civilly to a large degree depends upon what the US Attorney in that particular locality says. Despite everybody's talk about how it's improper evaluation by prosecutors, the fact is, they weren't bringing cases.

When asked whether Disney had actually sought a prosecutor to bring a case, the executive replied:

> Oh yes, and been declined on quite a few cases. In large part, it wasn't necessarily anything other than the offices having limited resources. I think this is, by the way, normal . . . management thinking. The US Attorney says, 'I have limited resources. I want to go after the person who is causing violence to my fellow citizens in my locality. I'm going to go after them rather than a copyright infringement which has a comparatively low guideline level, and as a result, I'm not going to bring it. I just don't have the manpower to do it or the money. And then we as copyright owners decide to go civilly. (Quoted in United States Sentencing Commission 2000, Intellectual Property/Copyright Infringement: Group Breakout Session Two, Day Two, p. 248.)

The systemic nature of the criminal process means that decisions taken in one institution will often have ramifications elsewhere. As we shall see in Chapter Eight, one of the most significant changes in the criminal process in the United States has been the introduction of sentencing guidelines, which serve to constrain the discretion of judges significantly in imposing criminal sentences. The guidelines have the effect of giving more power to the prosecutor, since the eventual sentencing outcome will be driven primarily by the charges laid (Standen 1993).

Discretionary power therefore becomes concentrated in the prosecutor, whose charging decisions will have significant bearing on the sentence ultimately imposed. In some cases this may militate in favour of leniency. As one US prosecutor commented in relation to the prosecution of juveniles (an issue discussed in more detail below):

> If the guideline does require a substantial prison sentence, is a prosecutor going to bring that case? Here's a case that everybody says the right answer is probation, but now I've got a guideline that says I don't have that option. If I prosecute this kid, he's going to jail for 16 months. (Quoted in US Sentencing Commission 2000, Intellectual Property/Copyright Infringement: Group Breakout Session Two, Day Two, p. 252.)

Table 9 – *Computer crime referrals and declinations, United States Department of Justice, 1992–2001*

	Fiscal year									
	1992	1993	1994	1995	1996	1997	1998	1999	2000	2001
Number of referrals for prosecution	115	126	155	201	197	292	417	497	807	853
Number of referrals disposed of	69	100	133	137	172	178	253	360	491	631
Number of referrals with prosecution declined	53	68	110	105	126	125	196	271	393	496
Number convicted after prosecution	12	26	18	23	33	37	47	72	81	107
Number not guilty after prosecution	4	6	5	9	13	16	10	17	17	28

Source: Matthew Scherb, JD candidate, 2004, Northwestern University, as published in Granick et al. (2003)

Patterns and Trends in Prosecution

An analysis of computer crime prosecutions by the United States Department of Justice between 1992 and 2001 (Granick, Hernandez, Young, and Tien 2003, p. 5) supports the notion that prosecutors are fairly selective. Annual referrals for prosecution increased sevenfold over the period, no doubt reflecting both an increase in computer crime and an increase in the law enforcement resources devoted to its investigation. The number of declinations also rose progressively over the period, registering a similar sevenfold increase. Of all the computer crime referrals disposed of by the United States Department of Justice each year, over three-quarters were cases rejected for prosecution. In other words, less than a quarter ever went to court (Table 9).

An analysis of dispositions in 1998 revealed that the most common reason for declining a prosecution was weak or insufficient evidence. Nearly a third of all declinations were attributed to lack of evidence of criminal intent, or lack of other admissible evidence. Another 30 per cent of declinations arose from the absence of a federal interest, the lack of deterrent value, or the fact that another jurisdiction intended to prosecute (Table 10).

Prosecutorial Priorities

In some places, matters will take on a higher priority depending on economic or political developments. One of the most compelling illustrations of this is the current status of offences relating to Internet child pornography in the criminal justice systems of many nations. Heightened concerns about sexual exploitation of children in the 1990s happened to coincide with the growth in telecommunications and computing technology. These technological developments played a large part in facilitating the production, reproduction and dissemination of

Table 10 – *Reasons for declining prosecutions in computer crime cases, US Department of Justice, 1998*

Reason for declination	Number	% of declinations	% of total dispositions
Lack of evidence of criminal intent	27	13.78	10.67
Weak or insufficient admissible evidence	34	17.35	13.44
Suspect to be prosecuted by other authorities	23	11.73	9.09
No federal offence evident	21	10.71	8.30
Minimal federal interest or no deterrent value	19	9.69	7.51
No known suspect	17	8.67	6.72
Juvenile suspect	10	5.10	3.95
Agency request	10	5.10	3.95
Civil, administrative, or other disciplinary alternatives	6	3.06	2.37
Office policy (fails to meet prosecutorial guidelines)	6	3.06	2.37
Jurisdiction or venue problems	5	2.55	1.98
Pre-trial diversion completed	5	2.55	1.98
Lack of investigative or prosecutorial resources	4	2.04	1.60
Witness problems	3	1.53	1.19
Suspect being prosecuted on other charges	3	1.53	1.19
Other	13	6.63	5.15

Source: Matthew Scherb, JD candidate, 2004, Northwestern University, as published in Granick et al. (2003)

child pornography. Additional developments such as the widespread availability of strong encryption have further assisted in concealing this activity from the attention of law enforcement agencies.

Responding to these concerns, governments in many nations enacted new laws, and allocated more resources to the investigation and prosecution of persons possessing or distributing child pornography. Because the stakes for the defendant are high (as we shall see below, courts in the United States impose severe penalties upon individuals convicted of these offences) charges are often defended aggressively. The jurisprudence of cyber crime is thus marked by an overrepresentation of child pornography cases. Many cases where the admissibility and authenticity of digital evidence have been challenged have involved alleged child pornography.

Another example of changing priorities is that of digital piracy or intellectual property (IP) crimes. In the United States, creators of music, video, software, and other valuable digital commodities have a great deal to protect. One might also argue that the future of creativity and indeed, the future of the information economy depends on the protection of intellectual property. Representatives of the affected industries succeeded in convincing Congress that this is the case, and in response, the Department of Justice formally designated intellectual property crimes as a priority in July 1999 (Goldstone 2001, p. 2). In May 2000, the US Congress enacted revisions to the US Sentencing Guidelines, with the effect of increasing penalties for electronic piracy and related offences.

Determining the Identity of the Offender

Since every computer connected to the Internet has a unique identifying number (the IP or Internet Protocol address) it would seem at first blush relatively easy to determine the source of a criminal communication. While this may indeed be the case for the unsophisticated offender who leaves bold electronic footprints, more sophisticated cyber criminals may be more difficult to identify. For example, an offender may alter or 'spoof' his IP address, and/or may 'loop' or 'weave' through a number of computers anywhere in the world before reaching the victim's computer. Moreover, IP numbers may be dynamic, attributed by the Internet service provider for a single communication. Under these circumstances, the source computer can only be identified through the assistance of the service provider concerned.

In addition, finding the source computer may not necessarily identify the perpetrator. So called 'Internet cafés' have many transient users. Even when a computer is located in a private home, a suspect may claim that he was not the only person with access to the computer in question, or even claim that his computer had been accessed remotely by an unknown person and used in furtherance of criminal activity. As we shall see in Chapter Four, successful prosecution may depend upon determining the true originator of the offending communication, and its route through each of the systems through which it has passed. In some cases, a search of physical premises is needed to catch the perpetrator red-handed or to find the conclusive evidence. Otherwise, the prosecution must make a case based on strong circumstantial evidence.

Framing the Charge

One of the more important challenges facing any prosecutor is to get the charge right. Whether in terrestrial space or in cyberspace, this means fitting the facts to the law. For example, in a homicide where evidence of premeditation is lacking, one does not normally charge a suspect with murder. Manslaughter (which does not require proof of intent to kill) is more appropriate.

Consistency in charging, whether in relation to cyber crime or terrestrial crime, is an understandable value under the rule of law. Given the differences in resources and priorities that may exist in some large jurisdictions such as the United States, occasional efforts are made to standardise prosecutorial practices. In September of 2003, the Attorney General of the United States sent a memorandum to all federal prosecutors, advising them of a general duty to charge and to pursue the most serious, readily provable offence in all federal prosecutions (Ashcroft 2003).

The goal of this policy was not only consistency across the federal system, but also an increase in the severity of sanctions. Nevertheless, 'overcharging' is a tactic sometimes used by prosecutors as an ambit claim in cases that may involve plea negotiations. That is, a prosecutor will charge the most serious offence imaginable with a view towards dropping it in return for a plea of guilty on a lesser charge.

The element of intent is no less important in framing charges in cyber crime cases than it is in terrestrial matters. As we shall see, the vocabulary of extenuation that is employed by offenders often extends to the apology that the person did not mean any harm, and did not foresee the consequences of his or her actions. Where the prosecutor has a good indication of intent, she will charge accordingly. To quote Martha Stansell-Gamm, Chief of the Computer Crime and Intellectual Property Section of the US Justice Department:

> If you intentionally damage data, whether you are an insider or an outsider, felony. If you are a hacker and you recklessly damage data, felony. If you are a hacker and you simply cause damage, misdemeanour. (Quoted in United States Sentencing Commission 2000, Intellectual Property/Copyright Infringement: Group Breakout Session One, Day Two, p. 230.)

The available evidence will usually determine the charge.

It is incumbent upon prosecutors to exercise great caution in drafting charges. Where the law has sought to keep abreast of technology, there may be new offences that can be applied to a given criminal act. Alternatively, time-honoured terrestrial charges, such as conspiracy to defraud, may be applied. Judges and juries may be more comfortable with a familiar statute than with one specifically crafted to address cyberspace illegality. Bell (2002) notes that it may be more convenient in the case of a hoax e-mail message to charge the accused with forgery. British prosecutors may forsake the *Computer Misuse Act 1990* for alternative charges under the *Data Protection Act 1984*, the *Telecommunications Act 1984*, or the *Terrorism Act 2000*.

One of the earlier prosecutions of computer crime showed how prosecutors may seek to stretch the law to meet new circumstances. In one case in the United Kingdom [**Case No. 8**], the accused had gained unauthorised access to a computer network and altered data contained on disks in the system. He was charged with damaging property under the *Criminal Damage Act 1971*; the *Computer Misuse Act 1990* was not yet in force. The prosecution faced a formidable challenge, as the Criminal Damage Act required proof of damage to tangible property. The prosecution succeeded in its claim that the disks and the 'magnetic particles' that they contained were one entity, and by altering the state of the magnetic particles, the perpetrator damaged the disks themselves. The accused was convicted at trial, and appealed. The appeals court affirmed the conviction, holding that it was sufficient to prove that tangible property had been damaged, not that the damage itself was tangible. Damage was defined broadly to embrace the 'temporary impairment of value or usefulness'. The subsequent enactment of the Computer Misuse Act was to pose new challenges for prosecutors, as we shall see.

Sometimes, legislatures are able to amend statutes enacted before the digital age to accommodate subsequent technological developments. This may still constitute a challenge for prosecutors, as defence counsel will seize upon any opportunity to contest the charges. Such was the case in a recent British matter [**Case No. 58**]. The accused had downloaded indecent images of children from the Internet and printed them out for his own use. The prosecution charged the defendant with making indecent photographs of children under the *Protection of Children Act 1978* as amended. Although the original Act referred to photographs, subsequent amendments applied it to data 'capable of conversion into a pseudo-photograph'. The defence, however, argued that the statute was ambiguous, in that the term 'make' implied the original act of creating, and did not encompass subsequent downloading or printing out of digital images.

The prosecution submitted that downloading is making, and that the Act was concerned not only with the original creation of images, but also with their proliferation. The court rejected the defence claim, holding that the words 'to make' must be given their natural and ordinary meaning, 'to produce by action, to bring about'.

One example of reliance on time-honoured legislation in response to a technologically sophisticated crime occurred in the United States from the Breeders' Cup betting scam in 2002. The defendant was a software developer for a company that maintains a network used to manage wagering systems at racetracks in North America. Using his access to the company's servers, he manipulated the system to enable a friend to win $3 million by 'picking' six consecutive winners in the 2002 Breeders' Cup race meeting. The defendant and his accomplices were charged with conspiracy to commit wire fraud (Associated Press 2002). A statute of sufficient breadth to embrace the conduct in question, 941 18 USC §1343, required the use of an interstate telephone call or 'wire communications' (which has been interpreted to include electronic communications) in furtherance of a scheme to defraud.

In the early years of the digital age, when legislation had yet to catch up with developments in information technology, many cases foundered on the failure of the prosecutor to fit the facts to the law. In the following chapter, we will see how the alleged creator of the 'Love Bug' virus escaped prosecution because what he was alleged to have done was not prohibited by the law of the Philippines. As close as authorities could come was to charge him with using a computer to obtain credit card or other personal information for a fraudulent purpose. This was not what he did, and indeed, was far wide of the mark.

Another such matter was an English case in which the accused had obtained access to a computer database owned by a telephone company by using customer passwords without permission. They were charged and convicted of contravening section 1(a) of the *Forgery and Counterfeiting Act 1981* (making a false instrument or device). They appealed on the ground that they had not made a false instrument, that is, a device on or which information was recorded or stored. The Crown appealed to the House of Lords, which held that the Crown was trying to force the facts of the case into the language of an Act not designed to fit them. The momentary holding of password details did not amount to recording or storing of information (*R v Gold and Schifreen* [1988] AC 1063; [1988] 2 All ER 186).

In some cases, prosecutors are able to fit pre-digital law to digital realities. Just as the law of theft was interpreted in some jurisdictions to include theft of intangible property (such as electricity), so too was the law of obscenity stretched slightly to embrace digital images. In a 1996 British case **[Case No. 29]**, the defendants were charged with various offences under the *Protection of Children Act 1978* and the *Obscene Publication Act 1959*, as amended in 1964, relating to indecent photographs of persons under the age of 16.

Section 1 of the Protection of Children Act made it an offence for a person

(c) to have in his possession such indecent photographs, with a view to their being distributed or shown by himself or another . . .

The defence maintained that data in digital form did not constitute a photograph. The court found that the data were a photograph 'in a different form'. The defence further maintained that the data were not 'distributed or shown' merely by its having been made available for downloading. Rather, the defence argued 'that which would be shown would be a reproduction called up by the person having access'. The prosecutor's original charging decision was vindicated when these defence claims were rejected.

A number of prosecutions have also foundered due to prosecutors simply choosing the wrong legislative provision when framing charges. In an early English case, the accused were officers in the Metropolitan Police who obtained car registration and ownership details from the Police National Computer. The data were obtained for their personal use, not police business. They were charged with, and convicted of, unauthorised access under section 1 of the Computer Misuse Act. They successfully appealed the conviction on the grounds that their access to the police computer was authorised; it was the subsequent activity that exceeded the bounds of their authorisation. The court observed that the defendants could have been successfully prosecuted under section 17(2) of the *Data Protection Act 1984*, which deals with improper use of data (*Director of Public Prosecutions v Bignell* [1998] 1 Cr App Rep 1). Legislation embracing Article 2 of the Council of Europe's *Convention on Cybercrime*, which prohibits unauthorised access to the whole or part of a computer system, would have covered this, as would 18 USC §1030, which includes 'exceeding authorised access'.

Shortly thereafter, the House of Lords clarified the meaning of unauthorised access for the purposes of the Computer Misuse Act by deciding that for access to be authorised, it must be authorised access to the relevant data or relevant program or part of a program. In that case one of the accused obtained bank account information from an employee of a credit card company and used it to forge credit cards, which he then used to make withdrawals from ATMs amounting to approximately US$1 million. It was decided that the employee of the credit card company had exceeded her authority by obtaining the account information for an improper purpose, and then passing it on to her co-accused (*R v Bow Street Magistrates Court; ex parte Government of the United States of America* [2000] 2 AC 216: **[Case No. 54]**.

In another British case, the accused gained unauthorised access to a computer with intent to commit a further offence relating to false accounting: **[Case No. 11]**. He was charged under section 1(1)(a) of the *Computer Misuse Act 1990* (UK) which made it an offence to '[cause] a computer to perform any function with intent to secure access to any program or data held in any computer'.

The defence argued that an essential element of the offence was the involvement of a second computer, and the evidence showed that the alleged activities were limited to one machine. Aglionby J agreed:

> It seems to me, doing the best that I can in elucidating the meaning of section 1(1)(a), that a second computer must be involved. It seems to me to be straining the language to say that only one computer is necessary when one looks to the actual wording of the subsection: 'Causing a computer to perform any function with intent to secure access to any program or data held in any computer.' It seems to me that had parliament intended that the section should cover the present situation the wording would be different, and the words 'that or any other computer' would have been added; but parliament has not said that.

In other legal systems, such as that of the Netherlands, judicial interpretation is more flexible, and a judge would have inferred that the legislature could not have intended such an outcome. But in this case, the charge was dismissed.

This was not a case of the prosecution having no choice but to 'shoehorn' the facts into an ill-drafted statute. Indeed, the judge himself noted that the activities in question would better have been dealt with under section 3 of the Act, which read:

> 3(1) A person is guilty of an offence if (a) he does any act which causes an unauthorised modification of the contents of any computer; and (b) at the time when he does the act he has the requisite intent and the requisite knowledge.

British courts have continued to rely on common law patches to legislation, as illustrated by a celebrated extortion case: **[Case No. 123]**. The defendants, two residents of Kazakhstan, obtained access to the victim's computer system in New York. (The victim, incidentally, was elected Mayor of New York City not long thereafter.) The two Kazakhs sent a series of e-mail messages declaring that the system had been compromised, and threatening to publicise this unless they were paid US$200,000. The victim contacted the FBI, and arranged to meet the alleged extortionists in London under circumstances which, unbeknownst to them, were under surveillance. The two were arrested and their extradition sought by the United States government. The extradition proceedings were based in part on a charge of causing an unauthorised modification of material in the victim's computer.

The defence argued that section 3(2)(c) of the Computer Misuse Act – 'to impair the operation of any such program or the reliability of any such data' – was confined to actions resulting in the computer's failure to record data, and did not extend to what they had done, which was to enter information that appeared to originate from one person when it in fact came from someone else. The court held that such electronic impersonation manifestly affected the reliability of the data, and allowed the extradition to proceed.

Prosecuting Juveniles

It has long been established wisdom in criminal justice that young people should face criminal proceedings only as a last resort. Authorities in Western criminal justice systems bend over backwards to avoid bringing the full force of the law against young offenders. Elaborate systems of counselling and diversion have been created to keep young offenders out of court.

Nevertheless, in cases of truly heinous conduct, such as homicide or sexual assault, or robbery, the last resort is occasionally exercised. One has also seen the prosecution of juveniles for extremely serious cyber crime.

Of course, until positive identification is made, the age and motive of a cyber criminal may not be immediately apparent. When a virus is released, when someone succeeds in obtaining unauthorised access to the information systems of a defence installation, or when an e-commerce site comes under attack, it may not be clear whether the perpetrator is the agent of a foreign government, a member of an organised crime syndicate, or just a 'techno-savvy kid'. Regardless of the perpetrator's identity, such conduct can inflict actual damage, or threaten potential damage, that can be very harmful. In the most serious cases, the harm or threat can be so grave as to demand that the offender be prosecuted, regardless of age.

The growth and diffusion of information technology provides juveniles with the capacity to do harmful acts that were simply unachievable before the digital age. The enormous growth in computing power and accessibility, and the relative technological sophistication of young people today, have given rise to some dramatic cases.

In 2000, a fifteen-year-old Canadian boy orchestrated a distributed denial-of-service attack against a number of prominent e-commerce sites, effectively shutting them down for several hours. Two years earlier, a juvenile in Massachusetts had pleaded guilty to disabling a telephone company computer servicing the control tower at Worcester airport. This put out of action both the main radio transmitter and a circuit that enabled approaching aircraft to send signals activating the runway lights (CNN 1998).

Prosecutors in the United States have shown little hesitation in bringing federal charges against juveniles alleged to have committed serious cyber crimes (DeMarco 2001). The conviction in the Worcester airport case was accompanied by a stern warning from federal prosecutors:

> This case reflects our intention to prosecute in federal court anyone, including a teenager, who commits a serious computer crime.
>
> Computer and telephone networks are at the heart of vital services provided by the government and private industry, and our critical infrastructure. They are not toys for the entertainment of teenagers. Hacking a computer or telephone network can create a tremendous risk to the public and we will prosecute juvenile hackers in appropriate cases, such as this one (United States Department of Justice 1998).

In relation to particularly young offenders, the prosecution may face additional obstacles in bringing a case to court. Most jurisdictions impose a minimum age for criminal responsibility, and some retain a further rebuttable presumption (known at common law as *doli incapax*) against criminal capacity. In Australia, for example, the minimum age of criminal responsibility is 10 years, while the further presumption against criminal responsibility operates until the age of 14 (see Urbas 2000b). The prosecution will only be able to rebut the presumption if it can prove that the young offender knew at the relevant time that his or her conduct was seriously wrong. Various forms of evidence will be relevant to this question, including general societal understandings of what constitutes serious wrongdoing, but a prosecution may face difficulties if there is a general lack of appreciation among youngsters – or the community generally – of the seriousness of hacking as punishable conduct. These issues are likely to become more acute as prosecutions of particularly young offenders are considered.

Prosecutors in some cases may have discretion to charge juveniles as adults. A person who was under the age of 18 at the time of the offence but over 21 at the time formal charges are filed may be prosecuted as an adult (see also Bowker 1999).

Authorities in the United Kingdom will also pursue juvenile computer criminals. Although they are unlikely to receive heavy sentences, there is a perceived need to proceed with prosecution in some cases in order to achieve general deterrence and to publicise the fact that the conduct in question is unacceptable and illegal.

Conclusions

Cyber crime vs conventional crime

At the dawn of the digital age, the novelty of computer crime, combined with the lack of technological sophistication in some prosecutors' offices and the inadequacy of some statutes to cope with new forms of crime, meant that some cases that might otherwise have been prosecuted were dropped. But as legislation began to adapt to emerging technologies and as prosecutors became more conversant with digital technology, there is less differentiation between cyber crime and conventional terrestrial criminality.

The bases for the decision to prosecute cyber crime are in many respects similar to those that apply to terrestrial crime. Considerations of severity of the alleged crime and sufficiency of evidence will continue to dominate. Serious offences where there exists a proverbial 'smoking gun', or an offender who identifies himself by boasting of his exploits, will be prosecuted. Those where the evidence (whether digital or physical) is weak will be declined.

Nevertheless, there are factors that continue to differentiate cyber crime from conventional terrestrial crime. One such factor arises from the tremendous capacity that digital technology has when placed in the hands of juveniles. Young people today are capable of (and have indeed succeeded in) launching attacks on critical infrastructure, disrupting large commercial enterprises, and influencing the price of shares traded on stock exchanges. Governments regard the most serious of these cases as requiring a deterrent response. As a result juveniles, who might otherwise be accorded more lenient treatment, are more often subject to prosecution. Achieving the goal of deterrence without appearing to direct the awesome power of the state against a teenage 'geek' requires new public relations skills.

Given the resource constraints upon most prosecutors, the availability of resources required to prosecute a case may determine whether a case goes ahead or not. This too applies to conventional crimes as well as crimes involving digital technology. Ballistics tests, behavioural profiling, DNA analysis, and other forensic procedures may be prohibitively expensive, except in the most major cases. The fact that cyber crime cases may be more likely than terrestrial crimes to involve offenders or crucial evidence located overseas means that cost may be a more salient factor in determining whether to proceed or not.

Cross-national comparisons

Despite significant efforts to achieve international harmonisation in law and policy with relation to cyber crime, considerable differences exist in prosecutors' responses to this type of case. The unique constitutional arrangements of the United States accord substantial protection to those who are the targets of criminal investigation and prosecution. The constraints that these constitutional protections place on law enforcement have invited involvement by prosecutors in the United States far earlier than occurs in other common law jurisdictions. This involvement is by no means limited to cyber crime cases; it also characterises other complex criminal investigations in the United States.

And of course, prosecutorial priorities will vary across jurisdictions, reflecting political cultures and political influences. The comparative zeal with which American prosecutors pursue perpetrators of piracy and intellectual property crime reflects the power of the software and entertainment industries in the United States. Elsewhere, prosecutors have what they see as competing priorities and more important domestic interests to protect.

CHAPTER FOUR

Cross-Border Issues

Introduction

One of the most important characteristics distinguishing computer-related crime from 'terrestrial crime' is the matter of jurisdiction. The global nature of cyberspace makes it much easier than ever before for a person sitting on one side of the world to commit a crime on the other side. The offending activity (whether it involves the sending of illicit images of children, malicious code, or fraudulent stock tips) can pass through numerous sovereign nations at the speed of light on the way to the target. Which of these nations can prosecute such cases: the jurisdiction where the activity was initiated, the place where it had its effect (that is, where the loss or damage was sustained), or a nation through which the offending communication may have passed on its path from origin to destination?

It is up to the prosecutor to decide whether a case should be prosecuted within his or her jurisdiction. It is up to the judge whether the court has jurisdiction to hear the case, on the basis of general statutory rules or the specific substantive offence with which the accused has been charged. Traditionally, jurisdiction required a substantial link with the territory in which the matter would be heard. Merely having been passed through by a communication en route from Country A to Country C was not always sufficient to achieve jurisdiction in Country B. A good deal of energy is now being devoted to expanding jurisdiction, as we shall soon see.

This transnational dimension of cyber crime poses four formidable challenges for prosecutors, especially those who may be involved from an early stage of investigations. The first is simply to determine whether the conduct in question is criminal in their own jurisdiction: prosecutors will be disinclined to expend their limited time and resources on matters that cannot lead to a prosecution. One of the most vivid illustrations of this comes from the classic book on hacking, a true story called *The Cuckoo's Egg* (Stoll 1989). What appeared first to be a trivial accounting error, discovered by a systems manager in a California research laboratory, turned out to be a major international espionage case. Prosecutors were initially disinclined to pursue a hacker who was apparently situated offshore until it became apparent that espionage may have been the purpose of his intrusions.

The second challenge is to assemble sufficient evidence to mobilise the law, that is, to obtain appropriate judicial authority for a physical search or for telecommunications interception. This is difficult enough when the offender is located within one's own borders. Even then, given the architecture of the Internet, evidence may be located in one or more foreign countries, and access to these may be difficult or impossible. It will normally require the assistance of authorities in the foreign country (or countries), who, for various reasons, may be unwilling or unable to assist. When the suspect himself is located abroad, these difficulties are compounded.

The third challenge is to identify the perpetrator, and to determine where he or she is physically located. This is easier said than done in an environment where technologies of anonymity and methods of stealing electronic identities can be exploited by a skilled offender to great advantage. The networked environment of cyberspace compounds this difficulty, as offences that appear to have originated in far-flung countries may in fact have been launched from across town. Conversely, apparently 'local' offences may have originated on the other side of the planet. Just as the identity and motive of the perpetrator may not be clear, so too may his or her whereabouts. Investigations by Hong Kong police following a complaint from a local woman that she was the victim of a cyberstalker led to a server in Colorado. Evidence obtained there revealed that the communications of the perpetrator, situated in Hong Kong, had been routed through the Colorado server (Lo 2002).

In addition, there are many circumstances where the nature of the offending conduct may not be immediately apparent. As we have noted, when an intrusion is first identified, one cannot be certain whether the perpetrator is an inquisitive teenager, a foreign government, or a member of a criminal gang. Moreover, what appears at first blush to be trivial may in fact be the loose thread of a much broader fabric. *The Cuckoo's Egg* espionage case is a vivid illustration.

Finally, there remains the decision of whether to leave the matter to authorities in the country where the suspect is physically situated, or to seek extradition of the offender to deal with him under one's own law. Not only can this latter course of action be both costly and time-consuming, it requires formal arrangements between countries. This chapter will discuss these challenges in more detail and will review cases that are illustrative of these problems and their management.

Jurisdiction

Sovereign states make their own criminal laws, and criminalise what they like (or rather, what they don't like!). The boundaries that separate conduct that is legal from criminal behaviour vary over time and from place to place. During the early nineteenth century in the United States, some states made it a crime to harbour a runaway slave, while others prohibited slavery per se. Today, slavery is universally condemned under international law.

The rapid development of digital technology, and its uneven adoption in the world today, have presented us with abundant examples of legislative efforts to keep abreast. Technology evolves faster than does the law. There are, moreover, significant differences across nations in both technological and legal development. These differences, and the efforts of the international community to overcome them, are discussed below in Chapter Six. In the present chapter, we seek to outline some of the challenges faced by prosecutors in deciding whether to encourage an investigation, and how to proceed against a suspect who is physically located beyond one's borders.

There are differences, of course, in the very basis of jurisdiction. Traditionally, the assertion of jurisdiction is based on four principles: territoriality; nationality; effects; and those matters that become the subject of universal jurisdiction (Tan 2000; Bellia 2001, note 33; Podgor 2002). According to the territoriality principle, sovereign states can assert jurisdiction over behaviour occurring within their territorial borders. The vast majority of criminal laws do just that. In practice, for the vast majority of terrestrial offences, the perpetrator, the victim and the act in question are all located in the same jurisdiction.

Cyber crime laws can also be territorially based. Article 3C of the *West Virginia Computer Crime and Abuse Act* states:

> Any person who violates any provision of this article, and in doing so, accesses, permits access to, causes access to or attempts to access a computer, computer network, computer data, computer resources, computer software or computer program which is located, in whole or in part, within this state, or passes through this state in transit, shall be subject to criminal prosecution and punishment in this state and to the civil jurisdiction of the courts of this state. (WVA CODE §61-3C-20)

Of course, authorities in West Virginia are probably not inclined to pursue every eligible offender, especially those whose communications may be incidentally routed through that state.

According to the nationality principle, states can assert jurisdiction over behaviour involving their citizens as perpetrators, regardless of where the alleged conduct occurred. Citizens of the United States, Australia, and many other places can be prosecuted in their home countries for having had sex with children anywhere in the world, even where such conduct may not constitute a criminal offence in those countries (see, for example, Australia's *Crimes (Child Sex Tourism) Amendment Act 1994* (Cth) which inserted new offences into the *Crimes Act 1914* (Cth)).

Under the effects principle, countries may assert jurisdiction over behaviour that affects their national interests, regardless of where it may have originated. Thus in 1989 the United States prosecuted the president of Panama for drug trafficking offences. A person who, on foreign soil, engages in an act of terrorism against an Australian citizen, or who assists others in entering Australia illegally, is similarly liable to prosecution in Australia.

Under principles of universal jurisdiction, countries can establish mechanisms to prosecute a person for conduct, regardless of where it was committed, that is deemed to be a crime against humanity, for example genocide or slavery. So it is that numerous countries have prosecuted persons for alleged war crimes committed both far away and long ago, particularly during World War II in Europe.

In Australia, the *Cybercrime Act 2001* (Cth) asserts jurisdiction where

- the conduct constituting the offence occurs partly in Australia or on board an Australian ship or aircraft;
- the result of the conduct constituting the offence occurs partly in Australia or on board an Australian ship or aircraft; or
- the person committing the offence is an Australian citizen or an Australian company.

These provisions are broadly consistent with the Council of Europe's Cyber-crime Convention. Thus, an Australian who travels to another country where hacking is not an offence and from there, hacks into a third country, could be prosecuted in Australia.

If an apparent crime is indeed worth investigating, assistance may be needed from authorities in the country where the offence originated, and/or from authorities in the country or countries through which the offending activity may have passed on its way to the target, or where evidence of the crime may be situated. There are two basic elements to cooperation: informal investigator-to-investigator assistance, and formal mutual assistance (AGEC 2001).

Informal assistance can be more expeditious, and is the preferred method of approach where compulsory powers (i.e. search warrants) are not required. It is based on good working relationships between police services of the countries in question, born of contacts made over time in the course of conferences, courtesy visits, and previous joint investigations.

Formal mutual assistance, on the other hand, is a more cumbersome process traditionally invoked pursuant to treaty arrangements between the countries in question, and involving the exchange of formal documents. It almost always requires that the offence in question be over a certain threshold of severity, and that it be a crime in both the requesting and the requested countries. This latter convention is referred to as 'dual criminality'.

There exists a web of bilateral mutual assistance treaties between pairs of nations as well as multilateral agreements such as the London Extradition Scheme, which provides for the rendition of fugitive offenders among members of the Commonwealth of Nations (Grabosky 1998).

Where was the Crime?

In some circumstances, it may not be immediately clear where a crime has occurred. At the very least, this initial obscurity can provide the accused with an argument. One of the more celebrated cases of the 1990s involved an attack against Citibank by a young Russian: **[Case No. 31]**. Using his own computer in Russia, the accused obtained unauthorised access to the bank's servers in the United States. He enlisted a number of confederates to open up bank accounts around the world, then instructed the Citibank computer to transfer funds to the various accounts. When the scheme was discovered and the accused identified as the perpetrator, an arrest warrant was issued in a US Federal Court. There was no extradition treaty at the time between Russia and the United States, but the accused made the mistake of visiting England to attend a computer exhibition. British authorities were obliged to cooperate in extraditing him to face charges in the United States. Under the extradition arrangements in force between the United Kingdom and the United States, UK authorities could assist as long as the offence with which the accused was charged had some equivalent in UK law. The accused applied for a writ of habeas corpus challenging the extradition, arguing *inter alia* that the appropriation had taken place in Russia, where his computer keyboard was located, not in the United States. The court held that the accused's physical presence in St Petersburg was of less significance than the fact that he was operating on electromagnetic disks located in the United States. Moreover, the acts with which the accused had been charged had clear equivalents in the *Computer Misuse Act 1990*; had he been operating from the United Kingdom rather than Russia, English courts would have had jurisdiction. The accused was eventually extradited to the United States, where he was convicted and sent to prison.

A more recent case involved a resident of Melbourne who was accused of stalking a woman in Canada: **[Case No. 147]**. The alleged offending communications included telephone calls and conventional letters; reference was also made to a website and to e-mail messages sent to others in Canada. The Canadian woman, who had never set foot in Australia, complained to Toronto police, who contacted Victorian police with the allegation that the communications in question had caused fear on her part about the Melbourne man's intentions.

The likelihood that Canadian authorities would seek extradition for a relatively minor offence was small, and Victorian police proceeded under section 21A of Victoria's *Crimes Act 1958*, which came into operation in January 1995. In July of 2000, the defendant denied that any harm was done to the Canadian woman, and argued further that if harm had been done, it was experienced in Canada and not in Victoria. The magistrate observed that the relevant section of the Crimes Act contained no express provision relating to the extraterritorial application of the law, and that the fear or apprehension, an essential element of the offence, had to be experienced within the borders of Victoria. The magistrate dismissed the charge, ruling that she did not have jurisdiction to hear the case.

The Director of Public Prosecutions appealed against dismissal of the charge, claiming that the Parliament of Victoria did have the power to create an offence with extraterritorial application, and that the magistrate did indeed have jurisdiction.

The Supreme Court set aside the magistrate's ruling, holding that in this age of modern technology, Parliament could not have intended to confine the legislation to actions and effects occurring solely in Victoria:

> Criminals are not respecters of borders. State and international boundaries do not concern them. They commit their evil acts anywhere and without thought to location.
>
> Movement between countries is much greater now than in the past and subject to less restrictions. Technology has reached the point where communications can be made around the world in less than a second. The Internet provides a speedy, relatively inexpensive means of communication between persons who have access to a computer and a telephone line. Access is not confined to ownership of a computer and businesses have sprung up offering access to the Internet for a small charge.
>
> The law must move with these changes ([2001] VSC 43, 1 March 2001, per Gillard J at par. 61–63).

Notably, the Victorian legislature has since acted to clarify that the offence is to be understood as covering cyberstalking and operating extraterritorially: *Crimes (Stalking) Act 2003* (Vic), in effect from 10 December 2003.

The nature of some cyber crimes is such that their effects are felt simultaneously in a number of nations around the world. This raises questions about whether harm occurring across a number of jurisdictions might be aggregated for the purpose of determining the seriousness of crime (and the severity of punishment). As Scott Charney of Microsoft commented:

[T]he denial of service attacks via 'LoveBug' – These were global events. To what extent are we going to calculate in global harms as part of this process? Are we going to expect every country to prosecute the defendant and each get their piece of this person for the damage he did in that country, or are we going to start thinking about how to aggregate the losses in one country and maybe sentence him there for the good of the entire planet? (Quoted in United States Sentencing Commission 2000.)

The flip side of every affected nation wanting a piece of the prosecutorial action is the situation in which no nation wants to go to the trouble of bringing an offender to justice. It would appear to be easier to let a matter 'fall between the cracks' than it would be to see justice done across a number of sovereign states. In practice, however, this is unlikely to happen. In transnational cases involving serious harm, the state with the greatest interest or with the most resources would be likely to proceed with prosecution.

Foreign Prosecution

Perhaps the easiest solution is to leave the matter to authorities in the country from which the perpetrator undertook the alleged criminal activity (if the perpetrator is still there). For fairly mundane matters, where the alleged activity is a crime in both countries and there is a degree of trust that justice will be done, this tends to be a preferred option. It is a much less costly and time-consuming path to take than extradition. This is what Canadian authorities sought to do in the stalking case.

Perhaps the most publicised example of allowing the host country to handle things was the case of the 15-year-old Canadian youth whose distributed denial-of-service attacks against Yahoo, Amazon.com and other prominent e-commerce sites in February 2000 earned him global notoriety. Few if any countries are prepared to extradite juveniles, and in this case, the extradition of a juvenile was precluded under Canadian law. Confidence on the part of US authorities that the young accused would be dealt with appropriately by their Canadian counterparts was not misplaced. In September 2001, he was sentenced to eight months in a youth detention centre.

Another illustration of such deference to the host country can be found in an Australian case relating to securities fraud: [**Case No. 87**]. In May of 1999, a resident of Melbourne obtained access to a number of e-mail servers and sent more than three million messages to addresses in Australia and the United States. The messages contained information purportedly reporting the results of research that predicted a 900 per cent rise in the price of shares in a US corporation that was listed on the NASDAQ Exchange.

In the heady days of the tech boom, share prices were particularly volatile and speculative buying rife. Relying on this, the accused, through a broker in Canada, had bought 65,000 shares in the target company at 38 cents per share, some four days earlier. When the NASDAQ opened for trading on Monday, 10 May, it appeared that the accused's mass e-mailing had been heeded by at least some of its recipients. Trading in the company's shares was approximately ten times the average daily volume and the share price doubled. The accused then instructed his broker to sell his shares, and made a profit of US$12,750.

Following the dramatic rise in the price of its shares, trading was suspended and the company issued a press release denying the statements made in the e-mail messages. Unfortunately for some investors, and eventually for the accused himself, the information in his e-mail messages had been false. When trading resumed the next day, the company's shares fell from an opening price of 53 cents to a closing price of 23 cents per share.

Not only did the accused manipulate the price of shares, his use of a number of servers to disseminate his three million e-mail messages necessitated that down time had to be taken for system maintenance, and gave rise to concerns for the security of the commercial enterprises whose servers had been compromised.

What the accused did made him liable to criminal charges in at least two countries: Australia and the United States. In relatively minor cases of sharemarket manipulation, it is common for authorities in the United States to proceed civilly, seeking disgorgement of the ill-gotten gains and a permanent injunction against the perpetrator not to reoffend. The Securities and Exchange Commission in the United States obtained judgment against the defendant in the District Court of Colorado for about US$15,800; the precise amount would be determined by the amount of interest due on the date of eventual disgorgement. Rather than mobilise the federal criminal process and seek to extradite the defendant, US authorities were happy to leave prosecution to Australia.

In Australia, the maximum penalty for the kind of sharemarket manipulation with which the defendant was charged was a fine of A$20,000 (US$15,000) or imprisonment for five years, or both. The offence of interrupting or obstructing the lawful use of a computer carried a maximum penalty of imprisonment for ten years.

The defendant pleaded guilty to two counts of making statements or disseminating information that was false in a material particular, or materially misleading and likely to induce the purchase of securities by other persons, contrary to the Corporations Law. He also pleaded guilty to one count of interfering with, interrupting or obstructing the lawful use of a computer contrary to section 76E of the *Crimes Act 1914* (Cth). He was sentenced to prison for three years, to be released on probation after three months subject to good behaviour.

Here we can see once again the deference to Australian justice. US authorities chose not to incur the costs or risk the uncertainties for an outcome not significantly more severe than that likely to flow from the Australian criminal process.

There are circumstances, however, when not everything will fall into place. Authorities in the country from which criminal activity is launched may lack the legal capacity to act. That is, harmful though it may be, the activity in question may not be a crime where it was committed.

Perhaps the most notorious case of this kind involved the creation and release of the 'I Love You' or 'Love Bug' virus in the year 2000. In early May of that year, a virus spread rapidly around the world, infecting Microsoft Windows operating systems. Victims would receive an e-mail message with an attachment, and with 'ILOVEYOU' displayed as the subject heading. When the attachment was opened, it hid or damaged files in the computer, then replicated itself by sending a similar message with attachment to all addresses in the infected computer's address book or network-shared drives. Some of the world's largest corporations were affected. Many had to shut down their systems to purge the virus, or for security checks. Calculating costs incurred as the result of such attacks is always risky; the estimated losses to businesses worldwide from the 'Love Bug' virus ranged from US$6.7 billion to US$15.3 billion in computer down time and software damage (Beh 2001; Grossman 2000).

Investigators quickly traced the virus to an Internet service provider (ISP) in the Philippines. Within a day of the attack, the ISP, Philippine authorities and the FBI identified a residence and telephone connection from which the virus appeared to have originated, but then matters stalled. Three days passed before a warrant could be executed. The boyfriend of the resident was arrested, but then released. On 30 June 2000, charges were laid against the resident's brother, a computer science student. The accused, who was remanded in custody, admitted that he might have released the virus, but did not admit to having created it. More importantly, because the creation and distribution of computer viruses were not defined as criminal acts under the laws of the Philippines, he had been charged under the only remotely applicable statute, the Access Devices Regulation Act – which made it a criminal offence to use a computer to obtain credit card or other personal information for a fraudulent purpose. When the Prosecutor's office determined that no crime had been committed under that Act, charges against the accused were dropped, and he was once again a free man. The lack of dual criminality precluded any extradition to the United States.

The 'I Love You' case provided a vivid illustration of the problems posed by the lack of harmonisation of laws. The international reaction to the lack of appropriate law appears to have caused some discomfort to Philippine authorities. In June of 2000, while the ill-fitting charges against the accused were still pending, the Philippines Congress enacted the *Electronic Commerce Act 2000* (Republic Act No. 8792). Section 33 of the legislation states that persons convicted of 'hacking or cracking' – the unauthorised access to or interference with a computer system/server or information and communication system; or any access in order to corrupt, alter, steal, or destroy using a computer, 'including the introduction of computer viruses and the like' – shall face a minimum fine of 100,000 pesos (about US$1770) and a maximum commensurate to the damage incurred, as well as mandatory imprisonment of six months to three years. The principle of non-retrospective application, however, protected the accused from being charged under this Act.

Another case where the element of dual criminality was lacking but which did eventually result in a successful prosecution was that of a 21-year-old Argentinian: **[Case No. 25]**. Toward the end of 1995, the young man, who lived at home in Buenos Aires with his parents and three younger brothers, used his PC and the facilities of Telecom Argentina to obtain unauthorised access to accounts in the Harvard University computer system. He achieved this by installing a 'sniffer' program that captured the user ID and passwords of legitimate Harvard users. He then set about using these accounts to access other systems, including those of NASA, the US Department of Defense, and the Los Alamos National Laboratory, among others. While he did not appear to have gained access to highly classified material, he was able to view and copy sensitive data on radar technology and aircraft design. When his intrusions became apparent, the target agencies were required to spend substantial sums to re-secure their systems.

In what appears to have been the first time in the United States that court-authorised electronic surveillance was used to identify and locate the perpetrator of a crime committed over the Internet, investigators from the FBI and the US

Naval Investigative Service, working with a federal prosecutor, were able to trace the intrusions to computer systems in Buenos Aires. The hacker's use of the nickname 'el griton' ('the screamer' in Spanish), also used as the name of his electronic bulletin board, led local authorities to the suspect's residence.

Although the Argentine authorities exchanged information and cooperated with their US counterparts, prosecution was to prove elusive. In March 1996, the accused was charged under US law with three offences:

- knowingly and with intent to defraud, possessing fifteen or more unauthorised computer passwords, user identification names, codes and other access devices: 18 USC §1029(a)(3);
- the illegal interception of electronic communications: 18 USC §2511(1)(a);
- fraudulent and destructive activity in connection with computers: 18 USC §1030(a)(5).

Unfortunately for prosecutors in the United States, the accused challenged their extradition request by claiming that the offences in question had no counterpart under Argentine law, and that the element of dual criminality necessary for extradition did not exist. He successfully argued before an Argentine court that extradition arrangements between the United States and Argentina did not extend to the offences in question. As one United States prosecutor later observed, 'We couldn't do anything until it became extraditable, or until he became extradited – or until he returned to this country for another reason. If he came into this country, then we could arrest him' (Amy Rindskopf, Office of the US Attorney for the District of Massachusetts, quoted in Stutz 1997). Some legal systems allow proceedings *in absentia* if the accused has been properly summoned. In the event of conviction, execution of the verdict is possible if the convicted person enters the jurisdiction.

The accused remained in Argentina, beyond the reach of US law, but neither out of sight nor out of mind. Merely to set foot in any other jurisdiction whose laws permitted extradition to the United States for the offences in question ran the risk of rendition to the US and a lengthy stay there (as the unfortunate Russian involved in the Citibank matter had recently discovered). Offered the opportunity to plead guilty to reduced charges, the accused waived extradition and travelled to the United States voluntarily in May 1998, where he was convicted of unlawfully intercepting non-classified communications and damaging files on NASA and Department of Defense computers. He was fined $5000 and sentenced to three years of probation (Reuters 1998).

Even if the activity in question is an offence under the law of both countries, authorities in the other country may lack the technical capacity to assist. They simply may not have the forensic skills necessary to provide the assistance required. Their involvement may, knowingly or unwittingly, indicate to the target of an investigation that he or she is under scrutiny.

Moreover, domestic law determines the extent to which mutual assistance can be given to another state. Some countries do not require dual criminality. Others do, but only when coercive measures are to be applied. Others restrict the instruments available.

Legal and technical capacity to assist are necessary, but still not sufficient, to ensure cooperation. No less essential is the political will to assist. Priorities differ across nations; what is of burning importance in Country A may be relatively unimportant in Country B. If relations with one's counterparts in another country are not close, one is less likely to go the extra mile. Even where a treaty places an obligation on parties to cooperate, the use of tortuous bureaucratic procedures, delay, and a search for exceptions may cause matters to grind to a halt. When authorities in another country are disinclined to cooperate, for whatever reason, investigations can be complex and legally murky. It may be possible to identify a perpetrator in cyberspace, but bringing him or her to justice can, under these circumstances, be very difficult.

Authorities in some countries have devised quite elaborate deceptions to overcome some of these jurisdictional impediments. One of the more intriguing [Case No. 155], involved two skilled Russian hackers (United States Department of Justice 2000). By exploiting a vulnerability in Windows NT, the two residents of Chelyabinsk, Russia launched a number of intrusions against Internet service providers, online banks and e-commerce sites in the United States. The offenders succeeded in stealing over 56,000 credit card numbers and other personal financial information of the sites' customers. They then sought to extort money from the victims by threatening to publish customers' data and damage the companies' computers. They manipulated eBay auctions by using anonymous e-mail accounts to be both seller and winning bidder in the one auction. The online payment system PayPal was also defrauded by using cash generated from stolen credit cards to pay for various products. Attacks of this degree of severity, embarrassing though they may be, are not in the victims' interest to conceal, and these gave rise to a nationwide FBI investigation. One of the pair was identified when he sought to collect an extortion payment.

In an undercover operation that would be prohibited by law in many other countries, FBI agents posing as representatives of a security firm called 'Invita' made contact with the two Russians in mid 2000, ostensibly to discuss employment opportunities in the United States. At the invitation of the undercover agents, the two Russians demonstrated their hacking skills from Russia against a test network that had been established for the purpose. They were then invited to Seattle with the prospects of employment. The two flew to Seattle, all expenses paid, and were 'interviewed' about their computing skills. In the course of their presentation, one of the suspects accessed his computer system back in Russia. The interview took place in offices that were well equipped, with technologies that enabled the FBI to record their interviewees' keystrokes. The two were then arrested and charged with an assortment of offences including fraud, extortion, and unauthorised computer intrusions.

Shortly thereafter, the FBI notified Russian consular authorities that two of their nationals had been arrested. This raised the prospect that the offenders' families and eventually their colleagues in Russia would soon learn of their predicament and destroy any evidence on their Russian computers or otherwise keep it beyond reach of the investigators.

Mutual assistance agreements between Russia and the United States did not extend to the investigation of computer crimes. After several unsuccessful attempts to enlist the assistance of Russian authorities, FBI investigators went ahead and copied data from the suspects' servers back in Russia (Lemos 2001). The data were preserved unread until approval from FBI headquarters and the Department of Justice, and a search warrant, were obtained. A warrant was necessary at this stage because when the copied data entered the territory of the United States, that material became subject to the protections of the Fourth Amendment.

After the fact, the investigators notified Russian authorities through official channels that the download had taken place. The Russians appear to have been less than pleased with these events; the Chelyabinsk branch of Russian counter-intelligence, the Federal Security Service, later charged one of the FBI agents with computer hacking. Three FBI agents who led the investigation were awarded the FBI Director's Award for Excellence. This was the first FBI case to involve the extraterritorial seizure of digital evidence.

The defence raised a number of objections, some relating solely to domestic legal matters, others with a cross-national flavour. One defendant claimed that the FBI violated the Fourth Amendment by using his password to access computers physically located in Russia and downloading data from them. That is, the remote cross-border search was unconstitutional. The court, citing the precedent of *United States v Verdugo-Urquidez*, 494 US 259 (1990), held that the Russian computers, which were the property of a non-resident and located outside US territory, were not subject to constitutional protection. The defence attempted to distinguish his case from *Verdugo* by arguing that his entry to the US was voluntary (thereby making him part of the 'national community' and providing the basis for Fourth Amendment protection), whereas Verdugo's was involuntary, subsequent to arrest. The court held that a single voluntary entry made for a criminal purpose was hardly sufficient to make the defendant part of the 'national community'.

The defence further argued that the search in *Verdugo* was a joint effort made lawfully, pursuant to Mexican law, whereas the search of the Russian computers was unilateral, done by fiat. The court observed that 'Nothing in the (*Verdugo*) opinion, however, indicates that the reach of the Fourth Amendment turns on this issue'.

Moreover, as the data in Russia were merely copied and remained intact and unaltered, there was no effect on the defendants' (or anyone else's) possessory rights, and therefore no seizure. The expeditious downloading of the data prior to obtaining a warrant was justified because the volatility of the evidence created exigent circumstances (see Westlaw: 2001 WL 1024026, (WD Wash., 23 May 2001)).

US law differs from that of some European countries, where evidence obtained through remote cross-border searches not authorised by the host country may be subject to exclusion. The *Council of Europe Convention on Cybercrime* specifies that parties must seek mutual assistance. Article 16 will provide the defendant with a clear defence if the procedure is not followed.

Practicalities

The framework of treaties and other agreements which can form the basis for mutual assistance is far from perfect. Soma, Muther and Brisette (1997, p. 326) refer to a patchwork of varying extradition standards. Moreover, costs associated with mutual legal assistance are borne by the party providing assistance. This creates hardship where small countries, which may never request mutual assistance of their own motion, are required to accommodate requests from more affluent countries such as the United Kingdom and the United States. Poor countries may thus be bound by treaty to subsidising the rich.

Suffice it to say that the web of international cooperation in the fight against cyber crime remains very loosely woven. Governments are often left to their own devices to craft solutions, some of which have been bold in the extreme. Perhaps the most dramatic example in terrestrial terms was the abduction of Nazi war criminal Adolf Eichmann by Israeli agents in 1961 and his transportation to Israel for prosecution (and eventual execution). The invasion of Panama and the capture of Panamanian President Manuel Noriega by US military forces in 1989 is another.

Despite the existence of an extradition treaty between the United States and Mexico, persons authorised by agents of the US Drug Enforcement Administration forcibly kidnapped a citizen and resident of Mexico from his home and flew him to the United States where he was prosecuted (*United States v Alvarez-Machain*, 504 US 655 (1992)).

These were all dramatic incidents, not the daily stuff of criminal justice, and undertaken in only the most extreme of circumstances. But if one extrapolates from the 'Invita' case referred to above, involving the Russian hackers who were lured to Seattle and whose server in Russia was the subject of a remote search, one can expect numerous occasions when the opportunity to conduct remote cross-border searches may arise.

Searches of this kind highlight a fundamental conflict between two fundamental interests: the need for Nation A to regulate extraterritorial conduct having harmful effects within its own borders, and the interest of Nation B in protecting its own citizens from harmful extraterritorial conduct (Bellia 2001). For investigators from one nation to enter another country clandestinely to collect evidence of a crime would be a violation of the host nation's sovereignty. The law relating to remote cross-border searches is murky, and seems likely to remain so. Issues of what kind of judicial authority should be required, and from which country, or indeed what kind of notification of the host country may be appropriate, have already begun to occupy the attention of legal scholars (Goldsmith 2001; Bellia 2001).

Through its *Convention on Cybercrime*, the Council of Europe has taken initial steps to address the issue of remote cross-border searches. While the Convention recognises expedited mutual assistance as preferable, it does provide for remote searches without consulting the other party, where the information in question is publicly available or with consent of the person who has the lawful authority to disclose the data. Some European states have also formed joint law enforcement teams, which are authorised to operate on both sides of a border to investigate certain serious crimes.

Meanwhile, some nations will, in cases they regard as most serious, opt for expedient solutions. There are states that consider cross-border searches to be a violation of their sovereignty, and others that do not (Kaspersen 2000). It seems likely that, in the absence of increased international cooperation, the 'Invita' judgment will not be the last word.

With the dramatic growth in digital technology, more evidence will exist in digital form. Not only is there likely to be digital evidence at an increasing number of ordinary domestic crime scenes, but as more crime occurs across national borders and in the networked environment of cyberspace, more evidence will be located in other countries. As Stein (2001, p. 376) reminds us, 'Whether we like it or not, the world is wired.'

Conclusions

Although transnational crime predates the digital age, digital technology has certainly facilitated it, and has posed new challenges for prosecutors. It is safe to assume that cross-border offences are more common today than in years past, and the need for cooperation between criminal justice agencies in different countries is greater than ever before. The traditional mechanisms of international cooperation, including letters rogatory, mutual assistance and other formalities with roots in the nineteenth century and earlier, are ill-suited to an era where offences can be committed from across the world at the speed of light.

Because international cooperation depends on a degree of commonality (if not uniformity) across nations, prosecutors have been active in the development of policy to achieve harmonisation in substantive and procedural law. To this end, prosecutors deal more with their foreign counterparts.

Differences across the common-law world in prosecutorial approaches are not especially pronounced, with perhaps one exception. In the United States, authorities appear to be less constrained in the use of undercover methods. So-called 'stings' and remote cross-border searches conducted without the authority of the host country, such as we saw employed under the guise of 'Invita', would probably not occur in Australia, Canada or the United Kingdom. These more robust investigative tactics may compensate for the constraints imposed on other methods by the US Constitution.

CHAPTER FIVE

Strategies of Cyber Crime Litigation

Introduction

As we have noted, even in matters where jurisdiction is not a problem, the vast majority of cyber crimes never go to trial. In those that do, the evidence may not be overwhelmingly indicative of guilt, or there may be some basis for challenging the processes by which it was obtained. In either event, the prosecutor can usually expect a vigorous defence. This chapter discusses some of the issues that prosecutors may have to confront, either during an investigation, on the steps of the courthouse, in the course of a trial, or in the event of an appeal.

We have seen that the involvement of the prosecutor in the planning and execution of an investigation will vary from country to country. The nature of cyber crime is such that prosecutors are more likely than not to become involved at an earlier stage. In the common law world, this is most pronounced in the United States, where, as we shall see, there is ample constitutional basis for challenging the admissibility of evidence.

Possible defence strategies that might be anticipated or contested by the prosecution may take a variety of general forms. The issue of jurisdiction was addressed above in Chapter Four. Depending on the nature of the alleged offence and the circumstances of the investigation, an accused may claim:

- that he or she was not the person who did the act;
- that the act or acts in question were not intentional;
- that the evidence in question was improperly obtained, and should be suppressed; or
- that the evidence in question was altered or interfered with, and therefore not credible.

In this chapter, we discuss these strategies and present cases that illustrate the challenges they pose for prosecutors.

Determining the Identity of the Offender

We noted earlier that there is more to identifying a cyber criminal than locating the computer that was used to commit the crime in question.

The defence bar is getting wiser, and it is not uncommon to encounter the claim 'the prosecution can't prove that my client was at the keyboard'. This line won't go far in defending the boastful hacker, but it is something that investigators and prosecutors may have to anticipate when dealing with a skilled offender intent on concealing her identity.

In some investigations, it might be possible to determine when the alleged offender is online, and to conduct a physical raid on the location while the alleged offender is at the keyboard. But more often, it is necessary to introduce circumstantial evidence showing that the accused was operating the computer in question at the time of the offence. One resident of Broken Arrow, Oklahoma was charged with transmitting child pornography from his home: **[Case No. 73]**. The accused, who shared the residence with another person, maintained that the state failed to prove that he, the accused, exercised sufficient dominion and control over his computer to necessitate that he sent the images in question. By suggesting that the housemate could have sent the images, the defendant sought to engender reasonable doubt on the part of one or more jurors. To rebut this claim, the prosecution presented evidence pointing to the defendant. The Internet service account used to transmit the images was in his name. The defendant admitted to using the 'handle' IAMZEUS which was linked to the offending transmission. In addition, a document examiner testified for the state that it was probably the defendant's handwriting that appeared on a document containing a file name resembling that which held the offending image. The defendant was convicted.

Challenging the Admissibility of the Evidence

In general, the admissibility of evidence in criminal cases will depend not only on the lawfulness with which it is gathered, but also on its inherent integrity. This relates to its reliability, the transparency of the processes by which it has been selected, gathered and presented, and its being made available to the defence.

Most countries require that their law enforcement agents obtain some form of judicial authority before searching for and seizing private property. Among the exceptions are Italy, China and South Africa, where authority may be vested in prosecutors or police (Drozdova 2001, p. 205). In the United States, judicial authority is required. The Fourth Amendment to the US Constitution states: 'The right of the people to be secure in their persons, houses, papers, and effects, against unreasonable searches and seizures, shall not be violated, and no Warrants shall issue, but upon probable cause, supported by Oath or affirmation, and particularly describing the place to be searched, and the persons or things to be seized.'

Drafted nearly two centuries before the dawn of the digital age, the Fourth Amendment was inspired by the repressive practices of the British government in the late 18th century. Among these was the general search warrant. In the United States, unlike some jurisdictions around the world, information required in order to obtain a warrant must be very detailed and specific. The affidavit in support of the request for the warrant must provide probable cause that a crime has been committed, and must identify with considerable specificity what evidence is to be sought. The actual search must be within the scope of the warrant (Brenner and Frederikson 2001).

Details required for a warrant will vary depending on the location of the computer and the intrusiveness of the proposed search. Warrants conferring authority to intercept telecommunications (including e-mail in transit) are the most exacting. Warrants authorising surreptitious entry (sometimes referred to as 'sneak and peek') will also require more details than a warrant for an 'ordinary' search. Although access to a computer in a suspect's possession also requires a search warrant, a suspect's stored e-mail (but not e-mail in transit) can be obtained from a service provider by a subpoena. Basic customer or subscriber information (but not the content of messages) may be obtained from a carrier or service provider through a court order.

There are exceptions to the warrant requirement, such as consent or exigent circumstances (United States Department of Justice 2002). An example of the latter is drawn from a US case (*United States v David*, 756 F Supp 1385 (D Nev, 1991)). After flying from Hong Kong to Las Vegas in April 1990, the suspect was taken into custody by customs agents and charged with conspiracy to import more than 20 kilograms of heroin into the United States. Discussions commenced between government officials and the accused's defence counsel, with a view towards enlisting the assistance of the accused in return for a favourable plea bargain. A preliminary agreement was reached under which the accused would meet periodically with investigators and share information with them under the terms of an 'off the record' proffer. It was explicitly agreed that none of the information provided by the accused would be used against him in the event that negotiations collapsed. The agreement did not make reference to records, documents or other materials that the accused might possess.

The accused possessed a computer notebook in which were stored, *inter alia*, phone numbers of his associates. Government agents had not been given permission to access the electronic notebook. During one meeting with government investigators, one of the investigators saw the accused delete some data from the notebook, and thereupon seized it.

At this point discussions between the government and the defence collapsed. The notebook was seized and searched, without a warrant, and the accused was indicted by a federal grand jury in June 1990. He filed a pretrial motion to suppress all evidence contained in the notebook and all additional evidence derived from that information. The court found that the seizure was lawful under the exigent circumstances exception to the warrant requirement, as there was probable cause to believe that the item seized constituted evidence, and reasonable belief that by deleting data, the accused was destroying relevant evidence.

The prosecution foundered, however, when the court held that the investigators should have obtained a warrant to search the computer that they had seized. In other words, the seizure was valid, but the subsequent search was not. The prosecution's argument that a search was essential before the computer's batteries died, risking the automatic deletion of further evidence, was rejected. Indeed, one investigator testified that he subsequently accessed the computer without changing batteries. All information that the government had obtained from the notebook, and all further evidence derived from it, was inadmissible.

Depending upon the prevailing laws of their jurisdiction, prosecutors may expect challenges to the validity of search warrants, and to searches and seizures conducted pursuant to these warrants. One example of a search that got out of control began at an apartment in Manhattan, Kansas (*United States v Carey*,

172 F 3d 1268 (10th Cir, 1999)). The resident of the apartment had attracted the attention of police for reasons quite unrelated to digital technology. He had been under investigation for some time for matters relating to the sale and posses- sion of cocaine. Indeed, undercover investigators had previously made controlled buys from the suspect at his apartment. When investigators arrived at the apart- ment with an arrest warrant, they saw in plain view a device commonly used for smoking marijuana, and what appeared to be a quantity of the drug itself. The officers obtained the suspect's consent to search the apartment, and discovered additional quantities of marijuana, cocaine and hallucinogenic mushrooms. They also seized two computers, which they assumed might contain evidence of drug dealing.

The officers obtained a warrant to enable them to search the computers for 'names, telephone numbers, ledger receipts, addresses, and other documentary evidence pertaining to the sale and distribution of controlled substances'. At the police station, a detective and computer technician began their search. They copied the contents to another computer and began searching the copied files, using keywords such as 'money' and 'accounts'. No files relating to drugs were found. The detective did, however, encounter a JPG file, which, when opened, appeared to contain child pornography. The detective then downloaded 244 JPG files onto 19 disks before resuming his search for evidence of drug transactions.

It should be noted that the authority under which the detective was executing the search was limited to evidence relating to drug transactions. He justified his initial opening of the JPG file on the grounds that it might have contained an image depicting a 'hydroponic growth system'. In any event, the correct proce- dure would have been for the detective, upon discovering child pornography, to have ceased his search, and to obtain a new warrant to search for evidence of the additional crime.

The defendant was charged with one count of possessing a computer hard drive containing images of child pornography. He had entered a provisional plea of guilty, but then sought to suppress the evidence on the grounds that it was obtained as the result of a general warrantless search. Prosecutors sought in vain to rebut the defendant's assertion that the government's search exceeded the scope of the warrant. They tried to argue that the defendant's consent to the search of his apartment carried over to his computers, and that the images came into 'plain view'. The JPG files listed in the computer directory, which the detective viewed, were identified by sexually suggestive names. Moreover, after viewing the first JPG file, the detective had probable cause to believe that the rest contained similar material. These claims were ultimately rejected. The appeals court concluded that the detective exceeded the scope of the warrant, and that the evidence was the result of an unconstitutional general search.

Managing Large Volumes of Evidence

The annals of white collar crime are replete with cases involving masses of doc- uments. Not surprisingly, many computer-related offences also involve large vol- umes of evidence, albeit in digital form. Among the challenges faced by today's investigators is the enormous increase in storage capacity of today's computers, and the challenges to effective and efficient searches that this entails. Pollitt (2003) reports that hard drive capacity increased by over 6000 per cent during the five-year period ending in 2002. A typical laptop can now hold hundreds of thousands of pages of data. Not only does this complicate the task of finding evidence that one knows exists, it greatly increases the challenge of looking for evidence that may exist.

Drafting and executing search warrants in the digital age are particularly challenging tasks, as the material sought might be commingled with vast amounts of other data, irrelevant to the matter under investigation. Moreover, the medium in which they are stored may be integral to the operational information system of an otherwise legitimate enterprise. Unless the system itself was an instrument of the alleged offence, seizure of the entire system might cause undue loss to proprietors or to innocent clients. A classic illustration of this was the case *Steve Jackson Games, Inc. v United States Secret Service*, 36 F 3d 457 (5th Cir, 1994), in which the United States Secret Service seized hardware and data files from a small Texas games manufacturer and Internet service provider, nearly putting it out of business. Neither the company nor its principal was ever prosecuted; the material seized was thought to contain evidence of an offence by one of the company's customers.

The requirement that warrants be as specific as possible (and the search and seizure be minimally intrusive) pose significant challenges to prosecutors, as judges in the common law world frown on trawling expeditions.

One Australian case gives some idea of the sheer volume of material that can be involved in a search, and the problems this can entail: *Hart v Commissioner of Australian Federal Police and Others* [2002] FCAFC 392.

On 9 and 10 September 1996, a number of warrants were executed in Brisbane, under the *Crimes Act 1914* (Cth), leading to the removal of a large volume of documents from a company that was under investigation for a range of tax-related offences.

As it was not practicable to examine the material on the premises, electronically stored information was copied onto storage devices brought to the premises by the executing officers, and was then removed for further examination. The items included electronic copies of material equivalent to about 260,000 pages. In addition, police removed more than 9000 hard copy documents comprising over 95,000 original pages. The officers assumed that the removal of the copied material itself constituted a seizure, and that they could spend a reasonable amount of time examining it in order to make their case.

The court held that the downloading and copying of the relevant material did not constitute a seizure, but rather removal of the material for the purpose of off-premises examination, with a view towards determining which if any elements were susceptible to seizure within the terms of the warrant. Moreover, the court found that the agents failed to demonstrate that they had sufficient basis for this removal. To be authorised to seize it, they would have had to consider whether there was 'evidential material' in the body of electronic data that they had downloaded, and to determine that by some initial examination. They were therefore not entitled to remove any of the material in electronic form.

Managing Encrypted Evidence

Just as digital technology in general is becoming more pervasive, so too is the technology of encryption. At the dawn of the digital age, encryption technology required such computing power that it lay beyond the means of all but the largest organisations. The pioneering work of Diffie and Hellman (1976) led to its democratisation. Although the United States government sought to discourage the widespread marketing of encryption software, fearing its exploitation by criminals and terrorists, the 'genie was out of the bottle' and it soon became available to anyone who could afford it.

When evidence exists in encrypted form, investigators may be stymied. Without a key to the encrypted data, the content is practically impossible to decipher. One case where investigators went to exceptional lengths to obtain an encryption key was the investigation of a member of a prominent organised crime family on the east coast of the United States **[Case No. 110]** (Electronic Privacy Information Center 2003). The individual was under investigation for illegal gambling and loan-sharking. On 15 January 1999, pursuant to a warrant, FBI agents surreptitiously entered the subject's business office to search for evidence. During the course of their search, the agents came across a personal computer, but were unable to access an encrypted file that they suspected contained evidence of criminal activity.

The FBI obtained two additional warrants, authorising them to undertake another surreptitious entry, and to install on the subject's computer a device developed by FBI engineers known as a key-logger system (KLS) in order to record the password to the encrypted file. The investigators successfully obtained access to the subject's encrypted file, and based on the evidence obtained, charged him with a number of offences.

In a hearing before a federal judge on 30 July 2001, the accused's attorneys sought to have the court suppress the evidence obtained from his computer on the grounds that the KLS may have been operating when the accused (or anyone else at his computer, for that matter) was communicating via modem over telephone lines. This would constitute interception of wire communications, which requires a special warrant pursuant to 18 USC §2510. Reassurances from the prosecution that telecommunications were not intercepted did not allay the accused's concerns, and his attorneys sought full details of the KLS, its operation, and its interface with the computer modem, Internet communications, e-mail and other computer functions. Because of the sensitive nature of KLS technology, the government expressed its concern that disclosure could jeopardise national security and compromise other criminal investigations. On 7 August 2001 the court ordered the government to file a report explaining the technology to the defence.

On 23 August, federal prosecutors moved to invoke the *Classified Information Procedures Act* (Title 18, United States Code, Appendix III, §1 *et seq.*), and provide not the full report, but only an unclassified summary. The defence opposed this, seeking access to the full report.

On 26 September the court held an in camera, ex parte hearing where FBI agents and senior officials of the US Department of Justice gave a top-secret briefing to explain the KLS technology to the judge.

On 4 October, the court denied discovery of the classified information and granted the government's motion. The FBI provided the defence with an unclassified description of the KLS, but the defence moved once again to suppress evidence.

The prosecution had demonstrated to the satisfaction of the court that in the course of the investigation, the KLS was configured in such a manner that when the modem was operating, no keystrokes were recorded. On 26 December 2001, the court upheld the FBI's use of KLS and denied the defence motion to suppress evidence obtained through the technique.

The accused entered a plea agreement with the government in February 2002, the terms of which precluded appellate consideration of the matters raised in the case.

The reason that authorities in the United States must go to such extraordinary lengths in order to obtain encryption keys is because the Fifth Amendment protects individuals against self-incrimination. The right to remain silent applies to the disclosure of encryption keys no less than to other potentially incriminating information. To compensate for this constitutional impediment, US federal authorities have introduced legislation that would make it an offence to use encryption to conceal incriminating communication relating to a crime that someone is committing or attempting to commit.

Those countries unconstrained by a bill of rights have devised a simpler solution to the challenge of encryption. They simply require individuals to disclose encryption keys or face criminal charges. In the United Kingdom, this can entail imprisonment for up to two years, and in Australia, six months (*Regulation of Investigatory Powers Act 2000*, ss. 49–55; *Crimes Act 1914*, s. 3LA). In Europe, Article 6 of the Rome Convention could be a barrier to such compulsory disclosure, although the European Commission on Human Rights has restricted the scope of the article to oral statements. Nevertheless, European procedures for compulsory decryption would have to be formulated precisely in order to withstand judicial scrutiny.

Lack of Criminal Intent

Many jurisdictions make it a criminal offence to possess certain materials, most commonly digital images depicting children engaged in explicit sexual activity. Whatever the nature of the content, the defendant may try to argue that he or she was unaware that the files in question were stored in the computer, or unaware of the incriminating nature of their content.

Possession

A contentious issue which arises from time to time in computer crime cases is that of possession. The essential elements of possession are (a) control and (b) knowledge. The defences are obvious, and the burden of proof is on the prosecutor.

Control

A Western Australian prison officer was found not guilty in Perth Magistrates Court of using a computer service to 'obtain possession of an article knowing it to be objectionable material' (*Censorship Act 1996*, s. 101(1)(b)). The defendant claimed that he received the image as an attachment to an unsolicited e-mail message and, without reviewing it, saved it with a number of other messages for his later perusal. Upon opening it some time later, he was confronted by an image of a man forcing a woman to engage in sexual activity while suspended above him by a large cargo hook. The defendant claimed to have attempted to delete the image immediately. However, it was later found on his office computer in a locked file to which the defendant himself had no access. The defendant claimed that he had no previous computer training, and that his act of saving the offending image was inadvertent. The magistrate found that the accused did not know that the attachment to the e-mail was sexually explicit when he received it, and that as the image in the locked file was inaccessible to him, he lacked control and therefore did not have possession. Although the Court of Appeal upheld the magistrate's decision to dismiss the charge, it faulted her reasoning. The real issue, according to the court, was the prosecution's failure to prove that the defendant knowingly used a computer service to obtain the objectionable image ([2001] WASCA 146 (9 May 2001)).

The difficulties in proving possession became evident in a British case involving alleged possession of child pornography: [Case No. 66]. The accused, a university lecturer, was prosecuted under section 160 of the *Criminal Justice Act 1988* for possessing indecent images of children. A university employee and her spouse, having noticed a number of questionable files on the hard disk of the lecturer's computer, notified the police, and the lecturer was arrested. He maintained that he had browsed the Web and had visited some extreme sites out of morbid curiosity, but denied having downloaded any illegal content. Unbeknown to the defendant, the caching function of the Netscape browser software had evidently captured the images in question. Sites visited by mistake or through a misleading link could have had the same result. In any event, the defendant denied that he knowingly possessed the images in question. The court held that the 'offence of possession under section 160 is not committed unless the defendant knows he has photographs in his possession'.

In some cases, the task of the prosecutor is made easier by the defendant's behaviour. It is easier to rebut a defence such as the one run in the Western Australia case above when forensic examination of the computer reveals that the file in question has been downloaded repeatedly over a period of time.

Such were the circumstances in the case of one unfortunate defendant whose computer was found to be storing some 27,000 images, a significant number of which were child pornography. The accused maintained that he had accidentally run across the offending images, which were then automatically cached on his hard drive. Arguing that he did not want the images to be saved on his hard drive, he had manually deleted the images by dragging them to the recycle bin icon on his computer's desktop. He claimed that the images were not stored, but saved against his will, and only temporarily displayed. The government was able to prove that manual deletion of the files represented control over them, and that the images would not have been stored had the accused not 'volitionally reached out' for them. The fact that he had asked the operator of one website 'to be given access to pictures of "naked young girls"' and had purposefully visited websites containing child pornography suggested that he had knowledge: [Case No. 129].

Similarly, a British case [Case No. 115], addressed the question of whether the act of opening an e-mail attachment constituted the offence of 'making', as discussed in Chapter Three: [Case No. 58]. The prosecution was able to demonstrate that one of the two accused had reason to believe that the attachment contained, or was likely to contain, indecent images. He had previously sent images of the subject to a newsgroup, and requested that additional images be sent to him. His co-accused was charged with 'making' indecent images while searching the World Wide Web. The prosecution claimed that by merely selecting images from the Web to appear on his screen, or through subsequent automatic storage of indecent images in the computer's temporary cache, the co-accused was making the images. The co-accused, who was quite computer-literate and who knew about caches, argued that there was no intention to retrieve the images, since they were not saved in a specific directory. The court held that the act of voluntarily downloading an image from a web page to the computer screen, if only for a fleeting moment, is an act of making.

Can one knowingly possess data that have been deleted? This was an argument raised in **[Case No. 46]**, a child pornography case that raised a number of other interesting legal issues, some of which are discussed below. Among the evidence against the accused were 1400 sexually explicit images of children. The images had been deleted, but investigators were able to recover them using a utilities program and the 'undelete' function. The matter was raised on appeal, rather than at trial. The court did not decide the question of whether one could knowingly possess deleted (but retrievable) data. It concluded that any alleged error had had no effect on the verdict, but noted that '[t]he evidence showed overwhelmingly that the accused knowingly transmitted, received and possessed unlawful images prior to their attempted deletion; the recaptured images were perfectly competent evidence of crimes committed before their deletion'.

Knowledge

One of the more famous remarks in the annals of jurisprudence was made by US Supreme Court Justice Potter Stewart in a 1964 obscenity case. In referring to what was conventionally termed 'hard-core pornography,' Stewart said:

> I shall not today attempt further to define the kinds of material I understand to be embraced within that shorthand description; and perhaps I could never succeed in intelligibly doing so. But I know it when I see it . . . (*Jacobellis v Ohio*, 378 US 184, 197 (1964)).

These words, penned well before technology revolutionised pornography, reflect a persistent issue in present day law and policy: whether the consumer of child pornography knows what he (and it is almost always a he) is viewing.

In the Australian state of Victoria, 'child pornography' means 'a film, photograph, publication or computer game that describes or depicts a person who is, or looks like, a minor under 16 engaging in sexual activity or depicted in an indecent sexual manner or context' (*Crimes Act 1958*, s. 67A). It is a defence to prosecution under this section that the defendant 'believed on reasonable grounds that the minor was aged 16 years or older or that he or she was married to the minor' (*Crimes Act*, s. 70(2)(c)). The prosecution must bear the burden of proving that the belief was unreasonable; this is obviously more difficult as the child approaches the age of 16.

In addition to considerations of a child's apparent age, child pornography may be produced without the involvement of children, or indeed, of any other person. Photographic images can be created, enhanced or altered in a manner that gives the appearance of child subjects. An image may be created *ex nihilo* (as is the case with cartoons) or transformed by technical means (the colloquial term for this is 'morphing'). It is not always possible to determine whether the product is fictional or real. Jurisdictions that aggressively pursue child pornography frame their legislation in terms of 'appearance' to overcome this technological challenge. Victoria's legislation is illustrative: as long as the image *appears* to depict a person who *appears* to be under the age of 16 and the person is engaged 'in sexual activity or depicted in an indecent sexual manner or context', it is covered by section 67A.

In the United States, attempts to criminalise child pornography resulted in the *Child Pornography Protection Act of 1996*. In response to the emerging use of digital technology to generate and modify images, this statute sought to criminalise not only actual depictions of children, but also 'virtual' depictions created without using minors (in contrast to the applicable age in Victoria, this means someone under the age of 18). To criminalise this virtual content, the US statute contained the language of subjective judgment, including the terms 'appears to be' and 'conveys the impression.'

The age of majority is not the only thing that distinguishes Victoria from the United States. The First Amendment to the US Constitution, which protects freedom of speech, has no counterpart in Australian law. To the surprise of no one, the Child Pornography Protection Act was challenged on the ground that terms of subjective judgment such as 'appears to be' are overly broad. The US Supreme Court struck down the Act, using classical as well as digital examples: 'the literal terms of the statute embrace a Renaissance painting depicting a scene from classical mythology' as well as contemporary interpretations of Shakespeare's *Romeo and Juliet* (*Ashcroft v Free Speech Coalition* 122 S Ct 1389 (2002)).

In the aftermath of *Ashcroft*, it now appears that the government must prove not only that the image in question was that of a real child, but also that the defendant actually knew it to be so. This was affirmed in two subsequent cases in the United States ([**Case No. 141**], and see also Westlaw: *United States v Reilly*, 2002 WL 31307170, SDNY, Oct. 15, 2002). This makes a prosecutor's job more difficult, but not impossible. In the first of the two cases, the judge duly instructed the jury that it must find that the defendant 'knew that the child pornography depicted at least one minor, that is, an actual person under the age of eighteen'. The jury convicted. In discussing these developments, Kerr (2003) suggests that clever aficionados of child pornography may well begin to prefix all their files with the word 'virtual,' and to prominently display publications on computer-generated images. In the United States at least, the 'sham virtual pornography defence' began to pose an additional challenge to prosecutors (US Department of Justice 2003). Congress attempted a constitutionally impregnable 'patch' in the form of the PROTECT Act (Prosecutorial Remedies and Other Tools to end the Exploitation of Children Today), a comprehensive package relating to missing and exploited children. The provision relating to virtual child pornography refers to 'a digital image, computer image, or computer-generated image that is, or is indistinguishable from, that of a minor engaged in sexually explicit conduct' (18 USC §2256). Whether this will pass constitutional muster and make prosecutors' lives easier remains to be seen.

Of course, that the content in question 'records no crime and creates no victims by its production' is of no consolation to authorities in many jurisdictions outside the United States which accommodate subjective judgments worthy of Justice Stewart. The mere tendency of speech to encourage unlawful acts (as is argued by many commentators on child pornography) is not a sufficient reason for banning it in the US (*Ashcroft v Free Speech Coalition*, 122 S Ct 1389 at 1403), but prosecutors in jurisdictions less solicitous of freedom of expression will have fewer problems.

Challenging Private Involvement in Criminal Investigation

It has long been recognised that the police cannot be on every street corner. This is no less the case in cyberspace. Like frontier societies generally, the electronic frontier has seen a good deal of private involvement in policing. In some jurisdictions, the regulation of cyberspace (or at least some corners of cyberspace) depends on complaints by private parties. For example, in Australia, the regulation of offensive Internet content and of online gambling is, to a significant extent, complaint-based. Moreover, in a great many cyber crime cases the success of an investigation will depend upon assistance rendered by the victim or by others knowledgeable about information technology.

There are other circumstances in which third parties, such as computer repair people or Internet service providers, become aware of criminal activity by their customers and contact the police.

In the United States, the Fourth Amendment to the Constitution protects citizens from unreasonable searches and seizures by government agents. Evidence obtained by police through an illegal search can be challenged by the defence through a motion to suppress. However, evidence obtained by the efforts of private third parties may under certain circumstances be admissible. The question of third party involvement and the point at which it may be considered action by the state is therefore an important one for prosecutors who may be involved in the planning of an investigation, or who must be prepared to respond to a defence motion to challenge the admissibility of evidence obtained by private actors.

In the United States, there are three issues to which prosecutors must attend when a private search has been challenged. For the evidence obtained through a private search to be admissible:

- the government must not have encouraged or initiated the private action;
- it must not be aware of or acquiescent in the search; and
- the private actor must not have intended to assist law enforcement officers by conducting the search.

A leading case in this area involved a federal prosecution in Kansas (*United States v Kennedy*, 81 F Supp 2d 1103 (D Kan, 2000)). On a July night in 1999, a customer support specialist for a high-speed Internet service provider received an anonymous telephone call. The caller stated that he was at the home of a friend, where he was scanning other computers through the Internet, and had identified images of child pornography on what appeared to be the computer of one of the ISP's subscribers. The caller chose to remain anonymous for good reason: what he had done (remotely accessing other people's computers without their consent) was illegal. He gave the IP number of the subscriber's computer to the ISP and hung up. The ISP's employee gained access to the IP address and confirmed the presence of files mentioned by the caller. He called this to the attention of his supervisors, who contacted law enforcement authorities. The police obtained a court order, and were then given the subscriber's contact details and address. Based on this information, an FBI agent contacted the subscriber by telephone, and without identifying his true profession, inquired whether the subscriber was satisfied with his Internet service. With these details corroborated, the FBI obtained a warrant and searched the suspect's home and computer. Based on the evidence they obtained, the suspect was charged.

The accused argued that the subscriber information that the FBI obtained from the ISP was obtained in violation of the *Electronic Communications Privacy Act of 1986* (ECPA) and the *Cable Communications Policy Act of 1984* (CCPA), and that evidence obtained subsequently should also be suppressed as having been the 'fruit of the poisonous tree'.

The defendant's motion to suppress was denied. The court held that the initial searches conducted by the anonymous caller and the ISP were not subject to the Fourth Amendment. Even if the Internet service provider disclosed the subscriber's information improperly, neither ECPA nor CCPA provided a suppression remedy.

One of the more intriguing cases dealing with the question of when third party involvement is action by the state involved facts so fascinating that they could serve as the basis for a novel: **[Case No. 136]**. In July 2000, an officer of the Montgomery, Alabama police department received an unsolicited e-mail message, with an attachment, from a sender called 'unknownuser' with a Hotmail address. The message read:

> I found a child molester on the net. I'm not sure if he is abusing his own child or a child he kidnapped. He is from Montgomery, Alabama. As you can see he is torturing the kid. She is 5–6 years old. His face is seen clearly on some of the pictures. I know his name, Internet account, home address and I can see when he is online. What should I do?

The Montgomery police officer contacted a special agent of the FBI based in Mobile, Alabama, with whom there was a standing working relationship relating to child pornography cases. In a subsequent communication, 'Unknownuser' (who was never identified) revealed that he was from Istanbul, Turkey. At the request of the Montgomery police officer, he provided the suspect's IP address. For good measure, he added the suspect's name, address and fax number. Based on this anonymous tip, police obtained the appropriate warrants and arrested a local doctor. The doctor was later convicted and sentenced to 17 and a half years' imprisonment and three years' supervised release.

One of the reasons that Unknownuser sought to remain anonymous was that his access to the doctor's computer was accomplished by illegal means. Unknownuser had uploaded a file containing a version of the SubSeven Trojan horse to a pre-teen erotica newsgroup (Kerr 2002). He was then able to obtain remote access to the computers of people who visited the site. The unfortunate doctor was one of these.

The fact that the doctor had been the victim of a crime at the hands of Unknownuser was of no consolation, nor was it at all useful in his defence. Had Unknownuser been an FBI agent, defence lawyers would have moved, with every likelihood of success, to suppress evidence obtained in the illegal search. But Unknownuser was a private citizen who had conducted his search prior to contacting the Montgomery police.

United States authorities remained in contact with Unknownuser, who claimed to have found child pornography on the computers of at least 2000 people. They thanked him repeatedly for his assistance, and encouraged him to provide further information. He indicated that his investigative activities were ongoing, and (despite their patent illegality) at no time was he advised to discontinue them.

In one message he was told: 'Our Federal attorneys have expressed NO desire to charge you with any CRIMINAL offense.'

Unknownuser contacted United States authorities on a subsequent occasion alerting them to another alleged child pornographer. Although law enforcement moved quickly, and prosecutors had obtained a guilty plea, Unknownuser had become less useful. The defence claimed that Unknownuser was no longer a private actor, but as a result of his extensive contacts with police and their continuing acquiescence in and encouragement of his activities, he had become an agent of the state. The defence moved to withdraw the plea and for suppression of the evidence obtained as a result of Unknownuser's assistance. Prosecutors failed to rebut the contention that Unknownuser had been transformed from a private to a public actor (229 F Supp 2d 503 (ED Va, 2002)). The decision was reversed some eight months later by the Court of Appeals for the Fourth Circuit, which held that the government's communications constituted passive acquiescence, and fell just short of the active encouragement necessary to transform Unknownuser into an agent of the state.

Third parties often become aware of criminal activity in the course of normal professional activities. Employees of legitimate courier services from time to time detect evidence of contraband. Many will report suspicious activity to police. Computer repair technicians may also encounter evidence of illegality in the course of their work. Such was the case with the employees of Upgraders, a computer repair shop in Austin, Texas, as documented in **[Case No. 41]**. In October 1997, one customer left his PC with Upgraders for repairs. While checking the computer, an employee noticed a large number of image files on the hard drive. The employee opened several of the files and found them to be child pornography. The proprietor of Upgraders then called the local police. An officer of the Austin police department interviewed Upgraders' employees, and in the course of the interview, one of the employees showed some of the files to the officer. Without a warrant, he seized the computer and took it with him to his office at the Police Department. He then contacted a special agent of the US Customs Service, and (without mentioning that he had already viewed images or that he had seized the computer) inquired whether Customs was interested in pursuing a federal criminal investigation. Customs proceeded with the investigation. Based on information provided by Upgraders' employees, a warrant was obtained, the computer (which had been returned to Upgraders) was seized, and the defendant was convicted. He appealed, arguing that the warrantless seizure by municipal police tainted the investigation by federal authorities. The court held that the Customs warrant was independent of the illegal seizure by the Austin police officer and dismissed the motion to suppress the evidence.

It has been suggested that some computer repair technicians have either a personal inclination, or an informal arrangement with law enforcement officers, to check for potentially illegal material on computers. If so, under United States law at least, there is a risk that the searches that they conduct may be deemed government action, and thus require a warrant. According to the Tenth Circuit, the party conducting the search must have intended to assist law enforcement efforts *and* the government must know and acquiesce in the intrusive conduct: *Pleasant v Lovell*, 876 F 2d 787, 797 (10th Cir, 1989); *United States v Leffall*, 82 F 3d 343, 347 (10th Cir, 1996).

In European countries, private involvement in criminal investigations is a complex matter. In principle, private parties may assist the police, and even when they violate the law in gathering evidence, the evidence may still be admissible. Private persons acting with encouragement of police are prevented from acting under circumstances where police themselves would not have the power.

Imaginative Defences

In the digital world, human relationships are mediated by technology. While developments in digital video technology may one day change this, most of our contacts in cyberspace are impersonal – we often don't know each other and hardly ever see each other. Digital technology may contribute to an illusion of anonymity, and to circumstances in which the perpetrator does not envisage the consequences of his or her actions. When a defendant's liberty is at stake, prosecutors can anticipate a variety of defences, some of them desperate indeed, others more plausible.

Some states provide explicitly for exemptions from criminal liability in specific statutes, such as those exempting police from liability for possessing child pornography in the course of their official duties. Other specific exemptions in the substantive criminal law may relate to artistic, scientific or therapeutic purposes. Other states refer to factors that would make the criminal conduct justifiable in some circumstances as a general principle of criminal law.

Accident

As proof of intent is central to obtaining a conviction for many offences, the defence may argue that 'it was all an accident'. All else being equal, damage inflicted as the result of recklessness or negligence is regarded as less culpable than damage intentionally inflicted. If the argument that 'I didn't mean to do it' stands a chance of resonating with a jury, the prosecutor may offer to accept a plea to the lesser charge. In the first prominent case involving the release of malicious code over the Internet, the accused maintained that he had no intention of bringing down the Internet when he released his worm ([**Case No. 9**]; see Hafner and Markoff 1991, pp. 439–40). He went to trial, and the jury was not sympathetic. It was sufficient that he intentionally obtained unauthorised access to a computer system. His lack of intent to do harm did assist him somewhat at the sentencing stage.

In the law of some European countries, the principle of *dolus eventualis* will apply when an accused knowingly and willingly recognises a considerable chance that a given outcome will result. See, for example, information provided by the Dutch Ministry of Justice on criminal culpability: <http://www.minjust.nl:8080/ b_organ/wodc/publications/ob205_05.pdf>.

From time to time hackers argue that what they were doing was really a public service. They claim that they were really contributing to information security by identifying vulnerabilities in computer systems. Such claims of altruism are relatively easy to rebut, most obviously in those circumstances where the perpetrator takes no steps to bring the vulnerability to the attention of responsible systems administrators.

Legitimate Research

In some jurisdictions it may be possible to run the defence that incriminating materials were in the possession of the accused for purposes of legitimate research. In January, 2003, a legendary rock musician was arrested under the (UK) *Protection of Children Act* after police executed two search warrants at his home and business. In May 2003, he was given a formal police caution and placed on an official register of sex offenders. The musician acknowledged using a website advertising child pornography, but claimed that having been abused himself as a child, he was doing research for an autobiography. This was not a new argument.

In 1996, an award-winning journalist in the United States went online to conduct research on Internet child pornography and law enforcement responses. He had previously written a series of articles on the topic (Tridgell 2000). In the course of his current research, the journalist exchanged images of minors with other chat room participants. As it happened, one of his correspondents was an undercover FBI agent. Following a search of the journalist's home, investigators found two images of nude children and recovered a number of other deleted files; he was charged with eleven counts of receiving, and four counts of transmitting, child pornography over the Internet. The accused intended to claim constitutional protection for his news-gathering activities: the First Amendment states that Congress shall make no law abridging the freedom of speech or of the press. Prior to trial, the government moved successfully to prevent him from presenting any evidence or argument concerning journalistic activities, on the grounds that (1) his investigations did not give rise to a compelling need to transmit and receive child pornography and (2) even if he was acting as a journalist, the First Amendment does not guarantee the press access to information prohibited by law to the general public. A defence motion to reconsider was also denied. The defendant was sentenced to eighteen months' imprisonment and three years of supervised probation, and was fined $4200: **[Case No. 68]**.

In a subsequent case, the defendant, who was not a professional journalist, was charged with possessing and transporting images of minors engaged in sexually explicit conduct. The case went to trial, and the accused testified in his own defence that he, having been sexually abused as a child, was exchanging images with other Internet chat room participants for the purpose of writing a serious book relating to child abuse. He said that he had written a small number of pages over a very long period.

The defendant's lack of literary productivity was such that the government did not have to take the steps that it had taken against the journalist. The jury was given a written interrogatory to be offered if it convicted on one or more counts: 'Was the defendant's sole purpose in committing the offence or offences to produce a serious literary work?' Their answer was negative: **[Case No. 46]**.

The State of New York appears to be even less sympathetic to arguments based on professional activity. A licensed social worker who specialised in sexually related problems was prosecuted in New York for possessing 'a sexual performance of a child'. The accused testified that he downloaded the images in question in connection with his research on the development of therapeutic treatment methods for persons involved with child pornography on the Internet. The Supreme Court of New York held that while the defence of legitimate research protects the use of ordinary obscene material for scientific, educational or governmental purposes, a comparable defence did not extend to child pornography: 'The compelling State interest in protecting children from being defiled far outweighs the value of allowing the product of the child's defilement to be used for scientific purposes'. The defendant was sentenced to five years' probation, ordered to perform 550 hours' community service and fined US$1000 (affirmed on appeal): [**Case No. 64**].

The law in the United Kingdom seems slightly more flexible. The *Protection of Children Act 1978* s. 1(4)(a) and the *Criminal Justice Act 1988* s. 160(2)(a) permit research into child pornography for a 'legitimate reason'. In the case involving the university lecturer ([**Case No. 66**], discussed above) it was noted that each case is to be considered on its own facts, although 'courts are plainly entitled to bring a measure of scepticism to bear upon such an enquiry'. This is indeed what occurred in the lecturer's case.

Fantasy

One of the more interesting defences is the so-called 'fantasy defence', most common in cases arising from alleged attempts to lure children for illicit purposes, and in stalking cases. The accused claims that his or her actions were an expression of fantasy and not indicative of real intentions.

The basis of the fantasy defence was laid in a celebrated case involving a student at the University of Michigan (Platt 1996). The student was renowned in various Internet forums as the author of shockingly sadistic stories. Widely and openly disseminated in cyberspace, their author's identity and institutional affiliation both publicly known, they reached a large audience. One such composition, written in the first person, was so revolting that two readers contacted the University of Michigan and complained about the extracurricular activities of one of its students. An internal investigation by the university followed. The student freely consented to a search of his university Internet account, and to his stored e-mail. Among his correspondence was an exchange of more than forty e-mail messages with a young Canadian man, many of which contained grotesque descriptions of proposed abduction and rape. The student's difficulties were compounded when it became apparent that he had given the victim in one of his stories a name that happened to be the name of a fellow student. University authorities contacted the FBI and the student was arrested. He was charged with violating USC §875(c), which prohibits threats to injure or kidnap a victim. The offence carried a penalty of up to five years' imprisonment.

The defence claimed that the stories were nothing more than fantasies. The court dismissed the indictment, stating that a threat must be 'on its face and in the circumstances in which it is made, so unequivocal, unconditional, immediate and specific as to the person threatened, as to convey a gravity of purpose and imminent prospect of execution'. In this case, the fantasy defence prevailed even before the case reached the jury (*United States v Baker and Gonda* (1995), US District Court, Eastern District of Michigan, Criminal No. 95-80106, Cohn J: <http:ic. net/~sberaha/baker.html>).

Some years later in March 1999, a 34-year-old IT executive logged into an Internet chat room called 'dad&daughtersex.log' and made contact with one 'KrisLA,' who identified herself as a thirteen-year-old girl. Over the next several months, the executive, who was using the nickname 'hotseattle', expressed his interest in meeting KrisLA in Los Angeles and engaging in sexual acts with her. He claimed to be 'totally for real', and not just engaging in fantasy behaviour. They arranged to meet at the Santa Monica Pier on 16 September 1999. Unfortunately for 'hotseattle,' who was arrested upon his arrival in Santa Monica, he had been corresponding not with a 13-year-old girl but rather with one Bruce Applin, a special agent of the Federal Bureau of Investigation (Applin 2000).

The accused was indicted on three felony counts:

1) Interstate travel (from the state of Washington to California) with intent to engage in criminal sexual activity with a minor, in violation of 18 USC §2423(b);

2) Use of a facility of interstate commerce (the Internet) to attempt to induce a minor to engage in criminal sexual activity, in violation of 18 USC §2422(b); and

3) Possession of child pornography (images found on his laptop computer) in violation of 18 USC §2252A(a)(5)(B).

The defendant pleaded not guilty to the three counts, and claimed that he had no intention of having an illicit encounter with a child. Rather, he claimed to have been operating in the online fantasy world of cyberspace, that he visited fantasy-based chat rooms to relieve stress, and that he assumed most people there were role-playing. Therefore, his travel to Santa Monica was not for the purpose of committing a crime.

The defendant argued that almost everyone in chat rooms engages in what he called 'real-time' fiction, or role-playing, and that the person he would meet in Santa Monica could just as easily have been a 40-year-old woman. An expert witness for the defence stated that as many as two-thirds of participants in Internet chat rooms (in addition to undercover police investigators) state a false age or sex.

After four days of deliberation, the jury found the defendant guilty of possessing child pornography, but was unable to reach a verdict on the other charges. All but one of the men on the jury accepted the fantasy defence, while the six women did not. The defendant, who had been remanded to custody awaiting sentence, was released the following day when the Ninth Circuit Court of Appeals ruled that parts of the Child Pornography Protection Act, under which the defendant was found guilty, were overly broad and therefore unconstitutional: *Free Speech Coalition v Reno*, 198 F 3d 1083 (9th Cir (Cal, 1999)). 'Hotseattle', however, was reluctant to try his luck any further. Pessimistic about the prospects for a fantasy defence in a retrial, he pleaded guilty to interstate travel with intent to engage in criminal sexual activity. Rather than 35 years in prison, to which he could have been sentenced had he been convicted of the original charges, he was sentenced to nine months' in-home detention, fined $20,000 and given five years' probation: **[Case No. 61]**.

As part of his plea agreement, he offered to assist the FBI in developing technology to permit remote access of future suspects' computers. If successful, this will reduce dependence on KSL technology and on private vigilantes such as Unknownuser, with all their associated problems.

The fantasy defence continues to pose a challenge for prosecutors, but not an insurmountable one. One suspect, after having chatted for months with various undercover agents who were posing as a 12-year-old boy, invited 'him' to a New

York hotel room to meet. At his trial, the defendant claimed that he knew all along that the person with whom he had been communicating was really an adult. Prosecutors were able to introduce texts of all previous correspondence between the defendant and the 'boy', and to show a correspondence between them as well as other evidence found in the hotel room. A message had referred to rollerblading, and the defendant had brought rollerblades to New York. This, while not necessarily a 'smoking gun', suggested an element of belief in the age of the boy. In addition, to quote a Secret Service agent involved in the case, 'There was a video camera in a backpack and a tape that was kind of cued up and ready to go. There was a CD with child pornography on it in his briefcase. We seized a pornographic videotape and other sexual paraphernalia . . .'(quoted in Karp 2002).

The defence lawyer, Paul Dalnoky, was later quoted as saying, 'I truly believe that [the defendant] really felt that he was talking to people who were role-playing . . . If you don't believe that you're really talking to a 12-year-old, you haven't committed a crime. It's not a crime to talk to grown-ups' (quoted in Karp 2002). The jury was not convinced, and the defendant was convicted under US federal law of travelling across state lines to engage in sexual acts with a minor, using telephone lines and the Internet to entice a minor to engage in sexual acts, and transporting child pornography across state lines.

Prosecutors have begun to observe more cautious and sophisticated conduct on the part of subjects who may be laying the groundwork for a fantasy defence. Given the very real presence of undercover police in cyberspace, offenders are beginning to slip key phrases into their communications, such as 'We're just pretending, right?' or 'You don't sound like a child', in order to establish a basis for future fantasy defence claims. As one Miami prosecutor observed, 'They're becoming savvy enough to know. They have discussions about how to get around this. They know the case law as well as we do' (Cameron Malin, quoted in Karp 2002).

Dalnoky argued in a subsequent interview that in the New York case, law enforcement was creating a crime where one did not exist before. There was never a 12-year-old, and had investigators not 'created' one, no crime would have happened. This hints at entrapment, a defence that is even more difficult than fantasy to run.

Addiction

The idea of technological addictions has been around for some time (Griffiths 1990). Already the idea of Internet addiction has inspired a good deal of thought (Center for Online Addiction 2003). It is no longer novel to suggest that persons charged with computer-related crime have acted because of impulse control problems. Indeed, Hafner and Markoff (1991, p. 343) have referred to the compulsive behaviour of one of the most celebrated computer criminals. It is therefore not surprising that some defendants will try to run the argument that their alleged misdeeds arose from uncontrollable habits.

A student at the University of Edinburgh was charged, along with two of his colleagues, with conspiracy under the *Computer Misuse Act 1990*. The alleged offences related to obtaining unauthorised access to computer systems in a variety of organisations, unlawfully obtaining services from a prominent British service provider, modifying code at a major share index, and disrupting work at a cancer research centre.

The defendant claimed that he had become addicted to computer use, and was therefore unable to form the intent required by the Computer Misuse Act. Despite instructions from the judge that addiction did not negate intent, the jury acquitted. Following the acquittal, the defendant's barrister made a statement suggesting that he was laying a foundation for future similar defences:

> The child, whose best friend is a computer rather than a person, is not going to function normally in society. We need to be able to predict how he will behave and what treatments will restore him to normal health. Parents must demand that proper research is done into this important problem. <http://www.eff.org/Net_culture/Hackers/uk_court_acquits_teenage_hacker.article>

Despite the good fortune of the Edinburgh student, however, suggestions of addiction are likely to figure more prominently in sentencing decisions than as defences at trial. The case from Melbourne, noted in Chapter One above, is a good example: [**Case No. 15**]. It seems likely that, before or after the verdict, the theme of computer addiction will find its way into the courtrooms of many jurisdictions around the world.

Therapy

The argument that obscene materials may be useful for therapeutic purposes predates the digital age: see, for example, *R v Staniforth; R v Jordan* [1977] AC 699, [1976] 2 All ER 714, [1976] 2 WLR 849.

We saw above how 'hotseattle' cited stress reduction as one of the reasons for visiting some of the shadowy areas of cyberspace. A recent case in the Australian Capital Territory (Unreported decision, 27 February 2003) resulted in a disposition of 'no conviction recorded' after the accused maintained that he accessed illegal images for therapeutic purposes.

A Canadian civil case that touched upon both therapy and addiction involved the dismissal of a college professor for using his employer's equipment to download child pornography: [**Case No. 119**]. The professor, who had pleaded guilty to criminal charges, was given a suspended sentence and placed on probation for two years. He sought to challenge his discharge from the college on the grounds that it arose from a mental disorder that could be considered a disability under Ontario's Human Rights Code.

The professor, who lived under difficult circumstances with his ageing parents, claimed to have used the Internet as an escape from the sadness and isolation of his personal life. He claimed that he was unable to control his impulses. The court held that evidence did not support a conclusion that the professor was suffering from any form of medically recognised mental disorder. His inappropriate use of the college's computers was both selective and controlled, and the depression for which he was temporarily hospitalised was brought about by his impending dismissal from the college as a result of his misconduct. These findings served to neutralise any justification for therapeutic use, or extenuation based on compulsive behaviour. His dismissal from the college was upheld.

'Higher Purpose'

Defendants in cyber crime cases often invoke the public interest to justify their deeds. Although this usually occurs at the sentencing stage (and will be accorded much discussion below), it may occur during the course of the trial. Such was the case in a Hong Kong prosecution: [**Case No. 44**]. The defendant, an assistant to a radiologist at the Queen Mary Hospital, learned in passing that 'a very famous lady' had been admitted for a CT scan. Shortly thereafter, the news media reported a government press release that the Hong Kong Secretary for Justice had been admitted to the hospital 'for observation due to an entero-gastric disorder'. Correctly inferring that this was the VIP in question, the accused, who had been given access to the hospital's Radiology Information System, accessed the patient's CT scan report. Noting that the patient's condition was significantly more serious than had been disclosed in the press release, the accused faxed the report anonymously to two Hong Kong newspapers, *Ming Pao* and *Apple Daily*. The following day, both papers published stories about the Secretary's illness, including the CT report.

The defendant was charged under s. 161 of the Crimes Ordinance, which covers access to a computer with criminal or dishonest intent. Before the magistrate, the defendant claimed that his intent was not dishonest, nor did he realise any gain from his actions. Rather, he was angry with the government for deceiving the public, and he felt that the public had a right to know that their government had provided them with false information. This lofty argument failed to convince the magistrate, however, who concluded that the defendant did it for the thrill and excitement of embarrassing the government.

The court also held that the defendant's 'gain' from the deed need not have been monetary; simply gaining information was sufficient to sustain the charge. The absence of monetary gain did, however, help the defendant win a non-custodial sentence.

The line that 'I was only providing a security service' has tended to serve hackers poorly when they get to court. The reason for this, as we have noted, is that most hackers tend not to disclose the security flaw to the relevant systems administrator, confidentially or otherwise. A more successful use of the public interest defence was made by a hacker in Houston, Texas. When scanning for insecure networks around Houston in March 2002, he noticed that he could obtain access to the wireless computer network of the Harris County District Clerk. After demonstrating this to a county official and a newspaper reporter, he was charged with obtaining unauthorised access to a computer system and knowingly transmitting a command that caused $5000 damage. The fact that the hacker is reported to have informed a county official in the presence of a journalist suggests that embarrassment may have been a factor in the decision to prosecute. In any event, the public nature of the intrusion, combined with the jury's rejection of the argument that he had intentionally caused damage, led to his acquittal in 15 minutes (Leyden 2003).

Covert Facilitation and Entrapment

The cloak of anonymity afforded by the Internet can be very useful to law enforcement officers. In addition to the 'hotseattle' and New York cases, there have been countless cases of individuals who have distributed pornographic images to police, or who have used e-mail to 'lure' a child to a meeting place, only to find that they had been communicating with a police officer (for an early overview, see Gregg 1996). The use of undercover tactics by police, whether in terrestrial space or in cyberspace, has always had its critics and defenders (Bronitt and Roche 2001). There are those who would object to circumstances in which the police create crime that otherwise would not occur, or who engage in behaviour that is itself criminal. (In many jurisdictions, police are explicitly exempted from laws criminalising possession or transmission of child pornography when the conduct is done in the line of duty.) On the other hand, those who defend aggressive investigations argue that they are necessary to combat many activities that would otherwise escape police attention. For example, digital technology has transformed child pornography into a commodity that can be produced, reproduced and disseminated on a wide scale at negligible cost, and beyond the gaze of vice squad officers on their periodic visits to adult bookshops (Grant, David and Grabosky 1997).

In some legal systems, such as Australia and the United Kingdom, there is no defence of entrapment. It is up to the judge to rule on the admissibility of evidence obtained through 'unconventional' investigative techniques. In the United States, the entrapment defence is extremely difficult to make, and is rarely used in cybercrime cases or terrestrial cases.

For an entrapment defence to succeed in the United States, the defence must establish that the government originated the criminal design, that the disposition to commit the offence was implanted in the mind of an innocent person, and that the defendant committed the crime at the urging of the government. To defeat a defence of entrapment, it is sufficient to demonstrate that the accused was predisposed to commit the crime. While some individuals might visit 'pre-teen sex' chat rooms for research purposes, out of idle curiosity, or indeed, for purposes of fantasy, many have illegal motives. The prosecution must prove beyond reasonable doubt that the defendant was disposed to commit the criminal act prior to the first time he or she was approached by government agents. This is less difficult when the accused is apparently a habitual visitor in some of the more questionable corners of cyberspace.

Challenges to the Integrity of Evidence

One of the most significant differences between cyber crime and terrestrial crime is the nature of evidence. There are differences in how evidence is stored, where it is located, how it is found, and in the physical limitations of what it will tell you. Digital evidence is intangible. It is often volatile. As we have seen, evidence in digital form may also be massive in quantity, thereby posing substantial logistical challenges.

Brenner and Frederiksen (2001, p. 66) advise that 'the simple act of starting a Microsoft Windows system will destroy more than 4,000,000 characters of evidence, and the spoliation will be far greater if the system is used to run any programs'. By this, they mean that when a system is 'booted up', a number of system files may be modified. Depending upon the forensic procedures employed in the course of searching a computer, this may present the defence with an opportunity to challenge the integrity of evidence presented to the court.

Assembling this evidence and presenting it to a judge and jury in a manner that is intelligible and credible is a significant challenge for prosecutors. In those jurisdictions where conviction depends on the prosecution's ability to prove guilt 'beyond reasonable doubt', the defence has an interest in introducing uncertainties and ambiguities.

Struggles over Discovery

It is the role of the prosecutor to make life difficult for the defence, without interfering with the right to a fair trial. In one child pornography case, the trial judge directed that a defence expert be given access to the defendant's hard drive and allowed to prepare a mirror copy of it. The expert made the copy and removed it. Shortly thereafter, defence counsel was contacted by the prosecutor and advised that retaining the copy might be grounds for prosecution, because such material would not normally be allowed to leave police custody and federal law did not contain an exception for discovery in criminal cases. Although prosecution was not explicitly threatened, defence counsel returned the copied hard drive to the police. The defence then entered a motion to dismiss on the grounds that the prosecutor's actions were a denial of due process and effective assistance of counsel, and that they interfered with the defendant's right to a fair trial. The trial court concluded that defence counsel had been offered every reasonable accommodation to examine the evidence at the sheriff's office, and dismissed the motion. The judgment was affirmed on appeal **[Case No. 151]**.

Standard Forensic Procedures

There are three basic defence tactics for dealing with the use of electronic evidence. First, as discussed above, the defence may question the identity of the author of the evidence in question ('It wasn't me; it was somebody else.') Second, the defence can claim that the evidence was tampered with. Third, it can argue that the unreliability of computer programs created inaccuracies in the output.

In a Wisconsin case, the defendant was on trial for possession of child pornography: **[Case No. 70]**. During the trial, he sought to do a computer demonstration in order to impeach the credibility of the prosecution witness by showing that the witness, a detective, had modified the contents of his computer. The trial court denied the request, finding the evidence to be 'irrelevant, extraneous, and potentially confusing to the jury', as the defence had not alleged that the demonstration would show anything relating to the pornographic images.

Depending on the jurisdiction, there may be a large number of computers awaiting forensic analysis. This may bring about significant delay in proceedings and give rise to possible defence challenges that the evidence was altered or interfered with in some manner. Bell (2002, p. 314) notes that prosecutions in the United Kingdom are often abandoned before trial because careless handling procedures contributed to the contamination of evidence.

There are different methods for the examination of digital evidence. This proliferation of technology may provide an opportunity for the defence to challenge one method or another. In any event, as is the case with other types of evidence, it is important for computer forensics professionals to maintain a chain of custody. Prosecutors must anticipate challenges such as that raised in a case arising from a large-scale conspiracy to import and distribute cannabis in the United States Midwest. One of the conspirators contended that the computer printouts which were part of the evidence against him may have been based on alterations to data by a co-conspirator who became a cooperating witness. He maintained that allowing the co-conspirator access to the computer in the course of the investigation could have affected the integrity of the data. He claimed that with a few keystrokes, the co-conspirator could have easily inserted the defendant's alias ('Gator') into the file. Unfortunately for 'Gator', the other evidence against him was sufficiently persuasive, and the appeals court dismissed his assertion as 'wild-eyed speculation'. At worst, admission of the printouts would have been harmless error.

Efforts to standardise forensic procedures have occurred on a number of fronts. The Computer Crime and Intellectual Property Section of the US Department of Justice developed federal guidelines for searching and seizing computers in 1994. The guidelines have been revised and updated periodically since then (CCIPS 2002).

Standardised forensic procedures have also been developed by the FBI's Computer Analysis Response Team (CART). Courts too have given their imprimatur to certain standardised forensic practices. In one recent case, the courts summarised in great detail the procedures taken at each step by investigators, holding it out as a textbook example of best practice (*United States v Triumph Capital Group, Inc.*, 211 FRD 31 (D Conn, 2002)). In the United Kingdom, the Association of Chief Police Officers has drafted guidelines in relation to preferred forensic procedures. Bell (2002, p. 323) queries whether a statutory scheme under the *Police and Criminal Evidence Act 1984* would be a more appropriate alternative.

This developing standardisation of forensic practice (assuming that investigators adhere to these standards) will give the defence less opportunity to challenge investigative techniques. Of course, departures from recognised best practices, to the extent that they occur, are likely to be seized upon by defence counsel.

Errors in computer program

In some cases, the defence may challenge computer-generated evidence on the grounds that it may have been distorted as a result of computing errors. After all, a great number of computer mishaps arise from 'bugs' or defective code. To introduce this element of uncertainty into a case may introduce an element of doubt in the mind of a juror. In one case involving conspiracy to possess and distribute cocaine, the government introduced telephone toll records as evidence of communication between alleged co-conspirators (*United States v Salgado*, 250 F 3d 438 (6th Cir, 2001)). The defence challenged these records, querying the error rate in the telephone company's billing system. The court held that the government need only present evidence that the computer was sufficiently accurate for the company to rely on it in the conduct of its business. It was not necessary for the actual computer programmer to testify in order to authenticate computer records.

Conclusion

Developments in technology have led to a kind of leap-frog between cyber criminals and their pursuers. As investigators became more skilled in cyber forensics, criminals have made increasing use of encryption technology. This in turn has given rise to such new technologies as key-logging, and new means of surveillance and interception. Developments in trial tactics have followed a similar leap-frog pattern. As prosecutors have begun to anticipate the fantasy defence and are better equipped to rebut it, so too have defence counsel and offenders sought to shore up their defence by introducing turns of phrase designed ultimately to sow the seeds of doubt in a jury.

Cyber crime versus terrestrial crime

One element that differentiates cyber crime from conventional crime is that evidence may exist in encrypted form. Although a massive application of computing power may enable the decryption of suspicious content, the power of encryption often exceeds the technical capacity of the state to break it. This may then require alternative strategies. As we have seen, nations that do not accord their citizens freedom from compulsory self-incrimination may compel disclosure. Authorities in the United States use different methods, as we and the defendant in **[Case No. 110]** have seen.

There has been a massive increase in the storage capacity of computers. It is no longer remarkable that the contents of the Encyclopaedia Britannica can be accommodated comfortably in the hard drive of one's laptop. The exponential increase in the storage capacity of ordinary information systems will pose significant challenges to those engaged in the search of terabytes of data and the seizure of items of evidence that are legally relevant. Only when an organisation is itself a criminal enterprise is seizure of an information system warranted. Because seizure of an entire computer system may be economically catastrophic for the owner, creative means have been developed for copying evidence on-site and analysing it later.

The involvement of the private sector in the investigation of cyber crime appears to have a significant bearing on prosecutions. Computer repair services are in a position to identify illegal content on clients' computers. Internet service providers, if not themselves aware of criminal behaviour on the part of their users, may be called upon to assist police with their investigations. Individual citizens too may come across criminal activity through their own activities, legal or otherwise. Such third-party involvement in the detection and investigation of offences, if not unique to cyber crime, is certainly prominent, and has given rise to an expanding body of law.

The United States versus common law countries

The matter of decryption not only differentiates cyber crime from conventional crime; the way in which investigators (and prosecutors) approach it also varies from country to country. We noted that accused persons in the United States are protected by the Fifth Amendment against self-incrimination. Authorities there compensate for these constraints by mobilising aggressive investigative powers such as 'sneak and peek' warrants, 'stings', and the use of key-logging devices. We know that technologies already allow remote (and very illegal) searches by private individuals. Presumably technologies of remote search will soon be applied (subject to appropriate prosecutorial guidance and judicial oversight) by law enforcement agencies in the United States.

The importance of the Bill of Rights in distinguishing practice in the United States from that prevailing in other common law jurisdictions cannot be understated. The First Amendment protections of freedom of expression have been the basis of challenges to laws that criminalised virtual child pornography. Journalists (or would-be journalists) have sought First Amendment protection from prosecution for possession of illegal images. That they have usually been unsuccessful is beside the point. The fact that they are in a position merely to raise such a defence differentiates them (and their prosecutors) from their counterparts elsewhere in the common law world.

The constraints of the Fourth Amendment will continue to provide American defendants with a basis for challenging the legality of searches and the admissibility of evidence obtained from those searches. The United States is indeed a different place.

CHAPTER SIX

The Quest for Harmonisation of Cyber Crime Laws

The Need for Adequate Cyber Crime Laws

Cyber crime laws may be relative newcomers to the substantive criminal law of most jurisdictions, but their evolution has followed a more or less familiar path. The starting point has been the observation, whether driven by national or international experience, that certain harmful or potentially harmful behaviours appear to be beyond the reach of existing criminal laws. The identification of deficits in the criminal law may emerge from academic analysis or the work of law reform bodies, occasionally even a far-sighted legislature, but most often such problems show up first in prosecutorial failures. The inability to find appropriate charges to lay, or the failure or abandonment of criminal proceedings when it emerges that the criminal law does not in fact extend to the conduct alleged, indicate most clearly that a legislative gap may exist.

Few cases provide a better illustration than the infamous 'Love Bug' computer virus, discussed in Chapter Four. The inability of prosecutors in that case to obtain a conviction under the Access Devices Regulation Act prompted the Philippines legislature within weeks to introduce new laws relating to electronic commerce. From 15 June 2000, a penalty of six months to three years imprisonment applies to 'hacking', 'cracking' and computer virus offences in the Philippines, with fines ranging to a maximum commensurate to the damage incurred. The 'Love Bug' incident also caused legislators in other jurisdictions, both in the Asia–Pacific region and elsewhere, to review their own criminal laws to assess the adequacy of their cyber crime provisions in the face of similar attacks (Urbas 2001).

A report in the year 2000 by the McConnell International consulting firm on the adequacy of cyber crime laws in 52 countries concluded that many had not sufficiently updated their legislation in response to emerging threats. The basis used for comparison was a list of '. . . ten different types of cyber crime in four categories: data-related crimes including interception, modification, and theft; network-related crimes, including interference and sabotage; crimes of access, including hacking and virus distribution; and associated computer-related crimes, including aiding and abetting cyber criminals, computer fraud, and computer forgery' (McConnell International 2000, p. 3). Of the 52 countries, 33 did not have laws to address any type of cyber crime, nine had laws to address five or fewer types of cyber crime, and ten had updated laws to be able to prosecute six or more of the ten categories listed. Among the countries identified as having fully updated their laws in relation to the prosecution of cyber crime were Australia, Canada, Japan, the Philippines and the United States. Others, such as Brazil, China, Malaysia and the United Kingdom, were assessed as having partially updated their laws (McConnell International 2000, p. 4). Importantly, the McConnell International report also noted that cyber crimes are not treated uniformly across countries, or even in some instances within countries – such as Australia, which has an array of federal, state and territory laws in relation to unauthorised computer access and data modification – and that penalty levels vary widely. In some Asian countries, for example, there are heavy fines and lengthy terms of imprisonment that apply to computer crime and intellectual property offences, while in others penalties are low or non-existent (Urbas 2001).

Of course, such differences are not peculiar to the cyber crime area, and harmonisation both within and between different jurisdictions is often a slow and sporadic process. The development of national cyber crime laws exhibits a move towards gradual harmonisation, preceded by several earlier stages of reform.

Extending Existing Criminal Offences

The first response of prosecutors faced with emerging criminal misuse of computers was to seek to apply existing criminal laws such as those criminalising trespass, malicious damage, fraud and theft. In most cases, such legislation makes no reference to specific technologies, and so prosecutors and judges have had to interpret and apply the legislative provisions to new fact situations arising from the misuse of computer technology. As in the 'Love Bug' case, this does not always succeed.

Another example of the difficulties encountered in applying traditional criminal offences to computer misconduct is the early English hacking case [**Case No. 9**], discussed in Chapter Three. It will be recalled that the appellate court in that case was able to uphold a conviction under the *Criminal Damage Act 1971* (UK) on the basis that the statute required damage to tangible property, not that it required the damage itself to be tangible. While this kind of subtle reasoning may have helped the prosecution in this case, it cannot be assumed that laws framed in the pre-electronic age will be readily applicable to computer-related crimes. To see whether they are, we need to look in more detail at traditional offences.

Brenner (2001, par. 15) considers how computer-related crimes might be understood within the traditional classification of 'crimes against the person', 'crimes against property', 'crimes against morality', 'crimes against the administration of justice' and 'crimes against the state'. We shall consider these in turn.

Crimes against the Person

There is little doubt that traditional offences against the person such as homicide or inflicting bodily harm, if committed by computer-assisted means such as hacking into a hospital system and altering a patient's prescribed medication to a lethal dosage (Brenner 2001, par. 17), could be adequately prosecuted under existing criminal laws. Similarly, there are specific laws in many jurisdictions prohibiting the endangerment of life by interference with the guidance or control of aircraft or other forms of transport. There are also laws prohibiting the communication of threats, harassment or stalking activity, though it should be noted that some of these categories of offences against the person have only recently taken distinctive statutory form as offences distinct from assault. One recurring problem with common assault in some jurisdictions has been the requirement of an apprehension of *immediate* bodily harm on the part of the victim, so that remotely communicated threats of violence have not always sufficed. By analogy, threats imparted by means of electronic communication may prove difficult to prosecute as assaults, while they may also fall outside the scope of older statutory provisions dealing with 'documents' containing threats (such as s. 31 of the *Crimes Act 1900* (NSW)).

In order to avoid similar difficulties in relation to harassment and stalking, some recent legislation has specifically included reference to computer and e-mail misuse (in Australia, see s. 359B(c)(ii) of the *Criminal Code Act 1899* (Qld) and s. 21A of the *Crimes Act 1958* (Vic)). The term 'cyberstalking' has been used to distinguish stalking using online or computer technology from more physical analogues. Three types have been distinguished: 'e-mail stalking' involving direct communication designed to intimidate the recipient; 'Internet stalking' involving the posting of slanderous or threatening material on publicly accessible websites; and 'computer stalking', in which the computer of the targeted victim is taken over (Ogilvie 2000). Answers to the question of whether criminal legislation succeeds in capturing these various activities within the scope of stalking offences are emerging through case law.

In the Victorian stalking case discussed in Chapter Four, there was uncertainty as to whether s. 21A of the *Crimes Act 1958* (Vic) extended to causing the victim to fear for her safety where the victim resided not in Victoria but in Canada. On appeal by the prosecution, the Supreme Court remitted the matter to the Magistrates Court, observing that the proper interpretation of the statutory provision did not require that all elements of the offence including the fear induced in the victim had to occur within Victoria – it was sufficient that the acts that constituted the relevant stalking conduct had occurred within the jurisdiction: [**Case No. 147**]. Since then, the Victorian legislature has sought to clarify the matter by amending the statute. The *Crimes (Stalking) Act 2003* (in force from December 2003) now provides that conduct constituting stalking may include contacting the victim by e-mail or other electronic means, and it is immaterial that the victim may have been outside the jurisdiction at the time of the stalking.

Crimes against Property

It is clear that the development of Internet commerce has created unprecedented opportunities for long-distance fraud and theft. Moreover, whether for financial gain or for other reasons, deliberate interference in the form of computer 'hacking' and damage to electronic data, dissemination of computer viruses, and disruption of services can all be readily understood as forms of interference with property. Again, much of this activity can be prosecuted under existing criminal offences, subject of course to significant evidentiary and jurisdictional difficulties in the case of cross-border crimes.

However, different difficulties arise where either the property or the interference in question does not comply with the traditional forms covered by property offences. Information, the fundamental 'good' of the digital age, is not generally classified as a form of 'property' under criminal law (Hughes 1990). This is despite the fact that some legislation specifically includes 'intangible property' as something capable of being stolen or obtained by deception (see for example s. 83 of the *Crimes Act 1900* (ACT) and s. 71 of the *Crimes Act 1958* (Vic), both based on similar provisions in the *Theft Act 1968* (UK)). In fact, the difficulty in prosecuting theft of information may well relate more to another element: the intention permanently to deprive the owner of the property (Hughes 1990). Where the owner is not thus deprived, because all that has happened is that unauthorised use or a copy of the information has been made, it is difficult to argue that this traditional component of theft is made out. The situation is somewhat similar to the phenomenon of joyriding (unlawful use of a motor vehicle), which in many jurisdictions necessitated the enactment of a new statutory offence due to the difficulty of obtaining a prosecution for theft. In the case of 'theft' of information, similar legislative creativity is needed. Other appropriate remedies may lie in breach of confidence or copyright infringement actions instead.

A further difficulty in applying traditional property offences to misconduct using computers or digital communications concerns the notion of 'trespass'. Both criminal and civil remedies have long been available in relation to trespass against land, person and chattels. However, while there is a clear analogy between trespass and computer 'hacking' or other forms of unauthorised access, there is rarely a straightforward legal basis for prosecuting such cyber crimes as trespass, in the absence of a division of cyberspace into parcels of 'private property'. Still less is there a basis for the criminal prosecution of activity carried out with express or implied permission, such as sending messages to a commercial website in such a way or in such numbers that the system is overloaded, resulting in a 'denial of service' to the general public.

Crimes against Morality

The category of 'crimes against morality' covers matters such as the dissemination of pornography and the use of computer technology to facilitate the commission of sexual crimes. Discussion of these areas has always raised contentious issues of public policy and social attitudes, but there is nothing to prevent the boundaries established for other media from being imported to the electronic domain. Where content is of such an offensive nature that its creation, possession or distribution have warranted criminal sanction, then it has been relatively straightforward to adapt existing laws to new electronic media. After all, the same adaptations have had to be made with the introduction of radio broadcast, film, television, video and electronic games, and of course, computer networks. While there is always disagreement over where to draw the line between free speech and artistic licence on the one hand, and for example sedition, defamation or pornography on the other, there is usually no clear reason why the rules for electronic communication should be different from those that apply to traditional paper-based methods.

The most obvious example is the prohibition of child pornography and the prosecution of those who trade in it. However, even here, some difficulties in applying legislation arise. In numerous cases, courts have had to rule on whether persons accused of posting indecent images of children on the Internet could properly be convicted of 'publishing' the material. The same has been true of 'possession' offences where the accused has downloaded material but denied doing so consciously and voluntarily, or with knowledge of its offensive content.

And of course, where transmissions across boundaries are involved, there is the problem of establishing which jurisdiction a crime involving offensive content was committed in, and which substantive offences apply.

Difficulties also arise in relation to the control of access to adult pornographic material or other content deemed inappropriate for viewing by the general public. The problem is not one of how to prohibit distribution of the material as such, but rather how to regulate its availability. Increasingly, legal concerns have focused on the adequacy of technological barriers such as subscription or proof of age requirements, and the responsibility of Internet service providers where such measures are absent or ineffective. The protection of children is also a concern in relation to sexual predators' use of online chat rooms in order to establish contact with potential victims.

Clearly, there are cultural and historical differences between countries which shape their legislative responses to sexually explicit content. In Japan, computer crime laws have been in force since the 1980s, but laws prohibiting child pornography were only enacted as late as 1999. In the United States, constitutional arguments have been used to challenge laws such as the *Communications Decency Act of 1996* (see *Reno v ACLU*, 117 S Ct 2329 (US Pa, 1997)), and the *Child Online Protection Act of 1998* (see COPA Commission 2000). Phenomena such as virtual child pornography (in which no pornographic images of actual children are used) have tested the boundaries of the First Amendment guarantee of constitutionally protected speech (Cisneros 2002).

In Australia, where free speech protection has a less clear constitutional basis, the general approach to online content has largely been through the classification system that applies generally to film, videos and computer games. This comprehensive system aims to inform the public of, and restrict access to, particular types of content such as sexually explicit and violent material. The Office of Film and Literature Classification (OFLC) assigns a range of classifications including 'R' or 'X' ratings for films containing material that justifies their restriction to adults. Criminal penalties apply to the unlawful distribution or broadcasting of material that is restricted or refused classification. The Australian Broadcasting Authority (ABA) is primarily responsible for online content, and has to date banned around 285 Australian websites under the Online Content Co-Regulatory Scheme. Note, however, that the ABA has no power over websites operated overseas. In addition, Australian states and territories have specific offences relating to child pornography.

Crimes against the Administration of Justice and Crimes against the State

The remaining categories, 'crimes against the administration of justice' and 'crimes against the state', appear to represent little that requires new laws to be developed specifically relating to computers. Examples discussed by Brenner (2001) include the rise of 'vigilantism' on the Internet, the unauthorised publication of law enforcement details, and cyberterrorism. Certainly, the latter threat has assumed heightened importance for governments and security agencies since September 2001, but the precise extent of any increase in cyberterrorism activity is unclear. Nonetheless, the extensive response by legislatures in various countries to the resurgent threat of global terrorism has included a revision of computer security laws along with other aspects of national security.

In the United States, the *Provide Appropriate Tools Required to Intercept and Obstruct Terrorism* (PATRIOT) *Act of 2001* has expanded the definition of 'protected computer' in the *Computer Fraud and Abuse Act of 1986* so that not only can unauthorised intrusions into computers in the United States be prosecuted, but so can any hacking that occurs anywhere in the world, provided that some packet related to the activity travels through a US computer. Given the complex routing of Internet transmissions, there is no reason why this would not include cases where neither the offender nor any victim was in the United States.

In countries which have not introduced terrorism-related computer laws, it may be that existing laws protecting the organs of government and public infrastructure are adequate to deal with cyber threats. In some countries, the motivation for control of Internet communications appears to be based more on internal security concerns. Indeed, laws introduced ostensibly to protect the national interest may be used to protect entrenched political interests from criticism or dissent. China's Internet Security Law passed in December 2000 makes it a criminal offence to transmit over the Internet material including 'slander and rumours or harmful information', 'incitement of ethnic hatred or discrimination', and 'information in support of cults' (Urbas 2001).

Creating New Computer-Related Offences

Where existing offences have failed to keep up with criminal exploitation of new technologies, new offences have had to be created. Early accounts of criminal use of new computer technologies date back to the 1960s, but it was not until the late 1970s that legislatures began to see the need for specific laws in response (Sieber 1998; Goodman and Brenner 2002). For example, in the United States a Bill for the Federal Computer Systems Protection Act was introduced in 1977, then revised and reintroduced in 1979, which criminalised any knowing, wilful manipulation or attempted manipulation of federal government computers or those involved in interstate commerce, for fraudulent purposes. This innovation was adopted in state law, beginning with Arizona and Florida (Goodman and Brenner 2002).

In Europe and elsewhere, similar legislative changes were made in order to protect information that was increasingly being stored on computer networks. Sieber (1998, pp. 24–30) has identified six 'waves' of computer laws that have emerged over the past three decades.

Privacy

The 'first wave' identified by Sieber, which began in the 1970s and 1980s, concerned the protection of privacy. The emergence of powerful new technology allowing governments and other organisations to collect, store and process large amounts of information about individual citizens prompted the enactment of protections in the form of privacy laws. The earliest was in Sweden, in 1973, soon followed by the United States in 1974 and other Western countries thereafter. In 1981, the Committee of Ministers of the Council of Europe (COE) adopted the *Convention for the Protection of Privacy of Individuals with regard to Automatic Processing of Personal Data*, an instrument which came into force in October 1985 (Sieber 1998, p. 143).

Australian jurisdictions took longer to get around to privacy protection, with the enactment of the *Privacy Act 1988* (Cth) and more recent *Privacy Amendment (Private Sector) Act 2000* (Cth). There are also privacy laws in some of the Australian states and territories, such as the *Privacy and Personal Information Protection Act 1998* (NSW) and the *Information Privacy Act 2000* (Vic). However, Australian privacy laws are not particularly strong legislative instruments, as remedies for breach of privacy are generally by way of declaration rather than criminal punishment, and private sector compliance is largely through voluntary codes of practice. The protection of privacy in Australia arguably lags behind privacy protection in Europe, where various Privacy Directives have implemented protections under the *European Convention for the Protection of Human Rights and Fundamental Freedoms*. Recent measures include the Privacy Directive (95/46/EC) and the Privacy and Electronic Communications Directive (2002/58/EC).

An associated development, complementary to privacy legislation, concerned access to government information through 'freedom of information' laws. These laws are based on the principle that where the government has information about or directly affecting an individual, he or she has a right to know about it, to see it, and to have it corrected if it is wrong. In Australia, the *Freedom of Information Act 1982* (Cth) came first, with states and territories following suit. Again, this legislation is largely administrative and designed to facilitate access to information, rather than criminalising particular types of computer misconduct.

A notable exception to the general approach to the protection of privacy in Australia is section 222 ('Unlawfully obtaining confidential information') of the Northern Territory *Criminal Code*, added in 1983, which penalises any person who 'unlawfully abstracts any confidential information from any register, document, computer or other repository of information . . . with intent to publish the same to a person who is not lawfully entitled to have or to receive it'. This provision is unusual in that it seeks to protect the confidentiality of information rather than to restrict access. In the first prosecution under this provision, a police officer was convicted of providing names and addresses from a police database to her de facto husband, a private investigator. While the disclosure was flagrantly in breach of her duties as a police officer, the conviction under s. 222 was quashed on appeal as the information was not 'confidential' in any real sense – rather, it was access to the computer data that was restricted: *Snell v Pryce* (1990) 99 FLR 213. Subsequent computer crime legislation has tended to focus on access control rather than on the confidentiality of content.

Economic Crime

The 'second wave' of computer legislation was more clearly criminal in its coverage, dealing with economic crime. As it became clear that existing criminal laws did not always extend to the unauthorised manipulation of computer functions, legislatures began to revise their laws. The result was a new array of offences prohibiting such acts as unlawful access to computers and damaging computer data.

The United States introduced its *Computer Fraud and Abuse Act* in 1986; Australia similarly amended its *Crimes Act 1914* (Cth) in 1989; and the United Kingdom enacted its *Computer Misuse Act* in 1990. The offences added at federal level in Australia (Part VIA, comprising sections 76A–76F of the *Crimes Act 1914* (Cth)) criminalised unlawful access to or impairment of Commonwealth computers and data, and carried penalties of up to 10 years' imprisonment.

Examples of prosecutions under the Australian provisions include:

- the case of a tax officer who repeatedly altered Commonwealth data to show that certain taxpayers had been relieved from payment of income tax: **[Case No. 24]**;

- a telephone company computer technician who was sentenced to a $2\frac{1}{2}$-year term of imprisonment for fraudulently manipulating the company's computerised inventory system to obtain an illegal benefit: **[Case No. 38]**;

- a computer consultant who hacked into customer lists belonging to an Internet service provider and published details of its security vulnerability, sentenced to three years: **[Case No. 50]**; and

- a Social Security employee who was sentenced to three years and nine months for manipulating departmental computer programs to pay himself benefits to which he was not entitled **[Case No. 121]**.

It should be remembered, of course, that a great deal of economic crime carried out with the use of computers and digital communications technology has been prosecuted under existing fraud and related laws. For example, the prosecutions in Australia for 'share ramping' on United States markets (see Chapter Four) proceeded under securities legislation administered by the Australian Securities and Investments Commission (ASIC). Nonetheless, the enactment of specific computer offences in the Crimes Act greatly assisted the law enforcement response to misuse of technology.

In fact, several Australian states and territories had enacted computer-specific offences somewhat earlier than the Commonwealth (e.g. ss. 222 and 276 of the Northern Territory *Criminal Code* in 1983; and s. 9A of the *Summary Offences Act 1966* (Vic) in 1988). The latter provision carried the title 'Computer trespass' and provided that a person 'must not gain access to, or enter, a computer system or part of a computer system without lawful authority to do so', punishable by 25 penalty units (a fine amount as set by statute), or imprisonment for six months.

Unlike the Commonwealth's computer offences, which were limited to unauthorised access to or impairment of Commonwealth computers and data, the Victorian provision was very widely drafted. The section applied to any computer system, whether owned by government or privately, and it was left up to prosecutorial discretion and judicial interpretation to determine what constituted 'access', a 'computer system' and 'lawful authority'. In an early Victorian case **[Case No. 13]**, it was held that a computer operator employed by a bank and given access to its computer system for certain purposes nonetheless breached s. 9A when he used that access to reprogram a bank's ATM systems to dispense funds to which he was not entitled. (The section has recently been repealed in favour of provisions following the Model Code, discussed below.)

It is notable that few legislatures have thought it necessary or desirable to include a legislative definition of 'computer' in their statutes. Thus, it is left to courts to interpret all legislative reference to 'computers' and related terms, and to fit this with the facts before them. This omission is deliberate, ensuring that legislation does not become obsolete with technological developments, but it causes some concern over the potential scope of the provisions. For example,

s. 135L (Dishonest use of Computers) of the *Crimes Act 1900* (ACT) prohibits dishonest use of 'a computer or other machine, or part of a computer or other machine'. The term 'machine' is defined to mean 'a machine designed to be operated by means of a coin, banknote, token, disc, tape or any identifying card or article'. Conceivably, though this is unlikely given prosecutorial discretion, this provision would cover the case of someone inserting a washer into a vending machine. The offence carries a maximum penalty of 10 years imprisonment.

Intellectual Property Protection

The 'third wave' expanded long-standing regimes of intellectual property protection, such as copyright and patent law, to computer software and digital content. In Australia, the *Copyright Act 1968* (Cth) was amended in 1984 so that computer programs were explicitly covered, and the *Circuit Layouts Act 1989* (Cth) was enacted to provide specific legislative protection to integrated circuits. The *Copyright Amendment (Digital Agenda) 2000* (Cth) further reformed copyright law to deal with new forms of digital information and communication.

Interestingly, the most severe criminal penalties in the *Copyright Act 1968* (Cth) now apply to offences involving copyright infringement by converting a work from hard copy or analog form into digital or other electronic machine-readable form (s. 132(6AA)). There are also heavy penalties for dealing in unauthorised broadcast decoding devices (s. 135AS): up to five years imprisonment plus substantial fines. However, sentences imposed for copyright infringement in Australia (whether using digital technology or not) have rarely involved imprisonment (Urbas 2000a). This is in marked contrast to the severe sentences imposed under copyright laws in the United States, and in particular the *Digital Millennium Copyright Act (DMCA) of 1998*, which carries maximum penalties of 10 years imprisonment and fines to US$1 million (s. 1204).

The most well-known DMCA prosecution to date is the ElcomSoft case, in which a Russian programmer employed by that company was arrested while attending a hacker convention in the United States in 2001. The charges related to the distribution of computer software allowing users to bypass copyright protection on electronic books. Indictments against the programmer were dropped after widespread protests, and he agreed to give evidence in criminal proceedings against the company instead (United States Department of Justice 2001b). A California jury acquitted on all charges in December 2002.

However, other criminal computer copyright prosecutions in the United States are proving more successful. One of the largest recent operations by the Department of Justice, code-named 'Operation Buccaneer', has resulted in successful prosecutions against more than a dozen members of Internet software piracy group 'Drink or Die', including extradition proceedings against an Australian suspect from New South Wales indicted in March 2003 (United States Department of Justice 2002; United States Department of Justice 2003b).

It should also be noted that the Computer Crime and Intellectual Property Section (CCIPS) of the United States Department of Justice has pursued numerous successful prosecutions under the *No Electronic Theft (NET) Act of 1997*, which outlaws large-scale unauthorised distribution of copyrighted material such as games and entertainment over the Internet, even if this is done without commercial gain (United States Department of Justice 2003d). In addition,

criminal prosecutions have been partly successful in limiting the extent and operations of 'peer-to-peer' file-sharing networks such as Napster and Gnutella, which
facilitate the online distribution of copyright material such as music recordings.
However, newer and more distributed networks such as Kazaa, which is owned by
a company registered in Vanuatu with a domain name registered in Australia
and servers located in Europe, are proving more difficult to combat (Smith
2003).

Illegal and Harmful Content

The 'fourth wave' identified by Sieber concerns illegal and harmful content such
as pornography, hate speech or defamation over the Internet. This has been a
particularly vexed issue, with clear cultural and legal differences between countries. As noted earlier, there have been markedly different legislative responses to
the regulation of sexually explicit material on the Internet, and the same applies
to other types of content seen as offensive or harmful.

In Europe, there are numerous criminal laws prohibiting the dissemination of
extremist political content such as pro-Nazi propaganda. The application of one
such law to online content was tested in May 2000, when a French court ruled that
the US-based Internet media company Yahoo! Inc. was required to block access
by French residents to its auction sites, which 'banalised' the Holocaust by selling
Nazi memorabilia. The company's response was to deny that the French court had
jurisdiction over conduct which occurred in the United States, and also to deny
that there was any adequate technological measure that could ensure compliance
with the ruling. After a lengthy legal battle, the company announced in early 2001
that it had instituted a policy of monitoring its auction sites to try to prevent the
online promotion of such material (Fowler, Franklin and Hyde 2001; Katz and
Jones 2001).

Jurisdictional issues have also emerged in relation to civil actions involving
defamatory material posted on websites, as illustrated by the *Dow Jones v Gutnick*
case discussed in Chapter Two.

In Australia, several states and territories have enacted criminal laws prohibiting racial and religious vilification. But at the federal level, as with privacy, the
approach has been less punitive. The *Racial Hatred Act 1995* (Cth) added new
provisions to the *Racial Discrimination Act 1975* (Cth), prohibiting the dissemination of racially offensive material, but breach of these provisions does not carry
criminal penalties. Rather, a complaint can be made to the Human Rights and
Equal Opportunity Commission (HREOC), which can make appropriate orders.
In 2000, the HREOC ordered a website operated by a group based in Adelaide,
South Australia, to be closed down on the ground that in questioning the historical occurrence of the Holocaust, it vilified Jewish people and thus was unlawful
under the Racial Discrimination Act (*Jones v Toben*, HREOC 2001, on appeal to
the Federal Court in *Toben v Jones* [2002] FCAFC 158 (21 May 2000) and *Toben v
Jones* [2003] FCAFC 137 (27 June 2003)).

The issue of 'cyber racism' has also recently been addressed by the Council of Europe (COE). In May 2001, the Council's *Convention on Cybercrime* was
opened for signature, together with a First Additional Protocol concerning criminalisation of racist and xenophobic propaganda disseminated over the Internet.

The Convention was aimed at a harmonised approach to criminalisation of such content as well as to investigative issues and international assistance.

Criminal Procedural Law

The 'fifth wave' consists of procedural reforms such as those enhancing investigative powers in relation to electronically stored material. As noted by Brenner (2001, par. 57), search and seizure laws in most jurisdictions were drafted at a time when the only evidence that needed to be collected was in tangible form. Many jurisdictions have realised that the enactment of substantive cyber crime laws may not result in significant prosecutions unless additional steps can be taken to preserve electronic evidence and to ensure cooperation with investigating authorities by individuals and entities such as Internet service providers.

Recognising this problem, a substantial portion of the COE *Convention on Cyber-crime* is devoted to appropriate search and seizure measures for electronic evidence. This approach is starting to be reflected in national legislative amendments. For example, the Australian *Cybercrime Act 2001* (Cth) contains provisions allowing police and customs officials to obtain orders requiring people with knowledge of computer systems to provide information and assistance with access, decryption and copying of data. Failure to comply with such an order is punishable by six months' imprisonment.

Security Law

The 'sixth wave' is related to security issues, and concerns the use of access controls such as encryption to protect data, and the limits to which such controls may be put. Much of this law was initially concerned with the protection of privacy and data security, but increasing attention is now being directed to issues involving national security and terrorism. For example, investigative powers in relation to electronic communications have been expanded under recent legislation. In signing the PATRIOT Act into law on 21 October 2001, President Bush said:

> Surveillance of communications is another essential tool to pursue and stop terrorists. The existing law was written in the era of rotary telephones. This new law that I sign today will allow surveillance of all communications used by terrorists, including e-mail, the Internet, and cell phones. As of today, we'll be able to better meet the technological challenges posed by this proliferation of communications technology (United States Department of State 2001; *Washington Post* 2001).

Organisations such as the American Civil Liberties Union have warned that these legislative amendments greatly expand the scope for electronic eavesdropping on citizens by law enforcement authorities. The *Domestic Security Enhancement Act of 2003* further facilitates electronic surveillance, as well as including new penalties of up to 10 years' imprisonment for the use of encryption to conceal criminal activity.

National Harmonisation

The drafting and subsequent judicial interpretation of laws inevitably reflect jurisdictional constraints and national political considerations. In countries with federal legal systems, such as the United States and Australia, a perennial problem is legislative divergence among internal jurisdictions. This has also been evident in the early development of computer crime laws (Sullivan 1988).

Federal laws in both Australia and the United States generally require an appropriate connection with national government or some aspect of interstate commerce triggering federal jurisdiction, while state legislatures operate under no such constraints. In the Australian context, the constitutional limitations on Commonwealth legislative power meant that Commonwealth computer crime laws were initially restricted to acts involving, or data held on, a Commonwealth computer, defined as 'a computer owned, leased or operated by a Commonwealth entity' (see s. 476.1 of the *Criminal Code Act 1995* (Cth)). However, new offences added under the *Cybercrime Act 2001* cover unauthorised computer access, modification of data, or impairment of electronic communications where this is effected by means of a 'telecommunications service', defined (in s. 476.1) as 'a service for carrying communications by means of guided or unguided electromagnetic energy or both'. Importantly, this covers the use of the Internet to commit offences. This extension of Commonwealth legislative reach rests on s. 51(v) of the Constitution, which gives the Commonwealth legislative power with respect to 'postal, telegraphic, telephonic, and other like services'.

Current legislative attention is being directed to another threat to the functioning of global communications systems such as the Internet and mobile phone networks. This is the prevalence of 'spam' or unsolicited messages advertising anything from investment opportunities to pornography, and becoming increasingly more sophisticated in order to bypass filter mechanisms. While much of this activity constitutes a nuisance rather than anything intrinsically offensive or criminal, its sheer bulk now threatens to make the Internet unworkable or unattractive as a means of communication. Part of the growing response, worldwide, is in the form of legislative proposals to criminalise or otherwise restrict the practice of bulk unsolicited e-mail. In the United States, the *Controlling the Assault of Non-solicited Pornography and Marketing (CAN-SPAM) Act* was signed into law in December 2003 (CNET News 2003a). In Australia, the *Spam Act 2003* (Cth) was also enacted in December, with most sections coming into force in 2004, though the legislation provides substantial civil rather than criminal penalties (CNET News 2003b).

Jurisdictional limitations aside, different legislatures within federal legal systems have simply adopted different approaches in formulating computer crime laws. Recognising the largely unnecessary legal complexity that this entails, some countries have made concerted efforts towards national harmonisation of their criminal law.

Australia's Model Criminal Code Project

The driving force for the process of national harmonisation within Australia has been the Model Criminal Code Officers Committee (MCCOC) of the Standing Committee of Attorneys-General (SCAG), established in 1990 and comprising senior law officers from all jurisdictions. The Commonwealth enacted general Model Criminal Code principles in its *Criminal Code Act 1995* (Cth), and several subsequent amendments have added substantive provisions. These now include laws relating to foreign officials, United Nations personnel, terrorist activities, people-smuggling, treason and espionage, theft, fraud and bribery, crimes against humanity, war crimes, slavery and sexual servitude, firearms trafficking, money laundering, and lastly, computer offences.

In January 2001, the Model Code Committee published its *Report on Damage and Computer Offences*, which has largely influenced the shape of recent Australian cyber crime legislation (Model Criminal Code Officers Committee 2001). Based on this report, the Cybercrime Bill 2001 was introduced into the Commonwealth Parliament on 27 June 2001, and with some amendments after consideration by the Senate Legal and Constitutional Committee, was enacted. The *Cybercrime Act 2001* (Cth) came into effect on 1 October 2001. This legislation served both to modernise Commonwealth computer offences (previously largely contained in the *Crimes Act 1914*) and to provide a model for the states and territories to follow. There is, of course, a significant judicial task ahead in interpreting much of this legislation, and there can be little doubt that some of the differences between the laws of different jurisdictions will turn out to be of legal importance (Steel 2002).

The breadth of the new offences is illustrated by s. 477.1, which criminalises unauthorised access, modification or impairment by means of a 'telecommunications service' where the person intends to commit, or facilitate the commission of, a serious offence against a law of the Commonwealth, a state or a territory. A 'serious offence' is any crime carrying a penalty of five years or more, and its commission using the means attempted may be impossible. The penalty is as for the serious offence in question.

On 23 October 2003, the new Commonwealth Criminal Code provisions were reportedly used for the first time to charge a 17-year-old Queensland youth in relation to alleged unauthorised entry into the computer system of an Australian Internet service provider and a United Kingdom university (Findlaw 2003).

The Emergence of International Harmonisation

As noted in earlier chapters, the effectiveness of law enforcement responses to cyber crime is considerably hampered by differences among various nations' legislation, and the consequent difficulty of prosecuting transjurisdictional crimes. This has been at the core of concerted efforts to move towards greater international harmonisation of laws.

Minimum Requirements for Cyber Crime Laws

An important part of the process of international harmonisation has been the identification of minimum requirements for computer crime laws. The approach taken has been that, while it is extremely difficult to achieve international harmonisation on all aspects of cyber crime laws, particularly in areas where national sensitivities or cultural factors are salient, at least a basic standard for the development of legislation can be agreed. Several international organisations have contributed significantly to this process.

The OECD

An early start was made by the Organisation for Economic Co-operation and Development (OECD). In a 1986 report entitled *Computer-Related Crime: Analysis of Legal Policy*, the organisation recommended that member states pay particular attention to their coverage of specific knowingly committed acts under their national penal laws:

(1) the input, alteration, erasure and/or suppression of computer data and/or computer programs made wilfully with the intent to commit an illegal transfer of funds or of another thing of value;

(2) the input, alteration, erasure and/or suppression of computer data and/or computer programs made wilfully with the intent to commit a forgery;

(3) the input, alteration, erasure and/or suppression of computer data and/or computer programs, or other interference with computer systems, made wilfully with the intent to hinder the functioning of a computer and/or of a telecommunication system;

(4) the infringement of the exclusive right of the owner of a protected computer program with the intent to exploit commercially the program and put it on the market;

(5) the access to or the interception of a computer and/or telecommunication system made knowingly and without the authorisation of the person responsible for the system, either by infringement of security measures or for other dishonest or harmful intentions.

The OECD continues to contribute to international computer security policy, recently updating its *Guidelines for the Security of Information Systems and Networks* (OECD 2002).

The Council of Europe

In 1989, the Select Committee of Experts on Computer-Related Crime of the Council of Europe (COE) produced a 'minimum list' of computer crimes to be prohibited and prosecuted by international consensus (Goodman and Brenner 2002):

• *Computer fraud:* The input, alteration, erasure or suppression of computer data or computer programs, or other interference with the course of data processing, that influences the result of data processing thereby causing economic or possessory loss of property of another person with the intent of procuring an unlawful economic gain for oneself or for another person;

• *Computer forgery:* The input, alteration, erasure or suppression of computer data or computer programs, or other interference with the course of data processing, in a manner or under such conditions, as prescribed by national law, that it would constitute the offence of forgery if it had been committed with respect to a traditional object of such an offence;

• *Damage to computer data or computer programs:* The erasure, damaging, deterioration or suppression of computer data or computer programs without right;

• *Computer sabotage:* The input, alteration, erasure or suppression of computer data or computer programs, or other interference with computer systems, with the intent to hinder the functioning of a computer or a telecommunication system;

- *Unauthorised access:* The access without right to a computer system or network by infringing security measures;
- *Unauthorised interception:* The interception, made without right and by technical means, of communications to, from and within a computer system or network;
- *Unauthorised reproduction of a protected computer program:* The reproduction, distribution or communication to the public without right of a computer program which is protected by law;
- *Unauthorised reproduction of a topography:* The reproduction without right of a topography protected by law, of a semiconductor product, or the commercial exploitation or the importation for that purpose, done without right, of a topography or of a semiconductor product manufactured by using the topography.

The COE Committee also provided an 'optional list' on which it would be harder to reach international consensus (Goodman and Brenner 2002):

- *Alteration of computer data or computer programs*: The alteration of computer data or computer programs without right;
- *Computer espionage*: The acquisition by improper means or the disclosure, transfer or use of a trade or commercial secret without right or any other legal justification, with intent either to cause economic loss to the person entitled to the secret or to obtain an unlawful economic advantage for oneself or a third person;
- *Unauthorised use of a computer*: The use of a computer system or network without right, that either (a) is made with the acceptance of a significant risk of loss being caused to the person entitled to use the system or harm to the system or its functioning, or (b) is made with the intent to cause loss to the person entitled to use the system or harm to the system or its functioning, or (c) causes loss to the person entitled to use the system or harm to the system or its functioning;
- *Unauthorised use of a protected computer program*: The use without right of a computer program which is protected by law and which has been reproduced without right, with the intent either to procure an unlawful economic gain for oneself or for another person or to cause harm to the holder of the right.

Many elements of these 'minimum' and 'optional' lists have by now found their way into national computer crime legislation, along with significant improvements in criminal investigative powers and procedures. In Australia, similar minimum requirements were formulated in early stages of the development of the *Cybercrime Act 2001* (Cth) and its state and territory counterparts (Thompson and Berwick 1997).

The United Nations

The next significant step towards internationalisation came in 1990 with the Eighth United Nations Congress on the Prevention of Crime and the Treatment of Offenders, and the accompanying Symposium on the Prevention and Prosecution of Cybercrime (Sieber 1998, p. 162). The Congress passed a resolution calling on member states to intensify their efforts to combat cyber crime, in particular by modernising their national laws so as to:

(a) ensure that existing offences and laws concerning investigative powers and admissibility of evidence in judicial proceedings adequately apply, and if necessary, make appropriate changes;

(b) in the absence of laws that adequately apply, create offences and investigative and evidentiary procedures, where necessary, to deal with this novel and sophisticated form of criminal activity;

(c) provide for the forfeiture or restitution of illegally acquired assets resulting from the commission of computer-related crimes.

The United Nations also made significant contributions through the next decade, with the publication in 1994 of the *UN Manual on the Prevention and Control of Computer-Related Crime*; the inclusion of a workshop on computer network crime held in conjunction with the 10th United Nations Congress on the Prevention of Crime and the Treatment of Offenders in 2000; and increasing attention directed by specialist United Nations bodies such as the Office on Drugs and Crime (UNODC) and the Centre for International Crime Prevention (CICP) to organised crime activities using the Internet (United Nations 2003).

The Council of Europe's *Convention on Cybercrime*

The Council of Europe's *Convention on Cybercrime* is to date the most prominent achievement of the international response to cyber crime. Even during its long drafting stage (over four years and producing 27 drafts), it provided guidance for national legislatures outside the Council involved in developing their own legislation, including the *Cybercrime Act 2001* (Cth) in Australia (see Explanatory Memorandum for the Cybercrime Bill: <http://scaleplus.law.gov.au/html/ems/0/2001072001.htm>). The *Convention on Cybercrime* was formally adopted by the Council of Europe in Budapest in November 2001.

The Explanatory Report to the *Convention on Cybercrime* makes clear the primary motivation for the harmonisation of national cyber crime laws:

> This kind of harmonisation alleviates the fight against such crimes on the national and on the international level as well. Correspondence in domestic law may prevent abuses from being shifted to a Party with a previous lower standard. As a consequence, the exchange of useful common experiences in the practical handling of cases may be enhanced, too. International cooperation (esp. extradition and mutual legal assistance) is facilitated, e.g. regarding requirements of double criminality.

The substantive and procedural provisions of the Convention are designed to assist with the harmonisation process. Chapter I defines key terms:

• 'computer system' means any device or a group of interconnected or related devices, one or more of which, pursuant to a program, performs automatic processing of data;

• 'computer data' means any representation of facts, information or concepts in a form suitable for processing in a computer system, including a program suitable to cause a computer system to perform a function;

- 'service provider' means:

  i) any public or private entity that provides to users of its service the ability to communicate by means of a computer system, and

  ii) any other entity that processes or stores computer data on behalf of such communication service or users of such service;

- 'traffic data' means any computer data relating to a communication by means of a computer system, generated by a computer system that formed a part in the chain of communication, indicating the communication's origin, destination, route, time, date, size, duration, or type of underlying service.

The main provisions are then contained in Chapter II, which comprises both substantive and procedural criminal law. The substantive law provisions require member states to 'adopt such legislative and other measures as may be necessary to establish as criminal offences under its domestic law, when committed intentionally', a series of specified acts, organised as follows:

Title 1 – Offences against the confidentiality, integrity and availability of computer data and systems

Illegal access (Art. 2): the access to the whole or any part of a computer system without right (optionally with the requirement that the offence be committed by infringing security measures, with the intent of obtaining computer data or other dishonest intent, or in relation to a computer system that is connected to another computer system).

Illegal interception (Art. 3): the interception without right, made by technical means, of non-public transmissions of computer data to, from or within a computer system, including electromagnetic emissions from a computer system carrying such computer data (optionally with the requirement that the offence be committed with dishonest intent, or in relation to a computer system that is connected to another computer system).

Data interference (Art. 4): the damaging, deletion, deterioration, alteration or suppression of computer data without right (optionally with the requirement that the conduct result in serious harm).

System interference (Art. 5): the serious hindering without right of the functioning of a computer system by inputting, transmitting, damaging, deleting, deteriorating, altering or suppressing computer data.

Misuse of devices (Art. 6): without right, the production, sale, procurement for use, import, distribution or otherwise making available of a device, including a computer program, designed or adapted primarily for the purpose of committing offences under Articles 2–5; or a computer password, access code, or similar data by which the whole or any part of a computer system is capable of being accessed with intent that it be used for the purpose of committing such offences; or the possession of such an item with intent that it be used for the purpose of committing any such offences.

Title 2 – Computer-related offences

Computer-related forgery (Art. 7): without right, the input, alteration, deletion, or suppression of computer data, resulting in inauthentic data with the intent that it be considered or acted upon for legal purposes as if it were authentic, regardless whether or not the data is directly readable and intelligible (optionally with the requirement of an intent to defraud, or similar dishonest intent, before criminal liability attaches).

Computer-related fraud (Art. 8): without right, the causing of a loss of property to another by:

- any input, alteration, deletion or suppression of computer data,
- any interference with the functioning of a computer system,
- with fraudulent or dishonest intent of procuring, without right, an economic benefit for oneself or for another.

Title 3 – Content-related offences

Offences related to child pornography (Art. 9): without right, the following conduct:

- producing child pornography for the purpose of its distribution through a computer system;
- offering or making available child pornography through a computer system;
- distributing or transmitting child pornography through a computer system;
- procuring child pornography through a computer system for oneself or for another;
- possessing child pornography in a computer system or on a computer-data storage medium.

Title 4 – Offences related to infringements of copyright and related rights

Offences related to infringements of copyright and related rights (Art. 10): the infringement of copyright (possibly excluding moral rights) committed wilfully, on a commercial scale and by means of a computer system.

Title 5 – Ancillary liability and sanctions

Attempt and aiding or abetting (Art. 11): intentionally aiding or abetting, and (optionally) attempting to commit, any offences under Articles 2–10.

Corporate liability (Art. 12): a legal person can be held liable for a criminal offence established in accordance with this Convention, committed for its benefit by any natural person, acting either individually or as part of an organ of the legal person, who has a leading position within the legal person, based on:

- a power of representation of the legal person;
- an authority to take decisions on behalf of the legal person;
- an authority to exercise control within the legal person.

Sanctions and measures (Art. 13): as necessary to ensure that the criminal offences established in accordance with Articles 2–11 are punishable by effective, proportionate and dissuasive sanctions, which include deprivation of liberty (for natural persons), or criminal or non-criminal sanctions or measures, including monetary sanctions (for legal persons).

The offences contained in Chapter II of the Convention require that the acts be committed intentionally or wilfully, and 'without right'. Thus, there is no scope within the terms of the Convention for the criminalisation of conduct which is accidental or even negligent, or in relation to which the relevant parties consent or there is some other legitimate reason for the conduct. The precise interpretation of 'without right' in particular contexts is otherwise left to national legislatures (Rawlings 2001).

It should be noted that the Convention also incorporates provisions designed to safeguard human rights norms and privileges, such as requirements for judicial or other independent supervision, proportionality, respect for and consideration of the rights of third parties (Inman 2001). Given the strength of the provisions allowing search, seizure and surveillance, however, these have been criticised as inadequate by some privacy advocates (Taylor 2001).

The remainder of Chapter II of the *Convention on Cybercrime* deals with procedural measures. Sections are organised as follows:

Title 1 – Common provisions

Title 2 – Expedited preservation of stored computer data

Expedited preservation of stored computer data (Art. 16): powers and orders relating to the preservation of stored computer data, in particular data which is vulnerable to loss or modification.

Expedited preservation and partial disclosure of traffic data (Art. 17): sufficient disclosure to allow identification of service providers and the path through which communication was transmitted.

Title 3 – Production order

Production order (Art. 18): relating to specified computer data or subscriber information.

Title 4 – Search and seizure of stored computer data

Search and seizure of stored computer data (Art. 19): empowering competent authorities to search a computer system or computer-data storage medium.

Title 5 – Real-time collection of computer data

Real-time collection of traffic data (Art. 20): requiring service providers to cooperate in the collection of traffic data.

Interception of content data (Art. 21): requiring service providers to cooperate in the interception and collection of content data.

There are also provisions dealing with jurisdiction, and Chapter III of the Convention then goes on to deal with international cooperation, extradition and mutual assistance.

At the time of writing, the *Convention on Cybercrime* had 37 signatories, 33 of which are Council of Europe members, with four non-European members: Canada, Japan, South Africa and the United States. The Convention's entry into force required five ratifications, including at least three from member states of the Council. On 18 March 2004, Lithuania became the fifth member state to ratify, and the Convention thus enters into force on 1 July 2004 (Council of Europe 2004).

Conclusion

Considerable differences still exist in legislative responses to cyber crime. Despite common legal histories, there are differences in the definitions of offences, the extent of criminalisation, and the penalties applicable to various forms of computer misconduct. These differences are apparent both among national jurisdictions and, within federal systems, among internal jurisdictions. This diversity need not be surprising, as it reflects the position of criminal law generally. However, with the international nature of much cyber crime, there is increasing recognition that legislative differences can impede effective law enforcement. There is some convergence, given the fact that more countries are now treating cyber crime as a significant form of misconduct requiring criminalisation backed by serious penalties, and in drafting new provisions, jurisdictions have inevitably looked at existing models. In this regard, the emergence of the Council of Europe's *Convention on Cybercrime* as the dominant international model for cyber crime legislation is a positive sign. However, the quest for legislative harmonisation is by no means over – indeed, it is just beginning.

CHAPTER SEVEN

Judicial Punishment in Cyberspace

The Definition of Judicial Punishment

Grotius, the seventeenth-century jurist and philosopher of law, defined punishment as 'the infliction of an ill suffered for an ill done'. This definition contains the four essential elements of punishment:

- the deed complained of and the punishment inflicted are linked;
- punishments are intentionally inflicted for a reason;
- the individual who is punished is answerable for his or her actions; and
- the infliction of punishment is a socially regulated activity.

Judicial punishment, which is controlled by the state, should also be distinguished from punishments which are inflicted informally, such as by parents on children (see generally Hart 1968, Walker 1991 and Flew 1969).

Punishments differ from acts of personal revenge in that they are administered by the state and are subject to rules as to consistency and appropriateness. Certain categories of people are exempt from judicial punishment, namely, children under certain specified age limits (usually ten years of age); slightly older children (usually between ten and fourteen years of age) who do not know that what they did was wrong; and individuals who are unfit to plead or found to be legally insane. These rules exist to protect those whom society determines to be not legally responsible for their actions.

In cyberspace, however, the imposition of judicial punishment poses some difficulties, particularly where young offenders are concerned. On occasions they may have inflicted enormous damage, sometimes extending across the globe, as in the case of the creation and release of malicious code. In addition, difficulties arise where cyber crime has been committed not for malicious reasons but out of curiosity or for sociopolitical reasons: for example, simply to demonstrate that cyberspace is 'free' or that technology is vulnerable. The traditional task that courts are required to carry out – of balancing the aims of punishment with the circumstances of the crime and the background of the offender – often becomes complex.

The Objectives of Judicial Punishment

There are two broad categories under which the objectives of judicial punishment can be classed (Walker 1991): *retributivism* and *consequentialism*. Each of these approaches has particular features that punishment needs to accommodate, if it is to achieve its purpose. These features include proportionality, denunciation, incapacitation, deterrence, rehabilitation, and restitution. Applying these to the novel circumstances in which many cyber crimes occur raises some unique issues.

Retributive approaches

Retribution is the justification for punishment based on the moral desert of the offender. Although punishment may have beneficial consequences as well, these play no part in why we should punish. On some versions of the theory, only by punishing a wrongdoer do we achieve justice or 'undo' the damage done by a crime.

Proportionality

Retribution typically includes a principle of proportionality that governs the amount or severity of punishment required for particular offences. Proportionality, or 'just deserts', simply means that the severity of punishment should be commensurate with the seriousness of the wrong. It can be seen in the justification for punishment contained in the Judaeo-Christian ethic set out in *Leviticus* (24:19–20): 'as he hath done, so shall it be done to him; breach for breach, eye for eye, tooth for tooth'.

In the context of cyber crimes, this raises the problem of how we can match the seriousness of a crime, or its moral blameworthiness, with the range of sanctions available in modern society. Surveys of community perceptions of the seriousness of crime, such as we have seen in Chapter Two, make it clear that the public does, in fact, regard cyber crime as serious and harmful. In the PricewaterhouseCoopers *Global Economic Crime Survey* (2003), for example, 31 per cent of the 3623 senior managers of large companies across the globe who were interviewed considered cyber crime to be the type of crime of greatest concern for the future, second only to asset misappropriation. The two, of course, are by no means mutually exclusive. Similarly, research has challenged the commonly held belief that the public is indifferent or somewhat ambivalent towards white collar criminality. In a survey of 503 residents in Brisbane, Australia, for example, it was found that the public does perceive white collar offences as serious, with the degree of seriousness dependent upon the degree of harmful impact of particular types of offences on victims (Holland 1995; Grabosky, Braithwaite and Wilson 1987).

Some forms of cyber crime, however, may be perceived as being of minor seriousness because their impact is less obvious. Intellectual property infringements, for example, are often seen as having no demonstrable effects comparable to the infliction of physical harm. Young computer users, for example, often see no problem with downloading digital data such as films and music without regard to copyright and without paying any fee. Business proprietors often feel at liberty to share software among their staff in breach of licensing restrictions. The extent of such misuse is substantial, as we have seen. It was estimated, for example, that approximately 65,000 people had logged onto the website created by a 21-year-old American hacker from Wyandotte, Michigan, who had offered approximately 142 software programs for free downloading. He pleaded guilty to copyright infringement and was sentenced on 30 January 2001 by the United States Federal Court to three years' probation, home confinement, restitution, and community service (United States Department of Justice 2001a: [**Case No. 82**]).

Similarly, a 12-year-old girl from New York had illegally downloaded more than 1000 copyright song tracks using a file-sharing service on the Internet. The Recording Industry Association of America (RIAA) took civil proceedings against her mother, with the case settling in September 2003 for US$2000 (Teather 2003). The girl claimed that she did not understand that downloading the songs was not allowed, as her mother had paid a subscription fee to the file-sharing provider. The proceedings attracted widespread criticism of the RIAA for pursuing legal action against children, parents and even grandparents in this way (Wingfield and Baker 2003).

Copyright infringement can in fact involve considerable harm being inflicted on businesses whose financial viability may depend upon fees being paid each time a work is reproduced. For example, the creator of the first Chinese language word processing program, 'Chinese Star', claimed to have lost ten pirated copies of his program for every one sold, thus substantially reducing the success of his business (Forney 1996). The Australian *Copycats Inquiry* (House of Representatives Standing Committee on Legal and Constitutional Affairs, Australia 2000, p. 11) also received a submission from one individual, part of whose business was destroyed through infringement.

As we shall see in Chapter Eight, other types of cyber crime can result in untold harm being inflicted on both individuals and businesses. The types of damage can extend from environmental harm, psychological damage, loss of reputation, and substantial financial loss – either directly, through loss of funds stolen electronically, or indirectly where repairs to computers and networks are required.

Earlier, we noted the case of a Queensland individual who was sentenced to two years imprisonment after being found guilty of hacking into a local council's computerised waste management system. He was accused of causing millions of litres of raw sewage to spill out into local rivers and parks, killing marine life and causing offensive smells. He was apparently motivated by revenge after having been refused a job at the plant: [**Case No. 101**].

The case in which perhaps the most extensive financial loss was inflicted on a corporation involved an individual who was convicted of creating and distributing over the Internet a fictitious press release concerning a company that falsely stated that the company's chief executive had resigned, that its earnings were to be restated, and that it was under investigation. The fraudulent release was said to have caused the company's stock to plummet nearly US$61 per share in just 16 minutes, resulting in US$2.2 billion in lost market capitalisation and US$110 million in losses to investors. As a result of the action, the accused profited by more than US$240,000. He was sentenced to 44 months imprisonment, disgorgement of all the profits, and interest in the amount of US$353,000. He also received a civil penalty of US$102,642: [**Case No. 94**].

The victims expect severe punishment for the perpetrators of such activities. The punishment inflicted in the above case clearly reflects the seriousness of the harm caused, although this balance is not always achieved.

Cyber crimes raise new concerns about proportionality, as the consequences of some types of offending can be great, and yet the conduct itself involves no physical violence. An individual can, for example, manipulate the share price of a company in another country, as occurred in an Australian case in 2000, simply by sending out false information via the Internet. In that case over three million e-mail messages were disseminated to investors, resulting in the company's share price falling from US$0.71 to US$0.31. The offenders only profited by about US$12,750 but the effects on the company were considerable. A sentence of two years imprisonment suspended for 21 months was imposed on one accused, and a two-year sentence wholly suspended imposed on his accomplice: [**Case No. 87**].

Similarly, an Australian music file-swapping website reportedly attracted more than seven million visitors, placing it among the top 10 per cent of infringing Internet sites worldwide, and thus the largest online music piracy operation ever detected in Australia (International Federation of the Phonographic Industry 2003). In terms of the extent of the illegality, such an operation should be ranked as serious and warranting prosecution, despite the fact that only one website conducted by an individual was involved.

The difficulty facing courts in such cases is that the conduct may be covert and seemingly harmless, involving the establishment of a website or transmission of e-mail, and yet the consequences may be profound. Courts are often not made aware of the extent of the loss in victim impact statements and, indeed, in many instances, losses simply cannot be quantified. In the 'Love Bug' case, for example, a 22-year-old computer science student in the Philippines had allegedly disseminated a computer virus that was said to have caused losses to businesses worldwide ranging from between US$6.7 billion and US$15.3 billion in computer down time and software damage (Grossman 2000). As we have seen, the prosecution failed because of the absence of appropriate legislation in the Philippines at the time. Had the case proceeded, the amount of damage would have been taken into account as an aggravating factor. Had the defendant only acted out of curiosity or only intended to inflict minor harm, then the actual loss caused would far outweigh the degree of criminality involved.

In another famous case involving malicious code, the offender was sentenced in the Netherlands on 27 September 2001 to 150 hours community service for having released a worm on 11 February 2001, embedded in the picture of a famous tennis player. The relatively benign worm sent one copy of itself to each e-mail address in the victim's Microsoft Outlook address book and also, on 26 January of each year, displayed the home page of an innocent computer retail shop on the victim's web browser. It did not, however, damage files. One of the reasons for the light sentence was the difficulty in obtaining proof of estimated loss, as businesses were reluctant to admit that they had been infected. An appeal court affirmed the sentence (Evers 2002; [**Case No. 100**]).

Denunciation

Denunciation involves the imposition of sanctions in order to express the public's abhorrence of the crime committed. It acts as a symbolic statement that society considers a particular crime to be sufficiently serious to warrant punishment, and that society will not tolerate the law-breaking conduct of the offender.

Sentencing remarks of judges in those cyber crime cases that have come before the courts often denounce the conduct in question. In an early Australian hacking case in 1993, the judge said:

> I formed the view that a custodial sentence is appropriate in respect of each of these offences because of the seriousness of them, and having regard to the need to demonstrate that the community will not tolerate this type of offence. Our society is being increasingly served by and dependent upon the use of computer technology. Conduct of the kind in which you engaged poses a threat to the usefulness of that technology, and I think it is incumbent upon the courts in appropriate cases to see to it that the sentences they impose reflect the gravity of this kind of criminality . . . ([**Case No. 15**]).

In order to be effective in this sense, the denunciation that accompanies the imposition of a sanction must be widely publicised, and in cyber crime cases, this often occurs. The Internet in particular provides a ready source of information about the harm caused by notorious cyber criminals (see, for example, Greatest Hackers in the Whole World 2003). Unfortunately, this publicity is often more celebratory than condemnatory, giving rise to the risk that notoriety in cyberspace could actively be pursued by young people keen to make their mark in the world.

A related concern is that if detailed information about a particular crime is disseminated widely, this may have criminogenic consequences with potential offenders being well-informed about the ways in which new cyber crimes can be perpetrated. Disclosing information on security flaws in networks or the operation of malicious code are cases in point. There is also increasing concern about the ready availability on the Internet of detailed information on bomb-making techniques and other dangerous or criminal activities. Fortunately, the pace of technological change is such that by the time a case works its way through the courts, the novelty of the crime will have dissipated.

Consequentialist approaches

Consequentialist approaches to punishment think of it as a way of bringing about some result, such as effecting a change in the criminal's behaviour, compensating the victim, preventing the criminal from offending again, or preventing others from offending in the future.

Incapacitation

Incapacitation simply means that because the offender is isolated from society, generally through imprisonment, he or she will be prevented from committing further crimes of the same or similar nature while in isolation.

The utility of incapacitation depends upon the likelihood that the offender will reoffend if given the opportunity. This involves predicting what the offender will do in the future. Unfortunately, there is little evidence to support the predictive ability of the judicial system. That is, it is simply not known, in most cases, whether or not an individual will offend again.

Current methods of predicting recidivism tend to over-predict, which means that offenders are being incapacitated gratuitously. Most offenders, particularly perpetrators of homicide, will never offend again as the offence is often an isolated incident which arose out of specific circumstances. It is therefore a waste of resources to imprison such offenders for lengthy periods solely in order to prevent them from reoffending (though of course there may be other justifications for their incarceration).

Cyber criminals do occasionally show a clear and obvious predisposition to reoffending. The offender in [Case No. 39], for example, had been previously arrested four times for hacking during the 1980s and had served a one-year prison term. He began reoffending in 1992, violating the terms of his probation, and remained a fugitive until his capture in 1995. It was this likelihood of reoffending that led the District Court for the Central District of California to impose highly restrictive conditions on his parole.

Incapacitation also ignores the fact that criminal offences may still be committed while the offender is in prison; indeed, prison may cause some people to offend or provide them with information on how to offend more effectively. In the case of cyber criminals, prison has sometimes allowed them to continue their activities unabated, and we have seen cases of fraudulent scams and paedophile activities carried on from within correctional facilities through the use of prison computers and mobile telephones that have been smuggled in.

In one case, inmates of a prison at Lino Lakes, Minnesota compiled an extensive database on children from the surrounding area. The prisoners, who had access to information technology through a prison-based computer programming and telemarketing business, scanned children's photographs and collated other information from local newspapers. The annotated files on local children contained information about which girls took piano lessons or had entered children's beauty contests, and also included physical descriptions of the children. The towns in which the children lived were alphabetised and coded with map coordinates. It was unclear whether these data were collected purely for purposes of voyeurism or fantasy, for planning subsequent criminal activity following release, or for sale to child molesters (Bernstein 1996).

Finally, there is the view that although offenders may not repeat their offence while in prison, they often reoffend immediately upon release. A number of the cases of cyber crime we have examined for this book illustrate that imprisonment has been no deterrent to further offending, particularly in cases involving child pornography.

In [Case No. 129], for example, the offender was convicted of possession of child pornography under 18 USC §2252A(a)(5)(B) after having viewed images on the Internet. The United States District Court for the District of Utah sentenced him to five years imprisonment and took into consideration the fact that he had viewed computerised child pornography while on parole, following a conviction in 1990 of sexually abusing a child.

Even some of the early phone phreakers reoffended immediately on release from prison. The offender in [Case No. 5], for example, was convicted in Canada in 1987 of telecommunications fraud involving organised criminality and was sentenced to ninety days imprisonment with two years probation. Upon her release from prison, she moved to the United States where she continued to operate a nationwide voice mail computer fraud scheme, finally resulting in her receiving a 27-month sentence of imprisonment in Chicago – at the time, one of the most severe sentences for computer crime ever handed down (Clough and Mungo 1992, pp. 148–55).

Deterrence

Deterrence can take two forms, which were concisely summarised by Cesare Beccaria in 1764: 'punishment aims to dissuade the criminal from doing fresh harm to his compatriots (special deterrence), and to keep other people from doing the same (general deterrence)' (Young 1986).

In determining whether punishment is an effective deterrent to cyber crime, evidence is needed of the extent to which individuals are aware of the possible punishments that may result from their criminal conduct, and also of whether or not they are likely to act upon any such knowledge by modifying their propensity to commit crime. Unfortunately, serious doubts have been raised about both of these matters.

Surveys of offenders have found that they rarely know what penalties govern their conduct, although the hacking community is often quite knowledgeable about the exploits of other hackers and how they have fared in the courts.

It has also been found that offenders rarely make a rational decision to carry out their offence or not based on the possibility of being punished. A large body of research has sought to test this so-called 'rational choice perspective', mainly by the use of surveys of offenders which try to identify the matters taken into account at the time the crime was committed (see Cornish and Clarke 1986). This research has not examined cases involving cyber crime, but rather has focused principally on crimes of violence.

One study from the United States, which examined the motivations of offenders who carried out serious property crimes, involved a survey of sixty offenders who were serving at least their second term of incarceration for offences such as burglary and armed robbery (Tunnell 1996). All sixty respondents in the study reported that they and nearly every thief they had ever known simply did not think about possible legal consequences of their actions. Although the offenders knew that they were doing wrong and tried to avoid arrest, thirty-two did not know the penalty attaching to their act until after their arrest. Thirty-six of the respondents said that the possibility of incarceration was no threat to them and the remainder did not perceive it as being a great threat. Thus, incarceration could not be said to have acted as a deterrent to the majority of these serious repeat property offenders.

As we saw in Chapter Two, in the case of cyber crime, there are many impediments to a successful investigation and prosecution, resulting in very few cases reaching the courts. As a result the probability of detection and punishment is generally low.

It is widely known that increasing the certainty of detection through more effective and efficient policing has far greater deterrent effects than increasing the use of incarceration, or indeed other sanctions (see Wilson and Boland 1978). There is also historical evidence supporting the converse of this proposition: namely that where the possibility of detection is removed, crime will increase, as occurred in Melbourne in 1923 during an extensive police strike when looting was rife (Massingham 1977).

A further problem with deterrence of cyber crime through judicial punishment lies in the fact that many individuals believe that what they have done should not be illegal. Many cyber criminals have claimed that they had no malicious intention but were simply motivated by curiosity. They simply may not accept that what they were doing is wrong. As we have seen, some spurious defences have been raised by offenders who have sought to deny the illegality of their conduct, and as we shall see in the next chapter, many offenders have rationalised their conduct by claiming that it was motivated by a socially beneficial or productive aim such as alerting the networked community to the presence of security flaws.

In the case of software piracy, many offenders have claimed that they had no malicious intention but were simply motivated by a desire to share works with others. Some who have copied software illegally have believed it is their right to make use of anything that is provided online. Perhaps the most celebrated case involved an individual who was prosecuted for making US$1 million worth of computer software available on the Internet over a period of approximately six weeks.

The 21-year-old student at the Massachusetts Institute of Technology provided a clandestine electronic bulletin board for the receipt and distribution of unauthorised copies of commercially published, copyrighted software. Although he was at pains to impress upon his subscribers the need for circumspection, the worldwide traffic generated by the offer of free software attracted the notice of university and federal authorities. Because he sought no profit from his actions – actions that caused substantial economic harm to copyright owners – he could not be charged under the then current criminal provisions of the copyright law, and the United States District Court dismissed an indictment charging him with wire fraud, on the ground that his acts did not violate the wire fraud statute. His acquittal was affirmed on appeal (871 F Supp 535 (28 December 1994)). Even so, being the subject of a federal criminal prosecution may have deterrent effects, both for the defendant and for those who might otherwise seek to follow in his footsteps.

Similarly, a 17-year-old from west Wales implausibly claimed that he was authorised to access e-commerce sites because there was no warning that access was prohibited. He called himself the 'saint of e-commerce' on his Internet sites, insinuating that he wanted to force companies to take more security precautions in the interest of consumer protection. He wrote:

> I'm for e-commerce when concluded in a secure and sensible manner but this is a rare thing. Most companies put some kind of page together and wait for the money to roll in. These people are the criminals.

He was sentenced to three years probation including a program of community rehabilitation: [**Case No. 91**].

Nonetheless, the courts in many cases involving cyber crime have identified deterrence as one of the principal aims of punishment when sentencing. This has been emphasised because of the widespread use made of computers and the need for those in the community to use them legally. The role of deterrence has also motivated some legislatures to increase maximum penalties in the hope of reducing cyber crime (see Chapter Six).

Rehabilitation

Rehabilitation has gone through periods of support and criticism throughout history as an objective of punishment, but remains one of the main purposes relied upon by the courts in sentencing offenders (see the Victoria (Australia) Supreme

Court case of *R v Williscroft* [1975] VR 292, 303–4 *per* Starke J dissenting). Prisons see one of their roles as providing opportunities for rehabilitation by encouraging offenders to be productive, law-abiding citizens. Indeed, this is reflected in the use of less stigmatising names for such institutions, such as 'correctional facilities'. They seek to achieve this aim by changing the offence-related behaviour, encouraging responsibility for one's actions, promoting self-esteem and developing educational, social and living skills.

The way in which offending behaviour is changed depends upon one's view of its causes. If it is believed that offending behaviour is caused by a biological determinant such as psychiatric illness, then one may seek to treat the undesirable behaviour medically, through drugs or psychotherapy. If, however, it is believed that offending behaviour is learned, then one may seek to re-train the offender out of patterns of offending through the use of behaviourist approaches such as desensitisation.

Finally, if it is believed that criminal behaviour is caused by the social environment, then one may seek to change that environment, or at least help the offender to cope with that environment without offending.

On some occasions, it seems that punishment has indeed had a rehabilitative effect on cyber criminals. Arguably this has been due to offenders being compelled to understand the physical consequences of their conduct and to see that their seemingly insignificant actions carried out on a personal computer have resulted in the infliction of palpable harm. In time, we may see the application of these 'restorative justice' practices to cyber criminals.

One offender, aged 22, from North Wales, created some of the world's most prolific computer viruses, which were contained in e-mail attachments. Two of these viruses were designed to stop computers operating and to destroy material when the computer was rebooted. The viruses infected some 27,000 computers in 42 countries. The offender served eight months of a two-year sentence of imprisonment, and when he was released, commented:

> I've learnt from my mistakes. I would never try to create a virus again. I want to help companies improve their security systems. I never meant the bug to spread across the globe and I was shocked when the FBI became involved. Going to prison was terrible. It was the worst time of my life ([**Case No. 137**], *Sydney Morning Herald*, 15 September 2003).

Similarly, the offender in [**Case No. 94**] also expressed remorse for his conduct in affecting the share price of a company through the dissemination of false information online. He was reported to have said that he only realised the significance of his actions when he began receiving letters from people who had lost much of their life savings when the company's share price fell. He said he would try to do everything 'to give back to society what [he] took from them'. He also agreed to return the US$353,000 he had obtained as a result of his conduct and, in addition, to pay the civil penalty imposed of US$102,642 (Martinson 2001).

The challenge that faces us is how to ensure that potential offenders realise the significance of their actions *prior* to engaging in cyber crime.

Restitution

Restitution aims to compensate the victim for the injury caused by the criminal act. The main problem with restitution, and indeed other financial sanctions, is that offenders rarely have the means available to them to pay compensation or fines. They may, however, undertake community work or even unpaid work for the victim, although this also presents some practical problems. When victims are numerous and widely dispersed, as is often the case with those whose computers are infected by malicious code, restitution is not a viable option.

In the case of computer-assisted fraud, sometimes substantial orders for restitution are made. For example, in **[Case No. 95]** two company accountants who had illegally issued more than US$8 million worth of stock to themselves through the use of the company's computers, received sentences of 34 months imprisonment in addition to restitution orders amounting to US$7,868,637. As part of the plea agreements, they agreed to forfeiture of seized assets, including stock already liquidated for over US$5 million, and agreed to pay the difference between the value of stock issued and the amount the government would receive from sale of the seized assets.

Criminal trials are not, however, well-equipped to quantify the loss of the victim, a function that is arguably better left to the civil courts. Finally, there is the problem that restitution orders may result in inequity where offenders have access to different financial resources. In some cases, such as those involving the wide-scale dissemination of computer viruses, the extent of losses from the criminal act far exceeds the capacity of the offender to make restitution.

The Choice of Appropriate Punishment

Punishment entails something which is assumed to be unwelcome to the recipient. Flew (1969) speaks of punishment as an evil or unpleasantness to the victim while Hart (1968) says that punishment must invoke pain or other consequences normally considered to be unpleasant, such as loss of liberty through incarceration, disqualification from some activity, or loss of something of value, such as money or time. In the case of cyber criminals, access to computers and the Internet is of considerable value. Hence some courts have imposed conditional orders that seek to limit the use of these resources during periods of probation or parole.

Throughout history, the range of available punishments has changed from those that were directed at the body of the offender through the infliction of pain, to punishments directed at the mind of the offender in an attempt to alter that person's behaviour from within (see Foucault 1977; Spierenburg 1984; Sharpe 1990). Recent technological developments have led to the electronic monitoring of offenders through the use of bracelets or anklets that are required to be worn throughout a period of home detention, thus merging corporal and psychological punishment (Black and Smith 2003).

In Western democracies the range of judicial punishments generally available includes fines; restitution and compensation orders; forfeiture and disqualification (confiscation / driving disqualification); unsupervised release (suspended, deferred, conditional sentences); supervised release (probation, community service, intensive corrections); custodial orders (either full-time or periodic); and – in a few jurisdictions – capital punishment.

In general, the sanctions that are available vary in both severity and the extent to which they are used. Judicial punishments have been described as operating within an enforcement pyramid in which the most severe penalties (such as capital punishment and imprisonment), which are seldom used, sit at the top of the pyramid, while the less severe and more frequently used penalties (such as non-custodial orders and fines) are near the base of the pyramid. Other non-judicial regulatory responses such as warnings will form the base of the pyramid in that they will be used most often (see Ayres and Braithwaite 1992). The perceived severity of individual sanctions depends, however, upon the individual circumstances of the offender.

In addition, other consequences of wrongdoing may be invoked: adverse publicity, professional disciplinary sanctions, civil action, injunctive orders and, most recently, various forms of restorative justice responses such as reconciliation and community conferencing.

It has been argued that compliance with laws is best able to be achieved where there exists a hierarchy of sanctions in which the most severe forms of punishment, such as incarceration, are available but seldom used. In the words of Ayres and Braithwaite (1992, p. 19), 'the more sanctions can be kept in the background, the more regulation can be transacted through moral suasion, the more effective regulation will be'.

Research supports the view that it is generally not the type of sentence that determines an offender's future criminal career, but rather various social and personal factors including access to employment and family and community support. Recidivism rates for offenders who have received community-based penalties, for example, do not significantly differ from recidivism rates for offenders who have experienced incarceration. Recidivism rates, however, tend to be higher for offenders who have been sentenced for more serious offences, regardless of the type of sanction received, while offenders who have undergone community-based penalties are able to avoid the undesirable consequences of incarceration (Hawkins 1976).

It is widely known that increasing the certainty of detection through more effective and efficient policing has far greater deterrent effects than increasing the use of incarceration, or indeed other sanctions. Recent research has demonstrated, however, that it is not always necessary to impose the most severe sanctions in order to maximise deterrent effects. Weisburd, Wheeler and Waring (2001), for example, found that financial penalties deter future offending by white collar criminals far more than does imprisonment. The process of detection, investigation and arraignment for a white collar offender is likely to produce similar deterrent effects to actually serving a term of imprisonment. Indeed, Simpson (2002, p. 159) observed that 'excessively punitive interventions can produce defiance, lack of cooperation, antagonism toward regulators, and potentially higher crime rates'.

The confiscation of an offender's assets represents an effective means of general deterrence as long as such sanctions are widely publicised. Both adverse publicity and forms of reintegrative shaming can be effective in workplaces where reputations are important. Cyber criminals who abuse their online privileges in the workplace by downloading child pornography, for example, could well be deterred if they were at risk of having their conduct publicly exposed. Already this takes place in some workplaces where lists of websites visited by staff are prominently displayed (Grabosky, Smith and Dempsey 2001, p. 68).

Disqualification as a company director may in some cases be a far more effective sanction to impose for dishonesty than a severe fine. Similarly, adverse publicity can have profound effects in terms of shaming an offender in the community, perhaps more so than requiring the offender to undertake anonymous community service. The effect of sentencing on an offender's family and associates also needs to be considered.

In addition, instead of looking to sanctions, it has been suggested that those who demonstrate high professional standards of conduct should be given praise and rewards that would help to foster an ethical professional culture (Sampford and Blencowe 2002). This idea is not new in discussions of compliance, but could be used to positive effect in professional contexts (see Grabosky 1995). Positive inducements could, for example, be provided to employees who respect copyright and adhere to workplace e-mail and Internet ethics policies.

Those who believe that judges are too lenient in sentencing cyber criminals often seek to have maximum legislative penalties increased. As we have seen in Chapter Six, however, the maximum penalties that attach to cyber crime already reflect the seriousness of such conduct, with lengthy terms of imprisonment and substantial fines available. The extent to which lengthy terms of imprisonment constitute a deterrent to crimes of this nature is open to debate. While many property offenders behave more or less impulsively, financial cyber criminals are relatively more likely to engage in rational calculation, making some assessment of the prospective benefits and costs of a given fraudulent course of action. In these circumstances, the greater the perceived likelihood of conviction and the more severe the expected punishment, the less the inclination to offend. Individuals who are aware, for example, that their assets may be confiscated after a criminal conviction may consider that the benefits to be derived from offending are outweighed by the risks.

Individual Punishments for Cyber Crime

Cyber crimes have attracted the complete range of available sanctions, extending from capital punishment to the most lenient fines and unsupervised release orders, as is apparent from the cases set out in Appendix A. Although the considerations that govern the use of each available sanction are essentially the same as for other types of crime, particularly property crimes and white collar crimes, some sanctions have raised issues unique to cyber crime. It is these we shall now consider.

Capital Punishment

In those countries that still retain capital punishment, the possibility remains that cyber criminals could be put to death as a punishment for their conduct. However, capital punishment is only available with respect to some types of computer-assisted illegality, as no country has enacted legislation prescribing the death penalty for unauthorised access or other offences in which computers are the target of illegal conduct (see Chapter Six above). The few cases in which capital punishment has been imposed all come from China, where people continue to be sentenced to death for a variety of non-violent economic crimes ranging from tax evasion and value-added tax fraud to counterfeiting, embezzlement and credit card theft.

For example, in March 1997, an individual was given a death sentence with a two-year reprieve for alleged credit card theft of US$62,650. In Yunnan Province, on 24 December 1997, another offender was executed for embezzling US$72,289 from the bank where he worked (see Amnesty International 1998).

In June 2000, a 36-year-old computer hacker in Hangzhou Province, China was sentenced to death for embezzling 1.66 million yuan (about US$200,000) from a bank. As an accountant with the bank, he had counterfeited official bank documents and misappropriated funds from customers' accounts (*People's Daily Online* 13 June 2000 **[Case No. 72]**).

Restitution

Occasionally, courts have made substantial orders requiring those convicted of cyber crime to pay illegally obtained funds to victims or to the state as restitution. In one false investment case, for example, in which a 17-year-old had set up an investment website promising a 'guaranteed' return to investors of between 125 and 2500 per cent within specified periods of time ranging from three days to several weeks, there was a settlement in which the youth agreed to repay approximately $US900,000 of the US$1 million that he had illegally obtained from more than 1000 investors (AFP 2002; **[Case No. 105]**).

Where offenders have disposed of the proceeds of their crimes and have no other assets, restitution orders would not be appropriate.

Forfeiture of Computer Equipment

Seizure of computer equipment used in the commission of offences has also occurred and provides a clear illustration of proportionality, by linking the punishment with the means by which the offence was committed.

One of the earliest cases involving forfeiture occurred in 1992 when the State of New York County Court ordered the forfeiture of the personal computers of four university students after it was proved that they had created and spread a computer virus that interfered with the operation of the university's computer system. One of the accused had also created a false user account at the university. They were also required to pay restitution of US$6000 to the University and US$1365 to two victims, and to perform 520 hours community service: **[Case No. 12]**.

In another case involving forfeiture, a juvenile disabled a computer servicing Worcester Airport in Rutland, Massachusetts, and disabled the FAA tower by hacking into the airport's computer system. His actions also caused loss of telephone services to the Rutland area. In a separate incident the offender had hacked into a pharmacy's computer and downloaded prescription data in breach of patients' privacy. The court imposed an order of two years' probation, during which he was ordered to have no possession of a modem, to pay restitution to the telephone company, and to perform 250 hours' community service. A forfeiture order was also made in respect of all computer equipment used in connection with the commission of the offences: **[Case No. 30]**).

Although forfeiture of personal computers may be appropriate when they are owned by offenders and have been used to commit offences, difficulties may arise when hardware or software belongs to some other person or corporation, or the forfeited computer contains data that belong to others. In such cases, the effect of the order may be to punish persons who were not involved in the commission of the offence. In some cases in which computers have been seized in the execution of search warrants on lawyers' premises, claims of legal professional privilege have been made on the grounds that the computer records contained confidential client communications.

Restricted Access to Computers

One of the more controversial conditional orders imposed on some cyber criminals has been to prohibit them from using computer equipment during the period of their supervised release on probation, while on parole following release from a custodial sentence, or even during bail pending trial. At least a dozen cases have gone to court in various jurisdictions in which restrictions on computer usage or Internet usage were imposed, some of which have been found to be too broad and unlawful. Orders have been imposed in cases involving child pornography downloaded from the Internet, computer hacking, telecommunications fraud and theft of software. Generally, it seems that such restrictions will be appropriate as long as they are reasonably related to the statutory purposes underlying the order, involve no greater deprivation of liberty than is reasonably necessary, and are not overly broad (see Hyne 2002).

The first case in which such an order was made involved an offender who had posted pornographic images of children to bulletin boards from his home computer. The Ontario Provincial Court sentenced him to two years probation and 150 hours community service, and ordered him to seek psychological treatment, not to communicate with anyone under 16 years of age, and not to download erotic material from the Internet: [Case No. 19]. The obvious problem with such an order concerns its enforceability and the problems that probation officers would encounter in determining what material the offender had downloaded.

This case was followed by a decision involving a famous recidivist American hacker who, in addition to being sentenced to almost five years imprisonment and ordered to pay US$4125 in restitution and to assign to his victims any proceeds he might receive from selling his story, was subject to stringent conditions during his three-year period of parole. These included a complete prohibition (without prior approval of the probation officer) on the possession or use of almost any kind of electronic equipment with the ability to act as or access a computer system or network. In addition, he was prohibited from acting as a consultant or adviser to individuals or groups engaged in any computer-related activity.

The offender appealed against this order on the basis that it involved a violation of his First Amendment rights, and because it was said to be vague and overly restrictive. The Appeal Court, however, decided that the conditions were reasonable in view of his recidivist tendencies and in order to protect the public: [Case No. 39].

Other courts in the United States have imposed restrictions on the use of computers or the Internet as part of conditional probation orders in cases of hacking and wire fraud ([Case No. 79]); online software theft ([Case No. 82]); creation and dissemination of computer viruses ([Case No. 120]); fraudulent online purchase of computer equipment ([Case No. 143]); theft of credit card information and fraudulent purchasing of goods ([Case No. 152]); gaining access to a judge's personal e-mail and files ([Case 148]); and online sale of child pornography (324 F 3d 1025 (2003)).

Complete prohibitions on computer or Internet usage can sometimes be overly restrictive. In [**Case No. 135**], involving possession of computerised images of child pornography, the District Court for the Eastern District of Pennsylvania imposed a special condition on supervised release that the offender could not possess a computer at his home or use an Internet service without the permission of his probation officer for the 70-month period of his supervised release. An appeal court held that this restriction was too broad, as the offender had not tried to contact minors online but had merely obtained illegal images of children.

Similarly, in [**Case No. 138**] a trial judge in the United States District Court for the Southern District of Illinois imposed severe restrictions on computer usage despite the fact that the offender had been convicted of fraud offences and that child pornography had only inadvertently been discovered on his computer. On appeal, the order was found to be overly restrictive and the case was remitted for resentencing.

Finally, in another recent decision (326 F 3d 372 (2003)), again involving child pornography, the United States Court of Appeal for the Seventh Circuit overturned a restriction that the offender should not possess or use a computer equipped with a modem that allows access to any part of the Internet, e-mail service, or other online service, or possess software expressly used for connecting to an online service. The Appeal Court held that this restriction was too broad and imposed a greater deprivation on the offender's liberty than was necessary, as he would have been unable to pursue his work as an information systems technologist on his release from prison. The judge observed that 'for *anyone*, a total ban on all Internet use would render life exceptionally difficult, given that today, the government strongly encourages taxpayers to file their returns electronically, more and more commerce is conducted online, and vast amounts of government information are communicated via websites'. The judge suggested instead that various forms of monitored Internet use would be appropriate, such as carrying out random searches of his computer or use of filtering software.

Only two cases have been decided in Australia in which restrictions on computer usage were ordered. In [**Case No. 161**], the 69-year-old offender had been charged with possession and publication of child pornography. He was sentenced to two years imprisonment for the publication offence and five years probation for possession, with conditions that he not use any computer at any time connected to the Internet, and that he not be in the company of any person under the age of 18 without the specific written permission of a probation and parole officer. On appeal, a non-parole period was set at 12 months in view of the offender's age and state of health. As this case involved contact with children as well as possession of images, the terms of this order would seem to be in accordance with the principles developed in the United States.

The other case involved a 17-year-old, who, as we saw in Chapter Two, was alleged to have attempted to murder a man whom he met in an Internet chat room and with whom he had engaged in a sexual encounter following the online meeting. As part of the bail conditions the teenager was ordered not to use the Internet except for schoolwork, to obey a nightly curfew of 9.00 p.m., and to report to police three times a week until his next court appearance. His computer, allegedly used to make contact with the man, was seized by police (Melbourne Magistrates Court, 28 October 2003; see Milovanovic 2003).

Monitoring Computer Usage

Monitoring computer usage has also been used as a condition in cases involving cyber crime. In [**Case No. 81**], for example, the offender was convicted of committing a series of denial-of-service attacks and was sentenced to six months incarceration, to be served by three months in jail and three months in home confinement, followed by one year of supervised release. He was also ordered to perform 240 hours of community service, and was required to allow the probation authorities to monitor his computing activity during the period of supervision.

In the first prosecution to go to trial in Los Angeles under the *Computer Fraud and Abuse Act of 1986*, the federal statute covering computer abuse and spamming, an offender was sentenced to 16 months in a federal prison for having maliciously bombarded his company's server with thousands of spam e-mail messages. Following his release from prison, he was also required to submit to unannounced searches of his computer, to advise all future employers about this conviction, and to receive psychological counselling: [**Case No. 146**]).

The possibility of an unannounced inspection of one's computer may act as a specific deterrent to some forms of cyber crime. Problems could, however, arise if an offender's computer is shared by others, as the privacy of non-offenders could be infringed by inspecting an entire hard drive containing data belonging to third parties. These questions will, no doubt, need to be addressed by courts over time as orders of this kind continue to be made.

Home Confinement/Tagging

Some courts have also made orders that offenders be confined to their homes or be electronically monitored during a period of probation or parole. The difficulty with such orders is that unless restrictions on computer or Internet usage are also imposed, the offender could easily continue to offend during the period of home detention.

In [**Case No. 61**], a senior executive in the United States was sentenced to nine months home detention in addition to payment of a fine of US$20,000 and five years probation in respect of his use of an Internet chat room to engage in sexual correspondence with a person whom he thought to be a 13-year-old girl.

Similar problems of compliance would arguably have also arisen in [**Case No. 98**] where the offender was the head of a hacker group who had, among other things, broken into two computers owned and maintained by NASA's Jet Propulsion Laboratory located in Pasadena, California, and used one of those computers to host an Internet chat room devoted to hacking. The court imposed a sentence of four months imprisonment and four months home confinement without any orders regarding computer or Internet usage. He was also ordered to pay US$4400 in restitution to NASA.

Arguably a more appropriate sentence was imposed on the offender in [**Case No. 82**], who had made stolen software available online. In this case the offender was sentenced to three years probation, including 180 days of home confinement, restitution to software manufacturers, and 40 hours community service, and was prohibited from engaging in Internet activity without the approval of the Probation Department. He was also required to notify all owners of computers that he used about the terms of his sentence.

More recently, courts have imposed home confinement orders on cyber criminals in conjunction with electronic monitoring. The offender from North Wales in the United Kingdom, for example, who created one of the world's most prolific Internet viruses, was released on parole on condition that he be subject to electronic monitoring and adhere to a curfew which banned him from leaving home after 7.15 p.m.: [**Case No. 137**].

Electronic monitoring was also ordered in the case of a young American woman who was convicted of logging on to her employer's system remotely, using a colleague's user name and password without authority, and changing the password of the Chief Information Officer so that he no longer had access to the network. Her sentence of three years probation contained a special condition that the first seven months be served in home confinement with electronic monitoring. She was also ordered to pay compensation of US$15,346.71 to her former employer: [**Case No. 102**].

Community Service

In order to require offenders to confront and remedy the consequences of their actions, some offenders have been ordered to perform periods of community service. In June 1993, an Australian computer hacker was sentenced to 300 hours community service and a $500 good behaviour bond for six months, for hacking into computers in Australia, Finland and the United States: [**Case No. 15**]. Arguably such orders could be of greater effect if the offender were ordered to repair damaged computers as community service or perhaps conduct computer training at community centres. In [**Case No. 145**], a plea agreement entered into in Missouri included the payment of US$10,000 in restitution to the victim corporation and 250 hours of community service, which included instructing the public on the dangers of hacking.

Of course, the constructive use of computer skills in this way would be inconsistent with a prohibition on computer or Internet usage, although appropriate terms of a conditional order could be negotiated.

Adverse Publicity and Apologies

Finally, in some cases, courts have ordered the offender to express remorse and to agree to publicity of the sanction imposed. In [**Case No. 76**], for example, in addition to serving six months in a detention facility, the 16-year-old offender was ordered to write letters of apology to the Department of Defense and NASA, whose systems he had hacked. He also agreed to public disclosure of information about his case, which might not normally occur in a case involving a 16-year-old.

Conclusions

From these few illustrations of sentences imposed on cyber criminals in recent years, we can see that courts are beginning to adapt sanctions to suit the novel circumstances of the cases. The difficulty that courts face in sentencing is to impose an appropriate punishment that will have some deterrent effect, while at the same time devising orders that will be enforceable and not overly restrictive to the offender or to third parties, such as family members, employers or business associates, who might be co-users of an offender's computer. The decisions that have been imposed, however, are still in their infancy and we are only recently beginning to see decisions of appellate courts being handed down which explore the boundaries and appropriateness of some of the conditional orders imposed.

With respect to our central arguments, it seems that courts across the globe are facing similar issues in adapting the principles of judicial punishment to cases involving cyber crime. Accordingly, it seems that these cases raise few issues that make them different from conventional crimes. The main features distinguishing punishments available for use in cyber crime cases from other types of offence are that computers can play a role in the terms of conditional orders, thus providing an enhanced link between the nature of the crime and the form of punishment. In this sense, the digital age has enabled punishment to fit the crime more closely than in the past.

Restricting access to computers or the Internet can, as we have seen, have potentially profound consequences making punishments of this kind arguably more severe than traditional conditional orders. The simple prohibition on the use of a computer could deprive a person of the ability to find employment, which can reduce, not enhance, the possibility of rehabilitation.

The other characteristics of cyber crime punishments to which courts have difficulty responding is the potential attractiveness of severe punishments to offenders who may see themselves as martyrs to their cause or as undergoing a rite of passage in the hacking community. Carefully worded orders requiring positive publicity and apologies may go some way toward reducing this potentially counterproductive effect.

There are few differences among courts across the globe concerning their choice of punishments in cyber crime cases – with the exception of those countries that still retain capital punishment. Generally, courts are beginning to respond to the realisation that cyber crime involves serious illegality and should receive appropriate sanctions for general deterrent purposes. Choosing a sentence that reflects the objective seriousness of the conduct, balanced with the individual circumstances of the offender, often raises challenges for the sentencing judge, and it is to these issues that we shall now turn.

CHAPTER EIGHT

Sentencing Cyber Criminals

Introduction

Having examined the purposes of judicial punishment as applied in connection with cyber crime, and reviewed some of the sanctions that courts have used in recent decisions, we now consider the sentencing process itself and the extent to which certain punishments have been imposed. We also seek to find out the extent to which the presence of a computer in the commission of a crime affects the sentence imposed by the court. We shall do this by examining a small sample of cases decided in Australia and New Zealand involving serious fraud, some of which had computer involvement, and others of which did not.

In achieving the various aims of punishment, courts are required to take into account any aggravating factors (or what are known in the United States as 'enhancements' to the level of penalty applicable to the offence, as specified in the United States Sentencing Commission's *Sentencing Guidelines* (2003b)), in addition to mitigating factors raised on behalf of the defendant (or what are known in the United States as 'downward departures' from the Commission's Guideline sentences). This enables the court to adopt an individualised punishment adapted to the circumstances of the offender, while at the same time taking into consideration matters of more general import to the community as a whole, such as the need to demonstrate denunciation of the conduct in question and to achieve general deterrence. This chapter also examines the various aggravating and mitigating factors that have been raised in recent cases of cyber crime, and considers whether these raise considerations different from those raised in conventional cases.

We also consider the process of sentencing itself, which, in cases involving cyber crime, also presents certain difficulties. The principal problems relate to the presentation of electronic evidence concerning the operation of digital technologies to the court and jury in such a way as to allow non-experts to understand the factual issues fully, and also the difficulty of adducing accurate evidence of the true effect of some forms of cyber crime, particularly those involving damage to networks and computers.

The sentencing judge is often obliged to consider the fact that multiple counts of illegality may be involved – such as in cases in which millions of e-mail messages have been disseminated to manipulate the sharemarket or to locate potential victims of financial fraud. The sheer task of compiling evidence of the extent of some illegal conduct often becomes daunting, with the potential consequence that the court could be unduly influenced by the gravity of the conduct and the extent of the crime, when in fact it could have been perpetrated quite simply through the use of electronic bulk-mailing software. The possibility arises, therefore, that the perceived seriousness of the conduct might not match the seriousness of the objective acts carried out.

In addition, as we have seen, sometimes the financial consequences of the crime simply cannot be quantified with precision, as victim corporations simply might not know the full extent of any financial loss sustained. This makes the presentation of an accurate victim impact statement sometimes difficult. The process of examining the detail set out in a complex victim impact statement might also be both time-consuming and costly, and one which a criminal court is ill-equipped to undertake.

In view of the complexities associated with criminal trials dealing with allegations of cyber crime, it is necessary for all those involved to be thoroughly trained in carrying out their duties effectively. Witnesses, particularly forensic computing expert witnesses, need to be trained in the presentation of complex technological information to courts and juries in much the same way as expert medical witnesses have developed expertise in presenting complex medical testimony to courts in clear and simple terms. Legal practitioners also should be trained not only in the particular evidentiary and procedural rules that apply in such cases, but also in liaising effectively with computer specialists for the presentation of lengthy and complex evidence. Just as a specialist Bar is developing to deal with such cases in some countries, so a specialist sector of the judiciary may need to be cultivated in order to ensure that judges with appropriate experience and skills are available to hear these cases.

Finally, jurors and lay witnesses in these cases should be provided with information that will enable them to understand the technologies being discussed. Alternatively, complex cyber crime cases could be tried by a judge alone, or by a judge with a panel of specialist assessors. This would, arguably, reduce the length and cost of cyber crime trials and expedite the sentencing process. Many of these reforms have already been considered in a number of jurisdictions. For example, in Australia, the report of the Deliberative Forum on Criminal Trial Reform of the Standing Committee of Attorneys General (2000) contains various proposals to make criminal trials fairer and shorter by removing technicalities and procedures that lead to increased delay and cost.

The Use of Individual Sentences

Because the state of computer crime statistics remains in its infancy in most countries, it is not possible to undertake a comprehensive analysis of the use of various sanctions for offences of this kind. Some of the greatest problems associated with surveying computer crime sentencing patterns empirically are the imprecise and disparate definitions of computer crime that exist in many jurisdictions, the fact that many offences are prosecuted in lower level courts where the judge's sentencing remarks are often not transcribed or reported, and the fact that computer crimes have only recently become prevalent enough to warrant special judicial attention to the collection of empirical data.

Despite these limitations, a general indication of the extent to which individual sentences have been used in cases of cyber crime is apparent from the material presented in Appendix A. Not all of the 164 cases noted in Appendix A resulted in a sentence being imposed: some cases have not been finally determined while others were remitted to lower courts for rehearing or resentencing following successful appeals by the accused. In 139 cases, however, a sentence was recorded. This provides a sufficient sample to discern some general trends, although it is insufficient for more thorough statistical analysis. As already stated, the sources of information of the appended cases are limited, with a number of cases only noted in official media releases or in news reports. As such, we cannot be confident that the information recorded is complete or always accurate, and hence the following observations must be treated with some caution. As interest in cyber crime increases and as government agencies devote greater resources to compiling statistical information about cases that are reported to police and go to court, we will be able to reach more definitive conclusions. In the meantime, the following discussion is provided as a preliminary scan of the currently available jurisprudence.

In order to discern any apparent differences between the sentences imposed by courts in different geographical regions, we present a simple descriptive table setting out the principal categories of sentence and the main regions in which the courts were located. Of course, the crimes in question could have been perpetrated in other countries and the offender dealt with in a jurisdiction where the effects of the conduct were felt. Multiple entries were made for some cases, such as where a court imposed an order of community service in addition to a fine and a restriction on the use of computers during the period of probation. This information, therefore, considers the full range of sanctions used rather than the most serious sanction used in any given case. Had we noted only the most serious sanction used, such as imprisonment, this would have resulted in some of the more interesting information concerning conditional orders being omitted. Where multiple offenders were involved in any given case, only the sentence imposed on the one considered to be the most culpable, in terms of severity of punishment, was recorded.

Of course, any differences among the sentences imposed in different regions would reflect the maximum penalties available to each court in each country, and so it is not appropriate to say that one region imposed sentences more or less severe than another (other than in the case of China, where the death penalty was involved in one case). Similarly, different types of cyber crime were prosecuted in different regions, and therefore general comparisons across the range of offence types would be inappropriate.

Generally, however, we can see from Table 11 that the courts made full use of the available sentencing armoury in each country, extending from full-time custodial orders to a range of conditional orders.

It appears that custodial orders were used in numerous cases, detracting from the view sometimes expressed that cyber criminals are dealt with leniently. Of course, some of these cases involved serious offences to do with the possession of child pornography or large-scale financial fraud, which invariably attract long custodial terms regardless of whether computers were involved in their commission (see discussion below).

Table 11 – *Sentences imposed in cyber crime cases noted in Appendix A, by region*

Sanction	USA	Australia and New Zealand	Asia	UK	Canada	EU	Total
Apology	1						1
Publicity of sanction	3						3
Suspended sentence	1	6	2	1		1	11
Probation/supervised release/ conditional discharge	36	1		4	4		45
Seek medical treatment					1		1
Restricted use of computers and/or Internet	9	1			2		12
Forfeiture of computers	2						2
Monitoring of computer usage	2						2
Home detention	5						5
Electronic monitoring/ tagging	2						2
Community service	11	2	1	1	1	1	17
Compensation/restitution to victims	26	6	2				34
Periodic detention		3					3
Fine or payment of costs	16	2	4	7	2	1	32
Imprisonment full-time, 12 months or less	10	3	4	6	2		25
Imprisonment full-time, 13 to 23 months	10		1	2			13
Imprisonment full-time, 24 to 59 months	22	7	7	3			39
Imprisonment full-time, 60 to 119 months	4	4		1			9
Imprisonment full-time, 120 months or more	2		2				4
Life imprisonment	1						1
Death			1				1

Notes: Data are based on the 139 cases noted in Appendix A in which a sentence (or plea agreement) was stated. Multiple entries were recorded for cases. Data are case-based, not offender-based. In cases with multiple offenders, the most severe sentence is recorded. Cases remitted for rehearing are excluded. Sentence as altered on appeal is recorded.

Courts also regularly made orders for restitution or compensation to the victims of cyber crime, usually in cases of financial crime or where corporations had suffered loss as a result of the conduct. For example, loss of business or reinstatement and repair costs following the infection of a network with malicious code often resulted in compensation orders being made. What is not known, however, is whether offenders were able to comply with such orders, sometimes amounting to many hundreds of thousands of dollars.

The only sentences that raise issues relevant to computers as the instruments of the commission of the crimes were the many conditions attached to probation orders that involved either the forfeiture of computer equipment or restrictions on the use of computers and/or the Internet during the period of supervised release.

An analysis was also undertaken of the eight principal types of offence in those cases in which a sentence was recorded. Details of the sentence types are set out for each offence category in Table 12.

From Table 12 it is apparent that orders restricting the use of computers and/ or the Internet were often used in cases involving hacking or cracking; that compensation or restitution orders were used regularly in cases of fraud/theft and unauthorised access to or modification of data (as one would expect, since these cases invariably have financial repercussions); that fines were used in a number of cases of fraud/theft and unauthorised access; and that cases of obscenity and fraud often attracted lengthy terms of imprisonment. In drawing conclusions from these data, it should be recalled that cases from all regions were included, thus making it difficult to discern particular trends with respect to the use of sentences for individual offence types.

In order to limit the number of variables, we considered two specific types of offence, those involving child pornography and obscene materials, and cases involving hacking and unauthorised access offences. Tables 13 and 14 show sanction usage for each region for each of these two separate offence types. Within each cell, the relevant sentence for each case is shown; where two or three cases were recorded for a particular region, each sentence is indicated. Where four or more cases were recorded for a region, the mean and the number of cases are shown, rather than all individual figures.

From Table 13 we can see that generally severe sentences were imposed in cases involving child pornography and other illegal obscene materials obtained or exchanged on the Internet or stored on computers. Custodial sentences seem to be longer in the United States than in other jurisdictions, although the individual circumstances of the cases in question make such conclusions less reliable. As one might expect, very few cases involved fines or other non-custodial sentences, in view of the gravity of conduct of this nature.

In the case of hacking and vandalism offences, a much wider range of sentences was used. Many cases involved probation or conditional discharge or supervised release orders, and fines were occasionally used. Interestingly, many courts in the United States made orders for compensation or restitution to victims for sums extending from US$4125 to US$324,061, with a mean award of US$82,058. The period of custodial orders was also considerably lower than for offences involving child pornography and obscene materials. Australian and New Zealand courts, on average, imposed the longest custodial sentences for hacking, viruses and computer vandalism offences.

Aggravating Factors

Following this brief review of the use of various sanctions, we now turn to the considerations that courts take into account when arriving at a sentence. It must be emphasised that sentencing laws and practices vary considerably between countries, with the most notable difference being the highly refined principles that courts in the United States are required to follow. These principles are established by the United States Sentencing Commission (2003b), which publishes a comprehensive range of both aggravating and mitigating factors that enable a court to depart from a predetermined range of sentences deemed appropriate for any given offence. In the jurisdictions of the United Kingdom, Australia,

Table 12 – Sentences imposed in cyber crime cases noted in Appendix A, by principal offence type

	Fraud/Theft	Telecom/Phreaking	Viruses/Spam/DDOS	IP/piracy	Obscenity	Access/Modification	Hacking	Threats/Stalking	Total
Apology							1		1
Publicity of sanction			1	1			1		3
Suspended sentence	3	1			4	3	1		12
Probation/supervised release/conditional discharge	10	2	6	2	9	8	19	2	58
Seek medical treatment			1		1				2
Restricted use of computers and/or Internet	3		1	2	3	1	6		16
Forfeiture of computers			1				1		2
Monitoring of computer usage			2						2
Home detention			1	2	1	1			5
Electronic monitoring/tagging							1		1
Community service	3	1	5	1	2	2	4		18
Compensation/restitution to victims	12	2	1	3		10	17		45
Periodic detention	1	1				1			3
Fine or payment of costs	10		4	2	8	5	10		39
Imprisonment full-time, 12 months or less	6	3	1	2	2	5	10	2	31
Imprisonment full-time, 13 to 23 months	2		4	2	1	5	3		17
Imprisonment full-time, 24 to 59 months	17	3	1	3	4	8	10	2	48
Imprisonment full-time, 60 to 119 months	3	1			4	1	1		10
Imprisonment full-time, 120 months or more	2				2			1	5
Life imprisonment					1				1
Death	1						1		2
Total	73	14	29	20	42	50	86	7	321

Notes: Data are based on the 139 cases noted in Appendix A in which a sentence (or plea agreement) was stated. Multiple entries were recorded for cases and some cases involved multiple offence types. Data are case-based, not offender-based. In cases with multiple offenders, the most severe sentence is recorded. Cases remitted for rehearing are excluded. Sentence as altered on appeal is recorded. Offence types include:
Fraud / Theft – Cases where fraud or theft was the principal reason for the misuse of computers
Telecom / Phreaking – Obtaining telecommunications services dishonestly
Viruses / Spam / DDOS – All cases involving malicious code, viruses, dissemination of unsolicited messages, and distributed denial-of-service attacks
I.P / Piracy – Intellectual property offences
Obscenity – Possession or obtaining illegal child pornography or other obscene images
Access / Modification – Unlawful access to computers and modification of data
Hacking – External access to networks for curiosity or malicious reasons
Threats / Stalking – Online stalking or dissemination of threatening messages

Table 13 – *Sentences imposed for child pornography/obscenity, by region*

Sanction	USA	Australia and New Zealand	Asia	UK	Canada	EU	Total*
Apology							1
Publicity of sanction							3
Suspended sentence (period of imprisonment suspended)		5 months; 18 months	suspended	18 months			10
Probation/supervised release/conditional discharge	mean = 4.7 years; number of cases = 6	5 years		12 months	2 years for each of the three cases		36
Seek medical treatment					1		1
Restricted use of computers and/or Internet		1			1		11
Forfeiture of computers							2
Monitoring of computer usage							2
Home detention	9 months						5
Electronic monitoring/tagging							2
Community service	550 hours				150 hours		15
Compensation/restitution to victims							32
Periodic detention							3
Fine or payment of costs	mean = US$8525; number of cases = 4			US$900	US$1275; US$3750		25
Imprisonment full-time, 12 months or less	18 months			12 months	10m		24
Imprisonment full-time, 13 to 23 months	18 months						10
Imprisonment full-time, 24 to 59 months	37 months	24 months; 24 months		36 months; 30 months			39
Imprisonment full-time, 60 to 119 months	60 months; 78 months	78 months; 96 months					8
Imprisonment full-time, 120 months or more	121 months; 210 months						3
Imprisonment (full-time all periods)	mean = 101 months; number of cases = 5	mean = 55.5 months; number of cases = 4		mean = 26 months; number of cases = 3	10 months; number of cases = 1		
Life imprisonment	1						1
Death							1

Notes: Data are based on the 29 cases involving child pornography/obscenity, out of the 139 cases noted in the Appendix in which a sentence (or plea agreement) was stated. Multiple entries were recorded for cases. Data are case-based, not offender-based. In cases with multiple offenders, the most severe sentence is recorded. Cases remitted for rehearing or resentencing are excluded. Sentences, as altered on appeal, are recorded. Terms of imprisonment are maximum (head) sentences. Monetary amounts are given in US$; for other countries, these are equivalents.

*Total = total number of cases of all types of offence.

Table 14 – *Sentences imposed for computer hacking/vandalism, by region*

Sanction	USA	Australia and New Zealand	Asia	UK	Canada	EU	Total*
Apology	1						1
Publicity of sanction	2						3
Suspended sentence		12 months				3 months	10
Probation/supervised release/conditional discharge	mean = 3.3 years; number of cases = 26	6 months; 4 years					36
Seek medical treatment	1						1
Restricted use of computers and or Internet	9			2 years; 3 years			11
Forfeiture of computers	2						2
Monitoring of computer usage	2						2
Home detention	3						5
Electronic monitoring/tagging	1						2
Community service	mean = 420 hours; number of cases = 8	85 hours	100 hours			150 hours	15
Compensation/restitution to victims	mean = US$82,058; number of cases = 19	US$3250; US$656.50					32
Periodic detention		6 months					3
Fine or payment of costs	mean = US$56,485; number of cases = 10 (max. US$250,000)	US$6500	US$8990; US$1200	US$2970; US$2160; US$2160		US$488	25
Imprisonment full-time, 12 months or less	mean = 8.8 months; number of cases = 10		6 months	mean = 11 months; number of cases = 3			24
Imprisonment full-time, 13 to 23 months	mean = 18.6 months; number of cases = 7		21 months	18 months; 15 months			10
Imprisonment full-time, 24 to 59 months	mean = 38 months; number of cases = 12	24 months; 36 months	36 months	24 months			39
Imprisonment full-time, 60 to 119 months	60 months	90 months					8
Imprisonment full-time, 120 months or more							3
Imprisonment (full-time all periods)	mean = 21.3 months; number of cases = 27	mean = 44.3 months; number of cases = 4	mean = 21 months; number of cases = 3	mean = 15; number of cases = 6			
Life imprisonment							1
Death			1				1

Notes: Data are based on the 69 cases involving hacking/vandalism/viruses, out of the 139 cases noted in the Appendix in which a sentence (or plea agreement) was stated. Multiple entries were recorded for cases. Data are case-based, not offender-based. In cases with multiple offenders, the most severe sentence is recorded. Cases remitted for rehearing or resentencing are excluded. Sentences, as altered on appeal, are recorded. Terms of imprisonment are maximum (head) sentences. Monetary amounts are given in US$; for other countries, these are equivalents. *Total = total number of cases of all types of offence.

New Zealand and Canada, less formal control of judicial discretion is achieved through the use of Guideline Judgments which set out the factors to be considered when sentencing for particular offence types. To date, however, guideline judgments have not been given in relation to cyber crime offences, a situation which, arguably, needs to be addressed.

United States Sentencing Commission Guidelines

Recently, various amendments have been made to the United States Sentencing Commission's policies (2003a) following the introduction of the PROTECT Act relating to child exploitation and kidnapping, and concerning a range of other offences as well. Of relevance to cyber crime are both the amendments relating to child exploitation and kidnapping, and the extensive amendments concerning cyber security.

Various sentencing enhancements are specified in cases of trafficking in material involving the sexual exploitation of a minor; receiving, transporting, shipping, or advertising material involving the sexual exploitation of a minor; and possessing material involving the sexual exploitation of a minor with intent to traffic, generally based on the number of images involved. If more than 600 images are involved, for example, the sentence can be increased by five levels. These amendments are significant in cases involving obscene images transmitted electronically, as it is easy to accumulate multiple images. In one police investigation in 1998, 'Operation Cathedral', police in fifteen countries uncovered the activities of the W0nderland (sic) Club, an international network with members in Europe, North America and Australia who used the Internet to download and exchange child pornography, including real-time video images. The club used a secure network with regularly changed passwords and encrypted content. In Europe alone, over 750,000 images were recovered from computers, along with more than 750 CDs, 1300 videos and 3400 floppy disks (Australasian Centre for Policing Research 2000, p. 126).

These enhancements were used in one American case involving possession and distribution of child pornography (345 F 3d 471 (7th Cir, 2003), to enhance the base sentence by ten levels. The offender received a sentence of 120 months' imprisonment. The enhanced sentence was affirmed on appeal to the United States Court of Appeals, which found that the trial judge had acted correctly in enhancing the sentence because of the offender's prior conviction for engaging in sexual relations with a 17-year-old girl and because he had distributed child pornography over the Internet. Interestingly, the Court of Appeals rejected the offender's argument that he had not 'distributed' the images, even though he was not actually present at his computer. He had created an automated system on his computer which enabled users to download one megabyte of images from his hard drive in exchange for each megabyte of images they sent to him. The court found that his activities qualified as distribution under the sentencing guidelines and that his use of an automated file sharing system was irrelevant (see *Cybercrime Law Report* 2003, vol. 3, no. 20, p. 7).

The other relevant amendments to the Sentencing Commission's Guidelines relate to cyber security. These amendments address the serious harm and invasion of privacy that can result from offences involving the misuse of, or damage to, computers and implements. The directive in section 225(b) of the *Homeland Security*

Act of 2002, PL 107–296 required the Commission to review, and if appropriate to amend, the guidelines and policy statements applicable to persons convicted of offences under 18 USC §1030 (fraud and related activity in connection with computers) to ensure that they reflected the serious nature and growing incidence of such offences and the need for an effective deterrent and appropriate punishment (United States Sentencing Commission 2003a).

The amendments generally provide sentencing enhancements for offences that involve either a computer system used to maintain or operate a critical infrastructure or used for the administration of justice, national defence or national security, or an intent to obtain private personal information. A further enhancement is provided for 'a heightened showing of intent to cause damage' and offences involving 'substantial disruption of a critical infrastructure'. The amendment also encourages an upward departure for 'cases in which the disruption of the critical infrastructure has a debilitating impact on national security, national economic security, national public health or safety, or any combination of these matters' (United States Sentencing Commission 2003a).

Upward departures were also amended to include cases in which the offence caused or risked substantial non-monetary harm (e.g. physical harm, psychological harm, or severe emotional trauma), or resulted in a substantial invasion of a privacy interest (through, for example, the theft of personal information such as medical, educational or financial records). An upward departure would be warranted, for example, in an 18 USC §1030 offence involving damage to a protected computer, if, as a result of that offence, someone's death resulted.

Examples of critical infrastructures include gas and oil production, storage, and delivery systems; water supply systems; telecommunications networks; electrical power delivery systems; financing and banking systems; emergency services (including medical, police, fire and rescue services); transportation systems and services (including highways, mass transit, airlines and airports); and government operations that provide essential services to the public (United States Sentencing Commission 2003a).

Aggravating Factors Found in Surveyed Cases

Table 15 sets out the number of cases from each region in which certain aggravating factors were noted in the documents available. The most frequently mentioned consideration was the amount of financial loss or the cost of repairs to computer networks caused by the offender. The extent of the criminality was also important, as determined by the number of instances or counts alleged in the charge or indictment – which in the case of many cyber crimes can be extensive. The fact that a government agency's computers had been attacked, such as a national security or defence agency, was also considered important, even if damage had not been extensive, such as in the French case in which the offender modified data in a police computer by altering a drink-driving conviction and replacing it with a 'smiley' symbol: **[Case No. 134]**.

The presence of prior convictions or a breach of trust as an employee were also factors in a number of cases, while courts in Australia treated the abhorrent nature of pornographic images of children as grounds for increasing sentence. In one Australian case the judge, on appeal, quashed a two-year suspended sentence that had been imposed by a magistrate, agreeing with the Director of Public

Table 15 – *Aggravating factors raised in cyber crime cases by region*

Aggravating factor	USA	Australia and New Zealand	Asia	UK	Canada	EU	Total
Large financial loss or repair costs	24	8	9	5			46
Large number of counts or extent of illegality	5		1	2			8
Breach of government agency's security or computers	3	1		1			5
Prior convictions or repeat offender	2	2	1				5
Breach of trust as employee	1	2	3				6
Abhorrent crime (nature of child pornography)		2			1		3
Victim company forced into liquidation				2			2
Offences committed while on parole	2						2
Environmental harm		1					1
Presence of special skills (US enhancement)	1						1
Lack of remorse		1					1
Potential of physical harm to victims	2		1	1			4

Notes: Data are based on the 139 cases noted in the Appendix in which a sentence (or plea agreement) was stated, not all of which had aggravating factors mentioned by the sentencing judge (69 did). Multiple entries were recorded for cases. Data are case-based, not offender-based.

Prosecutions that it was inadequate and out of step with community standards. The judge said that the magistrate was wrong to say that the accused's rehabilitation chances were better served outside jail. He said the accused's crimes were repugnant and that deterrence had to be kept in mind: [**Case No. 156**].

Examples of the kinds of aggravating considerations that courts have considered in these cases are as follows.

Financial Loss

One of the most important considerations to be taken into account in sentencing is the financial loss resulting from the crime. Malicious code probably has the greatest financial consequences, although such consequences are not always causally related to the dissemination of a single virus, as often the solution to the receipt of a computer virus may be a decision to upgrade hardware or software generally. Nonetheless, in the case involving the 'Love Bug' virus, estimated losses to businesses worldwide ranged from US$6.7 billion to US$15.3 billion in computer down time and software damage (Grossman 2000).

In [**Case No. 105**], a young offender obtained approximately US$900,000 from more than 1000 investors in his dishonest investment scheme. In [**Case No. 123**], the accused hacked into the computer system of a news and financial information provider and demanded, via e-mail, US$200,000 not to disclose that the system had been compromised. The judge said in sentencing one of the accused, 'as the government has pointed out, your crime was a very serious one because of its threat to international commerce and the integrity of data that the financial community relies upon to do its business'.

Extent of Conduct

Because computers are able to disseminate massive amounts of data and communications with ease, it is relatively easy to duplicate criminal acts on a wide scale. The fact that the conduct involves repeated acts perpetrated against multiple victims or spam messages sent over a long period of time is often taken into account as an aggravating consideration in sentencing.

The offender in **[Case No. 82]**, for example, provided free copies of software to 65,000 people online, although he derived no personal gain from his actions, while the offenders in **[Case No. 87]** sent over three million spam e-mail messages in order to manipulate the share price of an American company. As the judge observed when sentencing one of the accused:

> As a result of your action, resources, both financial and personal, had to be expended to investigate the spam problem, to implement anti-spam defences and to deal with complaints. Some of the Internet addresses were blocked for a period, upsetting the ability of those businesses to communicate. All these matters gave rise to a concern about the negative effect upon their commercial operations. In addition, in relation to the first two counts, your conduct had the potential to result in loss to investors, in loss of investor confidence in the system and in adverse impacts on the integrity of the stock market (**[Case No. 82]**, County Court of Victoria at Melbourne, 30 October 2000).

Breaching Government Agency's Systems

Another factor related to the seriousness of consequences arises in cases where a government agency's computer systems have been attacked. In one American case, the offender was convicted of three separate counts of computer hacking. He admitted during the proceedings that he had hacked into 'hundreds, maybe thousands' of computers, including systems at various university campuses in Los Angeles and San Diego, NASA computers at Stanford University and at their Jet Propulsion Laboratory in Pasadena, and numerous other government computer systems. This hacking activity gave him control over all aspects of the computers, including the ability to modify files and alter security on the systems. The NASA computer systems at Stanford were used to develop sensitive satellite flight control software. As part of his guilty plea, he admitted that he had caused US$17,000 in damage to these computers (**[Case No. 79]**; United States Department of Justice 2003a).

Similarly, one 16-year-old offender in the United States illegally gained access to a total of thirteen NASA computers, using two different ISPs to initiate the attacks. As part of his unauthorised access, he obtained and downloaded proprietary software from NASA valued at approximately US$1.7 million. The software supported the International Space Station's physical environment, including control of the temperature and humidity within the living space. As a result of the intrusions and data theft, the NASA computer systems were shut down for 21 days. This shutdown resulted in a delivery delay of program software, costing NASA

approximately $41,000 in contractor labour and computer equipment replace-
ment costs ([**Case No. 76**]; United States Department of Justice 2003a).

Breach of Trust

Courts also treat a grave breach of trust as an aggravating factor in sentencing.
Usually this arises where a trusted accounting professional or employee abuses
trust to misappropriate funds, often through the use of computers. In [**Case
No. 142**], a financial consultant to an Australian government department transferred A$8.725 million (US$6.543 million) electronically to private companies in
which he held an interest, after logging on to the department's network using
another person's name and password. The judge imposed a sentence of seven
years and six months' imprisonment with a non-parole period of three years and
six months.

In [**Case No. 38**], the offender was a computer programmer engaged by a
telecommunications company. He altered data in the interface, causing monetary
credits to be added to his own personal accounts and certain accounts of a friend
of his, totalling about US$15,000. In sentencing the offender, the trial judge said
that he had

> . . . acted in grave breach of the trust that was reposed in him in his relationship with [the
> company]. Secondly, the question of general deterrence loomed large in the circumstances
> of the case . . . [C]omputer technology can be implemented only by means of the exercise
> of their skills by persons expert in the field. The integrity of the computerised system, and
> therefore confidence in it for those who either own it or who have a valid interest in it, is
> dependent upon the integrity and honesty of such experts.

Misuse of passwords enabling employees to gain access to systems without authorisation is also deemed to be an aggravating breach of trust. In [**Case No. 116**], a
former employee in the human resources department of an insurance company
had illegally gained access to hundreds of computer records, and deleted them.
The judge, in sentencing the offender to 18 months imprisonment, noted the
offender's abuse of the trust that the company placed in him by giving him access
to passwords to which other employees were not privy.

Clearly, the networked world, and particularly the world of electronic commerce, is greatly dependent upon the security of passwords and access codes.
When people in positions of responsibility abuse their trust, courts are bound to
take a serious view.

Effects on Victims

A clear aggravating factor is the effect of the crime on victims, be they individuals, corporations or government agencies. As we have seen, substantial numbers of children across the globe have been exploited and abused by those who
trade pornographic images online and others who arrange sex tourism using the
Internet.

Individuals have also lost substantial sums through online scams and some
businesses have been crippled through external denial-of-service attacks, viruses,
or intellectual property infringements. There are numerous other examples of
victims who have suffered considerably at the hands of cyber criminals, and for
them, the problem is of critical concern.

Special Skills

In the United States, paragraph 3B1.3 of the Sentencing Commission's Guidelines (2003b) provides for an increased sentence when a defendant has 'used a special skill, in a manner that significantly facilitated the commission or concealment of the offence'. In the case of *United States v Petersen* (98 F 3d 502, 506–7 (9th Cir (Cal), 1996)), the court concluded that the defendant's computer programming ability was a special skill and enhanced the sentence. More recently, in **[Case No. 88]**, the first federal computer hacking case that went to trial in the Southern District of New York, a special skills enhancement was allowed where the defendant hacked a firm's computers to obtain passwords and used one of these to gain access to another company's database, which he then deleted in full. He also left the victim a taunting message on its network saying: 'Hello, I have just hacked into your system. Have a nice day'. He was sentenced to 27 months imprisonment.

However, in *United States v Godman* (223 F 3d 320, 323 (6th Cir, 2000)), where the accused was convicted of having used Adobe PageMaker to copy United States currency, the court found that the defendant's computer skills were not 'particularly sophisticated', as required by the decision in *Petersen*, and thus found that the upward departure was unwarranted. Similarly, in **[Case No. 127]**, the court held that developing a basic website did not require 'special skills' for the purposes of the enhancement. In **[Case No. 127]**, the accused had created a fictitious website for the Honolulu Marathon. He copied the real marathon website at <www.honolulu-marathon.org> and modified it slightly to make the modified site available at <www.honolulu-marathon.com>. The accused's website charged users US$165 to 'register' for the marathon, a sum which he retained in full. The legitimate marathon website did not allow any form of online registration.

The outcome of these decisions is that, as Orin Kerr (2002b) notes:

> the use of a computer alone to commit a crime does not mean that a defendant should get a special skills enhancement. To qualify, a defendant needs to be a real computer whiz, and needs to use that wizardry to commit the crime.

Sophistication, Planning and Expertise

Related to the question of the offender's possession of specialist expertise that permitted the commission of the crime is the question of the extent to which the offender employed some sophistication or planning.

In **[Case No. 87]**, for example, the court noted that 'considerable deliberation, planning, care, skill and sophistication was involved in implementing [his] plan'. Apparently, on 27 April 1999, the accused had sent his accomplice an e-mail message that said: 'This is illegal but I like it. Just don't mention anything to anyone about anything until we purchase the stock, and always keep our true identity very concealed.' The judge commented in sentencing:

> . . . this illustrates that not only were you aware your planned conduct was unlawful but that you wished to proceed with it for personal gain. And that is what eventuated, as did steps taken to conceal your identity. When asked about that message in your record of interview, your answers were evasive and unconvincing. The message also makes it difficult to accept the submission made on your behalf that you had no real understanding of the consequences of your planned action.

Table 16 – *Mitigating factors raised by offenders for cyber crime cases by region*

Mitigating factor	USA	Australia and New Zealand	Asia	UK	Canada	EU	Total
Good character or no prior convictions		5	5	3	3		16
Belief that conduct was legal	2	1	1	3	1		8
Absence of harm to victim or public	1	1		1			3
Offender had health problems including mental health		3		2	1		6
Prank – no malicious intent	1	1	2	3			7
Expression of genuine remorse	2	1	2	1			6
Cooperation with police investigation	2	2	1	1			6
Young age of offender	1	1	2		1	1	6
Repaid some or all of loss	1	1	1				3
Acted at the direction of another person	1	1					2
Believed that conduct should not be illegal	2			1	1		4
No personal gain to offender	1	1	2				4
Presence of an addiction to computers or the Internet	1						1
Good prospects of rehabilitation		2					2
Had intended to alert victims to risks of computers	1						1
Excessive delay in prosecution and trial		1					1
Small amount of loss		2	1	1		1	5

Notes: Data are based on the 139 cases noted in the Appendix in which a sentence (or plea agreement) was stated, not all of which had mitigating factors mentioned by the sentencing judge (52 did). Multiple entries were recorded for cases. Data are case-based, not offender-based. Only those mitigating factors accepted by the court were counted.

Mitigating Factors

Turning now to the various mitigating factors that courts take into account, we can see from Table 16 that the courts have considered a wide range of matters. Many of these are the kinds of considerations taken into account in conventional cases, although some, as we shall see, have particular relevance to the presence of computers.

Previous Good Character and Absence of Prior Convictions

As is often the case with economic and white collar criminals, those convicted tend to be first offenders with the ability to adduce evidence of previous good character as a mitigating factor. In the cases recorded in Appendix A, only a few individuals had prior criminal histories. The fact that many cyber criminals are young also means that they are likely to be able to adduce evidence of good character.

Guilty Plea and Cooperation

Related to the presence of good character is the argument raised in the vast majority of plea hearings: that the offender has cooperated with the police investigation and pleaded guilty, often at the earliest available opportunity. In most jurisdictions this can lead to a substantial reduction in penalty, sometimes resulting in reduction in custodial sentence by one-third.

In a number of cyber crime cases where the offender has assisted not only with the police investigation, but with government agencies generally in investigating other similar cases, it has been argued that the sentence ought to be reduced. In [Case No. 61], for example, the US Attorney's office requested a substantial reduction in the offender's sentence based on his substantial assistance to the government. The recommendation was based on the significance, usefulness, completeness, timeliness and nature and extent of the offender's assistance to the government since his guilty plea, which apparently included the fact that he had engineered a remote cyber-tracking program for the FBI to use in tracing known and suspected paedophiles online. As a result, the offender was sentenced to nine months' home detention, a fine of US$20,000 and five years' probation in a case involving possession of child pornography and intention to engage in criminal sexual activity with a minor.

In [Case No. 120], the offender, who had created a computer virus, assisted the FBI's investigation of several major international hackers, leading to a reduced sentence of 20 months' imprisonment, a special assessment of US$100, a fine of US$5000, and three years supervised release with 100 hours of community service. Some two months after his arrest, for example, the offender had provided the FBI with the name, home address, e-mail accounts and other Internet data for the suspect in [Case No. 100] in the Netherlands. The FBI passed the information to authorities in the Netherlands and the suspect was arrested and later sentenced to probation. Also in 2001, the offender in [Case No. 120] recorded online discussions with the suspect in [Case No. 137], the author of another virus which infected Microsoft computer systems worldwide. The FBI contacted detectives in Britain, who arrested the suspect early in 2002, leading to his conviction and sentence of two years imprisonment in London.

Absence of Harm to Victims

The absence of demonstrable harm to victims is also a compelling mitigating factor that has been raised in a number of cases. Of particular relevance are cases in which networks have been hacked simply in order to demonstrate security weaknesses – although even in these cases victim organisations may be required to undertake lengthy and costly reviews of network security in order to prevent further attacks.

In cases involving the possession and dissemination of child pornography, few offenders can raise the argument that victims were not harmed by their action, except arguably where so-called virtual pornography has been created entirely electronically without the involvement of human actors.

In some cases, offenders have claimed that although they traded in child pornography, they did not make any contact with children or seek to arrange meetings for sexual encounters. In **[Case No. 41]**, the United States Court of Appeals rejected the argument that because the defendant had not actually abused any child or produced or distributed any child pornography, and had no inclination to do so, he should be entitled to a downward departure from the guideline sentencing range. The Court of Appeals decided that while a court may depart from the guideline sentencing range when it encounters an 'atypical' case, it must provide sufficient reason for doing so. Simply referring to the fact that the accused had not actually abused any child was insufficient evidence to take his case outside the guideline principles to justify a downward departure. The appeal court vacated the sentence of 12 months imprisonment followed by a three-year term of supervised release, and remitted the case for resentencing.

Mental Health Problems Including Computer / Internet Addiction

Cyber criminals have, in a number of cases, raised health and particularly mental health problems in mitigation. The accused in **[Case No. 91]**, for example, testified that he had lived an unremarkable life until the age of 14 when he fell and banged his head, suffering serious physical and mental side effects. It was shortly thereafter that he developed an interest in computers. At his trial in April 2001, the prosecutor said that 'he was obsessed by his crusade – he is a high-strung man going through an abnormal period in his life'. The court sentenced the offender to three years probation during which he was required to undergo psychiatric counselling (Andrews 2001).

Similarly, the accused in **[Case No. 130]**, who in October 2002 pleaded guilty to a 12-count indictment charging him with wire, mail and credit card fraud, identity theft and conspiracy, raised the fact of mental illness in mitigation, including depression and obsessive-compulsive disorder. He argued that his actions were not driven by greed, but by a psychiatric condition for which he was taking medication (Burkeman 2002).

There are resemblances between this argument and that which secured the acquittal of the young Edinburgh University student tried in 1993 under the English *Computer Misuse Act 1990* for computer hacking (see Chapter Five, above). The charges related to gaining access to various high-profile computer networks and systems, including those of British Telecom and Lloyd's Bank, and an EC computer system in Luxembourg. The jury acquitted him on the grounds of a purported clinical addiction to hacking, which meant that he had not formed the requisite criminal intent. His two co-accused pleaded guilty to certain offences and were sentenced to six months imprisonment.

Addiction to the Internet, where it amounts to a diagnosable mental health disorder such as an obsessive-compulsive neurosis or is associated with clinical depression, could give rise to leniency in sentencing, or the use of a conditional order requiring the offender to undergo some therapeutic intervention.

Generally, however, courts have been reluctant to entertain such an argument. In both *United States v Caro* (309 F 3d 1348) and *United States v McBroom* (124 F 3d 533 (3rd Cir, 1997)), involving child pornography, as well as in **[Case No. 125]**, involving conspiracy to commit copyright infringement online, courts rejected the Internet addiction argument. In **[Case No. 125]**, Judge Kennelly rejected the defendant's claim that he had a diminished capacity under paragraph 5K2.12

because he suffered from 'Internet addiction' which made it impossible to control his behaviour. The judge argued that even if Internet addiction could lead to a reduced mental capacity, there was an insufficient link between the defendant's Internet addiction in the present case and his decision to spend his time on the Internet committing copyright crimes.

Youth

One of the most difficult considerations in cyber crime cases concerns the submission that a lenient sentence ought to be imposed owing to the relative youth of the offender. Youth is relevant to sentencing in a number of ways: it potentially shows that the conduct was committed because of youthful exuberance, and that the person did not realise the seriousness of his or her actions. It is also arguable that a lengthy custodial term may harm a young person's chances of future development, and that because offenders have many years of life before them, they have a greater chance of rehabilitation. Finally, for a very young person, there has often been insufficient time in which to acquire a criminal record.

There is the difficulty, however, that serious harm can be caused to computers, businesses, financial systems, and individuals by the acts of very young individuals. For example, children as young as 12 years of age can engage in actions that seriously infringe copyright. As we have seen, in the United States, the mother of a 12-year-old girl from New York settled a case for US$2000 when the Recording Industry Association of America took proceedings in respect of her daughter's illegally downloading more than 1000 copyright song tracks, using a file-sharing service on the Internet (Teather 2003). Courts are therefore faced with the difficult task of balancing carefully the mitigatory influence of youth against the objective seriousness of the conduct. Often this can lead to disparities of sentence and overly harsh or lenient punishments.

As we can see from the cases noted in Appendix A, many cyber criminals are young and a number of them teenagers. The youngest offender in the cases examined was a 15-year-old Indonesian student living in Australia, who was arrested for hacking while in Singapore in 2000. He pleaded guilty to five counts of unlawful access to computers and was fined Sing$1500 (US$870) by the Singapore Juvenile Court: [**Case No. 69**].

Where serious harm has resulted from the acts of a young person, the courts may be compelled to impose some form of custodial sentence in order to demonstrate general deterrence. In [**Case No. 76**], for example, the District Court in Miami sentenced a juvenile aged 16 to six months detention in a juvenile facility for hacking military computer networks and illegally obtaining information from NASA, leading to restoration costs for NASA of some US$41,000.

Similarly, [**Case No. 105**], in which the accused fraudulently collected more than $US1 million from more than 1000 investors through the use of an Internet investment site and bulletin board, clearly demonstrates the substantial financial harm which can be caused by young people equipped with some basic computing skills.

From the cases noted in Appendix A, we can see that teenage offenders generally received non-custodial sentences involving supervised release or community service, rather than immediate terms of imprisonment.

Lack of Malicious Intent and Non-Acceptance of Illegality of Conduct

Further mitigating factors that the courts may consider arise when offenders submit that their conduct was not carried out for any malicious motivation, that they intended to benefit the community by alerting computer users to security weaknesses in systems, or that their conduct should not, in any event, be illegal. Of course, courts must sentence offenders on the basis of the existing laws at the time the offence was committed, and so the final argument may not result in any reduction in sentence. Non-acceptance of the illegality of conduct has been raised in cases of copyright infringement where the offender derives no personal gain and is motivated to make software freely available to other Internet users (see, for example [**Cases No. 82 and No. 91**]).

Lack of malicious intent or potential benefits to society that might arise from the conduct are, however, sometimes deserving of greater attention. In [**Case No. 27**], the British Columbia Provincial Court found the offending couple guilty of possession of child pornography and imposed an order of two years probation and a fine of Can$5000 (US$3750) despite the prosecution's indication that an absolute discharge would have been satisfactory. The offenders, who conducted an adult bulletin board service, had in their possession a CD-ROM that contained some illegal images. Although they did not know of the presence of the illegal files, the offence was one of strict liability, and lack of knowledge was no defence.

Delay in Investigation and Trial

Because cyber crime cases may be difficult to investigate and to prosecute, considerable delay can be involved prior to sentencing. In some cases, defendants have sought to rely on excessive delay in the judicial process as a mitigating factor. In [**Case No. 38**], for example, the delay between the offender's interview by the police in January 1996 and his being charged with offences in June 1997 was raised as a mitigating factor. Counsel for the defendant argued that the period was so long as to cause anxiety in the mind of the applicant, which itself acted as a kind of punishment. He also argued on behalf of the defendant that it is usually appropriate to take undue delay into account when rehabilitation is a real prospect. The trial judge took the fact of delay in the investigation into consideration and the Court of Appeal concluded that this did not involve an error. Accordingly, the application for leave to appeal against sentence was dismissed.

The other factors raised in mitigation of sentence raise matters with which courts are generally familiar, and do not generate any features unique to cases involving cyber crime.

The Effect of Computer Involvement on Sentence

Determining the effect of computer use in the commission of an offence on the determination of sentence is difficult, because so many interrelated aggravating and mitigating factors are also involved in the exercise of judicial discretion. The number of variables is so great that many thousands of cases would be needed to conduct an analysis of the influence of any one factor, such as the presence of a computer, when controlling for these many other variables, including different jurisdictional variations in available sanctions. Clearly this is not feasible at present.

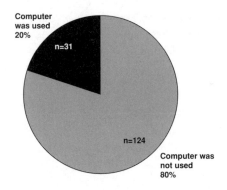

Figure 4 – Computer usage in offences
Source: Australian Institute of Criminology and PricewaterhouseCoopers (2003)

In order to limit the number of variables, however, we have drawn upon research undertaken by the Australian Institute of Criminology and PricewaterhouseCoopers (2003) in an attempt to discern any possible influence which the presence of a computer might have in determining sentence for one specific offence type – namely, serious offences involving dishonesty. The research was limited to Australia and New Zealand, and examined serious fraud cases prosecuted in the higher criminal courts in the years 1998 and 1999. Because serious fraud often involves the use of computers, this study provides an opportunity to compare cases of financial crime that did and did not involve computers as the instruments of the commission of these crimes.

The study examined 155 completed files relating to 208 accused persons from each of the Australian jurisdictions as well as New Zealand (ten jurisdictions in all). There were 165 males and 43 females, and 183 of the accused were convicted of offences. The study focused on cases involving 'serious fraud'. Files were, on the whole, selected by the police and prosecution agencies concerned, in accordance with the criteria of seriousness of the fraud involved and year of determination. Fraud is a generic category of conduct that involves the use of dishonest or deceitful means to obtain some unjust advantage over another. *Seriousness* was defined on the basis of the following:

- financial loss (generally over $100,000 unless other factors made the case of unusual seriousness or complexity), and/or

- sophistication in the planning and/or execution of the offence (such as through the use of computers, electronic transfers of funds, forged instruments, multiple false identities, etc.), and/or

- organisation of the offender(s) (such as the presence of multiple offenders, cross-border activities relating to the movement of individuals or funds, large numbers of victims, etc.), and/or

- whether the fraud offences were committed by professionals such as solicitors, accountants, financial advisers, mortgage brokers, etc. whose conduct involved breach of trust concerning clients' funds.

Computers were used in the commission of these serious fraud offences in only 20 per cent of files (31 cases) as shown in Figure 4 above.

Table 17 – *Most serious sentence imposed on computer crime/serious fraud offenders*

Most serious outcome	Computer used		Computer not used		Total	
	Number	%	Number	%	Number	%
Fine	1	2.3	2	1.4	3	1.6
Compensation	0	0	2	1.4	2	1.1
Suspended sentence (unsupervised release)	5	11.6	5	3.6	10	5.5
Deferred sentence (unsupervised release)	1	2.3	5	3.6	6	3.3
Supervised release – probation	1	2.3	7	5.0	8	4.4
Supervised release – community service	2	4.7	3	2.1	5	2.7
Periodic custodial order	3	7.0	9	6.5	12	6.5
Full-time custodial order	30	69.8	107	76.4	137	74.9
Total convicted	43	100.0	140	100.0	183	100.0
Acquitted	1		14		15	
No information recorded	3		7		10	
Total	47		161		208	

Note: Each percentage is the percentage of the total of those convicted, for which sentencing information was available.
Source: Australian Institute of Criminology (computer file)

The relatively low incidence of the use of computers could be explained because some of these offences took place a number of years prior to their being dealt with in the courts in 1998–99. Indeed, some cases involved criminality per-petrated in the early 1980s, when computers were a much less central part of domestic and business life than they are today.

Nonetheless, the study provides some useful data concerning the 31 cases in which computers were involved in the commission of serious fraud offences. The following analysis is based on the raw data from the study by the Australian Institute of Criminology and PricewaterhouseCoopers (2003) and has been undertaken with their permission by the current first-named author, who was the principal researcher in that study.

The categories of sentence imposed on the 183 convicted offenders are as shown in Table 17.

Comparing the raw percentages for the sentences imposed on offenders whose crimes involved the use of computers with those whose activities did not involve computers, we can see that full-time custodial sentences were used less often for computer offenders, and that suspended sentences without super-vision were used much more often for computer offenders than for non-computer offenders.

Table 18 sets out data on the mean length of sentence imposed on offenders who used computers and those who did not use computers for both maximum terms (the period the offender must serve if not paroled) and minimum terms (the period specified by the judge during which the offender is not eligible for release on parole). For maximum terms, the mean sentences were very similar, with computer offenders receiving only slightly lower mean maximum sentences. The mean minimum term awarded was, however, much higher where computers

Table 18 – *Mean period of full-time custodial sentences imposed on computer crime/ serious fraud offenders*

Custodial sentence	Computer used		Computer not used		Total	
	Number	Mean months	Number	Mean months	Number	Mean months
Maximum term	44	30.02	153	31.60	197	31.27
Minimum term	44	22.66	149	18.33	193	17.82

Note: Courts did not specify a non-parole period in respect of four offenders.
Source: Australian Institute of Criminology (computer file)

Table 19 – *Percentage of computer crime/serious fraud offenders whose maximum term of full-time custodial sentences fell within twelve-month intervals*

Custodial sentence maximum term	Computer used		Computer not used		Total	
	Number	%	Number	%	Number	%
0–12 months	13	29.5	59	38.6	72	36.5
13–24 months	4	9.1	19	12.4	23	11.7
25–36 months	13	29.5	22	14.4	35	17.8
37–48 months	5	11.4	20	13.0	25	12.7
49–60 months	7	15.9	12	7.8	19	9.6
61–72 months	1	2.3	9	5.9	10	5.1
73–84 months	0	0.0	3	2.0	3	1.5
85–96 months	1	2.3	3	2.0	4	2.0
97–132 months	0	0.0	6	3.9	6	3.0
Total	44	100.0	153	100.0	197	100.0

Source: Australian Institute of Criminology (computer file)

were used than where computers were not used, perhaps being indicative of the seriousness with which courts viewed computer fraud offences.

If, however, the distribution of sentences is compared, a somewhat different pattern emerges. Table 19 shows the percentage of each type of offender who received a maximum term of imprisonment for each twelve-month period.

From these data it is apparent that computer offenders tended to receive maximum terms in the categories of 25–36 months and 49–60 months much more often than did those whose offences did not involve computers. For maximum sentences higher than this, computer offenders tended to be less frequently represented than non-computer offenders.

Table 20 shows the percentage of each type of offender who received a minimum term of imprisonment for each twelve-month period.

From these data it is apparent that computer offenders tended to receive minimum terms in the categories 25–36 months and 49–72 months much more often than did those whose offences did not involve computers. For minimum sentences below 24 months, computer offenders tended to be less frequently represented than non-computer offenders.

Table 20 – *Percentage of computer crime/serious fraud offenders whose minimum term of full-time custodial sentences fell within twelve-month intervals*

Custodial sentence minimum term	Computer used		Computer not used		Total	
	No.	%	No.	%	No.	%
0–12 months	19	43.2	75	50.3	94	48.7
13–24 months	6	13.6	35	23.5	41	21.2
25–36 months	11	25.0	18	12.1	29	15.0
37–48 months	3	6.8	11	7.4	14	7.3
49–60 months	3	6.8	6	4.0	9	4.7
61–72 months	2	4.6	3	2.0	5	2.6
73–84 months	0	0.0	0	0.0	0	0.0
85–96 months	0	0.0	1	0.7	1	0.5
97–132 months	0	0.0	0	0.0	0	0.0
Total	44	100.0	149	100.0	193	100.0

Source: Australian Institute of Criminology (computer file)

Of course, with such a small sample and without matching mitigating and aggravating factors, these trends may not reflect the true way in which courts view computer-related financial crime in Australia and New Zealand.

What then were the various mitigating and aggravating factors raised by offenders, and how do these differ for those who did and did not use computers in the commission of their offences? Table 21 presents data on the primary mitigating factors raised by offenders, from which we can see the striking similarity in the rank order of types of mitigating factors raised by computer offenders and non-computer offenders. Pleading guilty and cooperating with the authorities were the two most frequently raised mitigating factors by both computer offenders and non-computer offenders.

The main mitigating factors in which differences were apparent concerned the offender's good chances of rehabilitation and low likelihood of re-offending, and mental health problems, both of which were raised more often by computer offenders than by non computer offenders. Similarly, computer offenders claimed to have no prior criminal history more often than non computer offenders. These considerations fit the stereotype of computer offenders as young, first-time offenders with poor social integration skills that could be indicative of mental health problems. Of course, the current data only relate to financial offences and a different picture might emerge if other types of cyber crimes were included, such as hacking or dissemination of offensive content.

When we turn to aggravating factors mentioned by judges in sentencing offenders, a similar pattern emerges. From Table 22 we can see that the offenders raised similar types of aggravating factors in cases in which computers were used and cases in which they were not. Breach of trust by a person in a position of trust or responsibility was the most frequently mentioned factor in both types of case, followed by the amount of money involved. As already noted in respect of mitigating factors, the absence of a prior conviction meant that this factor was mentioned by judges in no cases in which computers were used, but was an aggravating factor in 18 other cases. Similarly, only one computer offender had been in breach of a prior order.

Table 21 – *Mitigating factors raised by convicted offenders at the time of sentencing*

Mitigating factor	Computer used		Computer not used		Total	
	Number	%	Number	%	Number	%
Guilty plea	19	15.8	67	16.4	86	16.3
Cooperation with authorities	16	13.3	59	14.5	75	14.2
Previous good character/ contribution to community	7	5.8	36	8.8	43	8.1
No prior criminal history	10	8.3	32	7.8	42	8.0
Remorse	5	4.2	31	7.6	36	6.8
Health problem (physical)	5	4.2	23	5.6	28	5.3
Health problem (mental, e.g. depression, disorder)	8	6.7	20	4.9	28	5.3
Good chances of rehabilitation/ low likelihood of reoffending	9	7.5	19	4.7	28	5.3
Personal hardship/traumatic experiences/family broke up	7	5.8	20	4.9	27	5.1
Not a primary offender/ implicated by others	7	5.8	18	4.4	25	4.7
Has dependants	7	5.8	14	3.4	21	4.0
Gambling addiction	6	5.0	13	3.2	19	3.6
Assisted with police investigation	5	4.2	13	3.2	18	3.4
Career destroyed	2	1.7	12	2.9	14	2.7
Offered to repay	2	1.7	9	2.2	11	2.1
Made restitution in full or part	3	2.5	5	1.3	8	1.5
Served time in custody	0	0.0	8	1.9	8	1.5
Old age	2	1.7	4	1.0	6	1.1
Drug/alcohol addiction	0	0.0	5	1.3	5	1.0
Total	**120**	**100.0**	**408**	**100.0**	**528**	**100.0**
No information recorded	2		6		8	

Note: The sample pertains to 184 convicted offenders. These categories are not mutually exclusive, as offenders raised a number of mitigating factors (eight offenders raised one factor only). Percentages are percentages of the total number of factors recorded for each category of computer presence. For eight files, no information was available concerning the mitigating factors raised.

Source: Australian Institute of Criminology (computer file)

The conclusions that may be drawn from the research are that serious fraud offenders who made use of computers in the commission of their crimes tended to receive slightly more lenient sentences than offenders whose activities did not involve the use of computers, although, on average, full-time custodial terms awarded were similar. It appears, however, that computer offenders tended to receive maximum sentences of 25–60 months more often than non-computer offenders, and minimum terms of 25–72 months more often. Both mitigating and aggravating factors were similar for both types of offenders, although computer offenders tended to have more favourable previous history than non-computer offenders.

Conclusions

We have seen that the courts have been faced with some complex issues arising from the submissions made by prosecutors and defendants during the process of

Table 22 – *Aggravating factors noted during sentencing by use of computer*

Aggravating factor	Computer used		Computer not used		Total	
	Number	%	Number	%	Number	%
Breach of trust by a person in a position of trust/responsibility	20	23.8	34	14.3	54	16.8
Large sum involved	12	14.3	32	13.5	44	13.7
Long period of criminality involved	9	10.7	35	14.7	44	13.7
Sophisticated and planned acts	12	14.3	30	12.6	42	13.0
Repeated acts of dishonesty	7	8.3	14	5.9	21	6.5
Not remorseful	7	8.3	13	5.5	20	6.2
Prior conviction	0	0.0	18	7.6	18	5.5
Breach of order (e.g. breach of recognisance, offending on parole)	1	1.2	12	5.0	13	4.0
No reparation made	2	2.4	11	4.6	13	4.0
Failed to plead guilty	4	4.7	8	3.4	12	3.7
Principal offender	3	3.6	6	2.5	9	2.8
Theft of public money	3	3.6	6	2.5	9	2.8
Theft from elderly victims	1	1.2	7	2.9	8	2.5
Tried to blame/implicate others	3	3.6	2	0.8	5	1.6
Failed to cooperate with authorities	0	0.0	5	2.1	5	1.6
Low likelihood of rehabilitation	0	0.0	5	2.1	5	1.6
Total	**84**	**100.0**	**238**	**100.0**	**322**	**100.0**
No information recorded	4		17		21	

Note: The sample pertains to 155 convicted offenders. Some cases involved multiple aggravating factors. No information was recorded on computer usage for 21 convicted offenders.
Source: Australian Institute of Criminology (computer file)

sentencing. In the United States, where detailed guidelines exist to assist courts in achieving consistent and balanced sentences, the prosecution of cyber crime has led to reconsideration of some of these factors and amendment of the guidelines. In other jurisdictions, the sentencing jurisprudence associated with these cases remains in its infancy.

Despite this, the courts have approached their task in a careful and considered way and, on the basis of the cases presented in Appendix A, it appears that the sentences imposed have generally been appropriate and within the range of current sentencing laws and practices.

Our comparative review of the decisions has shown that the courts in different countries have not imposed sentences of a widely differing nature, taking into account the types of illegality involved and bearing in mind the different maximum penalties provided for in legislation. Even within countries, overt inconsistencies in decision-making are few.

With respect to differences between the sentences imposed in cases involving cyber crime and those imposed in conventional cases, our examination of the influence of the presence of a computer in the commission of serious fraud offences in Australia and New Zealand reveals few, if any, differences in approach. More rigorous statistical testing of this phenomenon must await further research when a larger sample of cases is available.

Sentencing practices in cases of cyber crime are, however, continuing to develop, and some sentences may seem overly lenient. Cyber crime is seen as a novel phenomenon, with some types of conduct only recently having been proscribed. On the other hand, courts have been required to emphasise the need for deterrence, and have actively made an example of those who break new laws.

Generally, it is the ability of those who use computers to inflict extensive damage upon multiple victims that makes these crimes so serious. The difficulty that courts face in sentencing is to impose an appropriate punishment that will have some deterrent effect while at the same time balancing the often compelling mitigating factors.

In the United Kingdom, Bell (2002) has identified a wide variety in the sentences imposed under computer crime legislation, and calls for sentencing guidelines to be promulgated from the English Court of Appeal. Generally, however, it is only after a considerable number of cases have reached the courts and inconsistencies in sentencing have become clearly apparent that appellate courts will establish guideline judgments. In **[Case No. 77]**, for example, the court declined to lay down sentencing guidelines for computer crime as requested by the lower court. It found that because fewer than ten prosecutions had proceeded under s. 161 of the Crimes Ordinance(Cap. 200), this was insufficient to enable all of the possible breaches of the section to have been explored by the courts.

In Australia, for example, the Australian government's response to the *Copycats Inquiry Report* (2000) supported the recommendation of the Committee that 'the Attorney-General bring to the attention of the Chief Justice of the Federal Court of Australia the system of guideline judgments instituted in the Supreme Court of New South Wales, with a view to developing guideline judgments in relation to copyright offences'. Guideline judgments in this area would, it is hoped, assist in ensuring consistency between judges in balancing the various considerations that are relevant to sentencing intellectual property offenders. However, the Chief Justice has pointed to the relatively small number of first instance copyright infringement matters heard in the Federal Court, and so it appears that this recommendation will not be adopted.

In addition, it might be appropriate for prosecution policies to be revised to deal with some of the specific challenges in the area of cyber crime, such as infringements committed by very young children, crimes which involve multiple instances, or offences committed against overseas victims.

Finally, it would be appropriate to establish programs for monitoring the types of offences and sentences that are dealt with by courts, with a view to gathering statistics on the use of individual sanctions and the various aggravating and mitigating considerations that courts take into account.

CHAPTER NINE

Conclusions

This book has provided the first international study of the ways in which cyber criminals have been dealt with by the judicial process. We have provided a preliminary analysis of some salient cases from around the globe and identified some of the principal concerns that face prosecutors and judges when dealing with the sometimes novel considerations raised by cyber crime.

Principal Conclusions

In relation to our central arguments, we are now able to offer some concluding observations.

Does Cyber Crime Raise Unique Problems?

First, we have found that the prosecution and judicial disposition of cases involving cyber crime do indeed raise certain considerations that make these cases different from cases involving conventional crime. Prosecutors have been presented with some truly novel arguments, such as the computer addiction defence. Difficult evidentiary issues have also been raised. When relevant and irrelevant data on a copied hard drive cannot be differentiated, the admissibility of the evidence is brought into question.

On the other hand, however, many computer-related cases raise the same conventional issues that prosecutors face in other complex cases involving financial fraud or dishonesty. It seems, for example, that a similarly high proportion of offenders plead guilty in cyber crime cases, making it unnecessary for full and protracted criminal trials to be conducted. Were this not the case, the difficulties associated with prosecution and trial would be greatly exacerbated.

As we saw in Chapter Six, over the past decade a number of legal problems have emerged which have created difficulties for the successful prosecution of cyber crimes. Their nature has sometimes been remarkably simple. For example, the omission of laws proscribing deception of computers as opposed to human actors can make it difficult to prosecute ATM-related fraud (*Kennison v Daire* (1986) 160 CLR 129). As these problems grew, various solutions were adopted. This too has created problems, as laws are now variable and conflicting across different jurisdictions.

Although the process of law reform relating to cyber crime has been slow, it is, arguably, quicker than in other areas of law – notably corporations and taxation law. Many of the legal issues concerning cyber crime relate not only to substantive computer crime offences but also to other types of cross-border crime, particularly economic offences. The seriousness of the cyber crime law reform problem is, therefore, not substantially different from other areas of international law.

The challenges posed by cyber crime for prosecutors also need to be placed in context. Although cyber crimes often involve voluminous information and data trails, so do other crimes. The recent prosecution of two Australians for killing twelve people and depositing their dismembered remains in barrels in a disused bank vault in Snowtown, South Australia, involved more than 1000 exhibits, 228 witnesses and 16,000 pages of court transcripts (Debelle 2003).

Similarly, prosecutors have had to deal with international criminals for many years in cases involving piracy on the high seas, illegal immigration, drug trafficking, and smuggling of contraband, not to mention serious fraud. Although these cases can often be protracted and slow, the mere presence of computers in the commission of the offence can hardly be said to raise new matters of jurisdiction and procedure with which courts are unfamiliar. The concern is, however, that the incidence of cross-border cyber crime will increase, placing additional burdens on already strained judicial resources.

Are There Differences of Approach Between Jurisdictions?

Secondly, it appears that the prosecutorial and judicial responses to cyber crime have been similar in North America, Britain and Australasia. Where differences exist, they largely arise from the presence of other legislative and procedural factors, rather than the fact that computers are involved. For example, the involvement of prosecutors in the United States in the planning and execution of investigations is attributable to constitutional exigencies and not to new technologies. There are different sentencing regimes in the United States, with its sophisticated system of sentencing guidelines, and in the United Kingdom and Australia where appellate court guideline judgments exist (although not, as yet, for cyber crime cases). These are more likely to be responsible for any perceived cross-national differences in sentencing practices than anything to do with computers. As our brief consideration of the sentences imposed in child pornography and hacking/vandalism cases showed, there appear to be few obvious differences in the ways in which courts in different countries approached these matters. All treated the possession and distribution of child pornography as warranting more severe sentences than cases of hacking and computer vandalism.

Are Cyber Crimes Treated More Seriously Than Conventional Crimes?

Thirdly, we found no conclusive evidence that the presence of computers in the commission of crime enhances the severity with which courts deal with those convicted of these crimes. Of course there are instances of extremely serious offences being facilitated through the use of computers, such as the possession and dissemination of child pornography, or the spread of malicious code which can disable computers across the globe in hours or days. But the fact that digital technologies have been used does not seem to result in the imposition of increased sentences. In fact, in some cases, the commission of crimes electronically could be said to *decrease* the seriousness of this conduct in the eyes of the courts. Stalking a victim through the use of e-mail, for example, could be said to pose less threat then actually waiting for one's victim outside her or his home. Similarly, engaging in sexually provocative discussion with a child in a chat room would seem to be less serious than engaging in physical sexual relations with a child – although, as we have seen, some sexual encounters can be initiated on the Internet.

In relation to financial crimes perpetrated electronically, our brief examination of the serious fraud cases decided in Australia and New Zealand showed that the presence of a computer did not obviously affect the sentence imposed, nor the aggravating and mitigating factors raised at the time of sentencing. This was, however, only a preliminary consideration of this variable; more extensive research is required to provide the basis for more rigorous statistical analysis.

Policy Implications

Our examination of the prosecution and punishment of cyber criminals has identified many fruitful avenues for policy reform. Although not all countries will agree on the most appropriate ways to respond to crimes of this nature, there are some issues that require urgent investigation, and on these all countries should, arguably, agree.

First, and of greatest importance, is the need for the process of legislative harmonisation to continue. The material presented in Chapter Six shows that there have been some important advances made already, such as the creation of the Council of Europe's *Convention on Cybercrime* and the *United Nations Convention against Transnational Organised Crime.* Individual countries need to continue their efforts to reform their own cyber crime legislation to ensure uniformity. This will help to facilitate the process of extradition as well as reducing inconsistencies in sentencing across countries. More importantly, the continuing process of legislative reform will help to ensure that unfortunate incidents, such as the failure of the prosecution in the 'Love Bug' virus case, will not be repeated.

Sufficient numbers of cases have now come before the courts that most prosecutors are aware of the many problems that can be encountered in court. This knowledge, arguably, needs to be used to ensure that prosecutors are appropriately trained and equipped to respond to some of the tactics that defendants raise to avoid responsibility for their actions. Prosecution policies may also need to be revisited to enable appropriate decisions concerning the acceptance of new cases for prosecution. Exactly when, for example, should a 15-year-old be prosecuted for having disseminated malicious code, and when is online copyright infringement serious enough to warrant the substantial costs associated with a multi-jurisdictional prosecution? Once again, organisations such as the International Association of Prosecutors could assist in devising effective policy reforms in this area and in achieving uniformity across jurisdictions.

Everyone involved in court proceedings, including prosecutors, defence counsel, solicitors, and jurors, needs to understand the sometimes complicated technological evidence that might be adduced in cases. In **[Case No. 90]**, for example, counsel for the accused, on appeal, criticised the trial judge for not understanding the facts of the case and for displaying confused reasoning. The Court of

Appeal also criticised some of the lawyers for not being familiar with the papers and being unable to answer questions about the case adequately. To overcome such problems, a specialist Bar might need to be established, and training courses offered for judges and lawyers. Similarly, the question of specialist units within prosecution agencies should be revisited, or a decision made as to whether it might be more cost-effective for the prosecution of some cyber crime cases to be outsourced to specially trained counsel in the private sector, rather than trying to maintain levels of expertise in this highly specialised area within public sector prosecution agencies. This problem, of course, principally arises for those jurisdictions in which prosecutors function solely within the public sector.

Resources may also need to be allocated to ensure that courtrooms are equipped with appropriate technologies for the presentation of electronic evidence in such a way as to make it readily understandable to jurors. Finally, in the most complex cases, jury trial may need to be made optional, in favour of trial by a judge assisted by a panel of trained assessors. At present, the number of cases that would benefit from reforms of this kind probably does not warrant considerable financial outlay, although as time progresses and more and more cyber crime cases reach the courts, the level of need will become clear.

Avenues for Further Investigation

Clearly, our book is very much a preliminary overview of the prosecution and sentencing of cyber criminals, and we would be remiss if we did not suggest possible issues and topics that could be worthy of attention by those who would follow in our path.

Improved Knowledge Base

Improved standards of information with respect to the prosecution and trial of cyber criminals must lie at the heart of any research agenda. Better and more extensive research needs to be carried out not only locally, but also internationally. Definitions of cyber crime need to be carefully framed and problems of accurate quantification addressed. In addition, the rapidly changing nature of cyber crime must be considered. One idea, for example, would be to include cyber crime issues in the next round of the International Crime Victimisation Survey.

Government statistical and census agencies should play a key role in conducting surveys of the population, as they are well placed to undertake research objectively. Public sector offices of crime statistics could, for example, ask some questions about cyber crime and security issues in their regular surveys on household use of information technologies. Official statistical data collection should also seek to explore more useful categorisation of cyber crime when collecting data from police, courts and correctional agencies. At present, conventional crime statistics simply do not enable any differentiation between cyber crimes and other types of offence.

Evidence also needs to come from those within industry. Persuading ISPs, financial institutions and merchants to be frank in disclosing cyber crime experiences is by no means simple, but some appropriate sharing of information must take place, even if conditions of confidentiality are imposed.

With improved levels of official information and more accurate surveys of cyber crime, we may then be in a position to direct resources appropriately to combat the problem. Courts and prosecutors should be better able to allocate resources and governments should be able to dedicate realistic levels of funding that would enable cases of this nature to be actively pursued through the courts.

Keeping Pace with Technological Developments

Of primary interest is the continuing game of 'leap-frog' being played by, on the one hand, those who perpetrate cyber crime, and, on the other, those who seek to control it. The pace of technological change is such that law and policy are subject to continuous challenge. With the increasing adoption of digital technologies and the increasing prevalence of computer literacy in the community, what once may have constituted 'special skills' under the United States Sentencing Guidelines are now mundane. Home computer users can counterfeit documents and establish their own fraudulent websites with ease.

Similarly, we have seen how post-release conditions imposed on offenders are now regarded as unrealistic and, indeed, counterproductive. In Western industrial societies at least, digital technology now pervades the lives of all but the most reclusive neo-luddites. Governments have set targets for electronic service delivery, which mean that those in the community will, except in extraordinary cases, be obliged to carry out their dealings with government electronically. And banks are now making it expensive and slow to transact business at a local branch with a teller. For courts to ban an offender from using computers, or place severe restrictions on their use, may make life close to unliveable. Certainly, the potential for rehabilitation could well be lost if workplace computers could not be used. Indeed, arguably the act of telephoning one's parole officer or calling a police station when on bail could infringe a ban on computer usage if one were to make use of a cellular telephone.

Further research is, therefore, needed on how offenders deal with such conditional orders. In addition, it would be worthwhile to conduct interviews with a sample of those who have been convicted of cyber crimes, to evaluate the 'rational choice' hypothesis. It could, for example, be possible to find out how many offenders knew the details of the offences they were committing and the associated punishments that were likely, and why they decided to commit their crimes nonetheless. We could also find out whether particular sanctions are perceived as having greater deterrent potential than others. Does, for example, the prospect of being banned from using the Internet produce a realistic deterrent to someone intent on dealing in child pornography online?

Further Investigation of Cases

The scope of our book has also prevented an in-depth discussion of individual cases. While some of the cases to which we have referred were relatively mundane, others raise complex questions about how they were able to be committed and why individual courts imposed the sentences they did. **[Case No. 61]**, for example, which involved an online 'sting' operation, the partial success of the fantasy defence, and contemporary challenges to the constitutionality of child pornography legislation in the United States, is one such case.

Explaining Attrition

One of the more interesting aspects of cyber crime prosecution is the attrition of cases before they get to the steps of the courthouse. The data reported in Table 9 of Chapter Three showed that 75 per cent of cases referred for prosecution to federal authorities in the United States were declined, primarily due to lack of evidence. An examination of attrition rates in a particular jurisdiction over time, or a comparison of jurisdictions with high and low attrition rates, might shed some interesting light on prosecution policies.

Police–Prosecutor Interactions

We noted in Chapter Three how prosecutors in some jurisdictions around the world are actively involved in the planning and execution of investigations, while elsewhere they are relatively passive recipients of briefs prepared and presented by the police. More intensive research on police – prosecutor relations in these jurisdictions could provide insight on how the demands of the courtroom are communicated back to the 'upstream' drivers of the investigation.

Defence Tactics

In addition, further research could be undertaken on the ways in which defence counsel approach their task of defending persons accused of cyber crime. Mann's (1988) study of white collar defence counsel provides a useful model. How trial counsel manage their clients and their adversaries – the prosecutors who are pitted against them – would make an interesting contrast with existing work, including our own, which tends to represent the point of view of the state.

Global Cooperative Action

Finally, despite the difficulties in investigating cross-national cyber crime, the annals of law enforcement contain celebrated examples of successful law enforcement cooperation across national frontiers. Operation Cathedral, the investigation of a global child pornography ring, resulted in simultaneous raids and over 100 arrests in Australia, Austria, Belgium, Finland, France, Germany, Italy, Norway, Portugal, Sweden and the United States in September 1998. Operation Buccaneer, an international software piracy investigation, involved the simultaneous execution on 11 December 2001 of more than 65 search warrants against alleged software pirates in the United States, the United Kingdom, Australia, Finland, Sweden and Norway. Operations such as these present unique opportunities for comparative analyses of prosecution and sentencing processes.

In the end, cases that come before the courts in the twenty-first century are likely to demonstrate many aspects of life as those of us in developed nations currently know it: activities that are heavily dependent on digital technologies, activities that involve participants in multiple countries, and activities that take place with an emphasis on speed. Prosecutors and courts need to be equipped with training and resources to respond effectively to such cases which, it may confidently be predicted, will become a regular feature in daily court listings. In order to maximise the efficiency of judicial processes, and to guard against the problem of history repeating itself, prosecutors and judges need to be made aware of the latest cases as soon as they come to light. Technology, which itself is deeply involved in the commission of modern crimes, will provide the best means of achieving such an objective. A century ago, the philosopher George Santayana said: 'Those who cannot remember the past are condemned to repeat it.' In today's digital environment, it may be said of prosecutors and judges that those who fail to anticipate the future are in for a rude shock when it arrives.

References

AFP 2002, 'Teen runs $1.9 million new scam', AFP, 8 January 2002: <http://www.afp.com>.

AGEC (Action Group into the Law Enforcement Implications of Electronic Commerce) 2001, *Mutual Assistance and Electronic Crime*: <http://www.austrac.gov.au/text/publications/agec/mutual_assistance.htm>.

AHTCC (Australian High Tech Crime Centre) 2003, 'World's law enforcers close in on Internet child sex abusers': <http://www.ahtcc.gov.au/>.

Amnesty International 1998, 'People's Republic of China: The Death Penalty in 1997', Amnesty International, New York. See updated information on this issue: 'Executed "according to law"? – The death penalty in China': <http://www.amnestyusa.org/regions/asia/document.do?id=806E474AFD57-DC5980256E5C00688E40>.

Andrews, R. 2001, 'Sins of "the saint of e-commerce"', *BBC News Online*, 6 July 2001: <http://www.bbc.co.uk>.

Applin, B. M. 2000, Affadavit of Bruce M. Applin: <http://www.cipherwar.com/news/00/naughton_fbi.htm>.

Armstrong, J. 2003, 'Computer Misuse Act 1990', Legal Commentary, 22 January 2003: <http://www.legalday.co.uk/lexnex/evershed03/e80220103a.htm>.

Ashcroft, J. 2003, Department Policy Concerning Charging Criminal Offences, Disposition of Charges, and Sentencing: <http://news.findlaw.com/nytimes/docs/doj/ashcroft92203chrgmem.pdf>.

Associated Press 2002, 'Programmer pleads guilty in Breeders' Cup case', 21 November 2002: <http://www.startribune.com/stories/693/3446165.html>.

Australasian Centre for Policing Research 2000, *The Virtual Horizon: Meeting the Law Enforcement Challenges*, Scoping Paper, Australasian Centre for Policing Research, Adelaide.

Australian Bureau of Statistics 1998, *Household Use of Information Technology, Australia 1998*, (Cat. No. 8146.0), Australian Bureau of Statistics, Canberra.

Australian Bureau of Statistics 2001, *Use of the Internet by Householders, Australia*, November 2000 edition (Cat. No. 8147.0), Australian Bureau of Statistics, Canberra.

Australian Computer Crime and Security Survey 2002, Deloitte Touche Tohmatsu, AusCERT, and New South Wales Police Crime Unit, Sydney.

Australian Federal Police (AFP) 1990–2001, *Annual Reports 1990–2001*, Australian Federal Police, Canberra.

Australian Institute of Criminology and PricewaterhouseCoopers 2003, *Serious Fraud in Australia and New Zealand, Research and Public Policy Series* No. 48, Australian Institute of Criminology/ PricewaterhouseCoopers, Canberra.

Australian Securities and Investments Commission 2000, *Complaints Made Under the EFT Code of Conduct 1999–2000*, ASIC, Sydney.

Ayres, I. and Braithwaite, J. 1992, *Responsive Regulation: Transcending the Deregulation Debate*, Oxford University Press, New York.

BBC News 2003, 'Briton may sue after FBI bungle', *BBC News Online (UK Edition)*, 26 February 2003: <http://www.bbc.co.uk>.

Beh, H. G. 2001, 'Physical Losses In Cyberspace', *Connecticut Insurance Law Journal*, vol. 8, no. 1, pp. 55–86.

Bell, R. E. 2002, 'The Prosecution of Computer Crime', *Journal of Financial Crime*, vol. 9, no. 4, pp. 308–25.

Bellia, P. L. 2001, 'Chasing Bits Across Borders', *University of Chicago Legal Forum*, 2001, pp. 35–101.

Bernardo, R. 2001, 'Man arrested for alleged computer hacking', *North County Times*, 21 January 2001: <http://www.nctimes.net/news/2001/20010121/qqq.html>

Bernstein, N. 1996, 'On prison computer, files to make parents shiver', *New York Times*, 18 November 1996, p. A1.

Black, M. and Smith, R. G. 2003, 'Electronic Monitoring in the Criminal Justice System', in *Trends and Issues in Crime and Criminal Justice*, No. 254, Australian Institute of Criminology, Canberra.

Bowker, A. L. 1999, 'Juveniles and computers: should we be concerned?', *Federal Probation*, December 1999.

Brenner, S. W. 2001, 'Cybercrime Investigation and Prosecution: The Role of Penal and Procedural Law', *ELaw: Murdoch University Electronic Journal of Law*, vol. 8, no. 2: <http://www.murdoch.edu.au/elaw/issues/v8n2/brenner82.html>.

Brenner, S. and Frederiksen, B. 2001, 'Computer Searches and Seizures: Some Unresolved Issues', *Michigan Telecommunications and Technology Law Review*, 8, pp. 39–114.

Brenner, S. and Schwerha, J. J. 2002, 'Transnational Evidence Gathering and Local Prosecution of Cybercrime', *John Marshall Journal of Computer and Information Law*, vol. 20, p. 347.

Bronitt, S. and Roche, D. 2001, 'Entrapment, the Art of Police Deception', *Australian Quarterly*, January/February 2001, pp. 20–4.

Burkeman, O. 2002, 'New York man admits Internet scam to defraud celebrities of $80m', *The Guardian*, 5 October 2002: <http://www.guardian.co.uk/internetnews/story/0,7369,805091,00.html>.

Business Software Alliance (BSA) 2003, *Eighth Annual BSA Global Software Piracy Study*: <http://www.bsa.org>.

Butcher, S. 2001, 'Ban urged on Internet bomb "recipes"', *The Age* (Melbourne), 17 January 2001, p. 7c.

Campbell, R. 2001, 'Consultant moved by greed, court told', *Canberra Times*, 24 April 2001.

CCIPS 2002, *Searching and Seizing Computers and Obtaining Electronic Evidence in Criminal Investigations*, US Department of Justice, Washington: <http://www.usdoj.gov/criminal/cybercrime/s&smanual2002.htm>.

Center for Online Addiction 2003: <http://www.netaddiction.com>

Chatterjee, B. B. 2001, 'Last of the Rainmacs: Thinking About Pornography in Cyberspace', in Wall, D. S. (ed.), *Crime and the Internet*, Routledge, London, pp. 74–99.

Cisneros, D. 2002, '"Virtual Child" Pornography on the Internet: A "Virtual" Victim?', *Duke Law and Technology Review* (2002/19): <http://www.law.duke.edu/journals/dltr/articles/2002dltr0019.html>.

Clough, J. and Mulhern, C. 2002, *The Prosecution of Corporations*, Oxford University Press, South Melbourne.

Clough, B. and Mungo, P. 1992, *Approaching Zero: Data Crime and the Computer Underworld*, Faber and Faber, London.

CNET News 2003a, 'Bush signs anti-spam bill into law', 16 December 2003: <http://www.msnbc.msn.com/Default.aspx?id=3662680&p1=0>.

CNET News 2003b, 'Australia's Spam Act to become law in April', 19 December 2003: <http://msnbc-cnet.com.com/2100–1028_3-5129683.html>.

CNN 1998, 'Teen hacker faces federal charges: Caused computer crash that disabled Massachusetts airport': <http://www.cnn.com/TECH/computing/9803/18/juvenile.hacker/>.

Computer Security Institute and Federal Bureau of Investigation 2001, *Computer Crime and Security Survey*, Computer Security Institute and Federal Bureau of Investigation, San Francisco: <http://www.gocsi.com>.

COPA Commission 2000: <http://www.copacommission.org/>.

Cornish, D. B. and Clarke, R. V. (eds) 1986, *The Reasoning Criminal: Rational Choice Perspectives on Offending*, Springer-Verlag, New York.

Council of Europe (COE) 2004, 'Entry into force of the Council of Europe Convention on Cybercrime' (Strasbourg, 18 March 2004): <http://press.coe.int/cp/2004/135a(2004).htm>.

Crang, M., Crang, P. and May, J. (eds.) 2001, *Virtual Geographies*, Routledge, London.

Cullen, P. 2003, 'Whiz kid scams $100,000', *The Mercury News* (Hobart), 23 August 2003: <http://www.themercury.news.com.au/printpage/0,5942,7040683,00.html>.

Debelle, P. 2003, 'End in sight for Snowtown jurors', *The Age* (Melbourne), 1 September 2003, p. 5.

De Frances, C. J. 2001, *National Survey of Prosecutors: State Court prosecutors in Large Districts 2001*, Bureau of Justice Statistics, Department of Justice, Washington.

DeMarco, J. V. 2001, 'It's Not Just Fun and "War Games": Juveniles and Computer Crime', *United States Attorneys' Bulletin*, vol. 49, no. 3, pp. 48–55: <http://www.usdoj.gov/criminal/cybercrime/usamay2001_7.htm>.

Diffie, W. and Hellman, M. E. 1976, 'New Directions in Cryptography', *IEEE Transactions on Information Theory*, vol. 22, pp. 644–54.

Drozdova, E. 2001, 'Civil Liberties and Security in Cyberspace', in Sofaer, A. D. and Goodman, S. (eds), *The Transnational Dimension of Cyber Crime and Terrorism*, Hoover Institution Press, Stanford, pp. 183–220.

Eckholm, E. 1999, 'China frees dissident to improve ties with US', *Sydney Morning Herald*, 26 December 1999.

Electronic Privacy Information Center 2003, Criminal No. 00–404 (DNJ): <http://www.epic.org/crypto/scarfo.html>.

Ernst and Young 2003, *Fraud: The Unmanaged Risk 8th Global Survey*, Ernst and Young, London.

Evers, J. 2002, 'Virus writer's conviction upheld', *IDG News Service*, 28 October 2002: <http://www.pcworld.com/news/article/0,aid,106443,00.asp>.

Farley, M. 1999, 'Electronic guerrillas breach blocks set up by the government to keep citizens from seeing unorthodox news and opinions on the Internet', *Los Angeles Times*, 1999.

Federal Bureau of Investigation (FBI) 2003, 'The case of the hacked South Pole': <http://www.fbi.gov/page2/july03/071803backsp.htm>.

Federal Trade Commission, United States 2002, 'Sentinel Top Complaint Categories: January 1–December 31, 2001', Federal Trade Commission, 7 January 2002: <http://www.consumer.gov/sentinel/images/charts/top2001.pdf>.

Federal Trade Commission, United States 2003, 'Sentinel Complaints by Calendar Year', Federal Trade Commission, 22 January 2003: <http://www.consumer.gov/sentinel/sentinel-trends/page3.pdf>.

Findlaw 2003, 'Computer hacker of prominent Internet service provider to face court': <http://www.findlaw.com.au/news/default.asp?task=read&id=17233&site=LE>.

Flew, A. 1969, 'The Justification of Punishment', in Acton, H. B. (ed.), *The Philosophy of Punishment*, Macmillan & Co. Ltd, London.

Forney, M. 1996, 'Piracy: Now We Get It', *Far Eastern Economic Review*, vol. 159, no. 7, pp. 40–3.

Fowler, B., Franklin, C. and Hyde, B. 2001, 'Can you Yahoo!? The Internet's Digital Fences', 2001 *Duke Law & Technology Review* 0012: <http://www.law.duke.edu/journals/dltr/articles/2001dltr0012.html>.

Foucault, M. 1977, *Discipline and Punish: The Birth of the Prison*, Penguin, London.

Fraud Advisory Panel 2001, *Cybercrime Survey*, International Fraud Prevention Research Centre, Nottingham.

Freiberg, A. 1992, 'Sentencing White-Collar Criminals', in Australian Institute of Judicial Administration (AIJA), *Sentencing of Federal Offenders*, Proceedings of a seminar for judges and magistrates held 1–2 November 1991, AIJA, Melbourne, pp. 1–19.

Frohmann, L. 1997, 'Convictability and Discordant Locales: Reproducing Race, Class and Gender Ideologies in Prosecutorial Decision-making', *Law and Society Review*, vol. 31, no. 3, pp. 523–556.

Gabriel, T. 1995, 'Reprogramming a convicted hacker', *New York Times*, 14 January 1995.

Geis, G. 1991, 'White-Collar Crime: What Is It?', *Current Issues in Criminal Justice*, vol. 3, no. 1, pp. 9–24.

Geurts, J. 2000, 'The Role of the Australian Federal Police in the Investigation of High-Tech Crimes', *Platypus Magazine: The Journal of the Australian Federal Police*, March 2000: <http://www.afp.gov.au/publica/platypus/mar00/intfrd.htm>.

Gibson, W. 1984, *Neuromancer*, Harper Collins, London.

Goldsmith, J. 2001, 'The Internet and the Legitimacy of Remote Cross-Border Searches', University of Chicago, Public Law Working Paper No. 16: <http://papers.ssrn.com/sol3/papers.cfm?abstract_id=285732>.

Goldstone, D. 2001, 'Deciding Whether to Prosecute an Intellectual Property Case', *United States Attorneys' Bulletin*, vol. 49, no. 2, pp. 1–8.

Goodman, M. D. and Brenner, S. W. 2002, 'The Emerging Consensus on Criminal Conduct in Cyberspace', *UCLA Journal of Law and Technology*, vol. 3: <http://www.lawtechjournal.com/articles/2002/03_020625_goodmanbrenner.php>.

Grabosky, P. N. 1984, 'Corporate Crime in Australia: An Agenda for Research', *Australian and New Zealand Journal of Criminology*, vol. 17, pp. 95–107.

Grabosky, P. N. 1995, 'Regulation by Reward: On the Use of Incentives as Regulatory Instruments', *Law and Policy*, vol. 17, no. 3, pp. 257–82.

Grabosky, P. N. 1998, 'Crime in a Shrinking World', *Trends and Issues in Crime and Criminal Justice* No. 83, Australian Institute of Criminology, Canberra.

Grabosky, P., Braithwaite, J. and Wilson, P. 1987, 'The Myth of Community Tolerance Toward White Collar Crime', *Australian and New Zealand Journal of Criminology*, vol. 20, pp. 33–44.

Grabosky, P. N. and Smith, R. G. 1998, *Crime in the Digital Age: Controlling Telecommunications and Cyberspace Illegalities*, Transaction Publishers/Federation Press, New Brunswick, New Jersey.

Grabosky, P. N., Smith, R. G. and Dempsey, G. 2001, *Electronic Theft: Unlawful Acquisition in Cyberspace*, Cambridge University Press, Cambridge.

Granick, J., Hernandez, C., Young, M., and Tien, L. 2003, Submission to the United States Sentencing Commission: <http://cyberlaw.stanford.edu/about/cases/1030%20Comments%202-19-03.pdf>.

Grant, A., David, F., and Grabosky, P. 1997, 'Child Pornography in the Digital Age', *Transnational Organized Crime*, vol. 3, no. 4, pp. 171–88.

Greatest Hackers in the Whole World 2003: <http://www.geocities.com/vienna/4345/>.

Gregg, J. 1996, 'Caught in the Web: Entrapment in Cyberspace', *Hastings Communications and Entertainment Law Journal*, vol. 19, pp. 157–97.

Griffin, P. 2001, 'Legal definition on hacking case', *New Zealand Herald*, 18 April: <http://www.nzherald.co.nz/storydisplay.cfm?storyID=183417>.

Griffiths, M. D. 1990, 'Addiction to Fruit Machines: A Preliminary Study Among Males', *Journal of Gambling Studies*, vol. 6, pp. 113–26.

Grossman, L. 2000, 'Attack of the Love Bug', *Time*, 15 May 2000, p. 49.

Hafner, K. and Markoff, J. 1991, *Cyberpunk: Outlaws and Hackers on the Computer Frontier*, Simon and Schuster, New York.

Hart, H. L. A. 1968, *Punishment and Responsibility: Essays in the Philosophy of Law*, Oxford University Press, Oxford.

Hawkins, G. 1976, *The Prison: Policy and Practice*, University of Chicago Press, Chicago.

Holland, R. C. 1995, 'Public Perceptions of White Collar Crime Seriousness: A Survey of an Australian Sample', *International Journal of Comparative and Applied Criminal Justice*, vol. 19, nos 1–2, Spring/Fall 1995, pp. 91–105.

House of Representatives Standing Committee on Legal and Constitutional Affairs, Australia 2000, *Copycats Inquiry: Cracking Down on Copycats: Enforcement of Copyright in Australia*, Commonwealth of Australia, Canberra.

Hughes, G. 1990, 'Computers, Crime and the Concept of "Property"', *Intellectual Property Journal*, vol. 1, pp. 154–63.

Hyne, D. 2002, 'Examining the Legal Challenges to the Restriction of Computer Access as a Term of Probation or Supervised Release', *New England Journal on Criminal and Civil Confinement*, Summer 2002, vol. 28, p. 215.

Inman, K. 2001, 'The Council of Europe's Convention on Cybercrime and Australia', *Cyber Law Research* 29: <http://www.austlii.edu.au/au/other/CyberLRes/2001/29>.

International Federation of the Phonographic Industry (IFPI) 2003, 'Police close down major online pirate site in Australia', 24 April 2003: <http://www.ifpi.org>.

International Intellectual Property Alliance (IIPA) 2000, *2000 Special 301 Report: Australia*, International Intellectual Property Alliance, Washington: <http://www.iipa.com/rbc/2000/AUSTRALIA_2000.PDF>.

International Intellectual Property Alliance (IIPA) 2001: <http://www.IIPA.com>.

Internet Fraud Complaint Center 2002, *IFCC 2001 Internet Fraud Report*: <http://www1.ifccfbi.gov/strategy/IFCC_2001_AnnualReport.pdf>.

Internet Fraud Complaint Center 2003, *IFCC 2002 Internet Fraud Report*: http://www1.ifccfbi.gov/strategy/IFCC_2002_AnnualReport.pdf.

Internet Fraud Watch 2001, *2001 Internet Fraud Statistics*: <http://www.fraud.org/internet/2001stats.htm>.

Internet Fraud Watch 2002, *2002 Internet Fraud Statistics*: <http://www.fraud.org/internet/2002stats.htm>.

Johnson, D. 2002, *The Japanese Way of Justice: Prosecuting Crime in Japan*, Oxford University Press, New York.

Karp, J. 2002, 'Imaginary crime yields real time: man accused of using Net to entice fictitious boy into sex ends up serving a not-so-fictitious sentence', *Tech TV*, 22 January 2002: <http://www.techtv.com/cybercrime/viceonline/story/0,23008,3367361,00.html>.

Kaspersen, H. W. K. 2001, Background Paper for the Workshop on Crimes Related to the Computer Network (A CONF. 187/10), in United Nations Asia and Far East Institute for the Prevention of Crime and the Treatment of Offenders (ed.), *The Global Challenge of High Tech Crime*, UNAFEI, Tokyo.

Katz, R. S. and Jones, R. A. 2001, 'National Boundaries in Cyberspace? Yahoo v LICRA', *Journal of Internet Law*, September 2001: <http://www.gcwf.com/gcc/GrayCary-C/News-Arti/Journal/0901_JIL.doc_cvt.htm>.

Kerr, O. 2002a, 'Computer hacker in a foreign country is a state actor for Fourth Amendment purposes, District Court holds: use of Subseven Trojan horse to search home computers for child porn violates the Fourth Amendment', *Computer Crime Updates*, 13 November 2002: <http://hermes.circ.gwu.edu/archives/cybercrime.html>.

Kerr, O. 2002b, 'Sentencing Guidelines: Ninth Circuit Limits "Special Skills" Enhancement for Use of a Computer', *Computer Crime Updates*, 24 July 2002: <http://hermes.circ.gwu.edu/archives/cybercrime.html>.

Kerr, O. 2003, 'Government must prove defendant in computer child pornography prosecution knew digital image was of an actual child, Southern District of New York concludes', *Computer Crime Case Update*, Pabon-Cruz, Reilly, 2 May 2003: <http://hermes.circ.gwu.edu/cgi-bin/wa?A2=ind0305&L=cybercrime&F=&S=&P=68>.

Kowalski, M. 2002, *Cyber Crime: Issues, Data Sources and Feasibility of Collecting Police-Reported Statistics*, Canadian Centre for Justice Statistics, Ottawa.

KPMG 2001, *Global e.fr@ud Survey*, KPMG Forensic and Litigation Services. http://www.kpmg.ca/english/services/docs/fas/efraud2001.pdf.

Lapthorne, K. 2003, 'Data whiz gets jail', *Herald Sun* (Melbourne), 20 September 2003.

Layton-Mackenzie, D. 2002, 'Criminal justice and crime prevention', in Sherman, L., Farrington, D., Welsh, B. and Layton Mackenzie, D. (eds), *Evidence-Based Crime Prevention*, Routledge, London, pp. 330–404.

Lemos, R. 2001, 'FBI "hack" raises global security concerns', C/net News.com, 1 May 2001: <http://news.com.com/2100-1001-256811.html>.

Leviticus, in *Holy Bible*, Authorized Version, British and Foreign Bible Society, London, 1964.

Leyden, J. 2003, 'Ethical wireless hacker is innocent': <http://www.theregister.co.uk/content/archive/29434.html>.

Lo, V. 2002, 'Police Training for Cyber-Transformation', paper presented at the Transnational Organized Crime Conference, Hong Kong, March 2002.

Louis Harris and Associates Inc. 1999, *Consumers and the 21st Century: A Survey Conducted for the National Consumers League*, Louis Harris and Associates Inc., New York.

Mann, K. 1988, *Defending White Collar Crime*, Yale University Press, New Haven.

Martinson, J. 2001, 'Judge jails Jesse James of the Net', *The Guardian*, 8 August 2001: <http://www.guardian.co.uk/internetnews/story/0,7369,533720,00.html>.

Massingham, C. 1977, 'When Police Strike: The Victorian Police Strike of 1923', in Milte, K. L. and Weber, T. A. (eds), *Police in Australia*, pp. 287–92, Butterworths, Sydney.

McConnell International 2000, *Cyber Crime and Punishment* ('The Cyber Crime Laws of Nations'): <http://www.mcconnellinternational.com> (choose 'Services', 'Strategies', then 'Global Strategies' to get to the page).

Mills, K. 1999, 'Christchurch youths sentenced on Internet card fraud', *Computerworld*, 30 August 1999: <http://idg.net.nz/webhome.nsf/ArchiveDate/ E5F7561E326D0217CC25684C000D4FEA!OpenDocument>.

Milovanovic, S. 2003, 'Student banned from Internet after stab charge', *The Age* (Melbourne), 29 October 2003, p. 3.

Minty, C. 2002, 'Phone terrorism research funded', *The Daily Oklahoman*, 6 April 2002: <http://www.newsok.com/cgi-bin/show_article?ID=870312&TP= getarticle>.

Miranda, C. and Shepherd, N. 2003, 'Musician Jailed Over Porn', *Daily Telegraph (Sydney)*, 8 September.

Model Criminal Code Officers Committee (MCCOC) of the Standing Committee of Attorneys-General (MCCOC / SCAG), January 2001, *Model Criminal Code – Chapter 4: Damage and Computer Offences; and Amendment to Chapter 2: Jurisdiction*: <http://www.law.gov.au/publications/Model_Criminal_Code/index.htm>.

Moitra, S. D. 2003, *Analysis and Modelling of Cybercrime: Prospects and Potential*, Max Planck Institute for Foreign and International Criminal Law, Freiburg im Breisgau.

Napier, B. 1994, 'Update on the Computer Misuse Act 1990', *Journal of Business Law*, p. 525.

National Criminal Intelligence Service 1999, *Project Trawler: Crime on the Information Highways*, NCIS, London: <http://www.cyber-rights.org/documents/ trawler.htm>.

National District Attorneys Association 1991, *National Prosecution Standards*. NDAA, Chicago.

National Office for the Information Economy (NOIE) and the Australian Computer Society 2000, *The Phantom Menace: Setting the Record Straight About Online Credit Card Fraud for Consumers*, National Office for the Information Economy and the Australian Computer Society, Canberra.

Newman, G. and Clark, R. 2003, *Superhighway Robbery: Preventing E-Commerce Crime*, Willan Publishing, Devon.

O'Connor, James R. 1973, *The Fiscal Crisis of the State*, St Martin's Press, New York.

Ogilvie, E. 2000, 'Cyberstalking', *Trends and Issues in Crime and Criminal Justice*, No. 166, Australian Institute of Criminology: <http://www.aic.gov.au/ publications/tandi/ti166.pdf>.

Oliver, M. 2000, 'Net pornographers face harsher sentences', *The Guardian*, 6 November 2000: <http://www.guardian.co.uk/internetnews/story/0,7369, 393646,00.html>.

Organisation for Economic Co-operation and Development (OECD) 2002, *OECD Guidelines for the Security of Information Systems and Networks – Towards a Culture of Security*: <http://www.oecd.org/dataoecd/59/0/1946946.pdf>.

Park, E. 2001, 'Analysis of Internet Crime In Korea and Countermeasures', paper presented to the Sixth Annual Conference of the International Association of Prosecutors, Sydney, Australia, 2–7 September 2001: <http://www. iap.nl.com/speeches2/internetcrime.html>.

Parker, D. B. 1983, *Fighting Computer Crime*, Charles Scribner's Sons, New York.

People's Daily Online 2000, 'Chinese hacker sentenced to death for embezzlement', *People's Daily Online*, 13 June 2000.

Platt, C. 1996, *Anarchy Online*, Harper Collins, New York.

Podgor, E. 2002, 'International Computer Fraud: A Paradigm for Limiting National Jurisdiction', *UC Davis Law Review*, vol. 35, pp. 267–317.

Pollitt, M. 2003, 'Digital Evidence in Internet Time', in R. Broadhurst (ed.), *Bridging the GAP: A Global Alliance on Transnational Organised Crime*, Hong Kong Police, Printing Department HKSAR.

PricewaterhouseCoopers 2002, *Intellectual Property Loss Survey Report 2001*, Pricewater-
    houseCoopers, Melbourne.
PricewaterhouseCoopers 2003, *Global Economic Crime Survey*, PricewaterhouseCoop-
    ers/Wilmer, Cutler and Pickering, New York.
Rawlings, J. 2001, 'The Council of Europe Draft Convention on Cyber-Crime:
    A European Perspective on a Global Problem', *Cyber Law Research* 13:
    <http://www.austlii.edu.au/au/other/CyberLRes/2001/13>.
Reuters 1998, 'Argentine hacker: case closed', *Wired News*, 20 May 1998:
    <http://www.wired.com/news/technology/0,1282,12416,00.html>.
Roberts, T. 2000, 'FBI targets computer crime', *Charlotte Business Journal*, 16 June 2000:
    <http://www.bizjournals.com/charlotte/stories/2000/06/19/focus1.html>.
Sampford, C. and Blencowe, S. 2002, 'Raising the Standard: An Integrated Approach
    to Promoting Professional Values and Avoiding Professional Criminality', in
    Smith, R. G. (ed.), *Crime in the Professions*, Ashgate, Aldershot, pp. 251–68.
SC Magazine 2001, vol. 4, no. 12, p. 10.
Sharpe, J. A. 1990, *Judicial Punishment in England*, Faber and Faber, London.
Sieber, U. 1998, *Legal Aspects of Computer-Related Crime in the Information Soci-
    ety*, *COMCRIME Study* prepared for the European Commission: <http://
    europa.eu.int/ISPO/legal/en/comcrime/sieber.doc>.
Simpson, S. 2002, *Corporate Crime. Law and Social Control*, Cambridge University Press,
    Cambridge.
Smith, R. G., Holmes, M., and Kaufman, P. 1999, 'Nigerian Advance Fee Fraud', *Trends
    and Issues in Crime and Criminal Justice* no. 121, Australian Institute of Criminology,
    Canberra: <http://www.aic.gov.au/publications/tandi/tandi121.html>.
Smith, R. G. and Urbas, G. 2001, *Controlling Fraud on the Internet: A CAPA Perspective.
    A report for the Confederation of Asian and Pacific Accountants*, Research and Pub-
    lic Policy Series No. 39, Confederation of Asian and Pacific Accountants, Kuala
    Lumpur, Australian Institute of Criminology, Canberra.
Smith, R. G. 2002, 'White Collar Crime', in Graycar, A. and Grabosky, P. (eds), *The Cam-
    bridge Handbook of Australian Criminology*, Cambridge University Press, Cambridge,
    pp. 126–56.
Smith, S. 2003, 'From Napster to Kazaa: The Battle over Peer-to-Peer File-
    sharing Goes International', *Duke Law and Technology Review* (2003/08):
    <http://www.law.duke.edu/journals/dltr/articles/2003dltr0008.html>.
Securities and Exchange Commission 2001, 'Litigation Release No. 17094', 8 August
    2001: <http://www.sec.gov/litigation/litreleases/lr17094.htm>.
Serious Fraud Office (UK) Annual Report 1997–98: <http://www.sfo.gov.uk/
    publications/1997_1998/section_05.asp#spelling (1998)>.
Soma, J. T., Muther, T. F. Jr, and Brisette, H. 1997, 'Transnational Extradition for Com-
    puter Crimes: Are New Treaties and Laws Needed?', *Harvard Journal on Legislation*,
    vol. 34, pp. 317–70.
Spierenburg, P. 1984, *The Spectacle of Suffering: Executions and the Evolution of Repression:
    From a Pre-industrial Metropolis to the European Experience*, Cambridge University
    Press, Cambridge.
Standen, J. 1993, 'Plea Bargaining in the Shadow of the Guidelines', *California Law
    Review*, vol. 81, pp. 1471–538.
Standing Committee of Attorneys General 2000, *Deliberative Forum on Crimi-
    nal Trial Reform* Commonwealth Attorney-General's Department, Canberra:
    <http://www.law.gov.au/publications/pubs.htm>.
Standler, R. B. 2002, 'Examples of Malicious computer programs': <http://www.
    rbs2.com/cvirus.htm>.
Stanko, E. 1981, 'The Impact of Victim Assessment on Prosecutors' Screening Deci-
    sions: The Case of the New York County District Attorney's Office', *Law and Society
    Review*, vol. 16, no. 2, pp. 225–39.

Steel, A. 2002, 'Vaguely Going Where No-one Has Gone: The Expansive New Computer Access Offences', *Criminal Law Journal*, vol. 26, pp. 72–97.

Stein, A. R. 2001, 'Frontiers of Jurisdiction: From Isolation to Connectedness', *University of Chicago Legal Forum*, pp. 373–406.

Stoll, C. 1991, *The Cuckoo's Egg*, Pan Books, London.

Stutz, M. 1997, 'Argentine hacker pleads guilty', *Wired News*, 5 December 1997: <http://www.wired.com/news/technology/0,1282,8996,00.html>.

Sullivan, C. 1988, 'The Response of the Criminal Law in Australia to Computer Abuse', *Criminal Law Journal*, vol. 12, pp. 228–46.

Suro, R. 1999, 'The hackers who won't quit', *Washington Post*, 1 September 1999: <http://www.washingtonpost.com/wp-srv/national/daily/sept99/global1.htm>.

Sutherland, E. H. 1940, 'White-collar Criminality', *American Sociological Review*, vol. 5, pp. 1–12.

Sydney Morning Herald 2003, 'I've reformed and want to Help, says ex-hacker', 15 September 2003: <http://www.smh.com.au/articles/2003/09/15/1063478121877.html>.

Tan, K. H. 2000, 'Prosecuting Foreign Based Computer Crime: International Law and Technology Collide', paper presented at the Symposium on the Rule of Law in the Global Village, 12–14 December 2000, Palermo, Italy: <http://www.undcp.org/adhoc/palermo/convmain.html>.

Taylor, G. 2001, 'The Council of Europe's Convention on Cybercrime and Australia: A Civil Liberties Perspective', *Cyber Law Research* 30: <http://www.austlii.edu.au/au/other/CyberLRes/2001/30>.

Taylor, K. 2001, 'New laws aim to close in on computer anarchy', *The Age* (Melbourne), 15 May 2001: <http://www.theage.com.au/news/2001/05/15/FFXB0M44PMC.html>.

Teather, D. 2003, 'It all turns out fine for 12-year-old Internet pirate', *The Age* (Melbourne), 12 September 2003, p. 9.

Thompson, D. E. and Berwick, D. R. 1997, *Minimum Provisions for the Investigation of Computer Based Offences*, Australasian Centre for Policing Research (ACPR): <http://www.acpr.gov.au/publications2.asp?Report_ID=13>.

Tinkler, C. 2004, 'Online porn crisis', *Herald Sun* (Melbourne), 25 January 2004: <http://heraldsun.news.com.au/common/story_page/0,5478,8484710%255E662,00.html>.

Tomasic, R. 1993, *Corporate Law Sanctions and the Control of White-collar Crime*, Centre for National Corporate Law Research, University of Canberra, Canberra.

Treasure, K. 2003, 'Magistrate made ill by child porn', *Illawarra Mercury* (New South Wales), 2 October 2003.

Tridgell, A. 2000, 'Newsgathering and Child Pornography Research', *Columbia Journal of Law and Social Problems*, vol. 33, pp. 343–91.

Tunnell, K. D. 1996, 'Let's Do it: Declining to Commit Crime', in Conklin, J. E. (ed.), *New Perspectives in Criminology*, pp. 246–58, Allyn and Bacon, Boston.

UNAFEI 1995, Criminal Justice Profiles of Asia. United Nations Asia and Far East Institute for the Prevention of Crime and the Treatment of Offenders, Tokyo.

United Nations 2003: <http://www.unodc.org/crime_ckp.html>.

United States Department of Justice (USDOJ) 1997, *Federal Prosecution of Violations of Intellectual Property Rights*: <http://www.usdoj.gov/criminal/cybercrime/intell_prop_rts/toc.htm>.

United States Department of Justice (USDOJ) 1998, 'Juvenile computer hacker cuts off FAA tower at regional airport: First federal charges brought against a juvenile for computer crime', press release, 18 March 1998: <http://www.usdoj.gov/criminal/cybercrime/juvenilepld.htm>.

United States Department of Justice (USDOJ) 1999, *Report on Cyberstalking: A New Challenge for Law Enforcement and Industry: A report from the Attorney General to the Vice President*: <http://www.usdoj.gov/criminal/cybercrime/cyberstalking.html>.

United States Department of Justice (USDOJ) 2000, Internet Fraud: Appendix B, Report of the Criminal Division's Computer Crime and Intellectual Property Section: <http://www.cybercrime.gov/append.htm>.

United States Department of Justice (USDOJ) 2001a, 'Man sentenced in Michigan for offering software programs for free downloading on "Hacker Hurricane" website', press release, 30 January 2001: <http://www.cybercrime.gov/baltutatsent.htm>.

United States Department of Justice (USDOJ) 2001b, 'Russian national enters into agreement with the United States on first Digital Millennium Copyright Act case', United States Department of Justice, press release, 13 December 2001: <http://www.usdoj.gov/criminal/cybercrime/sklyarovAgree.htm>.

United States Department of Justice (USDOJ) 2001c, 'Searching and Seizing Computers and Obtaining Electronic Evidence in Criminal Investigations': <http://www.cybercrime.gov/searchmanual.htm>.

United States Department of Justice (USDOJ) 2002, 'Operation Buccaneer', United States Department of Justice, various press releases: <http://www.cybercrime.gov/ob/OBMain.htm>.

United States Department of Justice (USDOJ) 2003a, Computer crime and Intellectual Property Section, Computer Intrusion Cases: <http://www.usdoj.gov/criminal/cybercrime/cccases.html>.

United States Department of Justice (USDOJ) 2003b, 'Defendant indicted in connection with operating illegal Internet software piracy group', press release, 12 March 2003: <http://www.usdoj.gov/criminal/cybercrime/griffithsIndict.htm>.

United States Department of Justice (USDOJ) 2003c, Fact Sheet: PROTECT Act: <http://www.usdoj.gov/opa/pr/2003/April/03_ag_266.htm>.

United States Department of Justice (USDOJ) 2003d, 'Man admits to distribution of pirated movies, music, computer software and games worth over $2.2 million', press release, 8 December 2003: <http://www.usdoj.gov/criminal/cybercrime/remyPlea.htm>.

United States Department of State, 26 October 2001, 'Bush comments on signing new antiterrorism law': <http://usinfo.state.gov/topical/pol/terror/01102600.htm>.

United States Sentencing Commission (USSC) 2000, Symposium on Federal Sentencing Policy for Economic Crimes and New Technology Offenses, 12–13 October 2000: <http://www.ussc.gov/2000sympo/2000sympo.htm>.

United States Sentencing Commission (USSC) 2003a, *Amendments to the Sentencing Guidelines* <http://www.ussc.gov/2003guid>.

United States Sentencing Commission (USSC) 2003b, *Sentencing Guidelines*: <http://www.ussc.gov/2002guid/tabcon02_2.htm>.

Urban, R. 2003, 'Police raids seize DVDs', *Sunday Age* (Melbourne), 7 September 2003, p. 3.

Urbas, G. 2000a, 'Public enforcement of intellectual property rights', *Trends and Issues in Crime and Criminal Justice*, no. 177, Australian Institute of Criminology, Canberra: <http://www.aic.gov.au/publications/tandi/tandi177.html>.

Urbas, G. 2000b, 'The age of criminal responsibility', *Trends and Issues in Crime and Criminal Justice*, no. 181, Australian Institute of Criminology, Canberra: <http://www.aic.gov.au/publications/tandi/tandi181.html>.

Urbas, G. 2001, 'Cybercrime Legislation in the Asia-Pacific Region', in Broadhurst, R. G. (ed.), *Proceedings of the Asia Cyber Crime Summit*, Centre for Criminology, University of Hong Kong, April 2001; revised version (August 2001) available at: <http://www.aic.gov.au/conferences/other/urbas_gregor/2001-04-cybercrime.html>.

Victoria Police 1993–2002, *Statistical Review of Crime 1992–2001*, Victoria Police, Melbourne.

Walker, N. 1991, *Why Punish?*, Oxford University Press, Oxford.

Washington Post 2001, 'Bush Signs Anti-Terrorism Legislation', 25 October 2001.   <http://www.washingtonpost.com/wp-srv/nation/specials/attacked/transcripts/bushtext_102601.html>.

Weisburd, D., Wheeler, S. and Waring, E. 1991, *Crimes of the Middle Classes: White Collar Offenders in the Federal Courts*, Yale University Press, New Haven.

Wenham, M. 2004, 'Child-sex trap snares first Net predator', *Courier Mail*, 15 January 2004: <http://www.couriermail.news.com.au/common/story_page/0,5936,8395589%255E421,00.html>.

Williams, M. 2001, 'The Language of Cybercrime', in Wall, D. S. (ed.), *Crime and the Internet*, Routledge, London, pp. 152–66.

Wilson, J. Q. and Boland, B. 1978, 'The Effect of the Police on Crime', *Law and Society Review*, vol. 12, no. 3, pp. 367–90.

Wingfield, N. and Baker, N. 2003, 'RIAA targets surprised by music-piracy lawsuits', *The Wall Street Journal Classroom Edition*: <http://wsjclassroom.com/onlinemusic/story04.htm>.

Young, D. 1986, *Translation of Beccaria's On Crime and Punishments*, Hackett Publishing Co., Indianapolis.

Zmontana, J. C. 2000, 'Viruses and the Law: Why the Law is Ineffective', *Information Management Journal*, vol. 34, no. 4, October 2000, p. 57.

APPENDIX A

Case Summaries 1972–2003

Cases are arranged chronologically by the date of the most recent court proceedings noted. URLs were operative at 31 March 2004.

[Case No. 1]

Jurisdiction / Date: USA, California, 1972
Sex / Age of Accused: Male, 26
Facts / Loss: Accused used a children's toy whistle to produce 2600-cycle tone in order to obtain free telephone calls from a telecommunications company. He was apprehended by the FBI making calls from San Jose to Sydney to listen to the Australian Top Ten.
Legal Proceedings: Accused was charged with telecommunications fraud.
Sentence / Outcome: Convicted and sentenced to two months imprisonment (Lompoc Federal Prison, California).
Reference: Clough and Mungo 1992, p. 25; Parker 1983, pp. 170–80; <http://www.webcrunchers.com/crunch/>

[Case No. 2]

Jurisdiction / Date: England, Leeds Crown Court (conviction 20 July 1983); Court of Appeal, Criminal Division (appeal decision 22 March 1984)
Sex / Age of Accused: Male, age unknown
Facts / Loss: Computer programmer opened bank accounts in Kuwait, programmed bank's computer to transfer funds into these accounts from dormant customer accounts, went to England, transferred the money to banks there and withdrew. The total transferred and withdrawn was approximately US$81,000.
Legal Proceedings: Accused was charged with six counts of obtaining property by deception under s. 15 of *Theft Act 1968*. He argued that the court had no jurisdiction, as conduct occurred in Kuwait, but the Court of Appeal held that the deception had occurred in England when he requested the funds be transferred, and he had taken control of the funds in England; therefore it could hear the case.
Sentence / Outcome: Convicted and appeal dismissed. Sentenced to 15 months imprisonment on each count, concurrent.
Reference: [1984] 1 WLR 962; [1984] Crim LR 427

[Case No. 3]

Jurisdiction / Date: Australia, High Court of Australia (on appeal from court of summary jurisdiction in Adelaide), 20 February 1986 (appeal)
Sex / Age of Accused: Male, age unknown
Facts / Loss: Accused closed his bank account but did not return his card, and then used it when the ATM was offline to withdraw A$200 (US$150) in cash. When offline the machine was incapable of determining whether the cardholder had any funds in his account.
Legal Proceedings: The accused was convicted of larceny contrary to s. 131 of the *Criminal Law Consolidation Act 1935* (SA), as amended. The accused argued that the bank had programmed the ATM to allow the withdrawal to take place, but the court held that this did not amount to consent to the transaction for a non-account holder. The accused had acted fraudulently with intent permanently to deprive the bank of the A$200.
Sentence / Outcome: Convicted of larceny and appeal dismissed.
Reference: (1986) 160 CLR 129

[Case No. 4]

Jurisdiction / Date: Supreme Court of Hong Kong (appellate jurisdiction), 20 March 1986 (appeal)
Sex / Age of Accused: Male, age unknown
Facts / Loss: Senior employee at Far East Bank stole a cheque from book of a customer, entered large amount, forged her signature and drew it on himself. He also tried to manipulate computers into crediting her account with a similar amount. The amount of the cheque was HK$3,980,000 (US$517,400). The amount to be credited to the customer's account by the computers was HK$4 million (US$520,000).
Legal Proceedings: Accused was charged with theft of a cheque, uttering a false document, and false accounting.
Sentence / Outcome: Accused pleaded guilty; he was sentenced to two years imprisonment on each of three charges, concurrent; these were suspended for two years on appeal as court was persuaded that this was not a genuine attempt to steal money but a grudge-based attempt to embarrass the bank. He was also ordered to pay HK$5000 (US$650) in costs to the Crown. He had a good history at the bank, no criminal record, but considered himself grossly overworked and had tendered his resignation due to that. There was 'not the slightest chance' of the scheme working and he must have known this as all large transactions are verified.
Reference: CACC 16/1986

[Case No. 5]

Jurisdiction / Date: Canada (and USA: Chicago, Illinois), 1987 (Canadian conviction)
Sex / Age of Accused: Female, 35
Facts / Loss: Accused was convicted in Canada of telecommunications fraud, served her sentence, then went to the USA where she was again convicted of operating a nationwide voice mail computer fraud scheme involving more than US$1.6 million in telephone calls and computer services from various companies.
Legal Proceedings: Accused was charged in Canada with telecommunications fraud involving organised criminality. Similar charges were filed in the US.
Sentence / Outcome: Canadian sentence: 90 days imprisonment with 2 years probation. US sentence: 27 months imprisonment (the sentence was at the time one of the most severe that had been imposed for computer crime).
Reference: Clough and Mungo 1992, pp. 148–55

[Case No. 6]

Jurisdiction / Date: Australia, Court of Criminal Appeal, Queensland, 3 April 1987 (appeal decision)
Sex / Age of Accused: Male, age unknown
Facts / Loss: Accused used his bank card to withdraw the equivalent of A$778.97 (US$584.23) from his savings account at an ATM, in excess of the existing credit balance of A$181.03 (US$135.77), when the ATM was offline and programmed to permit withdrawals of up to A$500 (US$375) per transaction.
Legal Proceedings: Conviction affirmed on appeal. Although the bank had programmed the ATM to allow the withdrawal to take place, it did not consent to withdrawals in excess of the credit balance.
Sentence / Outcome: No information other than conviction affirmed on appeal.
Reference: [1987] 2 Qd R 753

[Case No. 7]

Jurisdiction / Date: Australia, Queensland District Court at Brisbane, 13 March 1987 (convicted at trial); Supreme Court of Queensland, Court of Criminal Appeal, 3 July 1987 (appeal judgment)
Sex / Age of Accused: Male, age unknown
Facts / Loss: Accused paid forged cheques into an account and withdrew A$150 (US$112.50) from the bank's ATM while it was offline and programmed to allow withdrawals of up to A$500 (US$375), even though this would overdraw the account.
Legal Proceedings: Accused was charged with imposing on the Commonwealth by making untrue representations to obtain money, contrary to s. 29B *Crimes Act 1914* (Cth), a section then in effect. He was convicted on one count of receiving, one count of stealing, seven counts of forging, seven counts of uttering and seven counts of imposition. Appeal court affirmed the conviction, deciding that a false representation may be made to a machine by placing a card in an ATM even though this did not involve another person.
Sentence / Outcome: Convicted. Appeal dismissed.
Reference: [1988] 1 Qd R 537, 84 ALR 537

[Case No. 8]

Jurisdiction / Date: England, Crown Court at Southwark (trial), 24 May 1990 (convicted); Court of Appeal (Criminal Division), 4 February 1991 (appeal judgment)
Sex / Age of Accused: Male; 21 at the time of appeal
Facts / Loss: Hacker gained access to the Joint Academic Network, and altered data and passwords. He deleted some data and caused computers to crash.
Legal Proceedings: Accused was charged with damaging property contrary to s. 1(1) of the *Criminal Damage Act 1971* (UK). Defence tried to argue a distinction between the disk itself and the data on it, which was not capable of damage as defined by law. This was rejected.
Sentence / Outcome: Convicted and appeal dismissed. Held that if particles on disk were rearranged to devalue the disk by altering data, that would (and did) amount to damage. Sentenced to 12 months imprisonment, four to be served, eight suspended. Offender was the first in Britain to be sentenced to imprisonment for computer crimes.
Reference: [1991] 93 Cr App R 25

[Case No. 9]

Jurisdiction / Date: USA, District Court (Northern District, New York) (trial), 22 January 1990 (found guilty), 4 May 1990 (sentenced); US Court of Appeals, Second Circuit (appeal), 7 March 1991 (appeal judgment).

Sex / Age of Accused: Male, 23

Facts / Loss: The accused, a university student (now a professor), launched a worm program that infected more than 10 per cent of the Internet. The cost of repair was estimated at over US$100 million.

Legal Proceedings: This was the first prosecution under 18 USC §1030. The accused was convicted under 18 USC §1030(a)(5) of intentional access of 'federal interest computers' without authorisation, thereby preventing authorised access and causing a loss in excess of US$1000. He argued unsuccessfully (both at trial and appeal) that his access to computers was in excess of given authorisation rather than 'unauthorised' and that he did not have the requisite intent. There were no similar cases available at the time to guide sentencing, and it was thought that the total dollar value loss overstated the seriousness of the crime.

Sentence / Outcome: Sentenced to probation for three years and 400 hours community service, fined US$10,050 and ordered to pay the costs of his supervision at US$91 per month.

Reference: Trial unreported; 928 F 2d 504 (2nd Cir 1991)(appeal); <http://www.rbs2.com/morris.htm> and see <http://www.pdos.lcs.mit.edu/%7Ertm/>; appeal at <http://www.austlii.edu.au/au/other/crime/Morris.html>

[Case No. 10]

Jurisdiction / Date: England, Southwark Crown Court, 1992

Sex / Age of Accused: Male, age unknown

Facts / Loss: Accused installed a program on a printing company's computer that included a facility to prevent access without the use of a password, thereby denying the company access to its printing facilities for a number of days, resulting in a loss of US$64,800 worth of business and leading to the company's being wound up. Accused claimed that the company owed him fees equivalent to US$4095.

Legal Proceedings: Defendant pleaded guilty to computer offence under *Computer Misuse Act 1990*, s. 3.

Sentence / Outcome: Two years conditional discharge and a fine equivalent to US$2970. The court noted that the offender's conduct was at the lowest end of seriousness.

Reference: Napier 1994

[Case No. 11]

Jurisdiction / Date: England, 3–4 June 1990 (trial); 16 June 1992 (Court of Appeal, Criminal Division) (first prosecution under 1990 Act)

Sex / Age of Accused: Male, age unknown

Facts / Loss: The former employee of a locksmith business entered a 70 per cent discount on the computer when making a purchase, without the knowledge or permission of the sales assistant, resulting in a purchase worth £213.29 (US$383.92) rather than £710.96 (US$1,279.73).

Legal Proceedings: Accused was charged under ss. 1(1) and 2(1) of the *Computer Misuse Act 1990* (s. 1(1)(a) creates the offence of 'causing a computer to perform any function with intent to secure access to any program or data held in any computer'). He was charged with securing unauthorised access to computer (count 1) with intent to commit the offence of false accounting (count 2). At trial, the court determined no case to answer on count 1 and found the accused not guilty on count 2. The judge accepted the argument that under s. 1(1), the accused would have to gain access to one computer and use this to commit the offence against another computer. On appeal, the court held that only one computer need be involved.

Sentence / Outcome: Convicted.
Reference: (1991) 22 IPR 444 (trial); [1993] QB 94 (appeal)

[Case No. 12]

Jurisdiction / Date: USA, County of Tompkins, State of New York County Court, 4 September 1992 (pleas)
Sex / Age of Accused: Four males; first and second accused each aged 19
Facts / Loss: The first offender wrote a computer virus and created a false user account at his university which the other offenders used to release the virus. The virus was relatively benign, but caused computers to crash, leading to a potential loss of data.
Legal Proceedings: Each of the accused was charged with 12 counts of computer tampering in the first degree and attempted computer tampering in the second degree, and (in respect of the first offender) five counts of computer tampering, forgery and falsifying business records. The first and second defendants pleaded guilty to one count of second-degree computer tampering in exchange for dismissal of other charges.
Sentence / Outcome: First and second defendants were sentenced to pay restitution (US$6000 to the university and US$1365 to two other victims) as well as to 520 hours community service, forfeiture of their computers, and probation. All four students were either expelled from the university or suspended for at least 12 months.
Reference: Indictment No. 92-072-A; <http://www.rbs2.com/cvirus.htm#anchor-MBDF>

[Case No. 13]

Jurisdiction / Date: Australia, Victoria, Supreme Court of Victoria, 2 October 1992 (appeal)
Sex / Age of Accused: Male, age unknown
Facts / Loss: The accused, a computer programmer employed by a bank, entered instructions into the bank's computer system to take an ATM 'off host' which meant that it could dispense up to A$200 (US$150) even if the account from which it was drawn contained less than this amount. He used this method to overdraw his debit account. He also altered the computer to permit his debit card to be used on his credit card account.
Legal Proceedings: The accused was charged with 12 counts of obtaining property by deception (s. 81(1) *Crimes Act 1958* (Vic), 29 counts of computer trespass (s. 9A *Summary Offences Act 1966* (Vic), two counts of making a false document (s. 83A(1) *Crimes Act 1958*), and 20 counts of using a false document (s. 83A(2) *Crimes Act 1958*). In defence, he argued that he had some authority to gain access to the system for some lawful purposes. However, the court found that as an employee he was still as guilty as a hacker if he exceeded the limits of the permission given to him to enter the system.
Sentence / Outcome: Accused was convicted of the first two charges. However, in respect of the false document charges (which related to his credit card account), although his conduct put him within the bounds of those offences, the account had not been overdrawn and therefore there was no evidence that the accused had intended to cause the bank prejudice.
Reference: [1993] 1 VR 406

[Case No. 14]

Jurisdiction / Date: England, Liverpool Crown Court, June 1993
Sex / Age of Accused: Male, 21

Facts / Loss: The accused, who was a nurse, hacked into hospital computer systems to produce false prescriptions (for no apparent reason other than a fascination with computers). Some of the prescriptions he created could have caused serious harm if taken. Some were innocuous.

Legal Proceedings: There were two charges of unauthorised modification of computer material under s. 3 of the *Computer Misuse Act 1990* (UK).

Sentence / Outcome: The accused pleaded guilty and was sentenced to one year imprisonment. The sentence took into consideration a serious road accident a few years earlier, which was alleged to have changed his personality. He offered no reasons for amending the computer data, but said there was no malicious intent.

Reference: *Computer Fraud and Security Bulletin*, February 1994, p. 4

[Case No. 15]

Jurisdiction / Date: Australia, County Court of Victoria, 3 June 1993 (trial)

Sex / Age of Accused: Male, 20 when offences committed

Facts / Loss: Accused was hacking into computer networks.

Legal Proceedings: In defence, the accused argued that the offence was committed out of curiosity and for entertainment, for the ego boost of being able to do something that others cannot.

Sentence / Outcome: Six months good behaviour bond with surety of A$500 (US$375).

Reference: County Court of Victoria, 3 June 1993, Smith J (unreported)

[Case No. 16]

Jurisdiction / Date: USA, New York, Federal Court, 3 July 1993 (plea); November 1993 (sentenced)

Sex / Age of Accused: Male, 21 at date of plea

Facts / Loss: Accused inspired thousands of teenagers to study the internal workings of the United States national telephone system by phone phreaking. He broke into computers belonging to a telecommunications carrier by installing back door programs to allow him to re-enter at will, and by making other modifications that cost the company approximately US$370,000 to correct. He waited until a week before trial to plead.

Legal Proceedings: Accused pleaded guilty to two felony counts: one count of conspiracy and one count of unauthorised access to computers.

Sentence / Outcome: 12 months imprisonment (10 months minimum term) in Pennsylvania's Schuylkill Prison, three years probation, 600 hours community service.

Reference: <http://www.geocities.com/Vienna/4345/mark.htm>; also see Gabriel 1995 and <http://www.exhibitresearch.com/kevin/nyc/abene/>

[Case No. 17]

Jurisdiction / Date: USA, District Court for the District of Connecticut, 17 December 1993; United States Court of Appeals, 13 January 1995

Sex / Age of Accused: Three males, ages unknown

Facts / Loss: Accused constructed a fraudulent ATM which, when used with copied PINs, enabled funds to be withdrawn from accounts without authorisation. Accused made counterfeit cards and used them to steal more than US$107,000 from various accounts.

Legal Proceedings: All three defendants were charged on an indictment containing many bank-fraud related counts. The first accused pleaded guilty to one count of bank fraud, in violation of 18 USC §1344, and to one count of producing counterfeit ATM cards, in violation of 18 USC §1029(a)(1). The third accused admitted that he conspired with the first and second accused to use counterfeit access devices to transport a stolen ATM machine and to commit bank fraud, and he pleaded guilty to one conspiracy count that included these terms. The second accused pleaded guilty to similar offences.

Sentence / Outcome: First and second accused: Two and a half years imprisonment each (followed by four years of supervised release) with an order for compensation to be paid to the victims of US$464,000. Third accused: Five months imprisonment, followed by three years supervised probation, and fined US$2500. First and third accused appealed against their sentences with the appeal court remitting their cases for further adjudication.

Reference: Sentencing Transcript No. 3-93-cr-146 (D Conn December 17, 1993); US Court of Appeals 44 F 3d 1141 (1995); *Computer Fraud and Security Bulletin*, Vol. 2, 1994, p. 2

[Case No. 18]

Jurisdiction / Date: England, February 1994
Sex / Age of Accused: Three males, age unknown
Facts / Loss: The accused used a computer to imprint bank account details obtained from supermarket till rolls onto plastic cards to obtain ATM access. Scheme failed on two occasions when bank machines kept the cards because PINs failed to match.
Legal Proceedings: Sentence / Outcome: Convicted; first accused sentenced to nine months imprisonment; second accused to three months imprisonment; third accused to six months imprisonment.
Reference: *Computer Fraud and Security Bulletin*, Vol. 2, 1994, p. 2

[Case No. 19]

Jurisdiction / Date: Canada, Ontario Court (Provincial Division), 6 April 1995 (trial), 20 July 1995 (sentenced)
Sex / Age of Accused: Male, 19 at time of offence, 20 at time of sentence
Facts / Loss: The accused posted child pornography to bulletin boards from his home computer. Among the bulletin boards was one called 'Gateway', a major site for obscene pictures.
Legal Proceedings: This was the first Canadian conviction for distributing child pornography by computer. The accused was charged with one count of distributing obscene pictures and one count of distributing child pornography by using a computer to upload files to a bulletin board. The accused argued that neither distribution in fact (i.e. his identity as the uploader) nor distribution in law (i.e. uploading doesn't amount to distribution) had been proved. In mitigation he put forward his youth, his lack of a record, his peaceable though solitary nature and the fact that he had not acted out his fantasies. Also, he said he had some legitimate plans for the future. Aggravating factors included the following: (1) A psychiatrist identified the material as the sort that paedophiles might possess (the accused refused to submit to psychiatric examination); (2) the accused used photos of real children from catalogues, which he 'doctored'; (3) he kept a scrapbook of sexual assault stories; and (4) the accused had in writing indicated a clear intention to act out his fantasies. The court held that the defendant was guilty of distributing child pornography by uploading files onto a bulletin board from which members of the public who had access to the site could download them. He was, however, acquitted of distributing obscene pictures.

Sentence / Outcome: Defendant was sentenced to two years probation and 150 hours community service, and was ordered to seek psychological treatment, not to initiate communication with anyone under 16 years old, and not to download erotic material.
Reference: (1995) 22 OR (3d) 748. Sentencing decision at [1995] OJ No. 2238

[Case No. 20]

Jurisdiction / Date: Australia, Victoria, Melbourne County Court, 3 April 1995 (trial); Supreme Court of Victoria, Court of Appeal, 27 July 1995 (appeal)
Sex / Age of Accused: Two males, both 30 at sentence
Facts / Loss: The accused, English language students from China, electronically caused '0055' telephone information numbers to ring continuously. Thirty-five per cent of the cost of these calls went to the telecommunications company and 65 per cent to the service provider, and some of that 65 per cent went to the accused. They deflected US$125,250 of the telecommunications carrier's money to the service providers, who then paid a proportion (US$18,000) to the accused as information providers.
Legal Proceedings: The accused pleaded guilty to 12 counts each. Among the charges were dishonestly obtaining a financial advantage under s. 82(1) *Crimes Act 1958* (Vic); defrauding a telecommunications carrier of a charge by means of device under s. 85ZF(a) *Crimes Act 1914* (Cth); and a series of offences under the *Financial Transaction Reports Act 1988* (Cth). In mitigation it was accepted that neither accused had prior convictions, nor had been in any trouble with the law before; they had a shortage of funds and their culture and background did not allow them to ask friends for financial help; they were introduced to the scheme by a third party and their actual profit was very small; and they pleaded guilty at an early opportunity.
Sentence / Outcome: The accused were sentenced to three years imprisonment each with non-parole period of two years; reparation to be paid to the carrier of US$17,507.15 in total (not each). Appeal against this sentence was allowed as sentence was 'manifestly too high'; it was reduced to six months imprisonment with release after four months on 12 months good behaviour bond on payment of A$100 (US$75) recognisance.
Reference: [1995] 82 A Crim R 39

[Case No. 21]

Jurisdiction / Date: Canada, Court of Appeal for Ontario, 21 September 1995 (appeal)
Sex / Age of Accused: Male, 67 at time of offence, 68 at appeal
Facts / Loss: Accused was in possession of more than 300 images of child pornography, mostly photographs rather than digital images.
Legal Proceedings: He was charged with possession of child pornography under Criminal Code s. 163.1(4).
Sentence / Outcome: The defendant pleaded guilty and appealed against sentence. Eighteen months imprisonment imposed by trial judge was reduced to 10 months on appeal. Court noted that defendant was not engaged in production or distribution. He had no prior convictions and a good work record; a psychological report showed a low risk of criminal sexual behaviour, but possessors of such material provide impetus for its production and distribution.
Reference: (1995-09-25) ONCA c21877, available online at <http://www.canlii.org/on/cas/onca/1995/1995onca10294.html>

[Case No. 22]

Jurisdiction / Date: England, May 1995 (trial), November 1995 (sentenced)
Sex / Age of Accused: Male, 26

Facts / Loss: Defendant spread the Pathogen virus, which corrupted data on hard disk. Pathogen contained a second virus, Smeg, which hid it from antivirus software. It was released in the UK by uploading an infected file to a bulletin board. The Queeg virus was also disseminated. Prosecutor claimed that one victim had suffered loss of half a million pounds due to the viruses.

Legal Proceedings: Defendant was charged under ss. 2 and 3 of the *Computer Misuse Act 1990* (UK) with five counts of unauthorised access to computers to facilitate crime; five counts of unauthorised modification of software; one count of inciting others to spread virus.

Sentence / Outcome: Convicted and sentenced to 18 months imprisonment. Judge said: 'Those who seek to wreak mindless havoc on one of the vital tools of our age cannot expect lenient treatment.'

Reference: <http://www.f-secure.com/v-descs/smeg.shtml>; <http://www.rbs2.com/cvirus.htm>

[Case No. 23]

Jurisdiction / Date: Australia, Supreme Court of the Australian Capital Territory, 16 March 1995 (original sentence), 4 December 1995 (appeal)

Sex / Age of Accused: Male; 30 at sentence

Facts / Loss: The employee of a government department took tax file numbers of 30 persons with same surname as himself, and took files relating to the tax affairs of some companies in liquidation. It was routine for departmental employees to access computers like this, although there is a difference between doing so to relieve boredom and doing so for financial advantage or other nefarious purpose (he claimed to have checked salaries of friends to help his future choice of vocation).

Legal Proceedings: There were two charges of obtaining access to data stored in Commonwealth computer: s. 76B(2)(b)(v) of the *Crimes Act 1914* (Cth); and one charge of taking property out of possession of Commonwealth: s. 30.

Sentence / Outcome: Defendant pleaded guilty. Magistrate dismissed two charges and imposed a 12-month good behaviour bond of A$500 (US$375) without conviction in respect of the other charge. Prosecutor appealed against the leniency of the sentence. The magistrate's decision was set aside on appeal, conviction recorded on each of the three charges. Sentence was deferred on recognisance in same terms as the magistrate ordered. Court said that tax affairs should be private, and it is unacceptable for government employees to access information for their personal amusement and edification.

Reference: No. SC 191 of 1995, [1995] ACTSC 132

[Case No. 24]

Jurisdiction / Date: Australia, New South Wales Local Court (trial); New South Wales Court of Criminal Appeal, 15 December 1995 (appeal decision)

Sex / Age of Accused: Male, age unstated

Facts / Loss: The accused used his government workplace computer to grant relief from taxation to members of the public, without authority. His motivation was due to his concern about suggested inconsistencies in determinations of applications for taxation relief. He also had a heavy workload and wished to expedite the process. He derived no personal financial gain.

Legal Proceedings: The defendant pleaded guilty to 19 counts of intentionally and without authority or lawful excuse inserting data into a Commonwealth computer, contrary to s. 76 of the *Crimes Act 1914* (Cth). The case was stated to the Appeal Court to determine whether the accused's acts were carried out with authorisation. Court of Appeal decided that these acts were not authorised.

Sentence / Outcome: Remitted to District Court for sentencing
Reference: Case No. 60488 / 95, available online at <http://www.austlii.edu.au/au/cases/nsw/supreme_ct/unrep209.html>

[Case No. 25]

Jurisdiction / Date: USA (offences), Argentina (his residence); March 1996 (first charged)
Sex / Age of Accused: Male, 21 at trial
Facts / Loss: The accused used a personal computer and facilities of Telecom Argentina to obtain unauthorised access to accounts in a university computer system by installing a 'sniffer' program, which captured the user ID and passwords of legitimate university computer users. These accounts were then used to gain access to other computers belonging to government agencies, including military departments.
Legal Proceedings: The accused was first charged in USA with knowingly and with intent to defraud possessing fifteen or more unauthorised computer passwords, user identification names, codes and other access devices; the illegal interception of electronic communications; and fraudulent and destructive activity in connection with computers. He was unable to be extradited from Argentina because of lack of dual criminality under Argentinian law. He pleaded guilty to reduced charges and travelled to the United States voluntarily in May 1998, where he was convicted of unlawfully intercepting non-classified communications and damaging files on government agency computers. While he did not appear to have gained access to highly classified material, he viewed and copied sensitive data about radar technology and aircraft design. When his intrusions became apparent, the target agencies were required to spend substantial sums to re-secure their systems.
Sentence / Outcome: Fined US$5000 and sentenced to three years probation.
Reference: <http://www.wired.com/news/technology/0,1282,12416,00.html>

[Case No. 26]

Jurisdiction / Date: USA, District Court (Western District, Tennessee) (trial); USA Court of Appeals Sixth Circuit (appeal); 2 December 1994 (sentenced); 12 March 1996 (rehearing denied)
Sex / Age of Accused: First accused male, second accused female, both aged 38 at time of sentencing
Facts / Loss: The accused were transporting obscene materials interstate.
Legal Proceedings: Federal obscenity charges were brought, concerning the operation of a computer bulletin board business violating 18 USC §§1462 and 1465. The allegedly intangible form by which computer-generated images moved from defendants' computer bulletin board in one state to a personal computer in another state did not preclude prosecution under statute prohibiting interstate transportation of obscene materials. Evidence of defendants' operation of a computer bulletin board business that advertised and offered sexually explicit computer graphic files to its members supported conviction, despite defendants' spurious argument that they had no knowledge, intent or expectation that members would download and print images contained in files. They also unsuccessfully argued lack of jurisdiction, and that the GIF files never left their home and therefore they had a constitutional right to possess them in private.
Sentence / Outcome: Convicted. Appeal dismissed. First accused was sentenced to 37 months imprisonment, and the second accused to 30 months imprisonment.
Reference: 74 F 3d 701 (6th Cir. 1996); 1996 Fed App 0032P (6th Cir)

[Case No. 27]

Jurisdiction / Date: Canada, British Columbia Provincial Court Surrey, 28 June 1996
Sex / Age of Accused: One male aged 27; one female, age unknown but young
Facts / Loss: A young couple running an adult BBS (bulletin board system) held obscene material on a CD-ROM without personal knowledge.
Legal Proceedings: The judge concluded that even though the accused did not know the illegal material was present on the CD-ROM, it was there through their own negligence, and therefore they were guilty. A subsequent appeal was dismissed: the judge agreed that the offence was one of strict liability.
Sentence / Outcome: Convicted. Two years probation and fined Can$5000 (US$3750).
Reference: [1997] BCJ No. 40; (unreported appeal), 28 June 1996, BC Prov Court, Surrey

[Case No. 28]

Jurisdiction / Date: England, Bow Street Magistrates' Court, June 1995 (charged); July 1996 (trial)
Sex / Age of Accused: First accused: male, approximately 16 at time of offences and 19 at time of trial. Second accused: male, 19 at time of offences and 21 at time of trial.
Facts / Loss: Defendants gained unauthorised access to US Air Force computer systems, causing some 200 security breaches. Their conduct was described as a 'schoolboy prank'; however, US military officials said that the first named defendant caused more harm than the KGB and was 'the number one threat to US security'.
Legal Proceedings: Both pleaded guilty to 12 specimen offences under the *Computer Misuse Act 1990* (UK). Prosecution did not proceed with charges of conspiracy.
Sentence / Outcome: First accused was fined £1200 (US$2160) with £250 (US$450) costs.
Reference: <http://rf-web.tamu.edu/security/secguide/Spystory/Hacking.htm>; *USA Today*, 23 March 1996; *The Toronto Star*, 12 April 1998; *Sunday Times*, 30 March 1998

[Case No. 29]

Jurisdiction / Date: England, Crown Court at Birmingham, 24 May 1996 (trial); Court of Appeal (Criminal Division), 27 September 1996 (appeal decision)
Sex / Age of Accused: Two males, aged 25 (first accused) and 27 (second accused)
Facts / Loss: A total of 18 charges were brought, under the *Protection of Children Act 1978*, *Obscene Publications Act 1959*, and the *Criminal Justice and Public Order Act 1994*. The first accused stored child pornography on his computer and made it available to Internet users to whom he gave a password. The second accused was one such user.
Legal Proceedings: The first accused pleaded guilty to four counts of possession of indecent photographs, contrary to *Protection of Children Act* 1978 s. 1(1)(c) and one count of publishing obscene articles, contrary to *Obscene Publications Act 1959* s. 2(1). The second accused pleaded guilty to distributing indecent photographs, contrary to s. 1(1)(b) of the Protection of Children Act. The arguments raised on appeal that a computer disk was not a photograph for the purposes of the Act and that data were not 'distributed or shown' within the meaning of the Act were both rejected. Appeal dismissed.
Sentence / Outcome: First accused: three years imprisonment; second accused: six months imprisonment.
Reference: [1997] 1 Cr App R 244

[Case No. 30]

Jurisdiction / Date: USA, Boston, Massachusetts, 10 March 1997 (offences committed)
Sex / Age of Accused: Male, age unknown but young
Facts / Loss: The accused disabled a computer servicing an airport in Rutland, Massachusetts by hacking and caused loss of phone services to the nearby area from 9 a.m. to 3.30 p.m. He also hacked into a pharmacy computer, downloading prescription data in breach of privacy laws.
Legal Proceedings: The defendant pleaded guilty.
Sentence / Outcome: Two years probation, during which he was to have no possession of a modem, to pay restitution to the telephone company, and perform 250 hours community service. All computer equipment used in the commission of the offences was forfeited.
Reference: <http://www.usdoj.gov/criminal/cybercrime/cccases.html>

[Case No. 31]

Jurisdiction / Date: England (extradition proceedings including appeal to House of Lords re writ of habaeus corpus)/ USA, District Court (Southern District, New York) (charges laid); crimes committed in 1994; UK appeal hearing 19 June 1997
Sex / Age of Accused: Male, 25 at the time offences were committed
Facts / Loss: The Russian accused used a computer terminal in St Petersburg to gain unauthorised access to a bank in New Jersey, USA and made 40 transfers from customers' accounts to accounts in other countries, which he or his associates controlled.
Legal Proceedings: Officials waited to arrest the accused in the UK, as Russia had no extradition treaty with the US. He was then charged with US federal offences including wire fraud, bank fraud, and certain charges of misuse of computers.
Sentence / Outcome: The accused was committed to prison in the UK on 66 charges of theft, forgery, false accounting and computer misuse, with a view to extradition to the US, and pleaded guilty in the US once extradited. He was there sentenced to three years imprisonment.
Reference: [1997] 3 All ER 289; also see <http://www.parliament.the-stationery-office.co.uk/pa/ld199798/ldjudgmt/jd970619/levin.htm>

[Case No. 32]

Jurisdiction / Date: England, Birmingham Crown Court, February, June and July 1997
Sex / Age of Accused: Five males; first accused 23, second accused 20, third accused 22, fourth accused 20, fifth accused 22, when arrested and charged
Facts / Loss: Thirteen men obtained companies' bank details, forged letterheads and signatures and ordered the banks to pay monies into their accounts. These five were the organisers. The remaining eight allowed their accounts to be used to collect transfers. The total loss was equivalent to US$3,432,146.40.
Legal Proceedings: There was a range of offences including conspiracy and obtaining property by deception; 12 of the 13 pleaded guilty or were convicted.
Sentence / Outcome: Sentences ranged from three years imprisonment to a £1000 (US$1800) fine. A BMW car used in the fraud was confiscated as was £32,000 (US$57,600) belonging to one defendant, who was also ordered to pay £1000 in prosecution costs.
Reference: Serious Fraud Office (UK) Annual Report 1997–98; <http://www.sfo.gov.uk/publications/1997_1998/section_05.asp#spelling>

[Case No. 33]

Jurisdiction / Date: Hong Kong, Court of Appeal (original sentence in District Court), 25 September 1997 (appeal judgment)

Sex / Age of Accused: Male, age unknown

Facts / Loss: The accused was an IT fault engineer contracted to repair computers at four companies. He installed commands to delete the operating systems after certain periods of time. The loss to the company that owned the equipment and employed the repairman, based on the hours necessary to fix the problems, amounted to US$194,400.

Legal Proceedings: The accused pleaded guilty to three counts of criminal damage under s. 60(1) of the Crimes Ordinance, Cap. 200. The court said that the catastrophic result of the crime was obvious. In his defence the accused argued that he had a solid character, he stood to gain nothing from the crime, he had pleaded guilty, he had made an admission and cooperated fully when first apprehended, he had displayed remorse, and 'it was a practical joke'. Other mitigating factors raised included a dispute between the accused and his supervisor, and the fact that the accused was completely absorbed by computers, and had never had a girlfriend. The defence at trial said 'he had only ever held hands with a computer'. The accused appealed only against the sentence.

Sentence / Outcome: Convicted on each of the three counts in District Court and sentenced to two years and eight months imprisonment to be served concurrently. The sentence was reduced on appeal to one year and nine months, concurrent on each count, due to the accused's voluntary payment of restitution to one of the injured companies of HK$60,000 (US$7,800).

Reference: CACC000245/1997 – [1997] HKCA 419, 25 September 1997

[Case No. 34]

Jurisdiction / Date: England, Central Criminal Court, 19 November 1997 (convicted); 20 November 1997 (sentenced)

Sex / Age of Accused: Male, 53 when sentenced

Facts / Loss: The accused created false documents and accounts in respect of fictitious offshore companies in order to persuade the victim company's auditors that funds were being properly directed, rather than diverted into a loss-making company.

Legal Proceedings: The accused was convicted on three counts of false accounting, one count of conspiracy to defraud and one count of perverting the course of justice. The jury was unable to agree on one count of attempting to pervert the course of justice.

Sentence / Outcome: The defendant was sentenced to five and a half years imprisonment and ordered to pay £20,000 (US$36,000) to the Crown in respect of costs.

Reference: Serious Fraud Office (UK) Annual Report 1997–98: <http://www.sfo.gov.uk/publications/1997_1998/section_05.asp#spelling (1998)>

[Case No. 35]

Jurisdiction / Date: USA, District Court (Central District, California), 10 February 1998 (convicted)

Sex / Age of Accused: Male, 21 at conviction

Facts / Loss: This was arguably the first US federal case involving hate crime on the Internet. The accused sent threatening e-mail messages to 59 students with Asian-sounding names. The message read in part: 'I personally will make it my life career to find and kill every one of you personally.'

Legal Proceedings: The accused was charged with two counts of violation of civil rights under 18 USC §245(b)(2)(A). He said he had sent the messages as a prank. The prosecution argued that the accused blamed the success of Asian students for his academic failure (he had previously failed at the University of California).

Sentence / Outcome: Defendant was convicted on the first count. A mistrial was declared on the second count and the government did not proceed with the prosecution. He was sentenced to one year imprisonment followed by one year supervised release.

Reference: <http://www.fbi.gov/hq/cid/civilrights/hatecases.htm>; <http://www.nytimes.com/library/tech/98/10/cyber/articles/01e-mail.html>. Appeal: 195 F 3d 454 (9th Cir (Cal), 1999) (appeal dismissed)

[Case No. 36]

Jurisdiction / Date: Hong Kong, Court of First Instance of Hong Kong (Appellate Jurisdiction), 2 April 1998 (appeal judgment); October 1996 (offences committed)

Sex / Age of Accused: Male, 32

Facts / Loss: The accused published 19 pictures of child pornography on an 'erotic children' newsgroup.

Legal Proceedings: The accused was charged under s. 21(1)(a) of the Control of Obscene and Indecent Articles Ordinance, Cap. 390. The defence addressed the following questions: Did the material constitute an 'article' under the Ordinance? Had there been publication? And if so, was it to the public or to a section thereof? The main argument for the defence was the same on appeal as at trial: that the statute should not be applied to something outside its contemplation at the time it was created (a stream of electricity as a 'publication'). This argument was rejected by the court.

Sentence / Outcome: Convicted and given a suspended sentence. Appeal against sentence dismissed.

Reference: HCMA 000728/1997

[Case No. 37]

Jurisdiction / Date: Australia, Supreme Court of Victoria (Court of Appeal), 20 April 1998 (appeal)

Sex / Age of Accused: Female, 27 when offences committed (1995–96)

Facts / Loss: Employee of Department of Social Security inserted and altered data in the computers to cause payments to be made for her benefit, receiving A$16,312 (US$12,234) in benefits.

Legal Proceedings: Accused was charged with four counts of altering data stored in a Commonwealth computer without lawful authority or excuse and 20 counts of inserting data without lawful authority or excuse into a Commonwealth computer: s. 76C(a) *Crimes Act 1914* (Cth).

Sentence / Outcome: Accused pleaded guilty and was sentenced to 18 months imprisonment, but was released immediately on a A$500 (US$375) recognisance to be of good behaviour for four years. Judge took into account the early plea of guilty, the fact that the defendant had resigned from the Department and used her returned superannuation contributions to make restitution, the absence of prior convictions and her excellent work record, and the likely effect of imprisonment on her children. Appeal by DPP on the light sentence was rejected.

Reference: [1998] VICSC 48

[Case No. 38]

Jurisdiction / Date: Australia, Supreme Court of Victoria, Court of Appeal; 21 April 1998

Sex / Age of Accused: Male, 32 when offence committed, 35 when sentenced

Facts / Loss: Case involved computer fraud by a computer programmer engaged by a telecommunications company.

Legal Proceedings: This was an appeal from a sentence imposed in the County Court on 6 March 1998. The accused was charged with altering data under the *Crimes Act 1914* (Cth) ss. 16G, 76A, 76E(a) and with deception under the *Crimes Act 1958* (Vic), s. 81(1). He pleaded guilty. Mitigating factors included his plea of guilty and early indication of that plea, his young age and previous good character, the good prospects of rehabilitation, the delay in prosecution and his loss of career path. Losses involved invoices to the value of US$11,080.50 not issued, and various accounts of the telecommunications company's customers incorrectly credited to the value of US$4233.75. The fact that he was in a position of trust and not likely to be discovered was considered an aggravating factor.

Sentence / Outcome: Imprisonment for two and a half years with effective minimum term of 12 months, with A$500 (US$375) bond for 12 months and reparation equivalent to US$12,853.66. The appeal was dismissed.

Reference: Supreme Court of Victoria, Court of Appeal, 21 April 1998, No. 37 of 1998: <http://www.austlii.edu.au/au/cases/vic/VICSC/1998/57.html>

[Case No. 39]

Jurisdiction / Date: USA, North Carolina and Los Angeles (case eventually consolidated in LA); US District Court (Central District, California) (trial); US Court of Appeals, Ninth Circuit (appeal), 14 May 1998 (appeal)

Sex / Age of Accused: Male, 31 at arrest in 1995

Facts / Loss: The accused carried out various schemes to 'defraud and obtain property by false pretences' from a number of major corporations, using unauthorised access to the computers of software manufacturers and illegal copying of software from these sites (among many other things). Total loss was believed to be millions of dollars.

Legal Proceedings: The accused pleaded guilty in LA to seven counts under 18 USC §1029(a)(3) of possession of unauthorised access devices with intent to defraud, and to one count in North Carolina. The prosecution pointed out that the accused had been arrested four times for hacking during the 1980s and served a one-year prison term. He began hacking again in 1992, violating the terms of his probation. He fled on Christmas Eve 1992 and remained a fugitive until his 1995 capture.

Sentence / Outcome: In North Carolina the accused was sentenced to 22 months imprisonment: 14 months for violating the terms of his 1989 supervised release, and eight months for access device fraud committed in that state. In California he was sentenced to 46 months imprisonment, three years probation, and was given transactional immunity for all crimes he admitted to having committed between February 1992 and February 1995. He was also ordered to pay US$4125 in restitution and to assign to his victims any proceeds he might receive from selling the story of his conduct. The court's conditions of release, included as part of his sentence, specified that without prior express written approval of the probation officer, he was prohibited from possessing or using (personally or through third parties, and for any purpose) cell phones, computers, any computer software programs, computer peripherals or support equipment, personal information assistants, modems, anything capable of accessing computer networks, and any other electronic equipment, whether available then or in future, which could act as a computer system or access a computer system, network, or telecommunications network. In addition, the accused was prohibited from acting as a consultant or adviser to individuals or groups engaged in any computer-related activity. On appeal, he argued unsuccessfully that the restrictions were in violation of his First Amendment rights and were too stringent.

Reference: <http://www.usdoj.gov/criminal/cybercrime/usamarch2001_7.htm>;
145 F 3d 1342 (9th Cir (Cal), 1998) (unpublished disposition)

[Case No. 40]

Jurisdiction / Date: USA, Massachusetts; offences committed January–June 1998
Sex / Age of Accused: Male, age unknown
Facts / Loss: Proprietor of an online bookseller intercepted e-mail from another online retailer with a view to building knowledge of its customers' purchases and gaining a market advantage. No confidential financial information about customers was obtained or misused but the company copied thousands of e-mail messages to which it was not party. The accused was charged with 10 counts of unlawful interception of electronic messages and one count of unauthorised possession of passwords with intent to defraud.
Legal Proceedings: Proceedings were taken under the Wiretap Act, 18 USC §§2510–22.
Sentence / Outcome: Defendant agreed to pay a total fine of US$250,000 as part of a plea agreement.
Reference: <http://www.usdoj.gov/criminal/cybercrime/cccases.html>

[Case No. 41]

Jurisdiction / Date: USA, District Court, 31 July 1998 (sentenced); 11 January 2000 (Court of Appeal)
Sex / Age of Accused: Male, age unknown
Facts / Loss: Employees of a computer repair shop in Austin, Texas identified what appeared to be child pornography on the hard drive of a computer that the accused had brought to them for repair.
Legal Proceedings: The accused was charged with receipt of visual depictions of minors engaged in sexually explicit conduct contrary to 18 USC §2252(a)(2), and possession of visual depictions of sexual activities by minors contrary to 18 USC §2252A(a)(5)(B). He pleaded guilty to the possession charge and the other charge was dismissed. Accused had not actually abused any child or produced or distributed any child pornography (and had no inclination to do so). The argument that the search violated accused's Fourth Amendment rights was rejected on appeal.
Sentence / Outcome: District Court found total offence level to justify a possible incarceration range of 27–33 months. After considering the facts of the case, the court sentenced him to 12 months imprisonment, followed by three-year supervised release. Appeal allowed and case remitted for resentencing.
Reference: 200 F 3d 321 (5th Cir, 2000); <http://caselaw.lp.findlaw.com/scripts/getcase.pl?court=5th&navby=case&no=9850888CR0>

[Case No. 42]

Jurisdiction / Date: Australia, Supreme Court of Victoria, Court of Appeal, 1 December 1998 (appeal)
Sex / Age of Accused: Male, 34 at time of appeal
Facts / Loss: Defendant used desktop publishing equipment to produce false birth certificates, student ID cards and a driver's licence, then used them to open bank accounts, deposit 'wages' cheques and make withdrawals before they had cleared, and various other frauds. A total of US$31,072.50 was withdrawn from banks. The defendant also committed fraud on the revenue, as evidenced by 44 sales tax refund claims, paid out to the amount of US$343,787.25.

Legal Proceedings: Groups of 14 and 44 charges were brought, mainly defrauding and attempting to defraud the Commonwealth: s. 29D *Crimes Act 1914* (Cth).

Sentence / Outcome: Defendant pleaded guilty and was sentenced to five years imprisonment with non-parole period of three years. He was ordered to pay compensation amounting to US$30,975 and reparation amounting toUS$343,787.25 to the Commonwealth. Appeal on sentence dismissed.

Reference: [1998] VSCA 119

[Case No. 43]

Jurisdiction / Date: China, Shanghai; 1999 (sentence)

Sex / Age of Accused: Male, 28

Facts / Loss: Staff member at a securities company broke into the company's computer system and changed five transaction records, manipulating prices on the Shanghai Securities Exchange. This caused turnover of two stocks to increase drastically, and a direct loss equivalent to US$356,399.79.

Legal Proceedings: The defendant was convicted of hacking into the computer system and manipulating share prices.

Sentence / Outcome: Three years imprisonment and a fine equivalent to US$1208.13, and an order to pay US$355,200 compensation.

Reference: 'Computer hacker sentenced to three years in prison', *People's Daily Online*, 15 November 1999; see also <http://mishpat.net/cyberlaw/archive/informer35.shtml>

[Case No. 44]

Jurisdiction / Date: Hong Kong, Court of First Instance of Hong Kong (Appellate Jurisdiction), 15 January 1999 (appeal).

Sex / Age of Accused: Male, 29 at appeal

Facts / Loss: The accused, a hospital technical assistant, accessed the hospital computer, printed out an X-ray of the Secretary of Justice and faxed it to newspapers. He received no financial gain.

Legal Proceedings: The accused was charged with obtaining access to a computer with a view to dishonest gain contrary to s. 161(1)(c) of the Crimes Ordinance, Cap. 200. In defence the accused argued that he was not 'dishonest' and had made no gain. In mitigation he said (and the appeal court accepted) that he was merely trying to correct what he thought was a misrepresentation by the government to the public as to the Secretary's health. The court said that 'gain' includes information not available prior to computer access. Gaining access without authority was the same as gaining access in excess of authority. Aggravating factors were the breach of confidentiality and intrusion into the privacy of a patient. The accused had concealed his identity when faxing the newspapers and the inference could be drawn that he knew it was wrong. He was well-educated and this counted against him: he should have known it was dishonest.

Sentence / Outcome: Convicted and sentenced to six months imprisonment, reduced on appeal to 100 hours community service.

Reference: [1999] 2 HKC 547; HCMA 723/1998

[Case No. 45]

Jurisdiction / Date: Hong Kong, Court of First Instance (Appellate Jurisdiction), 31 July 1998 (original sentence); 9 February 1999 (appeal)

Sex / Age of Accused: Male, age unknown

Facts / Loss: This was a case of shoplifting: a few items were taken from a supermarket. **Legal Proceedings:** The accused was charged with theft contrary to s. 9 of the Theft Ordinance, Cap. 210. On appeal the point taken was whether computer-generated till records were admissible in evidence to show that the accused had not purchased the goods at that or another branch of the shop, but had stolen them. **Sentence / Outcome:** Convicted and appeal dismissed. The accused was fined HK$2000 (US$260) and required to pay costs of HK$3000 (US$390). **Reference:** HCMA 797/98

[Case No. 46]

Jurisdiction / Date: USA, District Court (District of Maine) (trial); 12 February 1999 (appeal decision) **Sex / Age of Accused:** Male, age unknown **Facts / Loss:** Defendant used his then girlfriend's computer to store and transmit images of child pornography. He testified at trial in his own defence but did not deny sending and receiving child pornography over the Internet. Instead, he argued that he had been sexually abused as a child and that his exchanges of such images on the Internet with other chat room participants were done in connection with his preparation of a serious book relating to child abuse. He said that he had written a small number of pages, albeit over a very long period, as part of this project. **Legal Proceedings:** The defendant was charged with possessing and transporting in interstate commerce computer graphic images of minors engaged in sexually explicit conduct, the production of which involved the use of minors engaged in such conduct: 18 USC §2252(a)(1). **Sentence / Outcome:** He was convicted and sentenced to 78 months imprisonment; appeal dismissed. The Court of Appeals held that: (1) the search warrant for computer equipment was not too broad, even though it did not restrict items to be seized to items related to the suspected crimes; (2) the search warrant authorised recovery of previously deleted information; and (3) the defendant was not entitled to downward adjustment for acceptance of responsibility. He had prior convictions. **Reference:** 168 F 3d 532 (1st Cir, 1999)

[Case No. 47]

Jurisdiction / Date: UK, England, Horseferry Road Magistrates Court, March 1999 **Sex / Age of Accused:** Male, 23 at sentence **Facts / Loss:** This was a case of cyberstalking: the accused, a computer programmer, sent his girlfriend threatening e-mail messages after she ended their two-year relationship. **Legal Proceedings:** The accused was charged and convicted of harassment by e-mail under the *Protection from Harassment Act 1997*, the first prosecution recorded under this Act. **Sentence / Outcome:** Two-year conditional discharge. **Reference:** *Guardian*, 16 October 1999; *Daily Telegraph*, 24 March 1999

[Case No. 48]

Jurisdiction / Date: Hong Kong, District Court (trial); Court of Appeal of Hong Kong, 17 March 1999 (appeal decision) **Sex / Age of Accused:** Male, age unknown; female co-accused, age unknown **Facts / Loss:** The male accused's girlfriend was a claims processor with an insurance company. She paid 43 false claims into the male accused's account, from which he made withdrawals equivalent to US$31,590, although the prosecution only proceeded in respect of US$19,500 – 23 of the 43 incidents.

Legal Proceedings: The male accused was charged with 23 counts of theft contrary to s. 9 of the Theft Ordinance (HK). He and his girlfriend were both convicted of 21 of the 23 counts. The male defendant's appeal was dismissed. At trial each defendant sought to lay blame on the other, with the female defendant arguing that she sometimes shared computers with colleagues and that someone else must have made the transfers from her computer. The male accused argued unsuccessfully on appeal that he had not acted dishonestly and had no knowledge of the transfers to his account. Appeal court found both defendants equally culpable.

Sentence / Outcome: Each defendant was sentenced to two and a half years imprisonment.

Reference: CACC 268/1998

[Case No. 49]

Jurisdiction / Date: USA, California, April 1999 (plea)

Sex / Age of Accused: Male, 50 at time of plea

Facts / Loss: On the Internet, the accused impersonated a woman who had rebuffed him and posted messages in a chat room, apparently from her, saying that she wanted to be raped. No physical harm was inflicted, but six men visited her house offering to rape her.

Legal Proceedings: The accused was charged with one count of stalking under Californian Penal Code s. 646(9); three counts of soliciting others to commit rape; and one count of using a computer network to execute an unlawful scheme. He pleaded guilty to the first four counts.

Sentence / Outcome: Six years imprisonment.

Reference: *New York Times*, 29 April 1999: <http://www.nytimes.com/library/tech/99/04/cyber/articles/29stalk.html>

[Case No. 50]

Jurisdiction / Date: Australia, New South Wales District Court (trial); Court of Criminal Appeal (appeal); 27 March 1998 (sentence); 15 April 1999 (appeal decision)

Sex / Age of Accused: Male; 26 at trial

Facts / Loss: Defendant was refused employment with an ISP in 1994 and took revenge by illegally accessing the network, obtaining credit card details of customers and disclosing them to journalists. He also altered the company's home page to indicate that security had been compromised. Some of the credit cards were used to make fraudulent purchases, although the total value was not high. The details of 1225 credit cards were published; the loss to the ISP in customers and contracts was estimated at US$1,500,000.

Legal Proceedings: The defendant was charged with eight counts of obtaining unlawful access to a computer and one count of unlawfully inserting data into a computer under s. 76 of the *Crimes Act 1914* (Cth).

Sentence / Outcome: Pleaded guilty and appeal on sentence dismissed; three years' imprisonment with 18 months suspended. Sentence took into account the fact that the offences were regarded as grave and the great potential for harm from this type of computer abuse, as well as the recognition that society is increasingly dependent on computers.

Reference: Unreported decision of New South Wales District Court (27 March 1998); [1999] NSWCCA 69 (15 April 1999): <http://www.austlii.edu.au/au/cases/nsw/NSWCCA/1999/69.html>

[Case No. 51]

Jurisdiction / Date: USA, District Court (Central District, California), January 1999 (plea); June 1999 (sentence)
Sex / Age of Accused: Male, 22 at sentence
Facts / Loss: The accused e-mailed death threats to Latinos in universities, government agencies, and corporations across the US.
Legal Proceedings: The accused pleaded guilty to seven misdemeanour counts of interfering with federally protected rights, namely threatening to use force against his victims with intent to intimidate or interfere with them because of their national origin or ethnic background.
Sentence / Outcome: Sentenced to two years imprisonment.
Reference: <http://www.usdoj.gov/usao/cac/pr/129.htm>; see also <http://www.wired.com/news/politics/0,1283,20470,00.html>

[Case No. 52]

Jurisdiction / Date: China, Hangzhou Province, 28 July 1999 (sentence)
Sex / Age of Accused: Male, age unknown
Facts / Loss: The accused sold a slightly modified version of company software.
Legal Proceedings: Accused was charged with piracy.
Sentence / Outcome: This was the first conviction for software piracy in China. The defendant was sentenced to four years imprisonment and fined an amount equivalent to US$2400 and ordered to pay US$33,600 in compensation.
Reference: *China Daily*, 29 July 1999; <http://www.wired.com/news/politics/0,1283,21003,00.html>

[Case No. 53]

Jurisdiction / Date: New Zealand, Christchurch District Court; August 1999
Sex / Age of Accused: Three males, aged 17, 18 and 19 at sentence
Facts / Loss: This was a case of fraud using the Internet. The accused collected and used credit card numbers stored at commercial sites that the victims had visited on the Internet.
Legal Proceedings: The accused were charged with a number of offences including attempting to obtain by false pretence, obtaining possession by false pretence, unlawfully being found in a building, and obtaining by dishonest means. Although the accused were limited in the things they could buy (for example, pizza), as they could not produce an actual card, there was the potential for a more extensive fraud using the same methods.
Sentence / Outcome: All three were convicted. Two were sentenced to 85 hours of community service and ordered to pay reparation equivalent to US$103.34 and US$652.33; the third was sentenced to 45 hours of community service.
Reference: Mills 1999: <http://idg.net.nz/webhome.nsf/ArchiveDate/E5F7561E32 6D0217CC25684C000D4FEA!OpenDocument>

[Case No. 54]

Jurisdiction / Date: UK, England, Bow Street Magistrates Court (first instance decision 11 June 1997); Divisional Court (first appeal 13 May 1998); House of Lords (second appeal, judgment 5 August 1999)
Sex / Age of Accused: Male, age unknown; female, age unknown
Facts / Loss: Male accused obtained account information concerning 189 accounts from an employee of a credit card company (the female accused), who was employed

as a credit analyst. The information was used to forge credit cards which were then used to make withdrawals from ATMs. The card issuer lost approximately US$1 million.

Legal Proceedings: Accused were charged with conspiring to commit offences in the United States which for the purposes of an extradition warrant corresponded with offences under the *Computer Misuse Act 1990* (UK), namely: (1) securing unauthorised access to a computer system with intent to commit theft; (2) securing unauthorised access to a computer system with intent to commit forgery; and (3) causing unauthorised modification to the contents of a computer system. The decision was upheld in the Divisional Court. Further appeal by the government to the House of Lords was upheld: access was unauthorised if the person accessing the data did not have authority to access the particular data in question, even if he or she had authority to access other data in the system.

Sentence / Outcome: Remitted to magistrate for reconsideration.

Reference: [2000] 2 AC 216

[Case No. 55]

Jurisdiction / Date: USA, District Court (Northern District, Texas), September 1999 (sentence)

Sex / Age of Accused: Two males, 32 and 30 at sentence

Facts / Loss: The accused hacked into computer systems, including government computers and those of credit agencies, illegally obtained long distance calling card numbers and sold them. Their ultimate goal was to own the telecommunications network from coast to coast. This is the first case in which government authorities successfully used a high-speed data wiretap in a criminal case, capturing the keystrokes of the hackers.

Legal Proceedings: The accused both pleaded guilty to criminal fraud and related activity in relation to access devices and computers in violation of 18 USC §§1029(a)(3) and 1030(a)(4).

Sentence / Outcome: First accused was sentenced to 41 months imprisonment. Second accused was sentenced to two years imprisonment. Each was ordered to pay US$10,000 to the victim corporations.

Reference: <http://www.usdoj.gov/criminal/cybercrime/phonmast.htm>; Minty 2002: <http://www.newsok.com/cgi-bin/show_article?ID=870312&TP=getarticle>

[Case No. 56]

Jurisdiction / Date: USA, District Court (Eastern District, Virginia), 7 September 1999 (guilty plea)

Sex / Age of Accused: Male, 19 when sentenced

Facts / Loss: The accused designed a program to identify computers on the Internet that were susceptible to attack and used it to damage various government websites. He also admitted that he had advised others on how to hack computers at the White House in May 1999. His conduct resulted in a government website being closed down for eight days. In mitigation, the accused claimed that he had not attacked some websites himself but only instructed others how to do so. He admitted that his incursions had caused damage exceeding US$40,000.

Legal Proceedings: The accused pleaded guilty.

Sentence / Outcome: 15 months imprisonment, three years supervised release and ordered to pay compensation of US$36,240.

Reference: <http://www.usdoj.gov/criminal/cybercrime/cccases.html>

[Case No. 57]

Jurisdiction / Date: Australia, New South Wales Court of Criminal Appeal, 9 September 1999 (appeal decision)
Sex / Age of Accused: Female, 49 when offence was committed
Facts / Loss: An employee of a government department used her workplace computer to transfer government funds amounting to US$147,236.25 to personal accounts she had created. When she admitted the crime to her partner she and her children were attacked by her partner and seriously injured; this was taken into consideration in sentencing.
Legal Proceedings: The accused pleaded guilty to defrauding the Commonwealth of Australia, contrary to s. 29D of the *Crimes Act 1914* (Cth).
Sentence / Outcome: Two years periodic detention. Crown appeal against leniency of sentence dismissed in view of the extraordinary post-offending circumstances of the assaults.
Reference: [1999] NSWCCA 285

[Case No. 58]

Jurisdiction / Date: England, Cambridge Crown Court (25 January 1999); Court of Appeal (10 November 1999)
Sex / Age of Accused: Male, age unknown
Facts / Loss: Accused downloaded photographs containing indecent images of young boys from the Internet and either printed them out or stored them on computer disks for his own personal use.
Legal Proceedings: The accused was charged with 12 counts of having made an indecent photograph (*Protection of Children Act 1978*, s. 1(1)(a)), and nine counts of possessing an indecent photograph of a child under the age of 16 years (*Criminal Justice Act 1988*, s. 160). The defence argued that downloading an image did not constitute making a photograph, but Court of Appeal rejected this, arguing that downloading images onto a disk or printing them out does equate to 'making'. In mitigation the accused raised good character, the absence of breach of trust, no evidence of risk to the public, and no further dissemination of the material.
Sentence / Outcome: Four months imprisonment for the 1978 Act offences and three months concurrent for the 1988 Act offences; reduced on appeal to a conditional discharge for 12 months on all counts.
Reference: [2000] 2 WLR 1083; [2000] 2 All ER 418; [2001] QB 88

[Case No. 59]

Jurisdiction / Date: China; December 1999 (sentence)
Sex / Age of Accused: Male, 36
Facts / Loss: China Democracy Party founder sent e-mail messages to exiled Chinese dissidents in the United States and accepted overseas funds to buy a computer, *inter alia.*
Legal Proceedings: He was prosecuted for subversion.
Sentence / Outcome: Convicted and sentenced to 11 years imprisonment.
Reference: Farley 1999; Eckholm 1999

[Case No. 60]

Jurisdiction / Date: USA, District Court (Northern District, Texas), February 1999 (indictment); December 1999 (plea)

Sex / Age of Accused: Male, 24

Facts / Loss: The accused trafficked in computer passwords stolen from an Internet company. The company lost US$90,000 as a result of his and others' use of these passwords. He also possessed 20 electronic serial numbers for mobile phones, one telephone calling card number and five credit card numbers.

Legal Proceedings: The accused pleaded guilty to charges of possession of unauthorised access devices under 18 USC §1029(a)(3).

Sentence / Outcome: Sentenced to 21 months imprisonment and ordered to pay a US$3000 fine, and also ordered to pay US$89,480 in restitution to the Internet company.

Reference: <http://www.usdoj.gov/criminal/cybercrime/cccases.html>

[Case No. 61]

Jurisdiction / Date: USA, District Court (Central District, California), 16 December 1999 (jury returned judgment on first trial)

Sex / Age of Accused: Male, 34 at the time offence was committed

Facts / Loss: The accused, the executive vice-president of a corporation, used an Internet chat room to engage in sexual correspondence with an agent who was pretending to be a 13-year-old girl, then travelled to LA to try to meet 'her'.

Legal Proceedings: There were three felony counts: (1) interstate travel (from the state of Washington to California) with intent to engage in criminal sexual activity with a minor, in violation of 18 USC §2423(b); (2) use of a facility of interstate commerce (the Internet) to attempt to induce a minor to engage in criminal sexual activity, in violation of 18 USC §2422(b); and (3) possession of child pornography (images on his laptop computer) in violation of 18 USC §2252A(a)(5)(B). After a mistrial, the accused pleaded guilty to interstate travel with intent to engage in criminal sexual activity. As part of the plea agreement, the two other charges were dropped. At the first trial, the accused's defence was based on the fact that he was addicted to the 'online fantasy' world of cyberspace, that he visited fantasy-based chat rooms to relieve stress, and that he assumed most people there were role-playing. The jury could not reach a verdict on the charge that he had attempted to have sex with a minor, thereby ascribing some credibility to this defence.

Sentence / Outcome: Sentenced to nine months home detention, a fine of US$20,000 and five years probation.

Reference: <http://www.usdoj.gov/usao/cac/pr/pr2000/050.htm>; <http://www.usdoj.gov/usao/cac/pr/203.htm>

[Case No. 62]

Jurisdiction / Date: USA, District Court (Western District, North Carolina), Charlotte, January–February 2000 (trial)

Sex / Age of Accused: Male, 39 at trial

Facts / Loss: A former employee installed a 'code' or 'logic' bomb in all hand-held computers used by the company's 2000 sales representatives, with a date trigger that caused them all to cease operation at a given time. Company's operations were down for several days and its direct loss as a result was more than US$100,000.

Legal Proceedings: The accused was charged under the federal *Computer Fraud and Abuse Act of 1986* with knowingly causing the transmission of a computer code that disrupted and damaged a protected computer.

Sentence / Outcome: Convicted and sentenced to 24 months imprisonment followed by three years supervised release. Ordered to pay US$154,879 restitution to employer and US$39,730 to another company.

Reference: <http://www.usdoj.gov/criminal/cybercrime/cccases.html>;   see Roberts 2000: <http://www.bizjournals.com/charlotte/stories/2000/06/19/focus1.html>

[Case No. 63]

Jurisdiction / Date: USA, District Court (Eastern District, Wisconsin), 4 January 2000 (guilty plea)

Sex / Age of Accused: Male, 19 when sentenced

Facts / Loss: The accused hacked into and damaged the United States Army's website. Public access to the site was restored within two hours.

Legal Proceedings: The accused pleaded guilty to intentionally gaining access to a protected computer and causing damage.

Sentence / Outcome: Six months imprisonment, three years supervised release and defendant ordered to pay restitution of US$8054.00

Reference: <http://www.usdoj.gov/criminal/cybercrime/cccases.html>; and see Suro 1999: <http://www.washingtonpost.com/wp-srv/national/daily/sept99/global 1.htm>

[Case No. 64]

Jurisdiction / Date: USA, New York, Oneida County Court (trial); Supreme Court, Appellate Division, Fourth Department, New York, 16 February 2000 (appeal decision)

Sex / Age of Accused: Male, age unknown

Facts / Loss: Computer repair technician located child pornography on the accused's computer, which the accused had sent in for repair.

Legal Proceedings: The accused was charged and convicted of two counts of possessing a sexual performance by a child contrary to Penal Law §263.16. Appeal court affirmed the conviction, holding that a computer graphic file was a photograph within the meaning of the statute prohibiting possession of a sexual performance by a child; that the defence of using obscene materials in scientific research did not apply to child pornography; and that the defence of justification based on mistake of law was not available to the defendant. The scientific defence was based on his position as a social worker specialising in treating sexually related disorders, while the defence of mistake of law was based on his belief that possession was legal as long as the material was not exhibited to an audience.

Sentence / Outcome: Five years probation, 550 hours community service, and a fine of US$1000. The sentence was affirmed by the Appellate Division.

Reference: 704 NYS 2d 426 (NY App Div 2000)

[Case No. 65]

Jurisdiction / Date: Court of Appeal of Hong Kong, 10 September 1998 (original sentences); 21 December 1999 (appeal against convictions); 7 March 2000 (appeal against sentences)

Sex / Age of Accused: Three males, ages unknown

Facts / Loss: The accused were engaged in production of false credit cards, using a computer program with 39,000 credit card numbers and a point-of-sale machine which could approve transactions on false cards. There were actual transactions of US$3.69 million plus potential losses of US$5000 for each of 3503 unused accounts (for MasterCard accounts alone).

Legal Proceedings: The accused were charged with conspiracy to commit forgery and possessing equipment for making false instruments (s. 76(1) of Crimes Ordinance,

Cap. 200), possessing false instruments (s. 75(1) and (2)), possessing a forged travel document (ss. 42(2)(c)(i) and (4) of Immigration Ordinance, Cap. 115), and contravening a condition of stay (s. 41).

Sentence / Outcome: First and third accused pleaded guilty at trial; the second pleaded not guilty, arguing that that his machines were from a legitimate business and that he knew nothing of the fraud conspiracy, but he was convicted. First accused was given six sentences totalling 10 years imprisonment, reduced to eight years and eight months on appeal; second accused was given three sentences totalling 12 years, reduced to 10 years on appeal; third accused was given three sentences totalling six years and six months, reduced to five years and ten months on appeal. In arguments against severity of the sentences, it was claimed that some of the sentences should have been concurrent instead of consecutive. This was accepted. However, the submissions in mitigation that the second accused's willingness to agree to much of the evidence shortened the trial, and that the second accused was now attempting to turn over a new leaf and lead a constructive life in the future, were rejected because of the seriousness of the crime.

Reference: CACC 475/1998

[Case No. 66]

Jurisdiction / Date: England, Bristol Magistrates' Court (trial); Queen's Bench Divisional Court, 27 May 1999; Court of Appeal, 8 March 2000

Sex / Age of Accused: Male, 36

Facts / Loss: Indecent photographs of children were downloaded from the Internet and discovered in a directory in the drive of the accused's computer, and in the cache of that and another computer. He had deliberately stored the photographs in the computer's directory, but those found in the caches had been automatically retained by the computer in a store of recently viewed documents.

Legal Proceedings: The accused was charged with making indecent photographs of children, contrary to *Protection of Children Act 1978*, s. 1(1)(a) and possessing indecent photographs of children, contrary to *Criminal Justice Act 1988*, s. 160(1). The magistrate ruled that there was no case to answer on the charges of making obscene images because this offence required some form of creation and this did not apply to data that had simply been stored. However, the accused was convicted of the strict liability offences under section 160(1), as he had de facto possession of the images in the cache and knowledge was irrelevant. He was found guilty of 10 counts of possessing a pornographic image of a child and fined £3000 (US$5400). The accused's appeal against the convictions for possession was allowed because it was not proved that he had the necessary knowledge of the existence and operation of caches. The Crown's appeal against the ruling on 'making' was allowed in part because under s. 1(1)(a) of the Protection of Children Act, 'to make' means 'to cause to exist, to produce by action, to bring about'. By section 7(2) of the Act, the meaning of 'indecent photograph' included a copy of an indecent photograph, and accordingly, the accused had made indecent photographs in the computer's directory when he knowingly copied them. The case would be remitted for conviction on those charges. However, the accused was properly acquitted of 'making' photographs in the caches, as he did not have the necessary intention.

Sentence / Outcome: Remitted to magistrate for conviction and sentencing on charges of making indecent photographs by copying them to a computer directory.

Reference: [2000] 2 Cr App R 248

[Case No. 67]

Jurisdiction / Date: England, Southwark Crown Court, Court of Appeal, 30 June 1999 (trial); 6 April 2000 (appeal)

Sex / Age of Accused: Male, 28

Facts / Loss: Accused had published an obscene article on the Internet.

Legal Proceedings: Defendant was charged under the *Obscene Publications Act 1959*, s. 2(1) with publishing obscene articles. He argued that because the website was in the USA, there was no publication in England; the argument was rejected.

Sentence / Outcome: 18 months imprisonment, suspended for 2 years.

Reference: Case available through Westlaw: 2000 WL491456 (No. 99/5233/Z3 CA (Crim Div))

[Case No. 68]

Jurisdiction / Date: USA, District Court (District of Maryland)(trial); US Court of Appeals Fourth Circuit, 13 April 2000 (appeal decision)

Sex / Age of Accused: Male, 53

Facts / Loss: The accused, an award-winning journalist, sent and received child pornography over the Internet.

Legal Proceedings: The accused was charged with six counts of transmitting child pornography over the Internet in violation of 18 USC §2252(a)(1) and nine counts of receiving child pornography over the Internet in violation of 18 USC §2252(a)(2) (the *Protection of Children Against Sexual Exploitation Act of 1977*). The accused conditionally pleaded guilty to one count of receiving child pornography and one count of transmitting child pornography. He argued that he was working on an article about Internet child pornography and was protected by the First Amendment. This defence was unsuccessful. The court had serious doubts about the truth of his defence. Furthermore, although the First Amendment protects 'news-gathering' activities, it does not confer a licence on either the reporter or his news sources to violate valid criminal laws. On appeal, the Court of Appeals affirmed the conviction, holding *inter alia* that the First Amendment did not permit a reporter to trade in child pornography in order to create a work of journalism.

Sentence / Outcome: Defendant was convicted and sentenced to 18 months imprisonment, three years supervised release, and fined US$4200.

Reference: Original finding: 11 F Supp 2d 656; 209 F 3d 338 (4th Cir, 2000)): <http://www.law.emory.edu/4circuit/dec99/994183.p.html>; also see Tridgell 2000; Washington City Paper: <http://www.washingtoncitypaper.com/archives/cover/1998/cover0807.html>

[Case No. 69]

Jurisdiction / Date: Singapore, Juvenile Court, May 2000

Sex / Age of Accused: Male, 15

Facts / Loss: The accused hacked into a computer in Singapore from Australia.

Legal Proceedings: The accused was charged with 16 counts of computer misuse. Defence raised youth as a mitigating factor, as well as the fact that no loss was suffered. The defendant pleaded guilty.

Sentence / Outcome: Fined equivalent of US$8990.

Reference: Tan 2000: <http://www.undcp.org/adhoc/palermo/convmain.html>

[Case No. 70]

Jurisdiction / Date: USA, Circuit Court for Winnebago County (trial); State of Wisconsin, Court of Appeals, 24 May 2000 (appeal)

Sex / Age of Accused: Male, age unknown

Facts / Loss: The accused was in possession of child pornography.

Legal Proceedings: The accused was charged with 19 counts of possession of child pornography on a computer. Difficult issues were raised about whether the warrant to search was properly obtained, as police had been searching the computer for evidence of another crime (online harassment) when they discovered the pornography. As soon as it was discovered, a second warrant was sought to search for more. The court ruled that this was acceptable as the original discovery was of files that were 'in plain view' and so didn't constitute a breach of Fourth Amendment privacy rights, even though files had to be opened before the pictures were in plain view.
Sentence / Outcome: Convicted on 18 counts.
Reference: 2000 WI App 128

[Case No. 71]

Jurisdiction / Date: Hong Kong, Court of Appeal (original sentence in District Court), 11 April 2000 (appeal judgment); 24 May 2000 (reasons for judgment)
Sex / Age of Accused: Two males, ages unknown
Facts / Loss: The accused produced and used a computer program designed to assist in taking bets on overseas football matches.
Legal Proceedings: The accused were charged with conspiracy to engage in book-making contrary to s. 159A of the Crimes Ordinance, Cap. 200 and s. 7 (1)(a) of the Gambling Ordinance, Cap. 148. On appeal, the accused argued unsuccessfully that the charge was bad for being duplicitous, as they were charged both with engaging and assisting in gambling.
Sentence / Outcome: Each accused was convicted and sentenced to two years imprisonment; appeal dismissed.
Reference: Trial: DCCC 1422/1998; appeal: CACC 000524A/1999

[Case No. 72]

Jurisdiction / Date: China, Hangzhou Province; May–August 1990 (offences committed); June 2000 (sentence)
Sex / Age of Accused: 36 at time of sentence
Facts / Loss: Accountant at the Bank of Communications of China counterfeited official bank documents and took money from people's accounts; about $US 200,000 was embezzled.
Legal Proceedings: The accused was charged with embezzlement.
Sentence / Outcome: Convicted and sentenced to death.
Reference: 'Chinese hacker sentenced to death for embezzlement', *People's Daily Online*, 13 June 2000

[Case No. 73]

Jurisdiction / Date: USA, District Court (Northern District, Oklahoma) (trial); United States Court of Appeals, Tenth Circuit, 20 July 2000 (appeal judgment)
Sex / Age of Accused: Male, age unknown
Facts / Loss: The accused, a participant in a gay and lesbian chat room, was reported to police after he sent two pornographic photographs of children to one of his chat room correspondents.
Legal Proceedings: The accused was charged with transporting child pornography through interstate commerce via computer (18 USC §2252(a)(1)). Appeal court held that the warrant which authorised the search of his computer for evidence of child pornography was not too broad and not in breach of the Fourth Amendment, which requires that a search warrant describe the things to be seized with sufficient

particularity to prevent a general exploratory rummaging in a person's belongings. The court also held that the normal rules governing search warrants apply to computers. Officers must take extra care, however, as there is a high likelihood that relevant and irrelevant documents will be mixed together on a computer.

Sentence / Outcome: Conviction affirmed, appeal dismissed.

Reference: 221 F 3d 1143 (10th Cir, 2000); appeal decision: <http://www.ci. keene.nh.us/police/campos.html>

[Case No. 74]

Jurisdiction / Date: Hong Kong, Court of Appeal (original sentence in District Court), 11 August 2000 (appeal judgment)

Sex / Age of Accused: Female, 50 at time of trial in 1999

Facts / Loss: The accused was a restaurant bookkeeper who regularly stole from the amounts she was required to bank, and used her own computer to produce false paying-in slips to make it appear that she had banked the full amount. The loss amounted to US$137,583.91.

Legal Proceedings: At trial, the accused pleaded not guilty to one count of stealing cash and 10 counts of using a false instrument contrary to s. 73 of the Crimes Ordinance, Cap. 200. She argued that she did not commit the crime and it must have been someone else, and that she was influenced to confess when interviewed by police with threats of trouble for her family. In mitigation, her previous clear record was cited, and reference was made to her elderly dependent husband. However, her grave breach of trust extending over a long period of time and involving large amounts of money was regarded as an aggravating factor.

Sentence / Outcome: Convicted at trial. Appeal against conviction and sentence dismissed. Sentenced to three years and four months imprisonment on the main theft charge and 30 months in total for the other 10 counts (three months each), to be served concurrently with the main prison term.

Reference: CACC 000095/2000 on appeal from DCCC 1074/1999

[Case No. 75]

Jurisdiction / Date: USA, District Court (Northern District of Texas), 6 September 2000 (plea)

Sex / Age of Accused: Male, 20 at time of plea

Facts / Loss: From 1997 to 1999 the accused was the leader of a famous hacking organisation. He stole teleconference services from telephone companies by hacking telephone numbers and PINs and using them to make unauthorised teleconferences among the members of the hacker organisation. Accused admitted that all of his hacking caused damage of between US$1.5 and 2.5 million.

Legal Proceedings: He was charged with conspiracy to commit telecommunications fraud and computer hacking contrary to 18 USC §§371, 1029(a)(2) and 1030(a)(5).

Sentence / Outcome: 26 months imprisonment, three years supervised release and ordered to pay US$154,529.86 restitution.

Reference: <http://www.usdoj.gov/criminal/cybercrime/cccases.html>

[Case No. 76]

Jurisdiction / Date: USA, District Court, Southern District, Florida, 21 September 2000 (sentenced)

Sex / Age of Accused: Male, 16 when sentenced

Facts / Loss: Between 23 August 1999 and 27 October 1999 the accused hacked into a United States military computer network and illegally obtained information. He intercepted more than 3300 electronic messages to and from agency staff, as well as passwords, and obtained agency software worth US$1.7 million. Agency computers were shut down for 21 days, with repairs costing US$41,000. He was the first juvenile hacker to be sentenced to detention in the United States.

Legal Proceedings: The accused pleaded guilty to two acts of juvenile delinquency, which under adult statutes, would have been violations of wiretap and computer abuse laws.

Sentence / Outcome: His youth was raised in mitigation. He was sentenced to six months detention in a juvenile facility, ordered to write letters of apology to the agencies in question and ordered to permit public disclosure of information about the case.

Reference: <http://www.usdoj.gov/criminal/cybercrime/comrade.htm>

[Case No. 77]

Jurisdiction / Date: Hong Kong, Court of First Instance of Hong Kong (Appellate Jurisdiction), 21 March 2000 (pleas in Magistrates Court); 9 October 2000 (appeal); 16 October 2000 (reasons given)

Sex / Age of Accused: Three males; first accused: 19 at sentence; third accused: 16 when offences were committed

Facts / Loss: The accused used 'back door' program to obtain lists of user names and passwords, dishonestly obtaining free ISP access and music piracy. Only small sums of money were involved (ISP fees were charged to the account holders, whose details the second accused had hacked).

Legal Proceedings: All three accused pleaded guilty to obtaining access to a computer with view to dishonest gain under Crimes Ordinance, s. 161 and criminal damage under Crimes Ordinance, s. 60; dealing with proceeds of indictable offence under Organised and Serious Crimes Ordinance, s. 25(1); and infringing copyright under Copyright Ordinance, ss. 118–119. On appeal against the sentences, it was argued in mitigation that the first accused was young, had a clean record, had pleaded guilty, came from a stable home, had shown remorse and was unlikely to reoffend; and that the third accused was young, from a stable family, and was studying at the Open University. However, the court took the view that much greater loss could have been caused by similar actions if bank account details had been hacked. The court said that for s. 161 breaches a custodial sentence would almost always be appropriate, and that breaking into a computer could be 'likened to burglary'. The court declined to lay down sentencing guidelines for computer crime as requested by the lower court, on the basis that fewer than ten prosecutions had proceeded under s. 161 and this was not enough to have explored all possible breaches of the section.

Sentence / Outcome: First and third accused were sentenced to be detained in a detention centre; second accused was sentenced to six months imprisonment. Appeal against sentences dismissed.

Reference: [2000] 3 HKC 744 HCMA 385/2000

[Case No. 78]

Jurisdiction / Date: USA, District Court (District of New Hampshire), 20 and 21 October 2000 (offences committed); June 2001 (sentenced)

Sex / Age of Accused: Male, 28 at sentence

Facts / Loss: The accused was dismissed from his employment and hacked into his former employer's computer system, deleting hundreds of files, sending e-mail to clients containing false information and causing other damage.

Legal Proceedings: The accused was charged with unauthorised computer intrusion under 18 USC §1030.

Sentence / Outcome: He was convicted and sentenced to six months imprisonment followed by two years supervised release, and ordered to pay US$13,614.11 in restitution. The accused was the first federal criminal defendant in New Hampshire to be sentenced to federal prison for computer hacking.

Reference: <http://nsi.org/SSWebSite/Samples/20jul01.html>

[Case No. 79]

Jurisdiction / Date: USA, District Court (Central District of California), November 2000

Sex / Age of Accused: Male, 20 when sentenced

Facts / Loss: The accused hacked into NASA and other computers, used stolen credit card account numbers to make purchases and telephone calls. He purchased US$6000 worth of electronic equipment fraudulently and caused US$17,000 worth of damage to NASA computers, and a further US$50,000 damage to the ISP.

Legal Proceedings: The accused was charged with unauthorised access and wire fraud.

Sentence / Outcome: Sentenced on hacking counts to 21 months imprisonment and ordered to pay restitution of US$87,736.29 to the victims; supervised release for three years with conditions imposed on his future computer usage.

Reference: <http://www.usdoj.gov/criminal/cybercrime/cccases.html>

[Case No. 80]

Jurisdiction / Date: USA; District Court (District of Dallas County, Texas), December 2000 (plea)

Sex / Age of Accused: Male, 18 at plea

Facts / Loss: The accused entered computer systems of UPS, State of Texas, Canadian Department of Defence and others, and deprived owners of use of the systems.

Legal Proceedings: There were six felony charges of breach of computer security and one felony charge of third degree aggravated theft.

Sentence / Outcome: Pleaded guilty; sentenced to two years imprisonment on each of the six computer charges and 10 years for the theft charge, all suspended. Placed on five years supervised probation and ordered to pay US$45,856.46 in restitution to the victims. As a condition of probation, the defendant was also required to obtain a high school diploma or graduate equivalency degree, submit to random urinalysis, and participate in community service. His use of computers was restricted.

Reference: <http://www.usdoj.gov/criminal/cybercrime/cccases.html>

[Case No. 81]

Jurisdiction / Date: USA, District Court (District of Alaska), 19 January 2001 (sentenced)

Sex / Age of Accused: Male, age unknown

Facts / Loss: A former systems administrator for the United States District Court in Alaska launched three denial-of-service attacks against the United States District Court for the Eastern District of New York. The accused overwhelmed the server with e-mail to prove that it was vulnerable to external attack.

Legal Proceedings: Accused was charged with interfering with a government-owned communications system. In mitigation, it was stated that the accused had paid US$5300 in restitution to the New York Federal Court system and others at the time of sentencing.

Sentence / Outcome: Six months imprisonment to be served by three months full-time in custody and three months home confinement, followed by one year of supervised release. Also ordered to perform 240 hours community service and to permit the authorities to monitor his computer activity.
Reference: <http://www.usdoj.gov/criminal/cybercrime/cccases.html>

[Case No. 82]

Jurisdiction / Date: USA, Michigan, 30 January 2001 (sentenced)
Sex / Age of Accused: Male, 21 when sentenced
Facts / Loss: The accused offered approximately 142 software programs for free downloading from his hacker website.
Legal Proceedings: The accused pleaded guilty on 12 October 2000 to copyright infringement of computer software. He provided copies of programs to 65,000 people but derived no personal gain and questioned the appropriateness of his prosecution.
Sentence / Outcome: Three years probation, including 180 days of monitored home confinement, restitution to software manufacturers, 40 hours community service, and a prohibition from engaging in Internet activity without the approval of the Probation Department. He was also ordered to notify all owners of computers he used during the period of his probation of the fact of his conviction.
Reference: United States Department of Justice 2001a

[Case No. 83]

Jurisdiction / Date: USA, District Court (Northern District of California), alleged offences committed 1999; pleaded guilty 29 January 2004
Sex / Age of Accused: Male, 24
Facts / Loss: The accused was charged with hacking into a telecommunications equipment manufacturer while a graduate student in 1999, and penetrating computers belonging to various IT companies. He was also charged with defacing the website of an online auction site. He argued that other hackers used his computer to commit the crimes.
Legal Proceedings: The defendant raised numerous arguments during bail proceedings, including challenging his indictment on the grounds that it spelled his name entirely in capital letters.
Sentence / Outcome: Pleaded guilty; awaiting sentencing.
Reference: <http://www.usdoj.gov/criminal/cybercrime/cccases.html>; <http://www.securityfocus.com/news/7959>

[Case No. 84]

Jurisdiction / Date: USA, District Court (Middle District, Florida), 15 May 2000 (offence committed); 20 March 2001 (plea)
Sex / Age of Accused: Male, 32 at plea
Facts / Loss: While an employee of a company, the defendant entered certain commands into three different multi-state network computers used in interstate commerce and communication by the company. These commands caused the computers to delete electronic information stored on their hard drives and prevented anyone from interfering with this destruction of data. The damage amounted to a cost to the company of at least US$209,000.
Legal Proceedings: The accused was charged with one count of intentionally damaging protected computers, in violation of 18 USC §1030(a)(5)(A).

Sentence / Outcome: Pleaded guilty; sentenced to five years probation, with a fine and/or restitution of US$233,000.
Reference: <http://www.usdoj.gov/criminal/cybercrime/cccases.html>

[Case No. 85]

Jurisdiction / Date: USA, District Court (Northern District, California), 21 March 2001 (plea)
Sex / Age of Accused: Male, age unknown
Facts / Loss: Shortly before leaving employment with a company, the accused burned CD copies of company proprietary information (about the company's products and developmental projects). He then went to work at a competitor company and copied the information onto the competitor's network. The information he obtained was valued at more than US$5000.
Legal Proceedings: The accused pleaded guilty to charges under 18 USC §§1030(a)(2)(C) and 1030(c)(2)(B)(iii) of exceeding authorised access to a protected computer.
Sentence / Outcome: Under a plea agreement, the accused received three years probation.
Reference: <www.usdoj.gov/criminal/cybercrime/cccases.html>; <http://www.nacic.gov/news/2001/jun01.html#a7>

[Case No. 86]

Jurisdiction / Date: New Zealand, Court of Appeal of New Zealand, 18 April–28 May 1998 (offences committed); 11 April 2001 (appeal judgment)
Sex / Age of Accused: Male, age unknown
Facts / Loss: The accused fraudulently used a computer program downloaded from the Internet (Scavenger) to evade billing for international telephone calls. Depending upon the time of day calls were made, the carrier's losses amounted to US$55,250–107,900.
Legal Proceedings: The accused was charged under the *Crimes Act 1961*, s. 229A with use of a document for pecuniary advantage with intent to defraud. The defence argued unsuccessfully that a computer program and/or a hard disk on which a computer program is recorded is not a document. The crime was committed shortly after the accused's arrival in New Zealand and the court said there was an inference that he arrived with intent to commit the crime.
Sentence / Outcome: The accused was sentenced to 12 months imprisonment on three counts concurrent, suspended for two years, and to six months periodic detention. The appeal was dismissed and conviction upheld.
Reference: [2001] NZCA 71 (11 April 2001); see Griffin 2001: <http://www.nzherald.co.nz/storydisplay.cfm?storyID=183417>

[Case No. 87]

Jurisdiction / Date: Australia, County Court of Victoria, sentenced 30 Oct 2000 (first accused) and 22 May 2001 (second accused)
Sex / Age of Accused: Two males aged 24 (first accused) and 39 (second accused) at time of sentencing
Facts / Loss: The accused sent three million spam e-mail messages and online information to addresses in Australia and the US (and possibly elsewhere) in order to manipulate the sharemarket in relation to a particular company. First accused made A$17,000 (US$12,750) profit, A$7000 (US$5250) of which he gave to second accused.

Shares in the targeted company fell from an opening price of 71 cents per share to a closing price of 31 cents per share. Resources had to be expended to investigate and deal with the spam problem. Some of the Internet addresses were blocked for a period of time. There was potential loss to investors, loss of investor confidence in the system and an adverse impact on the integrity of the stock market.

Legal Proceedings: Both accused pleaded guilty to two counts of making statements or disseminating information that was false or materially misleading and likely to induce the purchase of securities by other persons contrary to the Corporations Law; and to one count of interfering with, interrupting or obstructing the lawful use of a computer contrary to s. 76E of the *Crimes Act 1914* (Cth). In mitigation it was accepted that the accused cooperated with police in a lengthy record of interview, answered all questions and made admissions; pleaded guilty at what was, in effect, the first opportunity; had no prior convictions and good personal circumstances.

Sentence / Outcome: First accused: two years imprisonment on each of three counts (concurrent); 21 months suspended upon entering into a two-year good behaviour bond with a surety of A$500 (US$375); second accused: two years imprisonment, wholly suspended.

Reference: <http://www.countycourt.vic.gov.au/judgments/hourmouz.htm>; *The Age* (Melbourne) 23 May 2001

[Case No. 88]

Jurisdiction / Date: USA, District Court (Southern District, New York), 12 June 2001 (sentence)

Sex / Age of Accused: Male, 27 at sentence

Facts / Loss: The accused hacked the computers of a firm to obtain passwords and then used one of these to access another company's database and delete it. The deleted database cost the company US$60,000 to repair.

Legal Proceedings: This was the first federal computer hacking case that went to trial in the Southern District of New York. The accused was charged with computer hacking and electronic eavesdropping. The district judge determined that the accused's sentence should be increased because he used a specialist skill, his computer expertise, to commit his crime.

Sentence / Outcome: Convicted and sentenced to 27 months imprisonment, and ordered to pay restitution of US$96,385 to the victim company.

Reference: <http://www.usdoj.gov/criminal/cybercrime/cccases.html>

[Case No. 89]

Jurisdiction / Date: Hong Kong Court of Appeal, 20 June 2001 (appeal decision)

Sex / Age of Accused: Male, 23

Facts / Loss: The accused hacked into the e-mail accounts of two women living in a university dormitory and altered data, inserting sexual images and threatening rape. Accused submitted that the acts were carried out as a joke, but the victims were subjected to extreme fear and a serious invasion of their privacy.

Legal Proceedings: The accused pleaded guilty to two counts of criminal intimidation contrary to s. 24 Crimes Ordinance, Cap. 200, and eight counts of criminal damage contrary to s. 60(1).

Sentence / Outcome: Sentenced to 12 months imprisonment on each count of intimidation and four months imprisonment on each count of criminal damage, all concurrent. Appeal court indicated that there was 'much to commend the deterrent approach of the trial judge'.

Reference: [2001] HKCA 199 CACC 000083/2001; see also <http://edition.cnn.com/2001/BUSINESS/asia/04/20/hongkong.cyberstalking>

[Case No. 90]

Jurisdiction / Date: Hong Kong Court of Appeal (original sentence in District Court), 25 July 2000 (trial); 3 July 2001 (appeal)
Sex / Age of Accused: Three males, ages unknown
Facts / Loss: The first accused stole a cheque, changed the name on it and cashed it. His two co-defendants possessed a computer and software that could produce false credit cards. The second accused defrauded banks by altering cheques to show a fictional drawee and opening false bank accounts to cash them. The cheque that the first accused cashed was for HK$326.50 (US$42.45), altered to HK$110,000 (US$14,300). The second accused cashed five cheques varying from HK$4958 to HK$295,695 (US$644.73 to US$38,440.35).
Legal Proceedings: The accused faced 25 charges including charges of conspiracy to defraud, attempted theft and theft and, for the second and third accused, possession of equipment for making a false instrument contrary to s. 76(1) Crimes Ordinance, Cap. 200. On appeal, the third accused was found to have no 'control' over the machinery. There was a dispute over identification of the second accused at a parade, and the evidence against him was argued to be largely circumstantial. The defence argued that the first accused could not have 'conspired' with anyone else, as his alleged co-conspirator was fully exonerated at trial. This was a complex case in which the lawyers on appeal criticised the trial judge for not understanding the facts and for displaying confused reasoning, and the court criticised some of the lawyers on appeal for not being familiar with the papers and for being unable to respond adequately to questions.
Sentence / Outcome: All three accused were convicted at trial of one or more of the 25 charges. The conspiracy charge against the first accused was overturned on appeal, but he was sentenced to 18 months imprisonment concurrent with eight months for breach of a suspended sentence. The second accused was sentenced to four and a half years imprisonment. The third accused's single conviction was quashed on appeal.
Reference: Trial: DCCC 315/2000; appeal: CACC 317/2000

[Case No. 91]

Jurisdiction / Date: UK, Swansea Crown Court, Wales, 6 July 2001 (sentenced)
Sex / Age of Accused: Male, 17 at time of offending, 19 at time of sentencing
Facts / Loss: The accused gained unauthorised access to the Internet and obtained details of 23,000 credit card accounts. He claimed that he was authorised to gain access to the websites because they contained no warning that access was prohibited. The defence claimed that the accused had suffered serious physical and mental side effects due to a head injury. His conduct caused one company to close and caused huge financial damage.
Legal Proceedings: The accused pleaded guilty to two counts of obtaining services by deception after illegally accessing credit card details, and eight counts of unauthorised access to customer databases of companies in the US, Britain and Canada, as well as two counts of obtaining services by deception and two counts of obtaining computer equipment and other items worth US$2,518.20 by deception.
Sentence / Outcome: Three years' probation including a program of community rehabilitation.

Reference: <http://www.guardian.co.uk/internetnews/story/0,7369,517864,00.
html>; <http://www.guardian.co.uk/Archive/Article/0,4273,3978377,00.html>;
<http://www.fbi.gov/congress/congress03/farnan051503.htm>

[Case No. 92]

Jurisdiction / Date: UK, England, Court of Criminal Appeal, 9 June 1997 (offences
committed); 27 April 2000 (sentenced); 12 July 2001 (appeal decision)
Sex / Age of Accused: Male, age unknown
Facts / Loss: The accused offered to purchase videotapes containing child pornography and was charged before the videotapes were delivered. He claimed as a defence
that he could not incite because the videotapes had not been delivered. Offender
derived no financial gain.
Legal Proceedings: The accused pleaded guilty to incitement to distribute child
pornography contrary to s. 1 of the *Criminal Attempts Act 1981*. Defence appeal
dismissed.
Sentence / Outcome: Fined the equivalent of US$900 and ordered to pay equivalent
of $US977.40 in costs.
Reference: [2001] EWCA Crim 1684; [2001] Crim LR 822

[Case No. 93]

Jurisdiction / Date: UK, England, Southwark Crown Court, 12 August 2000 (offences
committed); 27 June 2001 (trial); Court of Appeal; 17 July 2001 (appeal)
Sex / Age of Accused: Male, 47 at appeal
Facts / Loss: A disgruntled former employee modified websites of his former
employer's clients, without authorisation. The total cost of repairs amounted to
US$16,200.
Legal Proceedings: The accused pleaded guilty to unauthorised modification of data
under s. 3 of the *Computer Misuse Act 1990*. The victim company had to carry out
considerable work to reinstate the websites and apologise to its clients. The defence
said that the 'amateurish' offences were spontaneous and committed in anger and
while drunk. No software was damaged and the correct information was restored using
backup systems. In mitigation, the accused had pleaded guilty, expressed remorse
and apologised, and was of previous good character. However, the court held that
the accused had taken advantage of his knowledge and his skill to exact unwarranted
revenge by causing inconvenience to the company, and this amounted to a breach of
trust warranting a custodial sentence.
Sentence / Outcome: Appeal against sentence dismissed. Sentenced to imprisonment
for nine months on each of three counts, to be served concurrently.
Reference: [2001] EWCA Crim 1720, [2002] 1 Cr App R(S) 86

[Case No. 94]

Jurisdiction / Date: USA, District Court (Central District, California), 29 Dec 2000
(plea); 6 August 2001 (sentenced)
Sex / Age of Accused: Male, 23 at time of offences, 24 at sentence
Facts / Loss: The accused created and distributed over the Internet a fictitious press
release concerning a particular company. The release, which was issued on 25 August
2000, falsely stated that the company's chief executive had resigned, that its earnings
were to be restated and that it was under investigation. The fraudulent release caused
the company's stock to plummet nearly US$61 per share in just 16 minutes, result-
ing in US$2.2 billion in lost market capitalisation and US$110 million in losses to

investors. The accused profited by more than US$240,000. The SEC described the losses resulting from the fraud as 'the single most devastating in the short history of the Internet'. In mitigation the accused said, 'It was not until I saw what some of these investors went through that I realised what I really did cause.'

Legal Proceedings: The accused pleaded guilty to two counts of securities fraud and one count of wire fraud.

Sentence / Outcome: Convicted and sentenced to 44 months imprisonment, disgorgement of all profits and interest in the amount of US$353,000; civil penalty of US$102,642.

Reference: CR-00-1002-DT, CD Cal (Calif, Los Angeles); Martinson 2001; Securities and Exchange Commission 2001

[Case No. 95]

Jurisdiction / Date: USA, District Court (Northern District, California), 20 August 2001 (pleas)

Sex / Age of Accused: Two males, 30 and 35

Facts / Loss: The accused were company accountants who exceeded their authorised access to the company's computer system in order to issue company stock to themselves, illegally. The stock issued was worth almost US$8 million.

Legal Proceedings: Each of the accused was charged with one count of computer fraud under 18 USC §1030(a)(4); one count of conspiracy to commit computer and wire fraud under 18 USC §371; and three counts of wire fraud under 18 USC §1343. Both pleaded guilty to the count of computer fraud.

Sentence / Outcome: Each accused was sentenced to 34 months imprisonment and three years supervised release. Restitution of US$7,868,637 was required. As part of the plea agreements they agreed to forfeiture of seized assets including stock already liquidated for over US$5 million, and agreed to pay the difference between the value of stock issued and the amount the government would receive from the sale of the seized assets.

Reference: <http://www.usdoj.gov/criminal/cybercrime/cccases.html>

[Case No. 96]

Jurisdiction / Date: USA, District Court (Southern District, Florida), Miami, Florida, June 1998 (offence committed); September 2001 (convicted)

Sex / Age of Accused: Male, age unknown

Facts / Loss: Employee used confidential passwords to place computer virus in four US locations of a company. The virus disabled the victim company's computer system for several days and cost the company over US$75,000.

Legal Proceedings: The accused was charged under 18 USC §1030 with knowingly sending a computer virus to cause damage to computers used in interstate commerce.

Sentence / Outcome: He was found guilty of two counts of deliberately infecting the computer systems of his former employer.

Reference: <http://www.niscc.gov.uk/Monthly/NM_APR02.pdf>; <http://pub.bna.com/eclr/00434.htm>

[Case No. 97]

Jurisdiction / Date: New Zealand, District Court of New Plymouth (trial); Court of Appeal of New Zealand, 4 September 2001 (appeal judgment)

Sex / Age of Accused: Male, age unknown

Facts / Loss: The accused was charged with stealing computer equipment from his employer and deleting a program he was employed to develop. By way of mitigation, the defendant claimed to have taken the computer to work on it during his holiday and that the deleted program was redundant. He also claimed that he was owed overtime by his employer and was entitled to withhold the equipment as security. The laptop computer and the program on a disk had been buried in a remote location; the defendant refused to reveal their whereabouts and had checked into hotels using a false name in order to avoid arrest. The victim company suffered no loss, although its reputation and financial viability had been placed at risk.

Legal Proceedings: The accused was convicted of theft and wilful damage. Conviction was upheld on appeal but sentence varied.

Sentence / Outcome: Six months periodic detention and a fine of NZ$10,000 (US$6500), of which NZ$8000 (US$5200) was to be paid to his employer, and an order for payment of reparation of NZ$5000 (US$3250) to the managing director of his employer. On appeal, the NZ$8000 was ordered not to be paid to the employer but to the Crown, as s. 28(2)(b) of the *Criminal Justice Act 1985* does not allow compensation to be paid to a victim unless there is physical or emotional harm.

Reference: [2001] NZCA 269: <http://www.austlii.edu.au/nz/cases/NZCA/2001/269.html>

[Case No. 98]

Jurisdiction / Date: USA, District Court (Southern District, New York), 5 September 2001 (sentenced)

Sex / Age of Accused: Male, 20 at sentence

Facts / Loss: Among other things, the accused broke into two computers owned and maintained by NASA in California, and used one of those computers to host an Internet chat room devoted to hacking. He also intercepted user names and passwords traversing the computer networks of a computer owned by San Jose State University. In the chat room discussions, the accused invited other participants to visit a website which enabled them to view pornographic images, and he earned 18 cents from an unidentified company for each visit a person made to that website. According to the complaint, the accused earned approximately US$300–400 per week from this activity.

Legal Proceedings: The accused was charged with possession of stolen passwords and user names which he used to gain free Internet access, or to gain unauthorised access to still more computers, and with possessing stolen credit card numbers.

Sentence / Outcome: Pleaded guilty; sentenced to four months imprisonment and four months' home confinement; also ordered to pay US$4400 in restitution to NASA.

Reference: <http://www.usdoj.gov/criminal/cybercrime/cccases.html>

[Case No. 99]

Jurisdiction / Date: USA, District Court (District of Maryland), 24 July 2001 (plea); 24 September 2001 (sentenced)

Sex / Age of Accused: Male, 19

Facts / Loss: The accused was a systems administrator for a company acting as a subcontractor to the Internal Revenue Service. He placed destructive code on three servers at the IRS's computer centre prior to his dismissal.

Legal Proceedings: The accused pleaded guilty to intentionally causing damage to a protected computer.

Sentence / Outcome: Sentenced to 15 months imprisonment and fined US$109,000.

Reference: <http://www.usdoj.gov/criminal/cybercrime/cccases.html>; <http://www.gcn.com/vol1_no1/daily-updates/17454-1.html>

[Case No. 100]

Jurisdiction / Date: Netherlands; 11 February 2001 (offence committed); 27 September 2001 (sentenced)
Sex / Age of Accused: Male, 20 when offence committed
Facts / Loss: The accused created and disseminated a computer worm embedded in a picture of a famous tennis player, which sent the infected e-mail to every address in Outlook address books. The worm was relatively benign, as it did not delete any files from host computers.
Legal Proceedings: Charge not known.
Sentence / Outcome: Convicted and sentenced to 150 hours community service. One of the reasons for the light sentence was difficulty in obtaining proof of estimated loss. Businesses were reluctant to admit they were infected. This was the first conviction of a virus creator in the Netherlands.
Reference: Evers 2002: <http://www.pcworld.com/news/article/0,aid,106443,00. asp>; <http://www.rbs2.com/cvirus.htm#anchor111499>; <http://www.sophos. com/virusinfo/articles/koursentence.html>; <http://www.sophos.com/virusinfo/ articles/kourtrial.html>

[Case No. 101]

Jurisdiction / Date: Australia, District Court Queensland, November 2001 (sentenced); 10 May 2002 (appeal)
Sex / Age of Accused: Male, 49 when sentenced
Facts / Loss: During March and April 2000, the accused made 46 attempts to hack into a local council's computerised waste management system following the loss of his job at the plant. To sabotage the system he set the software on his laptop to identify itself as 'Pumping Station 4', then suppressed all the alarms. During the attack he had command of 300 supervisory control and data acquisition nodes governing sewage and drinking water. The attack caused millions of litres of raw sewage to spill into local rivers and parks, killing marine life and causing offensive smells.
Legal Proceedings: The accused was charged with 30 counts of unauthorised access to computer and was convicted following jury trial. Convictions on two counts were set aside on appeal, with no change to sentence.
Sentence / Outcome: Two years imprisonment.
Reference: *SC Magazine* 2001, vol. 4, no. 12, p. 10; <http://www.abc.net.au/ worldtoday/s406755.htm>; appeal: [2002] QCA 164

[Case No. 102]

Jurisdiction / Date: USA, District Court, Ohio, Northern District, 14 September 2001 (plea); 26 November 2001 (sentenced)
Sex / Age of Accused: Female, 30 when sentenced
Facts / Loss: The accused logged on to her employer's computer system remotely, using a colleague's user name and password without authorisation, and changed the password of the Chief Information Officer so that he no longer had access. Her employer had to check the system to determine whether anything else had been changed, and whether she had improperly obtained any data.
Legal Proceedings: The accused pleaded guilty to one count of computer fraud under 18 USC §1030(a)(5)(A).
Sentence / Outcome: Three years probation, with a special condition that the first seven months be served in home confinement with electronic monitoring. She was also ordered to pay compensation of US$15,346.71 to the victim firm.

Reference: <http://www.usdoj.gov/criminal/cybercrime/cccases.html>

[Case No. 103]

Jurisdiction / Date: USA, District Court (Eastern District, California), Sacramento, August 2001 (plea); 30 November 2001 (sentenced)
Sex / Age of Accused: Female; 21 at sentence
Facts / Loss: A bank employee accessed computers to get customer account information to give to friend who was starting a real estate business. Unknown to her, the information was also used by imposters who would take on the identity of the clients. There was no loss to customers, as all funds were federally insured.
Legal Proceedings: The accused was charged with obtaining unauthorised computer access to confidential customer information from a financial institution, in violation of 18 USC §§2, 1030(a)(2)(A), 1030(c)(2)(B)(i) and 1030(c)(2)(B)(iii).
Sentence / Outcome: Pleaded guilty; sentenced to 36 months probation.
Reference: <http://www.usdoj.gov/criminal/cybercrime/cccases.html>

[Case No. 104]

Jurisdiction / Date: USA, District Court (District of Columbia), Washington, 2001.
Sex / Age of Accused: Male, 44 at time of plea
Facts / Loss: The accused hacked several times into the Federal Court's computers, downloading millions of pages of data and avoiding fees of at least US$5000. The Administrative Office of US Courts estimated that it incurred expenses of at least US$40,000 for detection and repair.
Legal Proceedings: The accused pleaded guilty to one felony count of fraud in connection with computers, under 18 USC §1030(a)(2)(B).
Sentence / Outcome: Unknown.
Reference: <http:www.usdoj.gov/criminal/cybercrime/cccases.html>

[Case No. 105]

Jurisdiction / Date: USA, District Court (Southern District of New York), 13 December 2001 (complaint filed)
Sex / Age of Accused: Male, 17
Facts / Loss: The accused created a website and Internet bulletin board that promised a 'guaranteed' return to investors of between 125 per cent and 2500 per cent within specified periods of time ranging from three days to several weeks. The accused allegedly obtained US$900,000 from more than 1000 investors during a six-week period.
Legal Proceedings: The accused pleaded guilty to a prosecution by the Securities and Exchange Commission.
Sentence / Outcome: Consent order to repay US$900,000 to the defrauded investors.
Reference: AFP 2002; <http://www.usatoday.com/tech/news/2002/02/14/net-scammers.htm>

[Case No. 106]

Jurisdiction / Date: Hong Kong, Court of Appeal (original sentence in District Court), 22 December 2000 (trial); 11 December 2001 (appeal)
Sex / Age of Accused: Two males, ages unknown
Facts / Loss: First accused was an oil dispatcher for a large retailer that bought and sold oil. He was employed by the second accused. Someone at the retail company

fraudulently obtained oil from the supplier oil company without payment. The first accused authorised this and deleted evidence from the oil company's computer to disguise the dishonest transactions. The second accused was alleged to have caused requisition order forms with previously used numbers to be used, which enabled the deception to take place. The value of the oil stolen exceeded US$442,000.

Legal Proceedings: The accused faced 28 charges of theft. This was reduced to nine charges at trial. Both accused were convicted at first instance. The first accused's appeal was dismissed; the second accused's appeal was allowed. In defence, first accused argued that sometimes his user name was not logged on when transactions took place (although there was evidence that the prior user often failed to log off), and that door swipe records were unreliable as to who was in the room. Second accused argued that the case against him was wholly circumstantial. Evidence of first accused's good character was called in mitigation.

Sentence / Outcome: First accused convicted; appeal against conviction dismissed; remitted for sentencing. Second accused's appeal against conviction allowed; conviction quashed.

Reference: CACC 10/2001

[Case No. 107]

Jurisdiction / Date: USA, District Court (District of Connecticut), 13 December 2001 (sentence)

Sex / Age of Accused: Male, 32

Facts / Loss: The accused hacked into a company's computers, cracked passwords and stole computer equipment from the company. The company's loss amounted to over US$198,000. This included US$21,500 for stolen computer equipment and expenditure by the company of over US$176,000 to conduct a damage assessment and restore the network.

Legal Proceedings: The accused pleaded guilty to charges of interstate transportation of stolen property and computer intrusion.

Sentence / Outcome: He was sentenced to 12 months and one day's imprisonment, followed by three years supervised release, and required to pay restitution of US$198,458.31 to the victim company.

Reference: <http://www.usdoj.gov/criminal/cybercrime/cccases.html>; Bernardo 2001

[Case No. 108]

Jurisdiction / Date: USA, District Court (Northern District, California), 18 January 2002 (plea)

Sex / Age of Accused: Male, 34

Facts / Loss: The accused gained access to a company's computer and sent e-mail to 30,000 employees, purportedly from one of the other employees, containing insulting statements. This caused damage to the company of more than US$25,000.

Legal Proceedings: The accused was charged with three counts: unauthorised access to a computer recklessly causing damage (count 1); unauthorised access to a computer causing damage (count 2); and using a telecommunications device in interstate communications with intent to harass (count 3) under 18 USC §1030 and 47 USC §223.

Sentence / Outcome: The accused pleaded guilty to count 2. Sentencing details unavailable.

Reference: <http://www.usdoj.gov/criminal/cybercrime/cccases.html>

[Case No. 109]

Jurisdiction / Date: USA, District Court (Southern District of New York), 27 September 2001 (plea); 30 January 2002 (sentenced)
Sex / Age of Accused: Male, 28 when sentenced
Facts / Loss: The accused, a paralegal at a law firm representing one of the plaintiffs in a class action suit against a tobacco company, devised a scheme to sell his firm's trial plan to opposing counsel (actually an FBI agent) for US$2 million.
Legal Proceedings: The accused pleaded guilty to conspiracy to commit wire fraud, to transport stolen property interstate and to access a computer without authorisation.
Sentence / Outcome: Two years and six months imprisonment
Reference: <http://www.usdoj.gov/criminal/cybercrime/cccases.html>

[Case No. 110]

Jurisdiction / Date: USA, District Court (District of New Jersey), Newark, Plea entered 1 March 2002
Sex / Age of Accused: Male, 36 at plea
Facts / Loss: Government agents installed key-logging software on accused's computer to discover the password used to open a file which was found to contain incriminating evidence. The accused argued that as the computer was attached to a modem, the government was therefore intercepting 'communications' and should have obtained a wiretap order under 18 USC §2510. The court eventually rejected this argument.
Legal Proceedings: The accused pleaded guilty to loan-sharking and racketeering offences.
Sentence / Outcome: Defendant had multiple prior serious convictions. He was sentenced to 33 months imprisonment.
Reference: Criminal Action No. 00–404 (DNJ); <http://www.epic.org/crypto/scarfo/opinion.html> (Defence application to suppress evidence of the key-logging program); see also: <http://www.infoworld.com/articles/hn/xml/02/01/04/020104hncapture.xml>; <http://www.philly.com/mld/inquirer/news/local/2769774.htm>; <http://www.nytimes.com/2001/07/30/technology/30TAP.html?ex=997533714&ei=1&en=de6e97c1b31add5a>; <http://www.stratford.edu/techtalknews/techtalk070602newsletter.html>

[Case No. 111]

Jurisdiction / Date: USA, District Court (Northern District, Ohio), 7 August 2001 (both indicted); 9 October 2001 (first accused's plea); 21 November 2001 (second accused's plea); 8 January 2002 (first accused sentenced); 13 February 2002 (second accused sentenced)
Sex / Age of Accused: Male, 32 at sentence (first accused) and female, 26 at sentence (second accused)
Facts / Loss: While employed by Chase Financial Corporation, they knowingly and with the intent to further a scheme to defraud the company, gained access to Chase computer systems without authorisation or in excess of their authorised access. They thereby obtained credit card numbers and other customer account information pertaining to approximately 68 accounts, which they were not authorised to access in connection with their duties at Chase. They admitted that the aggregate credit limits for the targeted accounts totalled approximately US$580,700.00. They transmitted the information via fax to one or more individuals in Georgia, who in turn fraudulently used it to obtain goods and services valued at approximately US$99,636.08.
Legal Proceedings: Each was charged with two counts of computer fraud, under 18 USC §§1030(a)(4) and 1030(a)(2)(A).

Sentence / Outcome: Both pleaded guilty; 12 months and 1 day imprisonment each.
Reference: <http://www.usdoj.gov/criminal/cybercrime/cccases.html>

[Case No. 112]

Jurisdiction / Date: USA, District Court (District of New Jersey), 9 May 2000 (conviction); 26 February 2002 (sentence)
Sex / Age of Accused: Male, 39 at sentence
Facts / Loss: The accused, a computer network administrator whose employment was terminated after 11 years, intentionally caused irreparable damage to the company's computers by activating a 'Trojan horse' that permanently deleted all of its sophisticated manufacturing software programs. This resulted in a loss to the company of at least US$10 million in lost sales and future contracts.
Legal Proceedings: The accused was charged with fraud and related activities in connection with computers (count 1) and transporting approximately US$50,000 worth of computer equipment from the employer to his residence (count 2). At the time of conviction the case was believed to be one of the most expensive computer sabotage cases in US Secret Service history.
Sentence / Outcome: Convicted on count 1, but found not guilty on count 2 and sentenced to 41 months imprisonment.
Reference: <http://www.usdoj.gov/criminal/cybercrime/njtime.htm>

[Case No. 113]

Jurisdiction / Date: UK, Southwark Crown Court (trial), October 2000 (convicted); November 2000 (sentenced); Court of Appeal (Criminal Division), March 2002 (appeal)
Sex / Age of Accused: Male, age unknown
Facts / Loss: The accused published on the Internet gay pornography involving consenting adults. The material appeared on a US-based website, which is deemed lawful by US authorities and which is still online.
Legal Proceedings: The accused was charged with publishing an obscene article under the *Obscene Publications Act 1959* (UK). The argument that because the website was based in the US there was no jurisdiction was rejected at trial and on appeal. Nor was it a defence that only the investigating officer was proved to have seen the pictures – it was enough that the public might have seen them. Defendant also argued a European Convention on Human Rights (ECHR) ground of appeal that his freedom of expression was curtailed, but this was also rejected.
Sentence / Outcome: Defendant was convicted of publishing the less explicit 'preview' images, which can be accessed without charge. He was not convicted of publishing the hard-core, pay-to-view images. He was convicted on the basis that his company controlled the website and he was therefore liable for its content. He was sentenced to 30 months imprisonment. The accused was the first person convicted in Britain for publishing obscene material on the Internet.
Reference: [2002] EWCA Crim 747 (appeal judgment); <http://www.bailii.org/cgi-bin/markup.cgi?doc=/ew/cases/EWCA/Crim/2002/747.html&query=perrin&method=all>; Oliver 2000: <http://www.guardian.co.uk/internetnews/story/0,7369,393646,00.html>

[Case No. 114]

Jurisdiction / Date: China, March 2002
Sex / Age of Accused: No information

Facts / Loss: The accused fraudulently leased telephone trunk lines from state-owned telecommunications company, then billed customers in the United States for Internet-routed calls to Vietnam. During one week in 2001 he stole US$634,800 worth of services.

Legal Proceedings: The accused was convicted.

Sentence / Outcome: 11 years imprisonment

Reference: 'Web Expert Jailed for Phone Scam', *South China Morning Post,* 7 March 2002, p. 8

[Case No. 115]

Jurisdiction / Date: UK, England; first accused: Lewes Crown Court, December 2000 (trial); second accused: Luton Crown Court; October 2001 (trial); Court of Appeal; 7 March 2002 (appeal for both accused)

Sex / Age of Accused: Both male, age unknown

Facts / Loss: First accused received an image as an e-mail attachment. Second accused downloaded images from the Internet.

Legal Proceedings: First accused had asked for the offending picture to be e-mailed to him; second accused had more than 30 years of experience with computers so would have known that images viewed on the Internet are saved in the temporary cache. First accused was charged with making an indecent photograph or pseudo-photograph of a child under *Protection of Children Act 1978,* s 1(1). He argued that he had not 'made' a photo by simply receiving the file and not deleting it. This argument was rejected at trial and on appeal. Appeal court stated that receiving unsolicited e-mail might not give rise to liability if deleted immediately. Second accused argued that the images he had downloaded were stored only in a temporary cache, and although he viewed them he did not intend to look at them again. Appeal court ruled that viewing the images (and the process of an auto download into a cache) constituted 'making'.

Sentence / Outcome: First accused was convicted at trial and appeal dismissed; second accused pleaded guilty to seven counts of 'making' at trial and appeal dismissed. First accused: two years probation. Second accused: concurrent sentences of 12 months imprisonment.

Reference: 2002 EWCA Crim 683 (No. 2001/00251/Y1)

[Case No. 116]

Jurisdiction / Date: USA, District Court (Southern District, New York), 31 October 2001 (plea); 27 March 2002 (sentence)

Sex / Age of Accused: Male, age unknown

Facts / Loss: The accused was dismissed from his post at an insurance firm after allegations of harassment from a woman who rebuffed his advances. He then entered the computer system without authorisation, using a password belonging to another employee, and deleted files relating to employee compensation, as well as altering the female employee's compensation record. As a result, the employer was required to expend thousands of dollars making the system secure against future abuse.

Legal Proceedings: The accused was charged with accessing a protected computer without authorisation and deleting approximately 950 files. The judge increased the sentence because of the breach of trust by the accused: his employer had given him passwords to which other employees were not privy.

Sentence / Outcome: The accused pleaded guilty and was sentenced to 18 months imprisonment and payment of US$91,814.68 in compensation to the employer.

Reference: <http://www.usdoj.gov/criminal/cybercrime/cccases.html>

[Case No. 117]

Jurisdiction / Date: Court of Appeal of Hong Kong (original sentence in District Court); 8 June 2001 (trial); 23 April 2002 (appeal)
Sex / Age of Accused: Male, 21
Facts / Loss: A range of illegal conduct was involved, including stolen mail and possession of false and stolen credit cards as well as a computer which could alter information on credit cards. The court was prepared to take the 'potential for future loss' as a sentencing guideline rather than actual loss: there was no indication of how much actual loss there was.
Legal Proceedings: The accused was charged with 17 charges of theft under the Theft Ordinance; two charges of possession of identity card relating to another person under Registration of Persons Ordinance, s. 7(A)(1A); four charges of forgery under Crimes Ordinance, s. 71; two charges of possessing equipment for making a false instrument, Crimes Ordinance, s. 76(1).
Sentence / Outcome: The accused pleaded guilty to all 25 charges and was sentenced to four years imprisonment. He appealed against the sentence on grounds of trauma when his parents divorced, and requested a discount for guilty plea. The appeal was dismissed: the defendant had two previous convictions, one for a similar offence (using a forged credit card); he was actively engaged in producing false cards; it was his own enterprise; it was a planned and sophisticated operation; and the court stated that while no actual international dimension had been found, there was clearly the potential for that.
Reference: CACC 516/2001

[Case No. 118]

Jurisdiction / Date: USA, Court of Appeals, Second Circuit, May 2002 (appeal)
Sex / Age of Accused: Male, age unknown
Facts / Loss: The evidence showed that the defendant had used his home computer to trade child pornography with others over the Internet, and that he had collected more than 1000 images of child pornography that he stored on his computer and disks at home.
Legal Proceedings: The accused was charged with receiving child pornography over the Internet in violation of 18 USC §2252(a)(2)(A).
Sentence / Outcome: The defendant pleaded guilty. Under the Sentencing Guidelines, he was sentenced to 121 months imprisonment (the low end of the guidelines), plus three years supervised release. The District Court had imposed several special conditions of supervised release that would bind him for the three-year period after he was released from prison; among them was a requirement that he not 'access a computer, the Internet, or bulletin board systems at any time, unless approved by the probation officer'. The defendant appealed against this condition, arguing that it was not 'reasonably related' to the goals of punishment, and involved greater deprivation of liberty that is reasonably necessary. On appeal the Second Circuit agreed that the 'no computers' restriction in the sentence was too onerous.
Reference: 298 F 3d, 122 (2d Cir, 2002)

[Case No. 119]

Jurisdiction / Date: Canada; Ontario Arbitration Board, May 2002 (judgment)
Sex / Age of Accused: Male, 49 at arbitration
Facts / Loss: This was a civil case: an employment law arbitration between the union representing a professor who was dismissed for accessing child pornography on college computers, and the college that dismissed him.

Legal Proceedings: The accused pleaded guilty to possessing child pornography in contravention of s. 163.1(4) of the Criminal Code of Canada. He was given a suspended sentence and placed on probation for two years. One of the conditions of that probation was that he not use the Internet on any computer at any time. The union argued in the employment arbitration that the professor's difficult personal circumstances led him to suffer from a mental disorder that had manifested itself in the form of pathological Internet use. This mental disorder, according to the union, could be considered a disability under Ontario's Human Rights Code, imposing upon the employer a duty to provide some form of assistance.

Sentence / Outcome: It was held in the arbitration that the college was entitled to dismiss him, although his long, unblemished service with the college and his difficult home circumstances were taken into account.

Reference: Local 560, 109 LAC (4th) 334, File No. MPA/Y200927 (2002); Decision at <http://www.lancasterhouse.com/decisions/2002/may/carter-seneca.pdf>

[Case No. 120]

Jurisdiction / Date: USA, District Court (District of New Jersey), Newark, 26 March 1999 (offence committed); 9 December 1999 (plea); 1 May 2002 (sentence)

Sex / Age of Accused: Male; 35 at sentence

Facts / Loss: The accused created a computer virus which was designed to infect macros in documents used by the Microsoft Word 97 and Word 2000 programs. Macro viruses were not new; they had been known since 1995. The innovative feature of the virus was that it propagated by e-mailing itself to the first fifty addresses in the victim's Microsoft Outlook e-mail address book. This feature allowed the virus to propagate faster than any previous virus. The virus arrived in each new victim's in-box disguised as e-mail from someone known to him or her. It caused US$80 million worth of damage to computers worldwide.

Legal Proceedings: The accused was charged with fraudulent activity connected with computers, under 18 USC §1030(a)(5)(A).

Sentence / Outcome: Defendant pleaded guilty. He was sentenced to 20 months imprisonment, ordered to pay to the United States a special assessment of US$100 and a fine of US$5000. He was also sentenced to three years supervised release with 100 hours of community service, with the stipulation that 'the defendant shall not possess, procure, purchase or otherwise obtain access to any form of computer network, bulletin board, Internet, or exchange format involving computers unless specifically approved by the US Probation Office'. Because the defendant helped the FBI to investigate several major international hackers, the judge reduced his sentence.

Reference: Case Number 22:99-CR-730-01; see also *The Australian*, 23 September 2003; <http://www.sophos.com/virusinfo/articles/melissa2.html>; <http://www. sophos.com/virusinfo/articles/melissa3.html>; Standler (2002).

[Case No. 121]

Jurisdiction / Date: Australia, New South Wales District Court (trial); New South Wales Court of Criminal Appeal, 16 May 2002 (appeal decision)

Sex / Age of Accused: Male, age unknown

Facts / Loss: The defendant worked at a government benefit agency and issued Electronic Benefit Transfer cards. He used his user name and password to withdraw cash from ATMs with those cards. During some of the withdrawals he was at work, and it was argued that his user name had not been inactive long enough for him to have got to the bank to use the card. This argument was rejected by the trial judge. A total of US$15,142.50 was withdrawn illegally.

Legal Proceedings: Accused was charged with 40 counts of imposing upon the Commonwealth by an untrue representation: *Crimes Act 1914* (Cth), s. 29B.

Sentence / Outcome: He was convicted on 36 of the 40 counts, and sentenced to three years and nine months imprisonment with non-parole period of two years and six months, and issued a reparation order amounting to US$15,142.50 in favour of the Commonwealth. The course of criminal conduct was carried out over four and a half months, which would have required planning and involved serious breaches of trust. Appeal against conviction was dismissed, but appeal on sentence was allowed as the trial judge had exceeded the maximum permissible. However, the court simply recalculated the various terms of imprisonment to come up with exactly the same overall sentence.

Reference: (2002) 130 A Crim R 24; [2002] NSWCCA 149; [2002] ACL Rep 130 NSW 270 (16 May 2002): <http://www.austlii.edu.au/au/cases/nsw/NSWCCA/2002/149.html>

[Case No. 122]

Jurisdiction / Date: USA, District Court (Eastern District, California), 1 March 2002 (plea); 17 May 2002 (sentence)

Sex / Age of Accused: Male, 26 at sentence

Facts / Loss: The accused obtained confidential customer credit card information from an associate who was an employee of a credit union, and used it to make telephone and Internet bookings for airlines and hotels. Fraudulent purchases totalled more than US$116,000. No customers lost any funds, as all funds were federally insured.

Legal Proceedings: The accused pleaded guilty to three felony counts including wire fraud, conspiracy to obtain unauthorised computer access to customer account information from a financial institution, and credit card fraud.

Sentence / Outcome: He was sentenced to 27 months' imprisonment followed by three years' supervised release, and required to pay restitution of US$116,869.30.

Reference: <http://www.usdoj.gov/criminal/cybercrime/cccases.html>

[Case No. 123]

Jurisdiction / Date: USA, District Court (District of New York), 1 July 2003 (trial of first accused); England, Bow Street Magistrates Court (extradition hearing); Queen's Bench (Divisional Court) (appeal); 18 May 2002 (extradition decision); 20 March 2002 (appeal decision)

Sex / Age of Accused: Both male; first accused 29 at time of sentence in New York; second accused 39 at time of sentence

Facts / Loss: The accused hacked into computer system of news and financial information provider and demanded, via e-mail, US$200,000 not to disclose that the system had been compromised.

Legal Proceedings: The accused were prosecuted on four charges of blackmail, two charges of conspiracy: one to obtain unauthorised access to a company's computer and one to cause unauthorised modification of data therein: s. 3 of the *Computer Misuse Act 1990* (UK). Defence tried to argue that the s. 3(2)(c) offence applied to a computer that was impaired such that it no longer recorded information that had been input, and that they had simply input info which was untrue (bogus e-mail), which the computer recorded.

Sentence / Outcome: Convicted (and extradited to USA) and appeal dismissed. If a computer was caused to record information that showed it was from one person when in fact it was from another, that affected its reliability. (The first accused had made his demands via an e-mail message which purported to come from a password holder in the system, when it did not.) The first accused was sentenced to 51 months imprisonment in New York. Charges were not proceeded with in the USA against the second accused.

Reference: [2002] 2 Cr App R 33; <http://www.usdoj.gov/criminal/cybercrime/cccases.html>

[Case No. 124]

Jurisdiction / Date: Court of First Instance of Hong Kong (Appellate Jurisdiction), March 2002 (trial); June 2002 (appeal)
Sex / Age of Accused: Male; 24 at date of appeal hearing
Facts / Loss: Defendant recorded the ISP details of a computer brought to his shop for repair, and used them on his own computer to incur Internet charges of HK$286.81 (US$37.28) on the account of one of the ISP's customers.
Legal Proceedings: Defendant pleaded guilty to obtaining access to computer with dishonest intent to cause loss to another, contrary to s. 161(1)(d) of the Crimes Ordinance, Cap. 200.
Sentence / Outcome: Detention sentence order. Although the defendant was a first-time offender with a job and stable family, he had breached customer's trust. The sentence also took into account deterrence value. Appeal against sentence dismissed.
Reference: HCMA 000450/2002

[Case No. 125]

Jurisdiction / Date: USA, District Court (Northern District, Illinois), 14 June 2002 (sentence)
Sex / Age of Accused: Male, 32
Facts / Loss: The accused was charged with piracy and conspiracy to commit copyright infringement under the No Electronic Theft (NET) Act; loss estimated at US$1.4 million.
Legal Proceedings: The accused pleaded guilty.
Sentence / Outcome: The court rejected three grounds for reducing the sentence under the Federal Sentencing Guidelines (including an 'Internet addiction' theory) and accepted one, departing downward two points and reducing the sentencing range from 24–30 months to 18–24 months. The offender was sentenced to 18 months imprisonment. The court was persuaded by (1) the fact that he was a caregiver to a sick relative, (2) the fact that he had cooperated with the government 'with no realistic hope of getting anything from the government in return', and (3) the fact that the underlying guidelines governing loss were originally written for the case of 'for profit' infringement, and he was not engaging in his acts for profit.
Reference: 222 F Supp 2d 1009 (ND (Ill), 2002)

[Case No. 126]

Jurisdiction / Date: England, Stafford Crown Court (trial); Court of Appeal (Criminal Division); 16 January 2002 (plea at Stafford); 12 July 2002 (appeal)
Sex / Age of Accused: Two males, 40 and 37 at appeal
Facts / Loss: The accused made and sold 'cable cubes' which enabled cable customers to get channels without paying a subscription. Total profit from the sale of cubes was estimated at US$10,800.
Legal Proceedings: Both accused pleaded guilty to the charge of incitement to commit offences contrary to *Computer Misuse Act 1990*, s. 3. They argued that the business

was partly legitimate, and that they were of previous good character. The court held that a disclaimer that 'if customers are not sure about the legality of the product they shouldn't use it' was not effective, but it was taken as evidence that the accused themselves knew their actions were illegal. The accused appealed on sentence only.

Sentence / Outcome: Defendants were sentenced to seven months imprisonment at first instance. This was reduced to four months on appeal.

Reference: [2003] 1 Cr App R (S) 83; <http://www.fact-uk.org.uk/press%20releases/20_23%202002.PDF>

[Case No. 127]

Jurisdiction / Date: USA, 9th Circuit on appeal from a decision of the United States District Court (District of Hawaii), 12 July 2002 (appeal decision)

Sex / Age of Accused: Male, 37

Facts / Loss: The accused set up a fictitious website for the Honolulu Marathon. He copied the real marathon website, modified it slightly and made the modified site available online (using a domain name very similar to the original), but charged users US$165 to 'register' for the marathon.

Legal Proceedings: The accused pleaded guilty to wire fraud under 18 USC §1343.

Sentence / Outcome: At sentencing the government argued and the court accepted that Section 3B1.3 USSG (US Sentencing Guidelines Manual), the 'special skills' enhancement of the guidelines, applied to the accused. The special skills enhancement provides for an increased sentence when a defendant has 'used a special skill, in a manner that significantly facilitated the commission or concealment of the offense'. The Appeal Court reversed this decision, holding that the use of a computer alone to commit a crime does not mean that a defendant should get a special skills enhancement. A hacker could qualify, but would need to display extensive expertise.

Reference: 296 F.3d 792 (9th Cir, 2002)

[Case No. 128]

Jurisdiction / Date: USA, District Court (Northern District, Texas) (trial); USA Court of Appeals Fifth Circuit (appeal); December 2000 (convictions); August 2001 (sentences); August 2002 (appeal judgment)

Sex / Age of Accused: First accused: male aged 38; second accused: female aged 33 at conviction

Facts / Loss: The defendants owned a company that provided subscribers with access to websites featuring child pornography. Child pornography was also found on a computer at their home. The pornographic sites were not operated by the defendants, who only operated the payment system. The company was highly profitable, taking in as much as US$1.4 million in one especially lucrative month. It was the largest commercial child pornography enterprise uncovered to that time. Its website counted at least 250,000 subscribers, many of them living overseas. The defendants had a fee-sharing arrangement with foreign webmasters who maintained the child pornography sites. The company provided a customer screening and subscription service to those websites. According to testimony from their trial, the defendants grossed about US$5.7 million from subscribers and paid about 60 per cent to the foreign webmasters.

Legal Proceedings: The defendants were charged with 89 counts, including transporting visual depictions of minors engaging in sexually explicit conduct under 18 USC §2252, and transporting child pornography under 18 USC §2252A.

Sentence / Outcome: Both defendants were convicted. The first accused was convicted of 89 counts of possessing and distributing child pornography, and sentenced to life imprisonment (1335 years: 15 years for each of the 89 charges) and a special assessment of US$8900. The second accused was sentenced to 14 years' imprisonment and a special assessment of US$8700. Both sentences were vacated on appeal and the defendants were remanded for resentencing. In 2003, the sentences were revisited and they were given the same terms again. On appeal it was successfully pointed out that the District Court had imposed multiple sentences by counting each image posted as violation of two statutes that criminalise the same behaviour.

Reference: *New York Times,* 9 August 2001; <http://www.dcfpd.org/investigators/computer%20and%20internet%20crimes.pdf>;
<http://www.law.com/jsp/decisionstate.jsp?id=1030343771315>,
<http://www.newsbits.net/2003/20030513.htm>

[Case No. 129]

Jurisdiction / Date: USA, District Court (District of Utah) (trial); US Court of Appeals, Tenth Circuit (appeal); 16 September 2002 (appeal decision)

Sex / Age of Accused: Male, age unknown

Facts / Loss: The accused was viewing child pornography on the Internet.

Legal Proceedings: The accused was charged with possession of child pornography under 18 USC §2252A(a)(5)(B). The defendant argued that the search of his computer was illegal without suspicion of crime or warrant. This was rejected. At trial, defendant also argued that his possession of the images was not voluntary, as they had been automatically saved in the temporary cache, but this was rejected. Visiting the sites was therefore enough to constitute possession.

Sentence / Outcome: Accused was convicted, and appeal dismissed. He was sentenced to 60 months imprisonment, partly on the basis that he was viewing computerised child pornography while on parole after being convicted in 1990 of sexually abusing a child.

Reference: 150 F Supp 2d 1263, 1270 (D Utah, 2001); 305 F 3d 1193 (10th Cir, 2002)

[Case No. 130]

Jurisdiction / Date: USA, District Court (Southern District, New York), March 2001 (arrested); October 2002 (plea)

Sex / Age of Accused: Male, 32 when arrested

Facts / Loss: The case involved identity fraud using online information. There was no monetary loss, but US$80 million at risk.

Legal Proceedings: The accused pleaded guilty to twelve charges of wire and mail fraud, credit card fraud, conspiracy and identity theft. Defence raised mental illness (depression and obsessive–compulsive disorder). An aggravating factor was that a number of the victims were famous.

Sentence / Outcome: Unknown.

Reference: *New York Post,* 20 March 2001; *New York Post,* 4 October 2002, p. 21; *The Guardian* (UK), 5 October 2002

[Case No. 131]

Jurisdiction / Date: USA, District Court (Southern District, California), August–October 2000 (offences); November 2002 (plea)

Sex / Age of Accused: Male; 32 at plea

Facts / Loss: The accused hacked into the computer system of an e-commerce retailer and used his home computer to gain access to the files of the retailer over a three-month period, causing damage in excess of US$10,000.

Legal Proceedings: He was charged under 18 USC §1030(a)(5)(A) with intentionally damaging a protected computer.

Sentence / Outcome: Pleaded guilty and received three years probation and a fine of US$10,000.

Reference: <http://www.usdoj.gov/criminal/cybercrime/cccases.html>; <http://www.landfield.com/isn/mail-archive/2001/Dec/0077.html>

[Case No. 132]

Jurisdiction / Date: Hong Kong, District Court, 29 November 2001; Court of Appeal of Hong Kong, 7 November 2002

Sex / Age of Accused: Male, age unknown

Facts / Loss: The accused manufactured video compact discs and CD-ROMs containing copyright films and music. 46,050 infringing discs were recovered.

Legal Proceedings: Accused was charged with four counts of possession of infringing copies and copy-making equipment under s. 118 of the Copyright Ordinance, Cap. 528 (Hong Kong). On appeal, defence argued that the evidence of copyright ownership was inadmissible as hearsay because it had been obtained from a computer database. That argument was rejected, as was the argument that the defendant was licensed by the copyright owners to produce the discs.

Sentence / Outcome: Accused was convicted and sentenced to 28 months imprisonment; sentence was affirmed on appeal.

Reference: DCCC No. 556 of 2001; CACC 557A/2001

[Case No. 133]

Jurisdiction / Date: USA, California, 9 September 2002 (trial); 2 December 2002 (sentenced)

Sex / Age of Accused: Male, 35 at time of plea

Facts / Loss: Former employee gained access to a company's computer system and read e-mail for the purpose of gaining a commercial advantage for his new employer, who was a competitor. Approximately US$21,636 in damage and costs was caused to the victim company.

Legal Proceedings: Accused pleaded guilty to one felony count of obtaining information from a protected computer.

Sentence / Outcome: Five years' imprisonment and a fine of US$21,600.

Reference: <http://www.usdoj.gov/criminal/cybercrime/cccases.html>

[Case No. 134]

Jurisdiction / Date: France, Besancon, January 2003

Sex / Age of Accused: Male, 19 when sentenced

Facts / Loss: The accused modified data by altering the record of his drink-driving conviction on a police computer and replacing it with a 'smiley' symbol.

Legal Proceedings: The accused was charged with data modification.

Sentence / Outcome: Three months' imprisonment wholly suspended, three months' driver's licence revocation and fine equivalent to US$488.

Reference: *Liberation* newspaper, France, 22 January 2003

[Case No. 135]

Jurisdiction / Date: USA, District Court (Eastern District of Pennsylvania), 28 August 2001, (trial sentence); Third Circuit, 6 January 2003 (appeal decision)

Sex / Age of Accused: Male, 62

Facts / Loss: The accused possessed computerised images of child pornography. He acknowledged that he was a paedophile and had prior convictions in the 1970s and 1980s for child molestation.

Legal Proceedings: The accused pleaded guilty to one count of receipt and one count of possession of child pornography, contrary to 18 USC §2252.

Sentence / Outcome: District court's sentence of 70 months imprisonment, followed by supervised release with conditions, was vacated on appeal and remanded for resentencing. The appeal court found that the condition on his supervised release (that he was not allowed to possess a computer at home or to use an 'online computer service' without the permission of his probation officer for the period of his supervised release) was too broad a restriction and was in violation of 18 USC §2553. A complete ban on computer usage is unacceptable where the defendant only used his computer to collect images and had no actual contact with minors.

Reference: 316 F 3d 386 (3rd Cir, 2003); appeal decision: <http://vls.law.vill.edu/locator/3d/Jan2003/013475.pdf>

[Case No. 136]

Jurisdiction / Date: USA, Court of Appeals, Eleventh Circuit, 14 January 2003 (appeal)

Sex / Age of Accused: Male, 40

Facts / Loss: This was a case involving possession of child pornography pictures (the defendant with a child) on computer. It was discovered by an anonymous hacker in Turkey.

Legal Proceedings: On appeal, the defendant argued that the anonymous hacker's conduct that alerted authorities to the defendant's conduct violated the Fourth Amendment, the Wiretap Act, and the Stored Communications Act. The court rejected all three arguments.

Sentence / Outcome: Convicted and sentenced to 17 and a half years imprisonment and 3 years supervised release

Reference: <http://www.law.emory.edu/11circuit/jan2003/01-15788.opn.html> (appeal decision); see also <http://www.safeplace.net/ccv/bulletin/2001-11-10.htm>; <http://research.yale.edu/lawmeme/modules.php?name=News&file=print&sid=531>

[Case No. 137]

Jurisdiction / Date: England, Southwark Crown Court, 21 January 2003 (sentenced)

Sex / Age of Accused: Male, 22 at sentence

Facts / Loss: The accused created and released three computer viruses contained in e-mail. Two were designed to stop computers operating and destroy material when computers were rebooted; they infected 27,000 computers in 42 countries. The defendant said that one virus was not intended to cause harm.

Legal Proceedings: The defendant pleaded guilty. The further charge of possessing indecent images was not pursued.

Sentence / Outcome: Sentenced to two years imprisonment for each of three offences, concurrent.

Reference: 'Computer Virus Author Jailed', BBC world news website, 21 January 2003: <http://news.bbc.co.uk/2/hi/uk_news/wales/2678773.stm>; also see Armstrong 2003.

[Case No. 138]

Jurisdiction / Date: USA, District Court (Southern District, Illinois); Court of Appeals for Seventh Circuit, 21 January 2003 (appeal)
Sex / Age of Accused: Male, age unknown
Facts / Loss: The accused was charged with fraud, but child pornography was found on the defendant's computer while searching for evidence of fraud.
Legal Proceedings: Only fraud offences were charged.
Sentence / Outcome: The defendant was convicted and sentenced to 24 months imprisonment. Trial judge imposed severe restrictions on his computer use despite the fact that there was no charge in respect of the child pornography. On appeal against this condition of sentence, the appeals court ruled that the restriction was too broad and remitted the case for resentencing.
Reference: <http://www.ca7.uscourts.gov/op3.fwx?submit1=showop&caseno=01-4340.PDF>

[Case No. 139]

Jurisdiction / Date: Hong Kong, Court of First Instance of Hong Kong (Appellate Jurisdiction), 23 January 2003 (appeal)
Sex / Age of Accused: Male, age unknown
Facts / Loss: An assessor with the Inland Revenue Department accessed the Department's computer to get the identity number of a colleague, which he then used to sign her up for a World Wildlife Fund membership without her consent. He paid the subscription for her with his own credit card and in his own name. He abused the password privilege he was given to access the system only for limited purposes, took confidential information in breach of secrecy provisions of IRD and passed that information to a third party.
Legal Proceedings: The accused was charged with obtaining access to a computer contrary to s. 161(1)(c) of the Crimes Ordinance, Cap. 200.
Sentence / Outcome: The accused was acquitted at trial, with the magistrate finding that he had gained access to the computer system of the IRD which was a serious breach of procedure. However, she concluded that no dishonesty was involved and this was not in fact a criminal matter at all. He was found guilty on appeal and case was remitted to magistrate for conviction and sentencing. On appeal the court held that 'gain' within the section did not have to be monetary but could include information, and that the conduct in this case was 'dishonest'.
Reference: HCMA 723/2002

[Case No. 140]

Jurisdiction / Date: Australia, Federal Court; December 2002 (suspended sentence); February 2003 (sentence)
Sex / Age of Accused: Male, age unknown
Facts / Loss: The Australian Competition and Consumer Commission took action against a company and its directors, who had made unsubstantiated health and other claims for its product on its website. The ACCC argued that businesses cannot hide behind the Internet and use it as an excuse to ignore obligations under the *Trade Practices Act 1974* (Cth).
Legal Proceedings: The court found the directors guilty of breaches of the Trade Practices Act. The directors then failed to implement the court's orders (including publication of a correction notice on the website) and were held in contempt. The company was required to pay a fine of A$20,000 (US$15,000) and each director was

fined A$10,000 (US$7500) and given a suspended sentence conditional on compliance with the court's orders. The accused, one of the directors, failed to comply with the conditions of the suspended sentence. The court said that he was 'labouring under the delusion that he is head of a non-existent state' and therefore falsely believed he was outside the jurisdiction of Australia.

Sentence / Outcome: The accused was convicted of contempt and given a sentence of one month imprisonment.

Reference: [2003] FCA 49 (6 February 2003) 'Contempt imprisonment arising from Trade Practices Act Breach', 7 February 2003, Australian Competition and Consumer Commission Media Release MR 20/03: <http://www.accc.gov.au/content/index.phtml/itemId/88312>

[Case No. 141]

Jurisdiction / Date: USA, District Court (Southern District, New York), 4 February 2003 (appeal judgment)

Sex / Age of Accused: Male, 19

Facts / Loss: This was a case involving possession of child pornography.

Legal Proceedings: Following the Supreme Court case striking down the ban on 'virtual' child pornography, *Ashcroft v Free Speech Coalition*, 122 S Ct 1389 (2002), the important question was raised here: If it is unconstitutional for the government to criminalise virtual child pornography (that is, child pornography generated by computer, not based on pictures of an actual child), must the government in a child pornography prosecution prove not only that an image was real child pornography, but also that the defendant actually 'knew' that the image was real child pornography? The court held that the answer is yes.

Sentence / Outcome: The accused was convicted of one count of advertising for the receipt, exchange, and distribution of child pornography and one count of distribution of child pornography. This conviction was upheld on appeal. Although the government had to prove knowledge, they had done so to a degree sufficient for the jury to convict. Accused was sentenced to 10 years imprisonment.

Reference: 255 F Supp 2d 200 (SDNY, 2003) <http://www.usdoj.gov/usao/nys/Press%20Releases/July03/pabon-cruzsentence.pdf>

[Case No. 142]

Jurisdiction / Date: Australia, Australian Capital Territory, ACT Supreme Court, 25 September 2001; Court of Appeal, 10 February 2003; High Court, 6 November 2003

Sex / Age of Accused: Male, 32

Facts / Loss: The accused, a financial consultant to the Department of Finance and Administration, allegedly transferred funds electronically to private companies in which he held an interest by logging on to the Department's computers using another person's name and password. A$8.725 million (US$6,543.750) was transferred, and A$5.48 million (US$4,110,000) was still unrecovered as of 1999.

Legal Proceedings: The accused was charged with defrauding the Commonwealth under the *Crimes Act 1914* (Cth). Bail was refused.

Sentence / Outcome: Sentenced to seven years and six months imprisonment with a non-parole period of three years and six months. Appeal against sentence dismissed. Appeal against sentence to High Court dismissed.

Reference: ACT Supreme Court, 25 September 2001; [2003] ACTCA 2 (10 February 2003): <http://www.austlii.edu.au/au/cases/act/ACTCA/2003/2.html>; [2003] HCAT rans 451: <http://www.austlii.edu.au/au/other/HCATrans/2003/451.html>; Campbell 2001

[Case No. 143]

Jurisdiction / Date: USA, District Court (Central District, California), 28 February 2003 (sentence)

Sex / Age of Accused: Male, 20 at sentence

Facts / Loss: In 2001 the accused had participated in a scheme involving hackers in Romania who gained unauthorised access to a company's online ordering system and placed fraudulent orders for computer equipment. The equipment was then sent to premises controlled by the accused in Los Angeles and dispatched to Eastern Europe. The accused also purchased credit card numbers from hackers and used them to purchase computer equipment from other retailers. Hundreds of thousands of dollars worth of fraudulent orders were placed (estimated US$500,000).

Legal Proceedings: The accused was charged with wire fraud, conspiracy and credit card fraud. He pleaded guilty.

Sentence / Outcome: The accused was sentenced to 33 months imprisonment and ordered to pay US$324,061 in restitution to the victims. He was also made subject to supervised release for three years, during which time significant restrictions were placed on his use of computers.

Reference: <http://www.usdoj.gov/criminal/cybercrime/cccases.html>

[Case No. 144]

Jurisdiction / Date: USA, District Court (Eastern District, California), 22 January 2001 to 26 October 2002 (offences); March 2003 (plea)

Sex / Age of Accused: Female, 23 at plea

Facts / Loss: The accused, an employee of a credit union, used a computer to access customer information, then opened credit card accounts in their names and incurred charges. The estimated amount of fraudulent transactions was US$53,376. No customers lost funds, as all funds were federally insured.

Legal Proceedings: The accused pleaded guilty to obtaining confidential account information and making fraudulent account transactions in violation of 18 USC §§1030(a)(2)(A) and 1030(c)(2)(B)(i). In defence it was argued that no losses were incurred by the credit union's customers.

Sentence / Outcome: The defendant was not sentenced at the time of the report, but as part of the plea agreement she was barred from employment at any federally insured financial institution for 10 years, pursuant to 12 USC §1829(a).

Reference: <http://www.usdoj.gov/criminal/cybercrime/cccases.html>

[Case No. 145]

Jurisdiction / Date: USA, Missouri, 13 March 2003 (plea)

Sex / Age of Accused: Male, 43

Facts / Loss: An employee of a company gained access to its system beyond his authorisation and stored 5000 user passwords. The loss to the company was approximately US$10,000. This was the first conviction for computer hacking prosecuted by Missouri's Computer Crimes and Child Exploitation Unit.
Legal Proceedings: The accused pleaded guilty to unauthorised computer intrusion.
Sentence / Outcome: Plea agreement included the payment of US$10,000 in restitution to the company and the performance of 250 hours of community service, which involved instructing the public on the dangers of hacking.
Reference: <http://www.usdoj.gov/criminal/cybercrime/cccases.html>

[Case No. 146]

Jurisdiction / Date: USA, District Court (Central District, California), September 2000 (offence); 25 March 2003 (sentence)
Sex / Age of Accused: Male, 30 at sentence
Facts / Loss: The accused was a disgruntled former employee who maliciously bombarded the company's server with thousands of spam e-mail messages.
Legal Proceedings: This was the first case to go to trial in Los Angeles under the Computer Fraud and Abuse Act, the federal statute covering computer abuse and spamming.
Sentence / Outcome: The accused was convicted and sentenced to 16 months imprisonment, and was required to submit to unannounced searches of his computer. He was also required to advise future employers about this conviction and to receive psychological counselling. Conviction subject to appeal in October 2003
Reference: US Department of Justice website, 25 March 2003: <http://losangeles.fbi.gov/2003/la032503.htm>

[Case No. 147]

Jurisdiction / Date: Australia, Supreme Court of Victoria (Common Law Division), 1 March 2001 (trial); 7 April 2003 (appeal)
Sex / Age of Accused: Male, 47
Facts / Loss: A Melbourne resident allegedly stalked a female television actor in Canada, mostly via mail and e-mail.
Legal Proceedings: The accused was charged with stalking under s. 21A of the *Crimes Act 1958* (Vic). The charge was initially dismissed by the magistrate for lack of jurisdiction on the basis that stalking requires the arousal of fear in Victoria and this could only have occurred in Canada. On appeal by the Director of Public Prosecutions, the Supreme Court held that conduct (letters sent, etc.) took place in Victoria; therefore there was jurisdiction. This was so even though the harm occurred outside Australia. The case was remitted to the magistrate for trial.
Sentence / Outcome: Pending. An application to appeal against the rulings filed by the defendant was rejected in April 2003. Meanwhile, the Victorian legislature has amended s. 21A to clarify that it included cyberstalking and did not require the actual effect of stalking to occur within jurisdiction: *Crimes (Stalking) Act* 2003. (Vic), in effect from 10 December 2003.
Reference: Trial: No. 6562 of 2000 (unreported); appeal: [2003] VSCA 34 (7 April 2003). See 'In your footsteps', *The Age* (Melbourne), 24 April 2003.

[Case No. 148]

Jurisdiction / Date: USA, District Court (Western District of Pennsylvania), 23 January 2003 (jury returned guilty verdict); 11 April 2003 (sentenced)
Sex / Age of Accused: Male, 43
Facts / Loss: Accused gained access without authorisation to the e-mail account of a Common Pleas Court Judge and obtained personal e-mail and files.
Legal Proceedings: The accused was charged with three counts of unauthorised access to a protected computer.
Sentence / Outcome: The accused was convicted and sentenced to imprisonment for one year and one day. His use of computers was restricted for his five years of supervised release after prison.
Reference: <http://www.usdoj.gov/criminal/cybercrime/cccases.html>;
<http://www.pittsburghlive.com/x/tribune-review/pittsburgh/s_136331.html>

[Case No. 149]

Jurisdiction / Date: USA, District Court (Central District, California), 5 January 2003 (offences); 18 April 2003 (plea)
Sex / Age of Accused: Male; 28
Facts / Loss: A former employee hacked into the company's computer system and destroyed critical data including the customer database and other records, and effectively shut down the company's computer server, Internet-based credit card processing system, and website. Because employees could not use the computer system, the companies were unable to dispatch drivers to pick up clients and the companies suffered thousands of dollars in losses.
Legal Proceedings: The accused was charged with intentionally causing damage to a protected computer by knowingly causing the transmission of a program, information, code, or command, in violation of 18 USC §§1030(a)(5)(A)(i) and (B)(i), a felony.
Sentence / Outcome: The accused pleaded guilty. He was sentenced to five years probation and ordered to pay US$28,404 in restitution.
Reference: <http://www.usdoj.gov/criminal/cybercrime/cccases.html>;
<http://www.verdasys.com/company/howtofind.php>

[Case No. 150]

Jurisdiction / Date: USA, District Court (Central District, California), Los Angeles, June 2003 (plea)
Sex / Age of Accused: Male, 24
Facts / Loss: The defendant obtained control of Aljazeera.net during the war on Iraq by fraudulent representations to the American office where the domain name was registered, and then diverted incoming traffic and e-mail to a website of his own design featuring the US flag in the shape of the country. He had learned that the website contained images of captured American prisoners of war. Aljazeera was unable to receive e-mail during the period of the diversion.
Legal Proceedings: The accused pleaded guilty to wire fraud and unlawful interception of an electronic communication.
Sentence / Outcome: Three years probation, 1000 hours community service and a fine of US$2000 together with full restitution to the victims.

Reference: <http://www.usdoj.gov/criminal/cybercrime/cccases.html>;
<http://english.aljazeera.net/NR/exeres/4B9940BC-39AC-488E-BEE0-
01365405A36F.html>

[Case No. 151]

Jurisdiction / Date: USA, 175th Judicial Court, Bexar County, Texas (trial); Court
of Appeals, San Antonio, Texas, 11 June 2003 (appeal decision)
Sex / Age of Accused: Male, age unknown
Facts / Loss: The accused sent his computer for repair. The repair technician
advised that there was a virus and the hard drive would have to be wiped. The
accused asked him to back up photo files, which were found to contain images of
child pornography.
Legal Proceedings: The accused was charged with possession of child pornography; he pleaded guilty, then appealed. The court concluded that by asking the
technician to back up those files, the owner relinquished any 'reasonable expectation of privacy' and could not claim violation of the Fourth Amendment right
to privacy.
Sentence / Outcome: Ten years community supervision.
Reference: <http://www.4law.co.il/Le558.htm> (appeal decision)

[Case No. 152]

Jurisdiction / Date: USA, District Court (Eastern District, California), March 2003
(plea); 12 June 2003 (sentenced)
Sex / Age of Accused: Male; 19 at sentence
Facts / Loss: The accused hacked into various websites, including a military one as
well as another site from which he stole credit card numbers. He then used those
numbers to make purchases. Fraudulent credit card purchases totalled approximately US$7167.
Legal Proceedings: The accused was charged with fraud and related activity in connection with computers, and credit card fraud in violation of 18 USC §§1030(a)(4)
and 1029(a)(2).
Sentence / Outcome: Pleaded guilty; sentenced to imprisonment for one year
and one day, three years supervised release and a US$200 special assessment. Also
ordered to pay US$88,253.47 in restitution. Court imposed special conditions
restricting his computer use on release from prison.
Reference: <http://www.usdoj.gov/criminal/cybercrime/cccases.html>

[Case No. 153]

Jurisdiction / Date: Australia, Melbourne, Victoria, October 2002 (arrested); July
2003 (sentenced)
Sex / Age of Accused: Male, age unknown
Facts / Loss: This was a case involving the sale and distribution of pirated computer games. The accused was apprehended with thousands of pirated Playstation
games. Police raided his house to find a sophisticated pirating operation, with four
computers being used to copy the games to blank CDs.
Legal Proceedings: No information

Sentence / Outcome: Sentenced to one year imprisonment.
Reference: *Sydney Morning Herald*, 11 September 2003: <http://www.smh.com.au/articles/2003/09/10/1063191457679.html?from=storyrhs>; *The Age* (Melbourne), 10 October 2002: <http://www.theage.com.au/cgi-bin/common/popupPrintArticle.pl?path=/articles/2003/10/10/1065676130931.html>

[Case No. 154]

Jurisdiction / Date: USA, District Court (Southern District, New York), 10 July 2003 (plea)
Sex / Age of Accused: Male, 24 at plea
Facts / Loss: The accused installed key-logging software on company's computers and used information that he gained about customers to access bank accounts and to fraudulently open online bank accounts. He also sold copies of MS Office 2000 Professional online. In addition to the fraud, the key-logging software was capable of damaging the company's computers.
Legal Proceedings: The accused pleaded guilty to five counts of computer damage, fraud and software piracy.
Sentence / Outcome: Not sentenced at time of report
Reference: <http://www.usdoj.gov/criminal/cybercrime/cccases.html>; <http://www.securityfocus.com/news/6447>

[Case No. 155]

Jurisdiction / Date: USA, first accused sentenced by District Court (Western District, Washington) (4 October 2002); second accused sentenced by District Court (Connecticut) (25 July 2003)
Sex / Age of Accused: Both male; first accused 27 and second accused 21 at time of sentencing
Facts / Loss: From 1999 to 2000 the accused carried out computer intrusions from Russia to obtain 56,000 credit card account numbers, in order to defraud an online payment system provider and to extort money from companies in the US. Loss suffered totalled US$25 million.
Legal Proceedings: First accused pleaded not guilty and was convicted on 20 counts of conspiracy, various computer crimes, and fraud. Second accused pleaded guilty to conspiring to make unauthorised intrusions into computer systems owned by companies in the United States, eight counts of wire fraud, two counts of extortion, four counts of unauthorised computer intrusions, and one count of possessing user names and passwords for an online bank.
Sentence / Outcome: First accused was sentenced to 36 months imprisonment, and fined nearly US$700,000. Second accused was sentenced to 48 months imprisonment followed by three years supervised release.
Reference: Available through Westlaw: 2001 WL 1024026; <http://www.usdoj.gov/criminal/cybercrime/cccases.html>; <http://www.fbi.gov/page2/oct03/hack100703.htm>

[Case No. 156]

Jurisdiction / Date: Australia, New South Wales District Court, August 2003 (appeal decision)

Sex / Age of Accused: Male, 53 when sentenced
Facts / Loss: The accused was in possession of more than 50,000 images of child pornography.
Legal Proceedings: The accused was a famous musician with an exceptional career in music and teaching. He pleaded guilty to charges and had no prior convictions, had accepted that he was a paedophile and had taken steps to rehabilitate himself. His crimes were, however, abhorrent and deterrence was a consideration in sentencing.
Sentence / Outcome: Two years imprisonment, with non-parole period of one year (increased on appeal by Director of Public Prosecutions from the original sentence of two years imprisonment wholly suspended).
Reference: Miranda and Shepherd 2003

[Case No. 157]

Jurisdiction / Date: Australia, ACT Magistrates Court, 17 September 2003 (sentenced)
Sex / Age of Accused: Male, 27 when sentenced
Facts / Loss: The accused was charged with possession of 39 images of child pornography, which were discovered on a disk during a search of his car on an unrelated matter. The images had been downloaded from the Internet. The accused was arrested by police in respect of an unrelated motor vehicle offence.
Legal Proceedings: The accused pleaded guilty to possession of child pornography.
Sentence / Outcome: 18 months imprisonment wholly suspended. followed by a three-year good behaviour bond.
Reference: *Canberra Times*, 18 September 2003, p. 9

[Case No. 158]

Jurisdiction / Date: Australia, County Court of Victoria, 19 September 2003 (sentenced)
Sex / Age of Accused: Male; 22 when sentenced
Facts / Loss: The accused encoded data from his mother's bank card onto a games arcade card and reconfigured a disused EFTPOS machine to imitate terminals of 19 businesses. He then fraudulently deposited money into his mother's bank account, obtaining 102 refunds worth US$75,494.25.
Legal Proceedings: The accused was charged with obtaining and attempting to obtain financial advantage by deception.
Sentence / Outcome: Pleaded guilty; sentenced to two years and three months imprisonment with a minimum term of nine months. Defendant had left school at 14 and had more than 400 dishonesty convictions.
Reference: Lapthorne 2003; Cullen 2003

[Case No. 159]

Jurisdiction / Date: Australia, County Court of Victoria, Melbourne, 26 September 2003 (sentenced)
Sex / Age of Accused: Male, 39 at time of offences

Facts / Loss: The accused approached an under-age girl on the Internet and met her and her friends and sister for sexual encounters, for which he paid. Pictures of child pornography were found at his home.

Legal Proceedings: The accused pleaded guilty to seven counts of performing an indecent act with a child under 16, five counts of performing an indecent act in the presence of a child under 16, two counts of causing a child to take part in prostitution, two counts of production of child pornography, and one count of possession of child pornography. He claimed he did not know that the pictures were of under-age children. A psychologist found him not to be a paedophile and in no danger of reoffending. Although the defence argued that the accused was genuinely remorseful, the court considered him to show no remorse. It was also argued that the girls consented to the indecencies. The accused said he did it as a way to give them money and cigarettes, which they would otherwise have stolen. The court said that this method of production of child pornography negates the argument that its possession harms no one.

Sentence / Outcome: Eight years imprisonment with a non-parole period of six years.

Reference: Unreported, County Court of Victoria, Melbourne, 26 September 2003; *The Age* (Melbourne), 27 September 2003; see Tinkler 2004

[Case No. 160]

Jurisdiction / Date: Australia, Hobart Magistrates' Court, Tasmania, 24 September 2002 (arrested); 2 October 2003 (plea)

Sex / Age of Accused: Male, 41 at plea

Facts / Loss: 134 images and movies of child pornography were found on accused's home computer.

Legal Proceedings: The accused pleaded guilty to possession of child pornography. In mitigation, the accused said that he had only downloaded the images the day before at the request of a friend from California, whom he had met through an Internet chat room.

Sentence / Outcome: Five months' imprisonment, suspended on the condition of good behaviour for four years.

Reference: *Mercury News* (Hobart), 3 October 2003

[Case No. 161]

Jurisdiction / Date: Australia, Nowra District Court, New South Wales, 27 May 2003 (plea), 1 October 2003 (sentenced); 18 November 2003 (appeal)

Sex / Age of Accused: Male, 69 at plea

Facts / Loss: The court heard that the defendant had lured two boys, aged 13 and 14, to his home, partly by using his 1935 Chrysler and partly by sporting cards. Both boys were shown sex toys, pornographic photographs and Internet sites. When police searched his home they recovered 35 folders of young children involved in sex acts.

Legal Proceedings: The accused pleaded guilty to possessing and publishing child pornography.

Sentence / Outcome: The defendant was sentenced to two years imprisonment for the publication offence and placed on a five-year bond for possession. The conditions of the bond were that he not use any computer at any time connected to the Internet, and that he not be in the company of any person under the age of 18 without the specific written permission of a probation and parole officer. The pre-sentence report said the defendant had 'no insight' into the plight of the children and was unaware of the harm or threat to their safety or well-being. The accused appealed against the severity of the original sentence on the basis of ill health. The magistrate resentenced the accused to two years imprisonment with a non-parole period of 12 months.

Reference: Treasure 2003; <http://www.abc.gov.au/illawarra/news/200311/s991266.htm>

[Case No. 162]

Jurisdiction / Date: Australia, County Court of Victoria, 2 October 2003 (sentenced)
Sex / Age of Accused: Male, age unknown
Facts / Loss: A man had filmed and photographed his daughter while she was naked, on several occasions between 2000 and 2002. She was 12 at the time of the first offence. Police found a large encrypted file containing 895 images and video on his computer after complaints by his daughter. The file was decrypted after 19 weeks of using a police password-cracking program.
Legal Proceedings: The accused was charged with possession of child pornography, incest and performing an indecent act with a child under 16. In view of the computer evidence, he pleaded guilty to the charge of possessing child pornography. Jury convicted him of one count of incest and four counts of performing an indecent act with a child under 16. He was found not guilty of one charge of committing an indecent act and one other count of incest. He showed no remorse and failed to cooperate with the investigation.
Sentence / Outcome: Six and a half years imprisonment with a non-parole period of three and a half years.
Reference: *The Age* (Melbourne), 3 October 2003

[Case No. 163]

Jurisdiction / Date: Australia, Sydney, September 2003 (pleas); 18 November 2003 (sentenced)
Sex / Age of Accused: Three males, aged 19 (first accused), 20 (second accused) and 21 (third accused) at sentence
Facts / Loss: This was Australia's first criminal prosecution for Internet music piracy. The accused illegally distributed about A$60 million (US$4.5 million) worth of music on a website called 'MP3 WMA Land'. The magistrate said it was an impossible task to calculate the precise economic loss, although it was significant.
Legal Proceedings: The accused were charged with copyright infringement. The first accused, who founded and maintained the site, pleaded guilty to 22 charges of distributing and aiding and abetting the distribution of copyrighted material. The second accused, who helped to maintain and update the site, pleaded guilty to 17 copyright breaches. The third accused pleaded guilty to 29 less serious copyright breaches after providing the site with four albums he had compiled

from copyrighted material. [The Australian recording industry believes this is the world's first criminal prosecution for online music piracy. A spokesman from the Music Industry Piracy Investigations (MIPI) agency applied to the NSW Local Court to be heard on behalf of the victims during sentencing submissions because he said the DPP's case was deficient. The magistrate refused the application, saying it was 'totally inappropriate for an organisation such as MIPI to have a direct role' in sentencing procedure, and that there was no precedent to allow it.]

Sentence / Outcome: The first and second accused were sentenced to 18 months imprisonment, wholly suspended. The magistrate said the defendants had known their activities were illegal and had gone to some lengths to avoid detection, and that imprisonment was warranted. However, he suspended the sentences, taking into account their youth and the fact they did not profit from their website. The third accused was sentenced to 200 hours community service with a similar number of hours to be served by the first accused. The second accused, being medically unfit to undertake community service, was required to pay a fine equivalent to US$3750 fine and to undertake a three-year good behaviour bond.

Reference: 'Online piracy criminal prosecution hailed as a world first', *Agence France Presse*, 7 September 2003; 'Netting crims', *Gold Coast Bulletin*, 9 September 2003; '$60m CD pirates get "slap on wrist"', *The Australian*, 2 October 2003; 'Uni net pirates sentenced for $60m music sting', *Sydney Morning Herald*, 18 November 2003; Fans mourn the day the pirated music died', *Sydney Morning Herald*, 19 November 2003; <http://www.news.com.au/common/story_page/0,4057,7904997%255E15319,00.html>

[Case No. 164]

Jurisdiction / Date: England, Crown Court at Doncaster (trial), 20 July 2000 (plea); 10 August 2000 (sentence); Court of Appeal (Criminal Division), 23 November 2003 (appeal judgment)

Sex / Age of Accused: Male, 36 at plea

Facts / Loss: The accused supplied 'multi-mode boards' to cable TV customers, which enabled them to get all channels without paying subscription fees. The total turnover arising from the offences was equivalent to US$1080; the loss to cable companies US$25 each month per device.

Legal Proceedings: The accused was prosecuted not by the police but by FACT, the Federation Against Copyright Theft. The accused pleaded guilty to three counts of inciting the commission of an offence under s. 3 of the *Computer Misuse Act 1990*. He had put a disclaimer on his website to try to evade any liability that might arise, but the court rejected the validity of this. In mitigation, the defence argued that only 20 devices had been supplied over a period of three months; the accused had admitted the offence early; and he had submitted a guilty plea.

Sentence / Outcome: Four months imprisonment awarded at trial on each count, concurrent, together with prosecution costs equivalent to US$18,000. This was reduced on appeal to the costs plus 150 hours community service, in view of the relatively small scale of the manufacture, the costs award and the fact that the cable companies could themselves have taken steps to prevent such activities.

Reference: [2001] 2 Cr App R (S) 28

APPENDIX B

Selected Legislative Summaries

Note that values in local currency have been converted to US dollars at the exchange rates on p. xv.

Australia
(Commonwealth)

Criminal Code Act 1995 (Cth) as amended by the *Criminal Code Amendment (Theft, Fraud, Bribery and Related Offences) Act 2000* and the *Cybercrime Act 2001* (Cth)

Unauthorised access, modification or impairment with intent to commit a serious offence (s. 477.1)	Penalty: as for the serious offence (punishable by life imprisonment or a period of 5 or more years)
Unauthorised modification of data to cause impairment (s. 477.2)	10 years max.
Unauthorised impairment of electronic communication (s. 477.3)	10 years max.
Unauthorised access to, or modification of, restricted data (s. 478.1)	2 years max.
Unauthorised impairment of data held on a computer disk etc. (s. 478.2)	2 years max.
Possession or control of data with intent to commit a computer offence (s. 478.3)	3 years max.
Producing, supplying or obtaining data with intent to commit a computer offence (s. 478.4)	3 years max.

Note: Under s. 4B of the *Crimes Act 1914* (Cth), a court may impose a pecuniary penalty in addition to, or instead of, a sentence of imprisonment. The maximum amount for a natural person, expressed in penalty units, is 5 times the maximum term, expressed in months. One penalty unit is equivalent to US$82.50 (s. 4AA). For bodies corporate, a penalty 5 times that for a natural person may be imposed. Thus, for a 10 years max. offence, a penalty of US$49,500 may be imposed on a natural person, or US$247,500 for a body corporate.

(cont.)

Australia (States and Territories)

New South Wales: *Crimes Act 1900*, ss. 308–308I (added by *Crimes Amendment (Computer Offences) Act 2001*)

Unauthorised access, modification or impairment with intent to commit serious indictable offence (s. 308C)	Penalty: as for the serious indictable offence
Unauthorised modification of data with intent to cause impairment (s. 308D)	10 years max.
Unauthorised impairment of electronic communication (s. 308E)	10 years max.
Possession of data with intent to commit serious computer offence (s. 308F)	3 years max.
Producing, supplying or obtaining data with intent to commit serious computer offence (s. 308G)	3 years max.
Unauthorised access to, or modification of, restricted data (summary offence) (s. 308H)	2 years max.
Unauthorised impairment of data held on a computer disk etc. (s. 308I)	2 years max.

Queensland: *Criminal Code Act 1899*, s. 408D (added by *Criminal Law Amendment Act 1997*)

Computer hacking and misuse (s. 408D)	2 years max.; 5 years max. if with intent to cause detriment or damage, or to gain benefit; 10 years max. if with intent to cause detriment or damage, or to obtain benefit, of more than A$5000 value, or with intent to commit an indictable offence

South Australia: *Summary Offences Act 1953*, s. 44 (added by *Summary Offences Act Amendment Act 1989* and amended by *Summary Offences (Offensive and Other Weapons) Amendment Act 1998*)

Unlawful operation of computer system (s. 44)	US$1875 max., or imprisonment for 6 months if with intent to obtain benefit or cause detriment

Tasmania: *Criminal Code Act 1924*, ss. 257A–257F (added by Act No. 13 of 1990)

Computer-related fraud (s. 257B)	2 years max. or US$1500
Damaging computer data (s. 257C)	2 years max. or US$1500
Unauthorised access to a computer (s. 257D)	2 years max. or US$1500
Insertion of false information as data (s. 257E)	2 years max. or US$1500

Victoria: *Crimes Act 1958*, ss. 247A–247I (added by *Crimes (Property Damage and Computer Offences) Act 2003*)

Unauthorised access, modification or impairment with intent to commit serious offence (s. 247B)	Penalty: as for the serious offence
Unauthorised modification of data to cause impairment (s. 247C)	10 years max.
Unauthorised impairment of electronic communication (s. 247D)	10 years max.
Possession of data with intent to commit serious computer offence (s. 247E)	3 years max.
Producing, supplying or obtaining data with intent to commit serious computer offence (s. 247F)	3 years max.
Unauthorised access to, or modification of, restricted data (s. 247G)	2 years max.
Unauthorised impairment of data held on a computer disk etc. (s. 247H)	2 years max.

Western Australia: *Criminal Code*, s. 440A (added by Act No. 101 of 1990)

Unlawful operation of a computer system (s. 440)	1 year max. or US$3000

Australian Capital Territory: *Criminal Code 2002*, ss. 112–121 (replacing provisions under the *Crimes Act 1900*)

Unauthorised access, modification or impairment with intent to commit serious offence (s. 115)	Penalty: as for the serious offence (punishable by life imprisonment or a period of 5 or more years)
Unauthorised modification of data to cause impairment (s. 116)	10 years max. and/or US$75,000

(*cont.*)

Unauthorised impairment of electronic communication (s. 117)	10 years max. and/or US$75,000
Possession or control of data with intent to commit serious computer offence (s. 118)	3 years max. and/or US$22,500
Producing, supplying or obtaining data with intent to commit serious computer offence (s. 119)	3 years max. and/or US$22,500
Unauthorised access to or modification of restricted data held in computer (s. 120)	2 years max. and/or US$15,000
Unauthorised impairment of data held in a computer disc etc. (s. 121)	2 years max. and/or US$15,000

Northern Territory: *Criminal Code*, s. 222 and ss. 276–276F (added by *Criminal Code Amendment Act 2001*)

Unlawfully obtaining confidential information (s. 222)	2 years max.
Unlawful access to data (s. 276B)	10 years max.
Unlawful modification of data (s. 276C)	10 years max.
Unlawful impairment of electronic communication (s. 276D)	10 years max.
Unlawful appropriation of access time (s. 276E)	3 years max.

Sources: <http://www.austlii.edu.au> (Australasian Legal Information Institute); <http://scaleplus.law.gov.au> (Commonwealth Attorney-General's Department)

United Kingdom	*Computer Misuse Act 1990* (c. 18)	
	Unauthorised access to computer material (s. 1)	6 months max. and/or fine
	Unauthorised access with intent to commit or facilitate commission of further offences (s. 2)	5 years max. and/or fine
	Unauthorised modification of computer material (s. 3)	5 years max. and/or fine

Source: <http://www.bailii.edu.au> (British and Irish Legal Information Institute)

United States (Federal)	United States Code 18 USC §1029 etc. (added by *Computer Fraud and Abuse Act of 1986*)	
	Fraud and related activity in connection with access devices (§1029)	Penalties of 10 to 15 years max., or 20 years max. for subsequent offence, and/or fine
	Fraud and related activity in connection with computers (§1030)	Penalties of 10 years max., or 20 years max. for subsequent offence, and/or fine
	Communication lines, stations or systems (wilful or malicious injury) (§1362)	10 years max. and/or fine
	Wire and electronic communications interception and interception of oral communications (§2510 etc.)	5 years max. and/or fine
	Stored wire and electronic communications and transactional records access (§2701 etc.)	5 years max. and/or fine, or 10 years for subsequent offence
	Recording of dialing, routing, addressing and signaling information (§3121 etc.)	1 yr max. and/or fine

Source: <http://www.usdoj.gov/criminal/cybercrime/cclaws.html> (US Department of Justice)

Canada	Criminal Code (RS 1985, c. C-46), Part XI: Wilful and Forbidden Acts in Respect of Certain Property	
	Mischief in relation to data (s. 430(1.1))	Imprisonment for life if mischief causes actual danger to life; 10 years max. if mischief in relation to property which is testamentary instrument or exceeds US$3750 in value; 2 years max. otherwise

Source: <http://laws.justice.gc.ca/en/C-46/41802.html> (Department of Justice Canada)

New Zealand	*Crimes Amendment Act (No. 6) 1999* (No. 322-2 of 2001, in force from 1 February 2002)	
	Accessing computer system for dishonest purpose (s. 250)	obtain benefit or cause loss: 7 years max.; with intent to obtain benefit or cause loss: 5 years max.
	Damaging or interfering with computer system (s. 251)	knowing that danger to life likely to result: 10 years max.; in other cases: 7 years max.
	Making, selling, or distributing or possessing software for committing crime (s. 252)	2 years max.
	Accessing computer system without authorisation (s. 253)	2 years max.

Sources: <http://rangi.knowledge-basket.co.nz> (New Zealand Research Archive); <http://www.sli.net.nz/crimebill/bill (Internet NZ)>

China	*Regulations on Protecting the Safety of Computer Information* (Order No. 147 of the State Council of the People's Republic of China, 18 February 1994)	
	Deliberate input of computer virus or selling special safety protection products without permission	Warnings may be given, fines imposed and illegal income confiscated
	Revised Provisional Regulations Governing the Management of Chinese Computer Information Networks Connected to International Networks (promulgated in February 1996 and revised in May 1997)	
	Computer information networks conducting direct international networking required to use the international access channels provided by the national public telecommunications networks of the Ministry of Posts and Telecommunications (Art. 6)	Public security organs shall order those who violate these to stop networking, issue them a warning, and impose a fine of no more than US$1800; earnings from illegal activities shall be confiscated where applicable (Art. 14)
	New Internet networks must have the approval of the State Council (Art. 7)	
	Internet access networks must conduct international networking through Internet networks (Art. 8)	

(*cont.*)

Computer Information Network and Internet Security, Protection and Management Regulations (promulgated 30 December 1997)

Prohibition of use of Internet to: harm national security, disclose state secrets, conduct illegal activity etc. (Art. 4), punishable by relevant State regulations (Art. 19); transmit information inciting illegality or overthrow of the Government etc. (Art. 5)	Punishable by warnings, confiscation of illegal income, and fines of not more than US$600 for individuals or US$1800 for Internet service providing units (Art. 20)
Prohibition of activities harming the security of computer information networks including: unapproved use of computer networks or resources, change of network functions, adding/deleting/altering stored data etc.; creation or transmission of computer viruses	Punishable as for Art. 5

Internet Security Law
State Secrecy Protection Regulations For Computer Information Systems on the Internet (January 2000)

Prohibition of using the Internet to transmit a range of unlawful or harmful content

Source: <http://www.qis.net/chinalaw/lawtran1.htm> (China Law Web); <http://www.chinaonline.com> (China Online); <http://www.bakerinfo.com/apec/chinaapec.htm> (Baker & McKenzie)

Hong Kong	*Crimes Ordinance* (Cap. 200)	
	Extends definition of 'criminal damage to property' to include 'misuse of a computer', i.e. unauthorised function, altering, erasing or adding any program or data	5 years max. (s. 161); 10 years max. or life imprisonment if property intentionally destroyed so as to endanger life (ss. 59, 60, 63)
	Theft Ordinance (Cap. 210)	
	Burglary defined to include unlawful interference with computer (s. 11)	14 years max.
	Telecommunication Ordinance (Cap. 106)	
	Unauthorised access to computer by telecommunications	Fine of US$2600 (s. 27A)

Source: <http://www.justice.gov.hk/home.htm> (BLIS – Bilingual Laws Information System)

Index

In this index, **c followed by a number** signifies a numbered case in Appendix A (e.g., **c22** refers to Case No. 22). Page references followed by *tab* indicate tables